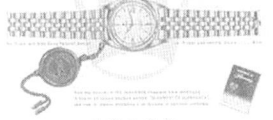

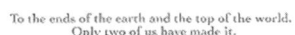

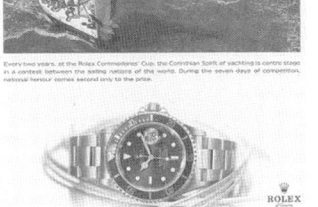

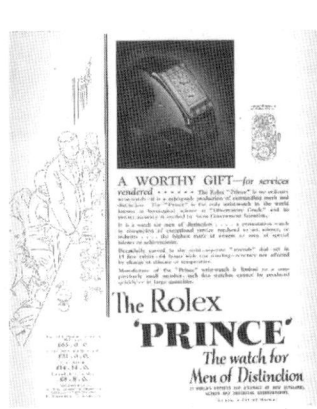

THE
ROLEX
REPORT

THE ROLEX REPORT

Revised & Expanded 4th Edition

AN UNAUTHORIZED REFERENCE BOOK
FOR THE ROLEX ENTHUSIAST

JOHN E. BROZEK

With a Foreword by
JEFFREY P. HESS

InfoQuest Publishing, Inc.®

Saint Petersburg, Florida 33716 USA

This book is dedicated to the memory of my parents

Richard and Jean Brozek.

CONTENTS

CONTENTS (continued)

FOREWORD

While it is curious that something as mundane and relatively common as a wristwatch gets so much worldwide attention, it is just plain amazing that one wristwatch in particular, Rolex, garners the far reaching and all encompassing and indeed almost "Hubble-esque" search for its very origins.

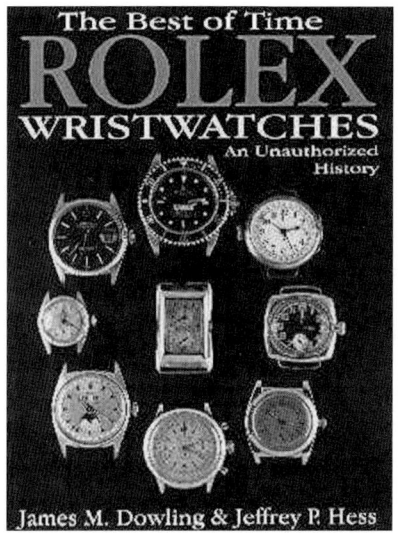

Studies have been done before and more will follow. What John Brozek has accomplished here is a substantial and well put together compilation of materials that collectors and students of Rolex alike will surely use on a daily basis.

Of particular use is the incredible macro photos of the many fakes and forgeries that continue to sully and denigrate what has been called the "greatest watch of all time" by many before me.

Jeffrey P. Hess
Co-Author, *The Best of Time, Rolex Wristwatches*

ABOUT THE AUTHOR

John E. Brozek has been a collector, appraiser and authenticator of Rolex (and other mechanical watches) for over ten years, and is a proud member of numerous horological organizations, including: the NAWCC *(National Association of Watch & Clock Collectors),* AWI *(American Watchmakers-Clockmakers Institute),* IWJG *(International Watch & Jewelry Guild),* BHI *(British Horological Institute),* and the IWCS *(International Watch Collectors Society),* as well as the NPA *(National Pawnbrokers Association).*

ABOVE: John E. Brozek with an F-16A *Fighting Falcon* of the 507th TFG based at *Tinker AFB*, Oklahoma, and on location at *Aviano Air Base*, Italy. Circa 1992.

BELOW: John E. Brozek is shown with the actor/auto racing legend Paul Newman at the Inaugural Grand Prix of St. Petersburg, 2003.

He has been an author, screenwriter, playwright, historian, freelance photographer and magazine contributing writer for over ten years, and his work has been featured in many prestigious publications, including: *International Wristwatch, InSync, Chronos,* the *Horological Journal,* and the *NAWCC Bulletin.*

Originally from Oklahoma, he graduated from the *University of Central Oklahoma,* and served in the United States Air Force while deploying to numerous overseas destinations, including: Italy, Austria and Germany. He is the founder and President of *InfoQuest Publishing, Inc.,* and currently resides in Saint Petersburg, Florida, where he lectures watch clubs and organizations on the identification of authentic and counterfeit Rolex watches and parts.

PREFACE

Like many of you, I've always had a bit of a curiosity with respect to Rolex—from the style and quality of their watches, to the romance and mystique surrounding this very secretive company. However, after purchasing my first Rolex nearly 10 years ago, that simple curiosity quickly evolved into a full-fledged obsession. I began reading books, like this one, and hunting for any information I could find on these incredible timepieces. Unfortunately, books with detailed, accurate information were few and far between.

Over the next few years, I began collecting different models and even acquired a few counterfeits for comparison's sake. By simple observations, I became quite proficient in identifying the counterfeit's features and even worked with a local jeweler in authenticating his Rolex watches.

Then in December of 1998, a colleague told me about a new online auction site called *eBay*, which he described as a "virtual garage sale". The concept fascinated me, so I logged on to check it out for myself. In those days, eBay was very new and they were still desperately trying to control the infestation of counterfeiters peddling their wares. Fake jewelry, designer clothing, and yes Rolex watches were being sold as the genuine article, and in quite large numbers I might add. Counterfeiters had already been selling fake Rolexes via the internet, but when eBay emerged, it was as if they had opened the flood gates.

After only a few minutes of navigating the site I was able to identify numerous counterfeit Rolexes up for sale. Some were the obvious: *"I found this watch in my attic... I don't have the box and papers, so please bid accordingly"*, while others were clever scams with believable stories. I spent the next few months compiling information for a reference book that would help educate the Rolex buyer on such topics as dating a vintage Rolex and identifying a counterfeit.

When I wrote the first edition of *The Rolex Report* in early 1999, I had no idea it would be received with such enthusiasm. What started as a small booklet on how to identify counterfeit Rolex watches, quickly grew into a comprehensive reference book with a history of the Rolex Watch Company, model identifications and subsequently a detailed price list.

Over the past three years, I've received orders from pawn shops and jewelry stores from all over the world, as well as from individuals and private collectors who simply wanted to further educate themselves on these incredible watches. I've exchanged e-mails with a number of these customers, which have developed into some great friendships. It seems the one thing they all had in common was the desire to learn more, as they persistently asked when the next edition would be available.

My goal for the fourth edition was simple: provide a well rounded resource that would be beneficial to the Rolex novice and aficionado alike.

With that being said, I would like to thank all my readers who have enjoyed my first three editions and I hope you continue to enjoy *The Rolex Report*.

ACKNOWLEDGEMENTS

There are a number of people whom I would like to thank for their assistance with the creation of this book, either directly or indirectly—please forgive me if I forget anyone.

I would like to express my sincerest gratitude to the following people:

To my family: Mike, Jay and Patti for their continual support over the years.

To Jerry VanCook and Linda McDonald at UCO, for their confidence and support which inspired me to write this book.

To Owen, Dave, Greg and the 'gang' at Central Cigars, for their input, as well as for putting up with my overwhelming obsession with this project.

To Roy Ehrhardt, for his valuable input and advice which was greatly appreciated.

To Matthew Bain & Massimo Barracca (watchcommander.com), Jennifer at Christie's, Syd Cain, Universal Pictures, National Geographic, Michael J. Rosenman, Jonathan Tee (passions.com.sg), bjsonline.com, Steven Oltuski (northerntime.com), Michael Benson, Jonathan Halliwell (rarerolex.com) and Ramin Cohen (Masterpiece Jewelry & Watches), who graciously allowed the use of their images in this book. A special thanks to Jon Todd (generalwar.com), for going out of his way to provide numerous images for this book, as well as the Daytona image used on the cover.

Many thanks to Michael Metzler, Harry Betz, and Craig Frank for their assistance in getting this project off the ground.

With a special thanks to Jeffrey P. Hess, for his incredible generosity, assistance and advice, as well as for writing the Foreword to this book.

INTRODUCTION

On March, 18, 1952, Raymond Lambert and Sherpa Tenzing Norgay, two distinguished members of a Swiss alpinist expedition, set a new altitude record when they climbed to within 200 meters/660 feet of the summit of Mount Everest—without the aid of oxygen. One year later, Tenzing returned to Everest with the British Himalayas expedition led by John Hunt and accompanied by Edmund Hillary. This expedition, following the famous *South Col* route, was first to reach the summit (at 29,035 feet) on May, 29, 1953. During these historic climbs, many expedition members were known to carry Rolex Oyster Perpetual Chronometers—a fact celebrated by Rolex in a number of advertisements.

To a climber, their equipment is critical, and thus by timing their ascent and measuring oxygen use, they quite literally bet their lives on the accuracy of these watches. It would later be learned that Tenzing received his Rolex as a gift from his long-time friend and fellow climber Raymond Lambert.

Fifty years later, Lambert and Tenzing returned to Everest—of course now it was Yves Lambert (son of Raymond Lambert), and Tashi Tenzing (grandson of Sherpa Tenzing Norgay) whom made the historic climb. This new expedition: "Geneva–Everest 1952–2002" reached the summit on May 16, 2002, and was again sponsored by Rolex—with expedition members proudly equipped with Rolex Chronometers.

Like these courageous climbers, Rolex has achieved a pinnacle of success with respect to watchmaking, and it is a celebration of this pioneering spirit for which this book was written.

Sherpa Tenzing Norgay standing at the top of the world— the summit of Mt. Everest on May 29, 1953.

Clocks slay time...
Time is dead as long as it is being clicked off by little wheels;
only when the clock stops does time come to life.
—William Faulkner

ABOVE: Vintage pocket watch fusee
movement *Bordier a Geneva.*
Circa 1795

PART I

Horology: The science of measuring time.

The Evolution of Clocks Through History
A Chronological History of the Rolex Watch Company
Rolex Wristwatch Profiles
Quick Reference for Rolex Model Evolutions

ABOVE: The ancient rock formation
at *Stonehenge* (England).

The Evolution of Clocks Through History

For thousands of years, ancient civilizations have used celestial bodies to measure the passage of time. The Sumerians tracked the movements of planets and stars to record the seasons, and even created ancient calendars to record lunar cycles. It is believed that around 4236 BC, the Egyptians discovered the 'Dog Star' in Canis Major, which we call Sirius. Rising alongside the sun every 365 days, it is believed to be "one of the earliest years recorded in history"[1]—and would later evolve into the current 365-day calendar. Though never proven, it has even been suggested that the massive rock formation at *Stonehenge* (in England), dated to over 4,000 years old, was used to measure seasonal or celestial events.

Ancient Egyptian shadow-clock
Cleopatra Needle

As early as 3500 BC, the Egyptians used giant obelisk-shaped sundials (or shadow-clocks) called *Cleopatra Needles,* which would cast shadows onto marks on the ground to track the 12 parts of the day. The significance of the number '12' during this period is unknown, however, some other examples include: the "twelve Giant Gods of Olympus, twelve Labours of Hercules, twelve Tables of Roman Law and twelve Apostles of Jesus Christ."[2] An obvious problem with these primitive timekeepers was that they could not be used at night or in inclement weather.

Ancient water-clock *Clepsydra*

Later, the Greeks and Romans created water-clocks called *Clepsydra*—a Greek word meaning 'water thief'. They would fill water into a large bucket with a hole in the bottom, so when the water spilled out it could be timed. Some examples have been discovered with a hollowed-out pearl (imbedded in the hole), used to eliminate the erosion caused by water flowing through the hole—thus, some may joke that this is the first example of a 'jeweled' movement. Water-clocks were also the first example of a timekeeper that did not rely on the observation of the stars.

Water-clocks were predominately used to signify the start and

17

stop of an event, such as speaking times allotted during court proceedings. While some would scoff at their accuracy, water-clocks were used for centuries and were even credited with aiding the advancement of astronomy.[3]

One drawback of the water-clock was the fact that they could not be used in the winter for fear of freezing. This limitation led to the invention of the *sand-clock*, which we commonly refer to as an hour-glass—two connected glass bubbles, narrow in the middle, which were filled with sand. These were obviously popular in Egypt, as they had no shortage of sand, however, some examples have been discovered containing powered eggshells, or even mercury.

Not only did the hour-glass operate similarly to the water clock, its purpose was similar as well. In churches for instance, they were used to mark the beginning and ending of a sermon, and onboard ships they were used to regulate the crew's shift on deck. Of course due to their size, they were only practical for measuring short periods of time and were only accurate if placed on a flat surface.

Sand-clock *Hour Glass.*

However, one successful use for the hour-glass was to calculate a ship's speed at sea. One would tie a knotted rope to a piece of wood and through it overboard. When the knots ran though one's fingers, it would be timed by the hour-glass. A rate of one 'knot' per $^1/_2$ minute would indicate that the ship was traveling at a speed of 1 nautical mile an hour—thus, the phrase *knots an hour.*

Another often forgotten timekeeper was that of the Chinese *fire clock* (or candle-clock) which was introduced around the 9th century. The clock consisted of a slow-burning taper (or candle) positioned beneath a set of weighted strings. When the candle burnt through the strings, they would drop the weights into a brass tray. This would display, as well as sound the hour with a 'clank'. Some say this could have been the inspiration for the hourly chime on clock towers centuries later, while others mark this as the earliest known alarm clock.

The first modern, or mechanical *clock*[4] was created sometime between 500-1000 AD in Europe, though the exact date is unknown. It used weights, which moved gears, which in turn moved a single hour hand. These clocks were very large and required the weights to be reset as many as four to five times per day. Over the many years that followed, large clock towers sprung up across Europe, possibly the first of which was the *Astronomical Clock* in the Strasbourg Cathedral in France (around 1352-4), which still operates to this day.[5]

It wasn't until centuries later that the next major hurdle in clock-making was reached, when the clock's driving weights were replaced with the invention of the 'coiled spring' by Peter Henlein (1480-1542), a locksmith from Nuremberg, Germany. This advancement led to clocks being made smaller and even more accurate.

In 1504, Henlein also invented the first portable-clock. Its odd-looking ball shape earned it the erroneous name: *Nuremberg Egg* when a translator mistook "little clocks" for "little eggs".[6] The clock was made of iron, had merely an

The Strasbourg Cathedral (France).

hour hand and no protective covering over the dial.

It wasn't until 1577 that Jost Burgi (1552-1632) invented the minute hand, designed for the Danish astronomer, Tycho Brahe (1546-1601), so he could more accurately track stars. Then in 1600, Burgi was also responsible for the first clock featuring minutes and seconds as well.

One of the greatest thinkers of the time, Galileo Galilei (1564-1642) was credited with the conception of the pendulum[7], after observing the consistent movement of a swinging lamp. Originally, his application was to the timing of the human pulse and it wasn't until shortly before his death in 1642, that he realized its value in connection to clock making.

The first construction of a pendulum clock, based on Galileo's design, was originally credited to his son. However, years later the distinction was bestowed upon Christian Huygens (1629-1695), a Dutch scientist who created a pendulum clock in 1656—its accuracy was said to be within one minute per day.[1]

The next few centuries saw the evolution of pocket watches. They became smaller, more accurate and very ornately designed. None was more responsible for this than Thomas Tompion (1638-1713), known as "the father of English watch making". His achievements included one of the first watches with a 'balance spring', and clocks of such accuracy they could run for a year without winding.

In 1704, Nicholas Facio (1664-1753), came to London with an idea that revolutionized the watch making industry, when he proposed using jeweled pivot bearings.

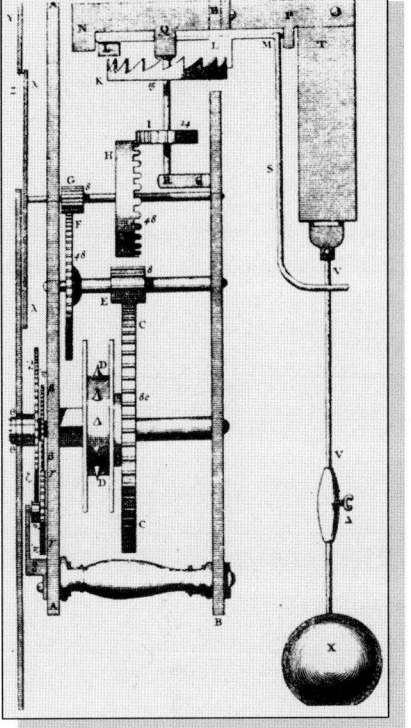

Courtesy of Science Museum, London

Christian Huygens' *Pendulum Clock* based on Galileo's design.

His idea was that a precious stone (or jewel) would not wear (or erode) as a metal pivot would, when under constant friction. The Commons' Committee declined his idea, stating that the invention was not original. They stated that Ignatius Huggeford had used the idea some years before, when he crafted a watch with a ruby mounted on the balance cock. The problem is that Huggeford's *ruby* was intended for ornate decorations and not to aid in the function of the watch. Unfortunately, this error was not discovered until years later, and Facio was not given the true credit he deserved until after his death.

Over the years that followed, the accuracy of watches found a new purpose. Motivated by a great sea disaster in 1701, the British Government passed an Act of Parliament in 1714, whereby granting a prize of £20,000 (worth millions today) for the first person to calculate "longitude onboard a ship to within one-half degree."[1]—this meant the watch's accuracy could not vary by more than six seconds per day, during the six week voyage.

Many people tried with limited success[8], until the son of a carpenter, John Harrison (1693-1776), set out to capture the prize in 1725. Unfortunately, it would not prove to be an easy task. While his timepiece successfully met every condition, collecting

Museum of the Worshipful Company of Clockmakers Guildhall, London

Huggeford's 'jeweled' watch.

the prize would take some forty years!

The British Government repeatedly "changed the rules" so to speak, setting additional conditions and awarding only a portion of the prize after each additional success. This forced Harrison to produce 4 additional timepieces—the best of which, simply named the *H.4*, varied by only 5 seconds!

It wasn't until 1765, when after decades of court battles, King George III intervened, and Harrison was awarded the balance of what ended up to be only £18,750, instead of the £20,000 prize he was originally promised.

Abraham-Louis Perrelet (1729-1826), has the distinction of one of the biggest advancements in clock-making when he designed the first self-winding watch in 1770. The pocket watch was called the "pedometer", named after the source of its power—a weighted lever that jerks as a man walks. This watch was then further developed by Abraham-Louis Breguet in 1777, and later patented by Louis Recordon in London in 1780. After this period, the self-winding watch seemed to fade into history, not to be resurrected until nearly one-hundred-fifty years later.

John Harrison's marine timekeeper, the H.4, which won him the Longitude Prize. Circa 1759

Courtesy of National Maritime Museum, London

Courtesy of perrelet.com

Early Perrelet automatic 'Pedometer'. Circa 1770

The first "wristwatch" was credited to Abraham-Louis Breguet (1747-1823), when it was commissioned for the Queen of Naples on June 8, 1810. The "oblong-shaped repeating watch for a wristlet took two years and a half to complete", and was said to be "of revolutionary construction and unprecedented sophistication."[9]

Breguet, who is considered by many as the finest watchmaker of all time, has also been credited with changing the appearance of watches from fat and clumsy to slim and modern.

While these many historic dates were important to the evolution of timekeeping, it was April 19, 1891, that changed "time" as we know it today. Due to a malfunctioning conductor's watch, two trains collided near Cleveland, Ohio, killing 11 people. News of this disaster quickly spread, launching a demand for all railroads (and communities) to adopt a timekeeping standard. Suddenly, the modern world developed a fascination with 'accurate' time.

[1] Quoted from the NIST online article, *A Walk Through Time*. http://physics.nist.gov/time

[2] Quoted from *Clocks & Watches*, by Eric Bruton.

[3] The Danish astronomer, Tycho Brahe used a water-clock when he made calculations, proving his discovery of a 'new star' in Cassiopeia.

[4] The word "clock" comes from the Latin word *clocca*, meaning "bell". Thus, signifying the early timekeepers which sounded the hour with a chime or bell.

[5] The original clock (built in 1352-4) was replaced in 1574, and again in 1842. The latter clock is still operational, and parts from the earlier clocks are exhibited in the Horological Museum at Strasbourg.

[6] According to *Clocks & Watches*, by Eric Bruton: *Ueurlein* (little clocks) was incorrectly translated as *eierlein* (little eggs).

[7] Galileo's Pendulum was originally called a *Horologium Oscillatorium*.

[8] Some notable thinkers who *unsuccessfully* made an attempt at the prize were: Sir Isaac Newton, Christian Huygens and Robert Hooke.

[9] Quoted from Breguet's website, *Inventions & Innovations* page. http://www.breguet.com

Hans Wilhelm Wilsdorf

ABOVE: Hans Wilhelm Wilsdorf
portrait by *Gasamaga Agayev*.

The Chronological History of the Rolex Watch Company

Hans Wilhelm Wilsdorf was born on March 22, 1881, in the small village of Kulmbach (near Nuremberg) in Bavaria—making him a German National Citizen. The prominent family business was that of ironmongers (hardware merchants), founded by his grandfather Carl Traugger Wilsdorf in 1842. Young Wilsdorf would have most likely followed the family tradition, had tragedy not struck when he was just 12 years old. In 1893, Ferdinand and Anna Wilsdorf died leaving he and his siblings in the care of their aunt and uncle. The family business was sold, and Wilsdorf was sent to a boarding school in the nearby town of Coburg. Hans was a highly intelligent young man and excelled in math and foreign languages (especially English). Upon completing his studies, Hans moved to Geneva, Switzerland, where he took work with a major pearl merchant in the exporting department—Wilsdorf's education of international trading thus began. It is worth noting that this company did not manufacture any products, but merely took advantage of the old adage *supply and demand*.

At the mere age of 19, Wilsdorf moved on and using his excellent language skills, accepted a job with the watch exporters Cuno Korten (located at 49, Rue Leopold Robert) for a wage of 80 Francs per year. His job was written correspondence (in English) with the company's British and U.S. clients. This afforded Wilsdorf an opportunity to develop important international contacts in the watch making community that would prove beneficial in the years to come. Cuno Korten was a highly profitable company, having an annual revenue of over one million Swiss francs. Therefore, Wilsdorf must have realized the possibilities in this industry, as he spent every available moment broadening his knowledge of watches and their construction. It became his passion and it is believed that this is when Wilsdorf decided to make *horology* his life's work. The more he learned, the more obsessed he became with the accuracy of watches. He would experiment night and day by setting a group of watches, then later comparing them for accuracy. After feeling quite confident, Wilsdorf took the three most accurate watches from the lot and submitted them (without permission) to the Neuchatel Observatory. All three watches passed the rigorous testing and Wilsdorf was praised by his superiors.

In 1903, and after only three years with Cuno Korten, Wilsdorf moved to London to work for another prominent watch making company (name unknown). Less than two years later, he decided to make yet another move and at the age of 24, went into business for himself. Wilsdorf took on an English partner, Alfred James Davis, and thus in 1905 the watch importing company *Wilsdorf & Davis Ltd.* was born. Wilsdorf, investing his inheritance, as well as money borrowed from his brother and sister, matched Davis' investment making them equal partners. Shortly thereafter, Davis married Wilsdorf's younger sister making the partnership even closer as they became family.

Originally, their offices were located in England at 83, Hatton Gardens (London), but soon moved to 44, Holborn Viaduct (near Clerkenwell). Early on, Wilsdorf & Davis sold watches in two main categories: *pocket watches* and the newly popular *travel clocks* (often referred to as purse or portfolio models). These folding clocks, covered in exotic leathers, were successfully exported in large numbers to the English markets.

Wristwatches of the time were small in number and primarily worn by women, as they were considered too feminine for a man. In fact, they were held in such disdain that many a gentlemen were quoted to say: "they would sooner wear a skirt as wear a wrist watch."[10]

W&D hallmark stamped inside case back. Circa 1914

Wristwatches were looked down upon by the established watch-making community as well. The opinion was that a wristwatch would never be able to withstand the rigors of human activity. It was also thought that a movement of such small size could never be made to maintain any level of accuracy.

It was not until around the turn of the century when wristwatches for men began to find a market, albeit small—this was around the time of the *Boer War* (South Africa 1899-1902). The climate in Africa was too hot to wear a jacket or vest, thus there was no place to carry a traditional pocket watch. The soldiers in these extreme climates began to wear small *pocket watches* on their wrists, attached with a primitive cupped leather strap to free up their hands during combat. Wilsdorf quickly recognized the demand and Wilsdorf & Davis began specializing in wristwatches to compete in this niche market.

Wilsdorf chose *Rebberg* movements from Herman Aegler's firm in Bienne, since successfully dealing with them from his days with Cuno Korten. They were known for producing small, accurate (lever escapement) movements at an affordable price. Furthermore, Wilsdorf was impressed

Early ladies Rolex with blank dial.

with their reliability, as well as the fact that replacement parts were easy to acquire.

Early, "pre-Rolex" models were made of silver and featured the company's hallmark: *W&D* (representing Wilsdorf & David) stamped on the movement and again inside the case back. The faces were left blank for the retailers to paint their own names on the dial for advertisement.

However, since the dials were primarily made of porcelain, and the enamel wouldn't accept the paint very well, it is common for these watches to now have *blank* dials—the painted names having long since been eroded after decades of cleaning. Early models still exist bearing the names of early retailers such as 'The Goldsmiths Company' (the world's first Rolex retailer) or 'Asprey' (London's most famous Jewelers) on the dial, along with W&D hallmarks inside.

In 1906, a London saddler, Alfred E. Pearson, took these wristlets a step further when he introduced the idea of "soldering wire loops to watch cases"[2], thereby allowing straps to be more easily

© 1900, Underwood & Underwood.

Royal Munster Fusiliers at Honey Nest Kloof, South Africa—Boer War. Circa 1900

Courtesy of Christie's Images, New York

Early Rolex 'Portfolio' watch. Circa 1928

ABOVE: Comparison of movements from a pocket watch (left) and wristwatch (right).

BELOW: Comparison of parts from a pocket watch and wristwatch movement, including escape and balance wheels. Note the considerable difference in size of these parts. Now imagine the difficulty involved in working with such miniature parts with 'turn of the century' technology.

Early ladies Rolex with porcelain dial. Circa 1914

attached. Also that same year, the expandable flexible bracelet was invented. Wristwatches could now be fitted to a wider range of sizes, thus a wider range of customers.

It was also around this time when companies discovered the advantage of having a trademark or logo to distinguish themselves from the competition. None was more evident than in 1888, when George Eastman named his new revolutionary camera the "Kodak". The explanation is thus: The name must be short, difficult to misspell, and it must mean nothing in any language, but yet easily pronounced in all European languages. Many companies followed suit, as did Wilsdorf & Davis, who on July 2, 1908, registered "Rolex" in Chaux de Fonds, Switzerland, and again in London on July 6, 1912. The origin of the word, or even who came up with it is unconfirmed to this day. Although, some believe it was derived from the French phrase: *Horlogerie Exquisite,* and yet others will say Wilsdorf himself named it after the sound a watch makes as it is being wound.

In 1910, Rolex sent their first movement to the School of Horology in Bienne, Switzerland—which later became one of the official institutes of time keeping tests. It was awarded the world's first wristwatch chronometer rating—with this accomplishment, the world had to take notice. It was also around this time that Wilsdorf recognized three major requirements for wristwatches to become truly successful: To keep accurate time, to be reliable and to be auto-winding.

With the *Chronometer Award*, Wilsdorf had achieved accuracy and now began to work on improving the reliability of his wristwatches. This was a timely problem due to the harsh elements they were being exposed to in the African and Far East markets.

In 1912, Wilsdorf traveled to Bienne and negotiated with Hermann Aegler (Jean Aegler's son) to supply *Wilsdorf & Davis* with additional movements. The contract was valued at £125,000 (five times greater than that of the entire capital of Wilsdorf & Davis), and was the largest contract of its kind ever signed. This was the start of a very profitable business relationship. In fact, over the years that followed, Wilsdorf would make numerous trips back to Bienne, placing new orders, as well as bringing new ideas for improvements.

On July 15, 1914, a Rolex was awarded the *Class "A" Certificate of Precision* from the famous Kew Observatory in England—the first ever given to a wristwatch. The rigorous testing lasted 45 days in five positions and three temperatures. It's extraordinarily noteworthy that prior to this, these certificates had only been awarded to marine chronometers.

After receiving the award, Wilsdorf decided that *all* Rolex timepieces would undergo similar testing, and that no Rolex would be sold again without its *Official Timing Certificate*. This meant that Rolex would not accept movements from Aegler unless they passed Rolex's own seven-day battery of meticulous tests. Rolex quickly began setting the industry standards for wristwatch accuracy, and customers started asking for them by name.

Over the next few years the name Rolex began to appear, not only on their movements and case backs, but also on the faces of their watches. This of course was not popular among their retailers, as it was still customary for the shops to place *their* names on the watches before selling them. It was a very slow transition that would take years to reach fruition.[11] First, labels were applied to the watch backs, then around 1921, some models slowly began to appear with the names of Rolex *and* the retailer side-by-side, or one above the other. This is often referred to as 'co-branded' or 'double named' watches.

Originally, Rolex was only meant to be the trademark used to market their watches, however, things quickly changed when war broke out in Europe in 1914. Public sentiment quickly shifted against Germany, as many German-owned companies were expelled from Britain, and anti-German riots began. Even though Hans was now a British citizen—having married his English wife a few years before—with a German sounding name like 'Wilsdorf' there was an obvious reason for con-

WWI soldier from the 166 Aero Squadron
in Loier Germany—note the wristwatch insert.
Circa 1914

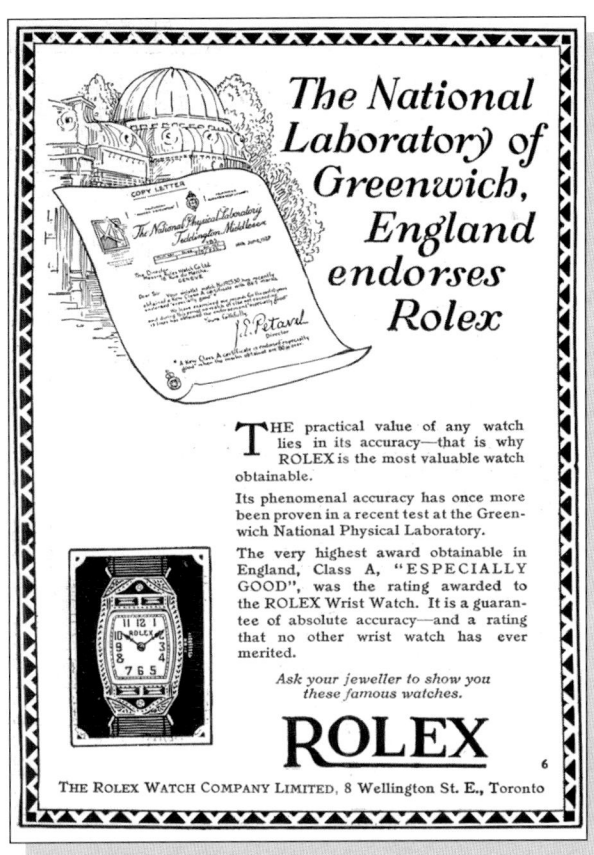

Rolex magazine advertisement celebrating the
Class "A" Certificate. Circa 1927

Early Dunklings/Rolex
double named pocket watch.

WWI Balkan soldier—note the wristwatch insert.
Circa 1917

cern. Although it was an expensive procedure, on November 15, 1915, Wilsdorf & Davis Ltd. was officially renamed: *The Rolex Watch Company Ltd.*[12]

Early Waltham wristlet
with pierced metal cover.

Like in the Boer War, the need for wristwatches in a combat setting was now at its peak. It is important to note that now more than ever it was considered important for these watches to become accurate. The wristwatches of the time, designed primarily for women, were quite small and not very reliable. These soldiers needed reliable, accurate watches so they could coordinate simultaneous troop movements and attacks. Pocket watches were impractical because they could not easily be accessed during combat situations. So like it or not, the wristwatch was the obvious choice, and many companies scrambled to fill the need. Rolex quickly found themselves in a strong financial position since they had already established themselves in the wristwatch market. Early models resembled very small pocket watches with "pierced metal covers" which allowed the hands' position to be read while still offering some level of protection, and sunk subsidiary seconds dials at the 6 o'clock position.

Around this time international-trading merchants (like Rolex) were faced with yet another problem. Since Germany was having difficulty restricting the flow of war supplies by the Allies, they adopted a new policy—unrestricted submarine warfare. This meant that German U-boats patrolling the British Isles were given orders to sink any allied merchant vessel on sight. Between February and September, 1915, fifty ships were hit by German U-boats, including the liner *Lusitania*. One hundred thirty-eight Americans were among the 1,198 lives lost on the *Lusitania*, which eventually led to Americas full involvement in World War I.

Cartier Tank watch.

As the war ended, wristwatches became much more acceptable and far less feminine. After all, no man would ever consider these very masculine soldiers of being anything but. Therefore, wristwatches were becoming more fashionable, and companies were creating new cutting-edge styles—none was more evident than Cartier's rectangular *Tank Watch*, thus named because it resembled the treads of a military tank.

The war did however strike one last blow to the Rolex company. On September 21, 1915, Britain imposed a duty of 33% on all imported watches, clocks and parts. This was followed by a government ban on all imported gold and silver a year later. With these tariffs making it prohibitively expensive to remain in England, Wilsdorf moved the center of operations for Rolex to the factory at Bienne, Switzerland, thus strengthening their relationship with Aegler. Then in 1919, Wilsdorf relocated to Geneva and founded *Montres Rolex S.A.* (located at 18 rue de Marche).

Also in 1919, the alliance between Rolex and Aegler was taken to the next level when Wilsdorf and Davis issued 6,960 shares of *The Rolex Watch Company Ltd* to Hermann Aegler (nearly 15% of their equity), making him a partner in exchange for a stronger business relationship. From that day forth, Aegler's company was known as: *Aegler Incorporated, Manufacturer of Rolex & Gruen Guild A Watches*[13] and they became the exclusive supplier of movements to Rolex. Thus, the movements were manufactured and tested in Bienne, then sent to Geneva where they were finished before being shipped to the retailers.

Since the new company was now a three-way partnership, with Aegler supplying movements to *both* Rolex and Gruen, an agreement was made with regard to distribution—Rolex would market their watches to Europe, Asia and the entire British Empire, while Gruen would sell only to the U.S.

As early as 1920, there began a major change in the ownership interest of Rolex. For reasons unknown, Davis began selling off his shares in the company to his partners. By 1924, he had sold (or gave away) his remaining interest in the company to Aegler, Wilsdorf, and Wilsdorf's wife May. What eventually happened to Davis and where he went from there is unknown. However, some speculate that his departure was in some way health related.

On May 2, 1925, Rolex trademarked the famous *crown* (or more accurately 'coronet') in Geneva, Switzerland—its 5-points allegedly representing 5-fingers, thus the watches "made by hand". However, the famous logo did not make its appearance on the dial until around 1939. In fact, it wasn't until around 1926, that the name "Rolex" finally began to appear on *every* dial. This occurred only after Wilsdorf launched an expensive advertising campaign, with an annual budget of one hundred thousand francs. The ads ran largely in English newspapers, and were designed to create product awareness.

Early version of the Rolex crown logo. Circa 1927

The campaign was an overwhelming success and Wilsdorf finally had the bargaining chip he needed. Wilsdorf now insisted that if it was the quality associated with the Rolex name that the customer wanted, then the name would be used on *all* Rolex made watches—and used it was. The Rolex name quickly became synonymous with quality and distinction and still is to this day.

As wristwatches began to evolve, attention was focused on trying to create a waterproof and dust proof case. Instead of the widely used 3-piece *Hunter* pocket watch style case: case body, back and bezel, whereas the back and bezel were 'hinged' to the case body, the new design moved toward a new 2-piece case.

Rolex pocket watch with 3-piece Hunter-style hinged case.

In an early design in Paris, Jacques Cartier's *Tank Watch* held the two pieces together via screws passing through from one half of the case to the other, thus creating a sealed unit. However, in Switzerland, the design moved toward threaded surfaces which were screwed together creating a much tighter hermetic seal.

Early on, Rolex used threaded cases made by Aaron Dennison's company—an American Ex-Patriot and founder of the *Waltham Watch Company* in 1854, he has often been called the "Father of American Watchmaking". Dennison's cases were of exceptional quality, and can easily be identified by the milled (or coined) edges on the bezel and back, which enabled the case to be tightened by hand. This same milled-edge design is still used to this day on all Rolex Oyster case backs.

Shortly after making the move to Bienne, Rolex began using cases from the Swiss maker, Francis Baumgartner. Baumgartner's *hermetic* design created a nearly waterproof case. The main drawback

Courtesy of Michael Benson

Early Rolex wristlet, featuring a 'milled' edge bezel—though this example is not a Dennison case, it bears a strong resemblance. Circa 1916

Dennison Watch Case Company
advertisement. Circa1942

Italian Rolex advertisement featuring a
Rolex Oyster inside a fish tank. Circa 1932

Courtesy of Christie's Images, New York

Rolex Oyster Precision worn by Miss Mercedes
Gleitze during her record swim across the English
Channel on October 21, 1927.

Courtesy of Passions of Singapore

Rolex Prince (model 971)
Brancard. Circa 1930

being that the whole of the watch (including the winding stem) was enclosed *inside* the outer sealed case. This meant that the bezel had to be unscrewed each day to allow access to wind the watch. This was unacceptable for mass appeal and these *tropical* watches were marketed almost exclusively in such areas as India and Burma.

Finally, on October 30, 1925, two first-time inventors, Paul Perregaux and Georges Peret filed a patent for a new moisture proof winding stem and button. Thus, finally curing Rolex's Achilles heel which was moisture entering the case via the winding button—the new design utilized springs and double helical screws, and has been likened to that of a submarine's hatch.

Shortly after hearing of the invention, Wilsdorf bought the patent from the two inventors and registered the world's first waterproof case: the *Oyster,* in Switzerland on July 29, 1926, and again in London on February 28, 1927.[14] It's believed that Wisldorf came up with the name while prying open an oyster at a dinner party.

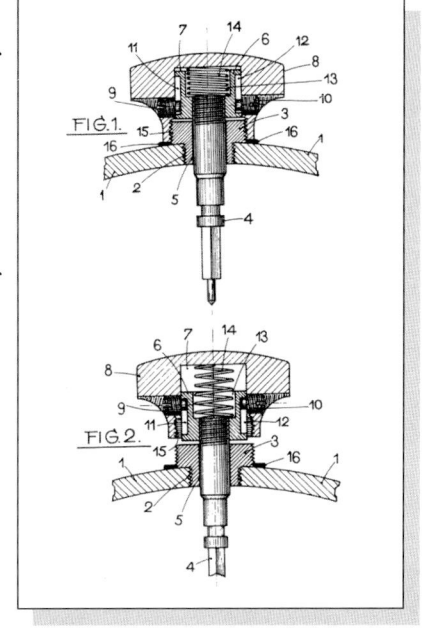

Early winding stem patent drawing. Circa 1925

It is worth noting that the synthetic crystal was also introduced at this time, thereby providing a watertight seal on three fronts: case back, crown and crystal.[15]

Wilsdorf quickly launched a massive advertising campaign to promote the new Oyster waterproof watch. On October 21, 1927, Mercedes Gleitze, a 26 year-old London typist became the first woman to swim the English channel—and the first to ever do it while wearing a watch. Her record swim lasted fifteen hours and fifteen minutes and was in the worst weather conditions imaginable, however, when she reached the shore her *Rolex Oyster* was in perfect condition.[16]

On November 27, 1927, Rolex took out an ad on the front page of London's *Daily Mail* at a cost of 40,000 Swiss francs. The ad featured a picture of Gleitze, with the headlines: "The Wonder Watch that Defies the Elements: Moisture Proof. Water Proof. Heat Proof. Vibration Proof. Cold Proof. Dust Proof.", and "the greatest Triumph in Watch-making."

Over the next few years, Wilsdorf continued to improve on the Oyster's design, and launched more outrageous (and highly successful) advertising campaigns to promote it. These even included *fish aquariums* displayed in the shop owner's windows, containing a submerged Oys-

London's *Daily Mail* front page insert. November 24, 1927

ter watch. Thusly, Rolex could now guarantee the Oyster waterproof to over 100 feet.

Even with the adoption of the waterproof winding stem in 1927, problems still arose. Many customers would simply forget to screw back the crown after winding it. Thus, the case would become flooded when submerged. Wilsdorf wouldn't rest until he had perfected the automatic self-winding movement.

In 1928, the *Rolex Prince* became an instant best seller (arguably the most successful of all Rolex

Harwood self-winding watch—note
the lack of a winding stem.
Circa 1920s

Unidentified automatic watch movement
based on Harwood design—note the
springs are mounted on the weight itself
rather than on a fixed bumper. Circa 1930s

Harwood self-winding movement—note
the semi-circular winding weight and bumpers.
Circa 1920s

Rolex *Bubbleback* case back
featuring the thick rounded shape
for which it was nicknamed.
Circa 1940s

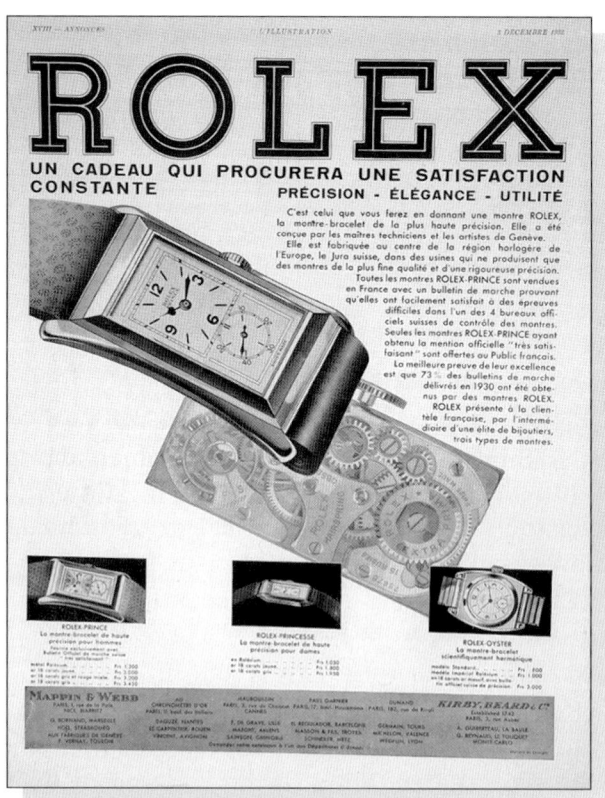

French magazine advertisement featuring the
Rolex Prince.
Circa 1932

watches), with its rectangular case and distinctive dual dial—hour/minute dial on top and seconds dial on bottom. It was known as: "the watch for men of distinction" and was frequently called "the doctors watch." Some say this was due to the increased accuracy and separate (clearly readable) seconds hand which simplified timing a pulse, while others say it was just too expensive for anyone other than members of society to afford.

Also in 1928, Rolex developed a new series of balances, available in three grades: 'Prima', 'Extra Prima' and 'Ultra Prima'—and were adjusted in 6 positions and all temperatures.

In the early 1920's, an Englishman named John Harwood introduced the first self-winding wristwatch, based on Perrelet's "pedometer" design of 1770. This unusual watch had no winding stem, thus solving the problem of dust entering the case, and the time was set by rotating the bezel. Its automatic movement utilized a semi-circular winding weight that pivoted at nearly 300 degrees—its swing interrupted by tiny bumpers on either side. However, the constant banging of this weight against the bumpers proved destructive (over time) to the watch's movement. While thousands of the watches were produced (over a two and a half year period) for the U.K., French and U.S. markets, they were never widely accepted. Ultimately, Harwood's patents expired and his company went bankrupt around 1930, shortly after the stock market crash of 1929.

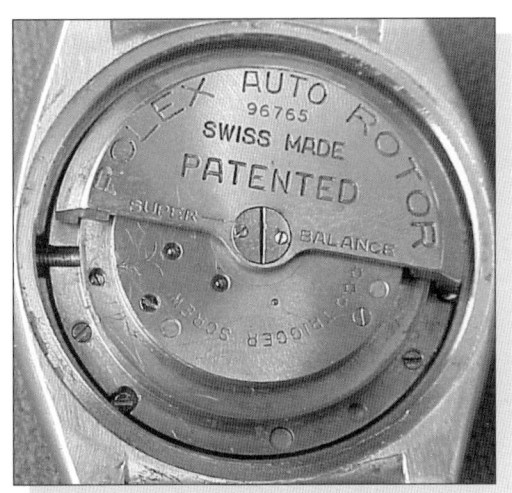

Rolex 'Auto Rotor' movement with Super Balance. Circa 1930s

Unlike others, Wilsdorf discarded this 'bumper' concept and never made any serious attempts at following Harwood's design. Instead, Wilsdorf believed the key lied in simple modifications to their existing movements—as usual, Wilsdorf was right. In 1931, the *Auto-Rotor* movement was designed from an existing Aegler (subsidiary seconds Hunter 8-3/4"') movement, and the first successful self-winding perpetual wristwatch was patented on January 14, 1932. The design is credited to Emile Borer, Herman Aegler's brother-in-law and the technical head of Rolex at the time. Its winding mass could turn (uninterrupted) both clockwise and counter-clockwise, and pivot freely a full 360-degrees on its staff in the center of the movement—thus a 'perpetual' motion. This design also added to the watch's accuracy, with the mainspring being held under constant tension. The watches were soon available in three sizes, so they could be marketed to women and men alike.

Due to the thickness of the case, to allow for the large semicircular-shaped rotor 'piggy-backed' onto the movement, it was subsequently nicknamed the *Bubbleback*[17], and has become one of the most sought after models by collectors. Later, the Auto Rotor was further improved on when, in 1935, a new 'streamlined' balance wheel was introduced as the *Super Balance*.

Throughout the 1920's, 30's and 40's, Rolex set records for accuracy, receiving numerous awards from the Kew, Geneva, Neuchatel and Besancon Observatories, respectively. By 1934, they were the first watch ever to receive class certificates from all four. From 1927 to 1940, these testing facilities issued a total of 21,561 chronometer certificates for wristwatches—Rolex received 19,155 of them! In fact, during a five month period in 1935, Rolex submitted 500 watches for certification. All 500 were issued chronometer certificates along with the accolade "honorable mention".[18]

By the mid 1930s, wristwatches had become more than just a passing fad, now accounting for 65% of all watches exported by Switzerland. They had proven themselves as being accurate, functional, waterproof and now self-winding. Wilsdorf's dream was becoming a reality and their business was

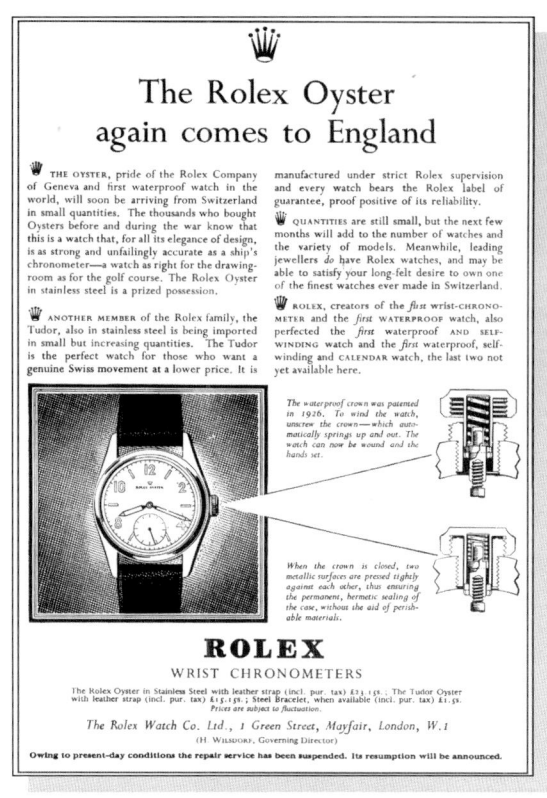

Magazine advertisement celebrating Rolex's return to England. Circa 1947

WWII vintage Rolex featuring the Roman/Arabic "California" dial. Circa 1940s

Courtesy of Passions of Singapore

First U.S. advertisement for the Rolex Oyster Perpetual. Circa 1944

Courtesy of Passions of Singapore

Rolex Chronograph (model 4768) with Valjoux movement. Circa 1940s

booming.

However, a new technology was on the horizon that would threaten the very existence of mechanical watches. In 1932, W.A. Morrison, working for Bell Labs, built the first Quartz clock—what would become the most accurate timepiece ever made, and would later prove to be accurate to within one second in over thirty years.

Then on September 21, 1935, a devastating blow hit Rolex—the devaluation of the English pound. Since Rolex's prices were set in English currency, the necessary increase caused exports to fall to a third. Rolex quickly scrambled to open new markets, thus lessening the financial blow. Those new markets included Italy, France and Argentina, as well as Latin America and the Far East.

By this time Gruen had sold off their shares to Aegler and Rolex, thus ending the three-way partnership which had lasted over a decade. Emile Borer took over Gruen's position on the board, and Rolex was now free to market their watches to the U.S.—which they would do just a few years later. It also meant that Rolex now had exclusive rights to *all* movements manufactured by Aegler.[19]

In 1937, Rolex joined the ranks of numerous other watch companies when they introduced their first *Chronograph* wristwatch. However, instead of designing the movement themselves, Rolex decided to use an existing movement from *Valjoux*[20]—which would continue to prove useful for nearly 50 years. In addition to timekeeping, a chronograph acts as a basic stopwatch. Early models used a simple one button control to start, stop and reset the seconds.

Wilsdorf, having the great business sense that he did, saw the need to market a line of lower priced watches without sacrificing the quality of Rolex. He registered numerous names such as Marconi, (named after the Nobel Prize winning physicist Gugliemo Marconi[21]), Omigra, Elvira, Marconi Lever, LON (named for the newly formed League Of Nations), Brex, Unicorn Lever and Rolco. (*Please Note: This is not a complete list and not all of these names were actually used.*) Wilsdorf was never happy with their success, and by the mid 1940's he had dropped all of the subsidiary lines.

By the start of the American involvement in World War II, U.S. watch companies were busy converting their factories to produce bomb fuses, gyroscopes, altimeters and other wartime instruments. Meanwhile, the 'neutral' Swiss companies were producing wristwatches at full speed. It is important to note that Rolex had not started exporting watches to the United States until the early 1940s.

In 1942, the War Production Board prohibited U.S. companies from manufacturing civilian watches. Military watches commonly featured Roman/Arabic dials, a version of which was patented by Rolex on May 30, 1941. Often referred to as the *California Dial*, it displays Roman numerals across the top half, with Arabic numerals across the bottom. Some military models even had an early 'hacking' feature, thereby making it easily synchronized with other watches during combat situations.

Even with this success, Rolex did not let their new presence in America distract them from servicing their European markets. In fact, Rolex watches were so popular in England that British pilots in the RAF (Royal Air Force) would decline the inferior government-issued watches in favor or Rolex Oyster Perpetuals, which they purchased with their own money.

To return the favor, Rolex had a standing wartime policy, whereas any *British* prisoner of war who lost his Rolex to his captors, could write to Geneva for a replacement. It is believed that this was Wilsdorf's own idea and he handled the correspondences personally. Apparently, the agreement was that the soldier would repay Rolex for the replacement watch, but not until after the war had ended.[22]

In 1944, tragedy struck Wilsdorf once again when his wife May died of a sudden illness. Also, in that same year, his friend and long-time business partner Hermann Aegler passed away leaving Wilsdorf as the sole owner of Rolex. With no heirs, and probably the fear that his company would go the same route of his father's after his death, Wilsdorf created the *Hans Wilsdorf Foundation* in 1945. This trust gave strict instruction on how the company was to be run after his death, ensuring that it

Rolex advertisement acknowledging their participation in the conquering of Mt. Everest. Circa 1954

Rolex advertisement celebrating the Oyster's success on Mt. Everest, as well as the record setting dive with the Bathyscaphe *Trieste*. Circa 1953

Timex magazine advertisement. Circa 1971

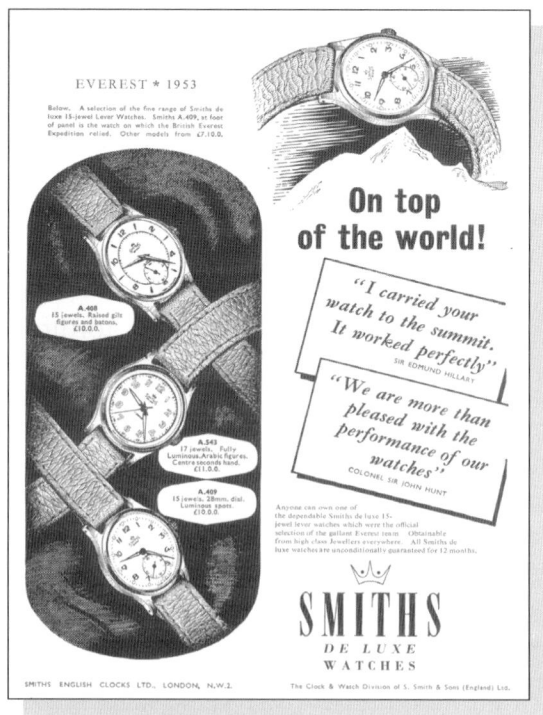

Smiths watch advertisement celebrating the use of their watches during the Mt. Everest expedition. Circa 1953

would never be sold and would never become publicly traded. To this day, the company follows his wishes and the *Hans Wilsdorf Foundation* allocates a large sum to charities and horological institutions.[23]

1945 marked the 40-year *Jubilee* anniversary of Rolex. It also marked three other very important achievements. On November 24, 1945, Rolex released the *Datejust* (model 4467), originally to be called the 'Victory'—to celebrate the Allied victory in WWII. This was their most expensive watch to date. Furthermore, it was the first calendar wrist watch with the numbered date automatically displayed in its dial window—changing automatically at midnight. Later in 1954, Rolex adopted the use of the glass bubble *cyclops* placed over the date which magnifies it 2 ½ times, making it much easier to read. It is worth noting that the *Jubilee* bracelet represented on the Datejust was so named for the Jubilee anniversary when it was introduced.

Also in 1945, Rolex launched what may have been their final attempt at a lower priced watch line: *Tudor*. Its symbol was originally a *rose*, representing the Tudor Rose, but was replaced with a *shield* by the 1960's. While it was nicknamed the "cheap-Rolex" and its quality scoffed at, Rolex insisted the Tudor line was "manufactured under strict Rolex supervision."[24] Finally, 1945 marked an achievement unprecedented in the watch industry when they received their 50,000[th] chronometer certificate from the testing bureau in Bienne.

LEFT: Original Tudor *Rose* logo
RIGHT: Current Tudor *Shield* logo

In the years that followed WWII, American watch companies struggled to catch up with the technological advancements of the Swiss 'jeweled' movements. This would prove to be a difficult fight, since the Swiss companies now accounted for 80% of the world's production of wristwatches.

One American success story to emerge from WWII was Joakim Lehmkuhl, a Norwegian electrical engineer who fled to America during the war. His company, *U.S. Time* would introduce a revolutionary yet inexpensive new watch in 1950, *Timex*. By 1955, Timex accounted for 15% of the U.S. Market in units and in 1959 sold over 8 million watches. Its success was greatly due to the fact that they were reliable and cheap—priced at just $25. Their subsequent TV campaigns would feature various 'torture tests' with the famous claim: "It takes a licking and keeps on ticking."

However, Rolex was busy with torture tests of their own. On May 29, 1953, Rolex participated in the conquering of Mt. Everest (at 29,035 feet) with the British Himalayas expedition led by Sir John Hunt. Expedition member Sherpa Tenzing Norgay was equipped with a prototype for the soon to be released *Explorer* (model 6098), which performed without fail. It was originally believed that Sir Edmund Hillary also wore a Rolex on the expedition. However, to Rolex's embarrassment, it was soon learned that he actually wore a watch made by the English company *Smiths,* when he endorsed the watch in a magazine advertisement (shown on the opposite page).

Around this time, Rolex expanded the size of their fa-

Courtesy of National Geographic

Mt. Everest expedition members Edmund Hilary and Tenzing Norgay. Circa 1953

cilities in Geneva which now employed 750 workers, with 450 more at the factory in Bienne.

Also in 1953, Rolex added two new models to their line: The *Milgauss* (model 6541), was the first watch specifically designed for people working around large electromagnetic fields, and the *Turn-O-Graph* (model 6202), which has been described as the predecessor for all modern sports models. Even with their notable contributions to the watch industry, they enjoyed only limited success.

Then in 1954, Rolex publicly released their most radical watch to date: the *Oyster Perpetual Submariner* (model no. 6204). This divers' watch featured an oversized steel case with rotating bezel, and was 'officially' rated waterproof to a depth of 180m/600ft. However, just a few months before, on September 30, 1953, a Submariner experimental watch simply known as *Deep Sea Special* was successfully tested to a depth of 3,150 meters (10,335 feet), when it was attached to the 'outside' of Professor Auguste Piccard's bathyscaphe *FNRS-2,* during the world depth record setting voyage.

Thanks to the growing popularity of Jacques Cousteau and the new sport of skin diving, the Submariner was an instant success. Certain models were even nicknamed the "James Bond" after being featured in a number of the spy films.[25] These watches were among the first of many to fit the *Professional* or *Tool Watch* category. Simply meaning, a watch that is designed for "use in specific professions or recreational pursuits."[26] While the Submariner was designed as a serious divers watch, most never see the depths for which they're rated—this sporty style has enjoyed enormous success as an everyday watch ever since.

That same year, Rolex released the *GMT-Master* (model 6542), named after Greenwich Mean Time—the world's standard time. It featured a 24-hour hand and bezel making it possible to read the time in any two time zones, simultaneously. Designed as an "aviators watch", GMTs were favorites among NASA astronauts in the 60's and 70's, as they still are today.[27] Chuck Yeager even wore one when he first broke Mach 1 (the speed of sound), on October 14, 1947—and again 50 years later.

However, when these watches were worn by astronauts in the *zero-gravity* conditions of space, they ceased to function after some 48 hours. This of course was due to the perpetual rotor which relies on gravity to auto-wind the watch. To overcome this, the astronauts had to wind the watches manually when in space.[28]

In 1956, Rolex took the Datejust one step further when they released the first *Day-Date* (model 6511), with the day of the week written out on the dial (now available in 26 different languages). This also marked the first *President* bracelet to celebrate the reelection of President Dwight D. Eisenhower. It is worth noting that this was the first model to bear "Superlative Chronometer Officially Certified" on the dial. Proving that the watch was not only elegant, but also incredibly accurate. Though the name President never appears on the watch (it was actually the *bracelet* that was named the President), it has become common place to refer to the Day-Date as a *President,* or *Presidential,* as nearly every President since Franklin D. Roosevelt has worn one. This fact was celebrated in the highly successful advertising campaign: "Men who guide the destinies of the world wear Rolex watches."

In 1955, the first Atomic clock was created, which used as its 'pendulum', the vibrating atoms of the metallic element, *cesium*—its frequency, 9,192,631,770 cycles per second, is said to give it an accuracy of "about 30 billionths of a second per year".[1] Finally, on January 3, 1957, the Hamilton Watch Co. introduced the first *electric wristwatch*—the mainspring replaced by a tiny energy cell (battery) that would last 18-months. This event sparked a revolution in the watch industry that would subsequently send many a watch company spiraling into bankruptcy decades later.

On January 23, 1960, a Rolex *test watch* was again part of a world record setting dive, when the Piccard (model 7205/0) accompanied the bathyscaphe *Trieste* on its journey into the Abyss. This new vessel was captained by Auguste Piccard's son Jacques Piccard, along with US Navy Lt. Donald

Hamilton Watch Company magazine advertisement celebrating the first electric wristwatch. Circa 1966

Rolex magazine advertisement celebrating the 50-year anniversary of Chuck Yeager's flight breaking the sound barrier (Mach 1). Circa 1997

Vintage RCA advertisement celebrating the invention of the Atomic Clock. Circa 1960s

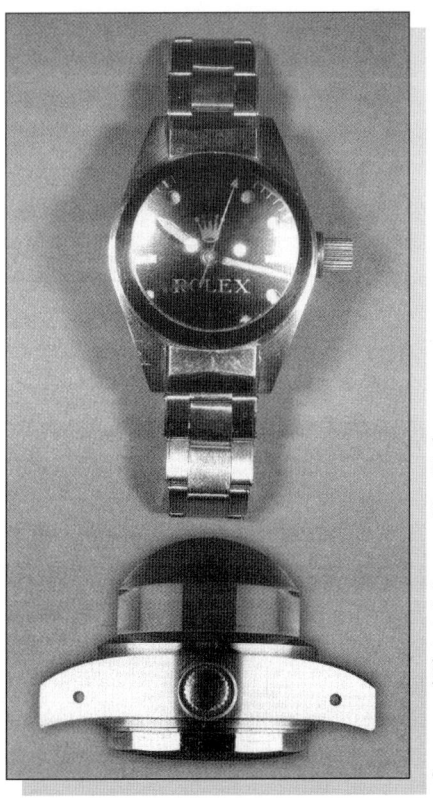

Courtesy of Christie's Images, New York

Rolex *Deep Sea Special*, experimental watch.

Walsh, and reached the deepest ocean floor in the world, the Challenger Deep of the *Marianas Trench* at 35,798 feet.

Unfortunately, Wilsdorf would never see the level of success to which his company would achieve, as he died on July 6, 1960, at the age of 79. Hans Wilsdorf had done more than just create a watch company—he created a legacy that would prove to be one of the most successful companies in the world. In 1963, running of the company was handed over to 41-year-old Andre J. Heiniger, as described in the provisions of the *Hans Wilsdorf Foundation.*

Also, in 1960 was the founding of the *Centre Électronique Horologer* (Electronic Watch Center) or C.E.H. in Neuchâtel. This consortium's prestigious membership included such names as Patek, Movado, Elgin, I.W.C., Enicar, Omega, Longines, Bulova, Le Coultre and Rolex, just to name a few. The purpose of this Swiss organization was to develop a quartz wristwatch movement.

Piccard's bathyscaphe *Trieste*, which journeyed to the deepest ocean floor in the world, the *Marianas Trench* at 35,798 ft.

Courtesy of Naval Historical Center, Wash DC

The C.E.H. publicly released their first production movement, the *Beta 21*, at the Basel fair on April 10, 1970. However, Rolex did not partake in this event, but instead conducted additional tests and publicly released their own model a few months later. Some say this was yet another example of Rolex's reputation for "over-engineering", as they refused to place their name or reputation behind anything without being extensively tested by their own engineers. Not to mention, they may still have had questions as to public demand for this product.

When the *Quartz Date* (model 5100) was first introduced on June 5, 1970, it was an immediate success—to Rolex's surprise. The watch was the first Rolex to feature a sapphire crystal, but did not utilize an Oyster case. Due to the very angular (or clunky) design, its success quickly faded, as did the *Beta 21*. Rolex discontinued this model by 1972 and pulled out of the C.E.H. in favor of continuing their own research. Contrary to popular belief, Rolex had been conducting research in electronic timekeeping for more than two decades, having filed patents for electro-mechanical watches as early as 1952.[29] Rolex introduced their improved *Oysterquartz* movement (calibre 5055) in 1977, which led to the *Oysterquartz Datejust* (model

Enicar Quartz OD, with the *Beta 21* movement. Circa 1970.

17000) and *Oysterquartz Day-Date* (model 19018), respectively. They featured new slimmer, angular cases, and now with the protection of the Oyster's screw-down crown and back—the accuracy of the Oysterquartz was guaranteed to err by less than one minute per year.

Unfortunately, despite these improvements, the Oysterquartz was a victim of bad timing—no pun intended. Around this time, Rolex was improving on the accuracy of their mechanical watches, having just developed the new 3030 movement which featured 28,800 BPH (or 8 beats per second), as opposed to the older 19,800 BPH (or 5.5 beats per second) movements. This advancement allowed Rolex to improve the accuracy of their watches by as much as 100%. Therefore, *accuracy* was not a motivating factor for one to jump ship from these mechanical watches.

The next blow to hit the Oysterquartz was the recent flood of *counterfeit* Rolex watches featuring quartz movements. As I'm sure you're aware, for years the tell-tale sign of a fake Rolex was the 'tick' versus 'sweep' second hand. Rolex has been known for having a fluid sweeping second hand and anything but was a sure sign of a cheap fake. This would certainly have been a difficult obstacle to overcome for Rolex dealers trying to sell the first Oysterquartz watches. Finally, the 'proverbial straw' that killed the Oysterquartz was the public opinion of quartz watches as being cheap. It became popular for companies to give away quartz watches at promotional events, thus making it difficult to maintain a level of value in the customers' eyes.

Rolex Oysterquartz Datejust

With these events all occurring within a relatively short period of time, the Oysterquartz had the deck stacked against them. Rolex was not blind to this, as they never turned their back on the product that built the company: *mechanical watches.* When Rolex released their first Quartz model in 1970, the total number never exceeded 7% of the company's total production. Even today, Rolex offers two Oysterquartz models: a Datejust and Day-Date, but the total production of these watches is now below 2%.

It is worth noting that the *Quartz Date* was not the first model in the Rolex catalog to feature a 'ticking' second hand. In 1954, Rolex released the *Tru-beat* (model 6556), which was also sold under the name *Metropolitan* in some U.S. markets. These watches featured a "dead beat" seconds hand, which actually stopped dead at each second before moving to the next—much the same as quartz watches today. The purpose of this unorthodox design was to provide a more easily readable seconds hand which would aide in measuring elapse time. Unfortunately, this was yet another example of Rolex being ahead of their time, as these models were avoided like the plague and were subsequently discontinued by 1960.

In 1971, Rolex introduced the *Sea-Dweller* (model 1665). Based on the Submariner design, it featured a reinforced case and *one-way gas escape valve* opposite the winding crown— to be used in decompression chambers after lengthy saturation dives. The watch was guaranteed to 660 m / 2,000 ft. In fact, early models were labeled on the dial in red: "SEA-DWELLER SUBMARINER 2000". The watch received several updates over the years, and in 1978, the depth rating was upped to an incredible 1,220 m / 4,000 ft (model 16660). Another notable feature of the Sea Dweller is the lack of a cyclops magnifier on the crystal.[30]

Over the years that followed, Rolex continued to release additional *Tool Watch* models, including: the *Explorer II, Yacht-Master* and updated 'Daytona' *Cosmograph* (now with

Courtesy of generalwar.com

Daytona Cosmograph (model 116528) with Paul Newman Dial.

an in-house movement), just to name a few. These models were a continued example of Rolex's commitment for the future being on mechanical watches, even under the recent frenzy of quartz watch movements.

During the 1970s and early 1980s, Japan was the new dominant force in the watch industry, with *Citizen* and *Seiko* producing inexpensive quartz watches in record numbers. The Swiss mechanical watches couldn't compete (on price), so many Swiss watch houses (with Rolex being one of the rare exceptions) eventually went toe-to-toe with the Far East markets by mass-producing quartz watches of their own. Unfortunately, these Swiss companies followed the quartz watch boom until it blew up in their collective faces. Thus, "such prestigious names as Omega, Longines, Blancpain, Tissot, Rado and Hamilton, were subsumed into a publicly owned consortium to avoid bankruptcy"[31]. This resulted in the Swiss watch industry seeing its position in the global market drop from 30% to 10%.

However, one rare Swiss success story to emerge was that of *Swatch*, who in 1983, entered the market with a new concept in watch production. While mechanical watches typically have in excess of 100 parts, these early Swatches had just 51. They had achieved major advancements in the mass production of inexpensive watches, which they marketed for just $25 to $35. Featuring colorful plastic cases, they were in essence 'disposable', as they were not designed to be repaired. Swiss watches were once again being produced in large quantity for global markets.

Early Swatch wristwatch.
Circa 1983

Meanwhile, Rolex had no intention of abandoning mechanical watches, but instead continued improving on their accuracy. In fact, from 1961 to 1985, Rolex received over 4.1 million chronometer certificates, making them by far the largest Swiss producer of chronometer wristwatches. However, this number still only represented about 1% of the total production of *Swiss Made* watches, thus Rolex epitomizes the saying "quality over quantity".

In 1992, Patrick Heiniger (son of André Heiniger) was appointed general manager by the Rolex board of directors. With a new commander at the helm, Rolex has continued to strive for perfection, with chronometer certificates for 1999 and 2000, totaling 584,607 and 635,209, respectively.[32]

While these numbers are staggering, the most impressive number thus far is actually the value placed on the company itself. According to *Interbrand* (the world famous branding consultants), Rolex closed out the millennium at number 55 on the list, with a total value of $3.56 billion, and a 1999 total sales figure of $1.451 billion. These are impressive numbers when one considers that this is a privately held company and the only watch company to appear on the list.

As we move into the 21st century, Rolex has once again proven their commitment to mechanical watches, with the creation of the *Watch Technicum* in the small town of Lititz, Pennsylvania. In this $9 million facility, students learn the art of mechanical watch repair, during an intense 3,000 hour course. The school accepts only 12 students per year, who attend tuition-free, but are required to provide their own tools. The school's director, Charles Berthiaume is also the vice president for Rolex USA, which co-founded the horological school with the *Watchmakers of Switzerland Training and Education Program*.

In the early 1980s, when the demand for mechanical watches began to decline, many watchmakers left the struggling industry for positions with defense contractors, where their micro-mechanical experience proved beneficial. Now, with the resurgence of mechanical watches, the need for experienced watchmakers has also risen. Unfortunately, there aren't enough people to fill the positions and the situation doesn't seem to be improving. According to Berthiaume, "the average age of a watchmaker in this country is in the mid 50s."[33] This along with the fact that there are currently less than a dozen watchmaking schools in the United States, has motivated Rolex to sponsor the school in hopes of building a force of watchmakers to maintain these mechanical timepieces into the new millennium.

[10] Quoted from *Timeless Elegance: Rolex,* by George Gordon.

[11] According to *Time in Gold, Wristwatches,* by Viola & Brunner: Rolex started by shipping only one watch marked "Rolex" in a box of six watches, a year later the number was increased to two, then a year later three, and so on...

[12] According to *The Best of Time, Rolex Wristwatches,* by Dowling & Hess: *"fees to the government alone were £74.00.00 (or $296 in 1915 dollars)."*

[13] The official name was *Aegler, Société Anonyme, Fabrique des Montres Rolex & Gruen Guild A.*

[14] According to *The Best of Time, Rolex Wristwatches,* by Dowling & Hess: Wilsdorf had a *"habit of reading every new patent applied for in Switzerland"*, thus he likely learned of the new design shortly after it was registered.

[15] According to *Time in Gold, Wristwatches,* by Viola & Brunner: Rolex invented the new "unbreakable synthetic material" (plastic) and it was produced in their own factory.

[16] After Miss Gleitze initial swim on October 8, 1927, many critics believed it to be a hoax and questioned her success. Miss Gleitze agreed to do it again, and on October 21, 1927, completed what has been called the "vindication swim". It was this event that Rolex participated in.

[17] In Italian it was known as *Ovettone,* meaning "little egg".

[18] Source: *Collecting Rolex Wristwatches,* by Osvaldo Patrizzi.

[19] During the 3-way partnership between Aegler, Gruen and Rolex, Aegler provided movements to both Gruen *and* Rolex. A notable example were the movements used in the Gruen *Techi-Quadron* and its sister model, the Rolex *Prince.*

[20] The name *Valjoux* was derived from the location of the factory

where they were produced: the *Vallée de joux*, high in the Jura mountains of western Switzerland.

[21] Marconi received the Nobel Prize for physics in 1909, for his accomplishment in sending radio signals over the Atlantic Ocean in 1901, and was considered one of the most contemporary thinkers of the time.

[22] James M. Dowling's Rolex webpage. http://www.ukwatches.com/

[23] According to *Time in Gold, Wristwatches*, by Viola & Brunner: *"A great portion of these funds goes, for example, to welfare projects (in memory of the founder's wife), another portion to such trade institutions as, for example, the Watchmaking School in Geneva (Industrial Arts Department), the School of Economic and Social Sciences at the University of Geneva, and the Swiss Watch Research Laboratory."*

[24] As quoted from *Britain's Horological Journal*, dated August, 1947, in *The Best of Time, Rolex Wristwatches*, by Dowling & Hess.

[25] In 1962, Sean Connery first donned a *Rolex Submariner*, when he portrayed James Bond in the film *Dr. No*.

[26] Quoted from *Vintage Rolex Sports Models*, by Skeet & Urul.

[27] While the 'official' wristwatch of NASA was the *Omega Speedmaster*, many astronauts favored Rolex GMT-Masters for their personal use and often carried them on space flights.

[28] Quoted from *The Best of Time, Rolex Wristwatches*, by Dowling & Hess.

[29] Rolex patented their first *electro-mechanical design* on April 7, 1952, as well as a *watch battery* on June 3, 1952.

[30] Due to the extra thickness of the crystal on the Sea-Dweller (3mm thick), the 'standard size' cyclops lens would not focus properly on the date, thus it was never adapted to this model.

[31] Quoted from *Through times of War and Peace, Rolex Has Kept Time With Style and Precision*, by Suzanne Rowan Kelleher. http://www.cigaraficionado.com

[32] Source: *Federation of the Swiss Watch Industry*. http://www.fhs.ch/index.htm

[33] Quoted from *Time to restore a craft*, by George Strawley, *The Associated Press*.

Rolex Wristwatch Profiles

Over the years, Rolex has produced a number of revolutionary watch styles which have become famous the world over. The following pages are dedicated to those watches. In this section, I will give an abbreviated background of their creation and evolution over the years. Unfortunately, this limited format prohibits me from covering every style within a particular model line. Instead, I will only discuss the more substantial events surrounding these watches. The watch models discussed are listed below in chronological order from when they were first introduced.

Furthermore, at the end of this section, I have included a *Quick Reference* of evolutions which occurred, affecting the Rolex watch line as a whole. Included in this discussion are: bracelets, hands, crystals, movements, etc...

PRINCE
BUBBLEBACK
DATEJUST
EXPLORER
TURN-O-GRAPH
SUBMARINER
MILGAUSS
GMT-MASTER
DAY-DATE "President"
COSMOGRAPH "Daytona"
SEA-DWELLER
OYSTERQUARTZ
YACHT-MASTER

(Please Note: Case & Lug sizes indicated for each model represent known sizes that have been identi-fied for that particular model. However, they may not represent every size produced for the given model—some exceptions are likely to occur on certain models.)

PRINCE

Year Introduced: 1928
First Model: 1343 / 971
First Movement: 1036

Model 1490, Circa 1930s

In 1928, Rolex introduced what would prove to be one of the most accurate wristwatches to date, the *Prince*. Compared by some to Cartier's *Tank* watch, the Prince featured a very modern rectangular case and was advertised as "the watch for men of distinction". Frequently called the "Doctor's watch", it featured separate dials for the hour/minute (on top) and seconds (on bottom).

Originally, the Prince was available in two different styles: the *Classic* (model 1343) which featured a rectangular case, and the *Brancard* (model 971) which was more flared in its design. Both models were available in sterling silver, 9kt and 18kt gold, but the Brancard was also available in a two-tone 18kt gold configuration.

By 1930, Rolex expanded the Brancard lineup to include two new versions, both featuring faceted end-pieces and the '971' designation. Model 971U was available in the metal configurations listed above, however, model 971A was known as the *tiger stripe* due to the two-tone 18kt gold stripes running along the top of the case. In the same year, Rolex began to offer the Brancard line with a solid platinum option, making it the most expensive model to date. Then in 1934, yet another option was added to the Brancard when it became available in steel.

In 1935, Rolex released the *Railway Prince* (model 1527) which featured stepped sides resembling those of a locomotive. At the same time, Rolex also introduced the H.S. movement, so named for *Heures Sautantes* (or Jumping Hours). On this unique design, the hour hand was replaced with a tiny aperture at the 12 o'clock position. Through this window one could view a miniature wheel displaying the hours 1 thru 12. When the

Courtesy of northerntime.com

Early Prince 'HS'
Jump Hour movement.
Circa 1936

minute hand passed the 60-minute mark, the wheel would turn, thus the hour marker 'jumping' into place at the start of each hour. The idea never really took off as they were considered too difficult to read. However, one might say that this is another example of Rolex being ahead of their time, since the design was resurrected a decade later as inspiration for the revolutionary Datejust aperture introduced in 1945.

One cannot discuss the Prince without mention of the "Quarter Century Club". This was a special series of watches made for the Eaton company, a large Canadian department store chain. When an employee completed 25-years of service, they were rewarded with a watch, thus the name Quarter Century. These watches featured a special dial with the inscription "$\frac{1}{4}$ CENTURYCLUB" replacing the normal hour markers around the dial. These watches also featured a special presentation engraving on the case back with the individual's name and years of service.

Prince (model 1490)
$\frac{1}{4}$ Century Club. Circa 1939

Courtesy of northerntime.com

Another rare and very odd model was called the *Sporting Prince*. This rectangular-shaped pocket watch, available in either conventional or "jumping hours", was carried in lieu of a wristwatch when participating in athletic events—particularly golf. When the hunting case was opened, a spring-loaded mechanism would tilt the movement up on a hinge so the dial could be easily read. This design has been described as an early shock-protecting device, thereby protecting the movement from harm during physical activity. Very rare (and very limited) versions were even created as wristwatches—with less than a dozen known to exist. According to Dowling & Hess, *The Best of Time, Rolex Wristwatches*: A number of these models have been faked by "using the Sporting Prince case with lugs soldered on."[34]

The Rolex Prince enjoyed success with numerous styles, include versions with sweep (or center) seconds and continued in production until around the mid 1940s when it was finally discontinued.

BUBBLEBACK

Year Introduced: 1933
First Model: 1858
First Movement: Ref. 520

	Gents	Ladies
Case Size:	31mm	24mm
Lug Size:	16mm	13mm

Model 3131, Circa 1940s

The story of the *Bubbleback* originated in the early 1930s when Rolex was developing their first self-winding movement. John Harwood's company had just gone bankrupt trying to perfect their 'bumper' design, and with their patents 'undefended', companies around the world were scrambling to succeed where he had failed—many of which offering only slight modifications to the aforementioned design. As usual, Rolex was the exception, and instead followed Robert Frost's advice and "took the road less traveled".

Wilsdorf had always felt the key to a successful automatic movement lied in simple modifications to their existing and 'already proven' designs. It was one of these movements, a subsidiary seconds 8-$\frac{3}{4}$''' Hunter, which was outfitted with the semi-circular rotor mechanism—actually bolted onto the back. In fact, it was this 'piggy-backed' rotor design which gave the watch its now-famous appearance and name. As it turns out, the Auto-Rotor was so thick it required the case back to have a 'bubble-shape' to house the oversized mechanism. Thus, the watch became affectionately known as the *Bubbleback*, and was also nicknamed the *Ovettone* in Italian (meaning "little egg").

While there has been some debate as to when the *first* Rolex Perpetual was released, it is believed that the Auto-Rotor design was developed as early as 1931, patented in 1932, introduced in 1933, and then publicly launched as "The watch sensation of 1934".

Courtesy of northerntime.com

Bubbleback (model 3131) with subsidiary seconds and featuring the Roman-Arabic or *California* dial. Circa 1942

One would think that the watch was an immediate success, however, that was not the case. Early public opinion was not favorable, probably due to the rash of unsuccessful self-winding models thrust onto the market during previous years. Rolex made many attempts at easing these concerns, not only for consumers, but also watchmakers who themselves were still quite skeptical of auto-winding designs—early Rolex models even contained instructions printed inside the case back to gain support from the watchmaking community.

The earliest Bubblebacks (probably model 1852 or 1858) were outfitted with a 3-piece case, reminiscent to the first Oyster Royal, but with a new deeper case back, and was subsequently powered by the Ref. 520 (subsidiary seconds), and Ref. 530 (sweep seconds)—with a substantially higher price for the 'sweep' versions.

In 1936, a 2-piece case was introduced with a new modified movement, now a 9 $^3/_4$'''. Model 3131 featured the Ref. 620 (subsidiary seconds), while model 3132 was powered by the Ref. 630 (sweep seconds).

It is worth noting that these early perpetuals were the first to be offered in the new stainless steel material *Steelium*, a Rolex term patented on December 18, 1931, as well as the steel and gold mixture *Rolesor*, also a Rolex term, patented on April 1, 1933.

In 1941, a ladies model was added, powered by the 7 $^3/_4$''' Hunter movement (Ref. 420), but only available with subsidiary seconds.

Over the years that followed, Rolex released numerous versions of the Bubbleback, including what subsequently evolved into the Big Bubbleback which led to the development of the Datejust in 1945. Versions of the Bubbleback and/or Big Bubbleback continued in production into the late 1950s and possibly even the early 1960s.

Courtesy of watchcommander.com

ABOVE: Bubbleback (model 3372) with sweep seconds. Circa 1940s

BELOW: Bubbleback (model 5028) with sweep seconds. Circa 1940s

Courtesy of watchcommander.com

LEFT: Bubbleback (model 5018) with 'Bombe' lugs. Circa 1950s

RIGHT: Early *Datejust* Big Bubbleback (model 6075) Circa 1948

DATEJUST

Year Introduced: 1945
First Model: 4467
First Movement: 740

(Big Bubbleback)			
Case Size: 31mm			
Lug Size: 20mm			
(Datejust)	Gents	Mid-Size	Ladies
Case Size:	36mm	31mm	26/29mm
Lug Size:	20mm	17mm	13mm
(Date)	Gents	Mid-Size	Ladies
Case Size:	34mm	31mm	24/26mm
Lug Size:	17/19mm	16/17mm	13mm

Courtesy of generalwar.com

Model 16233, Circa 2002

Rolex released the *Jubilee Datejust* (model 4467) in 1945, to mark the 40-year (or Jubilee) anniversary of the founding of *Wilsdorf & Davis*. Originally, Wilsdorf wanted to call it the Victory to celebrate the recent Allied victory in WWII, but it was changed to the Jubilee at the last minute. Shortly thereafter the name 'Jubilee' was dropped and the watch became simply known as the Datejust (although it didn't appear on the dial until some years later). The Jubilee name was then attached to the watch's bracelet, as it is known to this day.

The original Datejust was actually a version of the 'Big Bubbleback', which Rolex had been developing since the early 1940s. The new movement (caliber 740) featured two improvements: a sweep seconds hand, and a date wheel visible on the dial—through an aperture at the 3.

Like the Bubbleback, these early models were referred to as *Ovettone* (Italian for 'little egg'), due to the domed back, and show little similarity with today's Datejust models. They featured a 'coin edge' bezel (reminiscent to the Dennison cases used by Rolex in the 1920s), a date wheel which displayed alternating red and black numbers and a tiny Bubbleback vintage crown.

Over the years, the Datejust has seen numerous changes including a larger crown and new fluted bezel. Probably the most notable addition was when Rolex introduced the cyclops magnifying bubble on the DateJust (model 6605) at the Basel fair in 1954. Subsequently, the cyclops was added to every watch in the Rolex line to feature a 'date' wheel, with the exception of the Sea-Dweller and apparently was only *optional*

Courtesy of watchcommander.com

Early DateJust (model 6105)
Ovettone. Circa 1950s

on early model GMT-Masters.

In 1956, Rolex introduced a new Datejust (model 1625) known as the 'Thunderbird'. Named after the U.S. Air Force aerobatics flying team, it featured a gold Turn-O-Graph style bezel. Though a version of the watch is still available, it has enjoyed only limited success, even after numerous updates.

Initially, Rolex only offered the Datejust line in 18kt yellow gold, then around 1957 introduced it in stainless steel. By this time, examples in white gold and even platinum were in circulation, but only in very small quantities.

Around this time they also began to offer the Datejust with bracelet options: a Jubilee bracelet, Oyster bracelet or a leather strap. This coincided with the release of the Day-Date and with it the 'changing of the guard', as the Day-Date became the new flagship model.

Rolex was now relaxing their restrictions on the Datejust's configuration and introduced the first stainless and gold (also called the 'two-tone' or 'bicolor') models by 1962.

In the late 1970s, Rolex introduced two new improvements to the line. First was the 'Quick Set' feature, which allowed the date function to be set quickly (via the winding stem), without having to advance the hour hand past the midnight position. By 1983, all Rolex models were fitted with this Quick Set feature.

At this same time, Rolex began outfitting their watches with the new sapphire crystal. This improvement aided in the appearance, as well as the durability of the watch. This new crystal had a slimmer profile, yet was more waterproof and scratch resistant.

When Rolex completed these improvements, they began designating the watches with a new case reference number featuring five-digits, replacing the old four-digit number.

In addition to the Datejust, Rolex introduced the Oysterdate in the early 1950s. This watch is very similar to the Datejust, its case being just 2mm smaller. Rolex has also offered the Datejust in a 'mid-size' which is 80% the size of the standard Datejust.

Courtest of watchcommander.com

Early DateJust (model 5030)
Ovettone —Note the lack of a cyclops.
Circa 1950s.

Courtesy of bjsonline.com

Datejust (model 16264) fitted with the Turn-O-Graph (or Thunderbird) bezel. Circa 2001

EXPLORER

Year Introduced: 1953
First Model: 6098 / 6150
First Movement: A.296

Explorer
Case Size: 36mm
Lug Size: 20mm*
Explorer II
Case Size: 40mm
Lug Size: 20mm

* 19mm on 5500 models

Courtesy of generalwar.com

Model 14270, Circa 2002

The he origin of the Explorer dates back to the early 1950s, when Rolex began testing the durability of the Bubbleback as a utility watch. These early Explorer prototypes; model 6098, fitted with a white dial featuring arrow-shaped hour markers and hands; and model 6150, donned a black 'Quarter Arabic' dial with only the 3-6-9 marked with numerals—this model also featured large Mercedes-style hands. While both watches were powered by the prototype A.296 movement, neither actually bore the name Explorer on the dial.

Apparently, both models were given to mountaineers and expedition members to test the limits of these watches. Included in this experiment were members of the British Himalayas expedition who set out to conquer Mt. Everest in 1953. After the highly publicized success of this expedition, the watches quickly evolved, and the name "Explorer" was adopted.

In mid 1953, the 6098 was renumbered as the 6298, and was upgraded to the black Quarter Arabic dial, but retained the arrow-shaped hands. Also in late 1953, the 6150 was renumbered as the 6350, and was the first to bear the name Explorer on the dial—positioned above the 6.

During this period of renumbering, it is common for the inside case back to bear *both* numbers, with the earlier number being "struck through", and the newer number positioned below.

Over the next decade, the watch saw numerous changes, including four new models: the 6610, 5500, 5504 and 1016, respectively. Notable changes in the mid 1950s included: the introduction of flush-fit end pieces, the words "Officially Certified

Courtesy of watchcommander.com

Explorer (model 6350) with black honeycomb dial. Circa 1950s

Chronometer" positioned above the 6, and the name "Explorer" moving to its new home positioned below the 12. Also (for a short time), the 6610 featured a depth rating of "50m = 65ft" printed in red below the 12. Probably the most visible change was the evolution of the hands, from pencil-shaped to the more recognizable "Mercedes-style" we know today.

By the late 1950s, the dials began to read "Superlative Chronometer Officially Certified" above the 6. Around this same time Rolex also changed the wording at the bottom of the dial from *Swiss* to *Swiss T<25*, signifying the switch from Radium to Tritium as the luminous material. (*Please Note: Some models in the early 1960s will bear Swiss, with T<25 positioned on either side. This was due to the T<25 being added to the existing stock of dials that were already printed Swiss.*)

Courtesy of bjsonline.com

Explorer II (model 1655) with 'orange' hand. Circa 1970s

In the late 1950s, Rolex released a version of the *Air-King* (model 5500) with an Explorer dial. This dress watch is recognizable by its slightly smaller size, and fitted with a 19mm bracelet instead of the 20mm on standard Explorer models. The dial was also marked "Precision" or "Super Precision" above the 6—early version dials were in gloss black. Recent evidence suggests that these watches may have been sold to British military officers in the far east markets.

In 1963, Rolex launched what would prove to be the most sought after model in the Explorer line, the *Space-Dweller* (model 1016). This version of the Explorer was to commemorate a visit to Japan by NASA's Mercury astronauts. The watch was not released into all Rolex markets (sold primarily in Japan) and was not a major seller. Therefore, very few were produced, making it a highly collectable model. These models were, in fact, marked "Space-Dweller" below the 12.

2002 Explorer II (model 16570).

The next major change would come in 1971, when a new watch was introduced, the *Explorer II* (model 1655). This watch featured crown guards, a new fixed, engraved 24-hour bezel and an extra (orange) 24-hour hand, which when used against the bezel would distinguish AM from PM, and thus day from night. The watch was designed for speleologists (cave explorers), who spend days on end exploring deep caverns where its easy to lose track of time, not to mention daylight. By 1974, the extra hour hand was changed to *red*, instead of *orange* as on previous versions. Over the next decade, the watch saw few changes, until it was discontinued in early 1985.

By mid 1985, the new Explorer II (model 16550) featured the 3085 movement, and benefited from a major facelift as well. Updating its appearance was a new bezel, Mercedes hands (replacing the older, large stick hands), and a slimmer sapphire crystal. This model also borrowed its new extra hour hand from the GMT and with it the very popular 'jump-hour' feature. For the first time, this watch was now available in a black or white dial option.

Meanwhile, the 1016 carried on relatively unchanged until it was discontinued in 1989, and replaced by the new Explorer (model 14270). This completely redesigned model featured a new movement, case, dial and sapphire crystal.

TURN-O-GRAPH

Year Introduced: 1953
First Model: 6202
First Movement: A.296

All models
Case Size: 40mm
Lug Size: 20mm

Model 6202, Circa 1950s

In 1953, Rolex released the *Turn-O-Graph* (model 6202), its name labeled in very tiny print below the Rolex logo, positioned below the 12. Shortly thereafter, the name was repositioned (in larger print) to its new home, above the 6. Powered by the A.296 movement, it was depth rated to 165 feet (50 meters), though this designation was not marked on the dial until a few versions bore it in the mid 1950s. The watch featured a black rotating bezel to measure elapsed time, which Rolex referred to as a "time-recording rim". The bezel bore rounded numbers at the ten-minute marks and tiny circular minute divisions all the way around. However, the bezel did not feature a luminous bubble at the 12 until the late 1950s. It also sported a black dial, with round luminous markers on all the hours, save the 3-6-9, which utilized rectangular indices and the 12 featuring the now-popular inverted triangle.

Early versions were equipped with pencil-shaped hands and featured a seconds hand with a small luminous circle all the way on the tip. The more recognizable Mercedes-style hands were introduced to the Turn-O-Graph by the mid 1950s. Also around this time, the watch was upgraded to the A.260 movement. It is important to note that some (but not all) models featured "Officially Certified Chronometer" positioned above the 6, as far back as the early 1950s.

The watch was marketed to adventurer-types and world travelers, but due to the success of the Submariner and GMT, the Turn-O-Graph was eventually discontinued in the early 1960s.

Early Turn-O-Graph (model 6202). Note the pencil-shaped hands and second hand with luminous circle on the tip.

SUBMARINER

Year Introduced: 1953
First Model: 6200
First Movement: A.296

___All models___
Case Size: 40mm
Lug Size: 20mm

Courtesy of generalwar.com

Model 16610, Circa 2002

Over the years, Rolex has become famous for "over-engineering" their watches. They've exposed them to the most outrageous of conditions, dating back to the first *Oyster* which braved the English Channel, the *Explorer* conquered Mt. Everest and the *Milgauss* warded off massive electromagnetic fields. Rolex watches have broken the sound barrier and even experienced the zero-gravity of space, but these grueling tests pale in comparison to those the *Submariner* has faced.

On September 30, 1953, Rolex took the term 'torture tests' to a new level, when a Rolex experimental watch simply known as *Deep Sea Special* was successfully tested to a depth of 10,336 feet (3,150 meters). The watch was attached to the 'outside' of Piccard's famed bathyscaphe *FNRS-2*, during the world depth record setting voyage. It is worth noting that only seven of these experimental watches were made, #5 sold in June 2000, at Christie's in London for £75,250/$112,500.[35]

If this wasn't enough, Rolex pushed the envelope even further on January 23, 1960, with another experimental watch, now more fittingly named the Piccard (model 7205/0). This watch accompanied Piccard's new bathyscaphe, the *Trieste*[36], on its journey to the deepest ocean floor in the world, the Challenger Deep of the *Marianas Trench* at 35,798 feet (11,000 meters)—at this depth, the watch successfully withstood pressures of over seven tons per square inch!

There has been some discussion as to which, was in fact, the *first* Rolex diving watch. The short list includes the 6200, 6204 and 6205 models, respectively. There is evidence to support each claim, but for simplicities' sake,

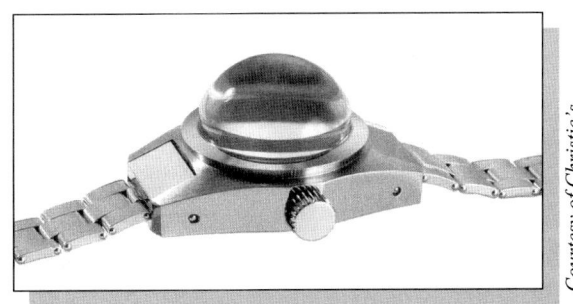

Courtesy of Christie's

Rolex Piccard (model 7205/0), which accompanied the bathyscaphe *Trieste* to the *Marianas Trench* at a depth of 35,798 feet.

I will favor a recent opinion which is gathering many followers.

Unlike current Submariner models, which are divided into two versions, date and non-date, the Submariners of the 1950s were divided into different depth ratings—many available in the Rolex catalog concurrently. This was due to the fact that in the 1950s, not every recreational diver *needed* a watch with a depth rating of 600+ feet. Therefore, Rolex offered different models, with different depth ratings, at different price points. Today however, all current Submariners are rated to 1,000 feet, whether it be the date, or non-date model—if one requires a deeper rated watch, they can simply opt for the Sea-Dweller with a 4,000 feet rating.

It is worth noting that Rolex model numbers (for the most part) ran in chronological order, therefore it is logical to assume that the 6200 would have preceded the 6204, and 6205, respectively. With that being said, it is believed by some that the first Rolex diving watch was the model 6200, released in 1953, and powered by the A.296 movement[37]. Early versions were fitted with a bi-directional bezel (with rounded numbers at the ten minute marks), and featured a dial strikingly similar to the Explorer prototypes (with numerals at the 3-6-9), which were also released in 1953. The case was thick and the winding crown oversized, bearing the mark *Brevet* (from the French word *brevette* meaning patented) under the coronet, and with it a depth rating of 660 feet (200 meters).

Brevet crown.

However, at this time neither the depth rating, *nor* the name Submariner were printed anywhere on the watch. It is also important to note that all of the early models (until around 1955) were fitted with pencil-shaped stick hands and featured a second hand with a small luminous circle on the tip.

The 6204 was *officially* launched as the first Submariner at the Basel Spring Watch Fair in 1954. Although, it is believed to have actually been released shortly after the 6200, in late 1953. The earliest versions (produced in 1953), were rated to 330 feet (100 meters), but by the time it was launched at Basel it had been upped to 600 feet (180 meters). This was the first version to bear the name *Submariner* on the dial (in very small print), positioned above the 6. However, many examples have surfaced where the name *Submariner* had been "obscured by black paint." [38]

The reason for this is unknown, but it has been suggested that there may have been a legal issue, concerning the use of the name Submariner, that had yet to be resolved. This theory is further supported by the fact that Rolex patented a number of model names from 1953 to 1954 which could have been used in lieu of Submariner. Those names included the following: *Deepsea* (Jan '53), *Frogman* (Feb '53), *Diver* (July '54), *Deep-sea Diver* (July '54), *Skin Diver* (July '54), *Dive-O-Graph* (Sept '54), and *Swimpruf* (Oct '54). It is worth noting that the name "Submariner' was not officially patented by Rolex until around 1960.

Also in 1954, Rolex released the 6205, which was almost identical to the 6204. Both watches were fitted with the A.260 movement, which was an improved version of the A.296 fitted to the 6200. They also shared a new dial, which closely resembles the style we are accustomed to today—round hour markers, with rectangles at the 3-6-9. One distinguishable difference was that the 6205 was only rated to 330 feet (100 meters), although it was not printed on the dial until around 1955.

In 1955, the 6204 was renumbered as the 6538, and the 6205 as the 6536, respectively. These new models were subsequently marked *Submariner*, in larger print above the 6. The 6536 was

Courtesy of bjsonline.com

Submariner (model 6536-1)
'Chronometer version'. Circa 1957

now fitted with the new 1030 movement and Mercedes hands, which the 6538 did not receive until the late 1950s, when a version was released as the 6538A—the 6536 and 6538 remained in production until 1965. Also in 1955, the 6200 received the Mercedes hands, and by 1958 it was available with either the standard Submariner, or Explorer styled dial.

By 1956, the Submariner bezel was redesigned, now featuring individual minute marks—to the first fifteen minutes. Soon thereafter, the triangle positioned on the bezel was painted red, and the watches' cases were being made thicker—similar to the 6200 model. The larger *Brevet* crown was being widely used as well. Also in 1956, the 6536 became available as the 6536/1, which featured a chronometer version of the 1030 movement.

In 1958, the 6200 was renumbered as the 5510, and the 6536/1 as the 5508, respectively. Both were fitted with the new 1530 movement, and remained in the product line until the mid 1960s.

By the late 1950s, the bezel was again redesigned, now featuring the squared font numbers we know today, and the triangle was no longer painted red. Also around this time, the word *Brevet* was removed from the winding crown, now simply featuring the Rolex coronet.

In 1959, Rolex launched the 5512, which was fitted with the 1570 movement and the first model to feature the crown guard—these earliest versions of the crown guards had square profiled ends. By the early 1960s, the 5512 was fitted with the 1560 movement, and with it bore the words *Officially Certified Chronometer* on the dial, positioned above the 6. Around this time, the crown guards had a more pointed appearance at the ends, but by the mid 1960s their appearance shifted to the more rounded profile, as they are today.

In 1962, the model 5513 was launched, powered by a non-chronometer 1530 movement, but was fitted with the 1520 movement by the mid 1960s. Around this same time, Rolex changed the wording at the bottom of the dial from *Swiss* to *Swiss T<25*, signifying the switch from Radium to Tritium as the luminous material used on the dial and hands. Some models in the early 1960s will bear *Swiss*, with *T<25* positioned on either side. This was due to the *T<25* being added to the existing stock of dials that were already printed: *Swiss*.

By the mid 1960s, chronometer models now read *Superlative Chronometer Officially Certified*, and the overall dial's printing switched from gold to white.

In 1966, Rolex launched the 1680 model, powered by the 1575 movement, and with it the first *date* feature on a Submariner. To allow the cyclops magnifying bubble to be positioned over the date aperture, the crystal was given a thick, yet flat profile (as opposed to the bubbled shape on other models). The

Submariner (model 5512) Circa 1963

Submariner (model 5513)
Circa 1960s

ABOVE: Fitted with current-style Submariner dial.

BELOW: Fitted with early-style 3-6-9 Arabic dial.

name *Submariner* was printed in red on the 1680 model as late as 1980, however, the white printed name began phasing back in as early as 1974.

By the early 1970s, the winding crown now bore the current *Triplock* markings—three dots positioned under the coronet.

In the early 1980s, the 1680 was renumbered as the 16800, and was now fitted with a scratch-resistant synthetic sapphire crystal, giving it a much slimmer profile—the depth rating was now increased to 1,000 feet (300 meters).

Triplock crown.

Also in the 1980s, Rolex added a new safety feature to the rotating bezel. Prior to this time, the bezel was able to turn both clockwise *and* counterclockwise. Now, the bezel was restricted to turning *only* counterclockwise. This was done to prevent the accidental movement of the bezel while diving, thus giving the erroneous indication of less time spent at depth. This could cause the diver to incorrectly pace his ascent, and therefore increase his chances of developing DCI (decompression illness), a potentially deadly condition often referred to as "the bends"

In 1996, the 16800 was replaced by the *current* Submariner (model 16610), now featuring the new Cal. 3135 movement. While a year earlier, in 1995, a new non-date Submariner (model 14060) was released, powered by the Cal. 3030. This watch was subsequently replaced in 2001 by the 14060M, which features the new Cal. 3130 movement.

Over the years, there have been a number of the Submariners adapted for military use. The first of which was in 1954, when a version of the 6204 was issued to the British Royal Navy. Then in the late 1950s, a version of the 6538 was modified for *both* the British Royal Navy *and* Royal Canadian Navy.

In 1968, a special version of the 5513 was issued to the British Royal Navy. This watch was fitted with a large diamond-shaped hour hand, with a similar shape on the tip of the second hand. Another distinguishing feature, was the letter "T" within a circle, printed above the *Submariner* name, which was positioned above the 6. This is said to signify the use of Tritium as the luminous material on the dial and hands. (*Please Note: These watches also featured T<25 at the bottom of the dial, signifying the luminous material as well.*)

ABOVE: Submariner (model 5513) as issued to the *British Royal Navy*, and fitted with 'military strap'.

BELOW: Reverse side of the same watch, with 'identifying service numbers' engraved on the case back.

In 1972, Rolex created the 5517, specifically designed for to the British Royal Marines. This watch looked nearly identical to the 5513 listed above, with the exception of the bezel, which featured individual minute marking all the way around—not just to the first fifteen minutes.

The three later watches (6538, 5513 and 5517) had the strap bars soldered in place, allowing the watch to be fitted with a military-style cloth strap, exclusively. It is also said that these watches feature "identifying service numbers" engraved on the case backs.

It is impossible to discuss the Submariner without a mention of *James Bond*, since the watch was featured in a number of the movies. As a child, I remember watching the spy films, and marveling at the gadgets Q had created for my hero. None was more memorable than the Submariner, which featured a bezel, spinning like a

saw-blade, allowing 007 to cut free the ropes binding his hands.

The success of the Submariner, has been (at least partially) credited to its presence in these spy films—after all, who wouldn't want a Submariner after seeing James Bond wear one? You can liken this to the success of Ray Ban's *Wayfarer* sunglasses, after Tom Cruise donned them in the film *Risky Business*.

Over the years, I've received numerous inquires as to which Submariner model was *officially* considered the James Bond model—unfortunately, the answer isn't that simple. While most collectors categorize *all* Submariners without crown guards as James Bond models, Rolex purists would argue that only the 6200, 6204, 6536 and 6538 deserve this distinction. Another qualifying factor for many is the presence of the larger 'Brevet' crown.

With that being said, there's also the matter of the 5513, which Roger Moore used in *Live And Let Die*. While it doesn't fit the description mention above, it's probably the most memorable Submariner to be featured in the spy films. The actual movie prop used in the film is shown in the images below.

Movie prop Submariner (model 5513) Note the 'modified' bezel which has been re-cut to resemble a saw-blade.

This watch sold at a Christie's auction in 2001 for £26,523.

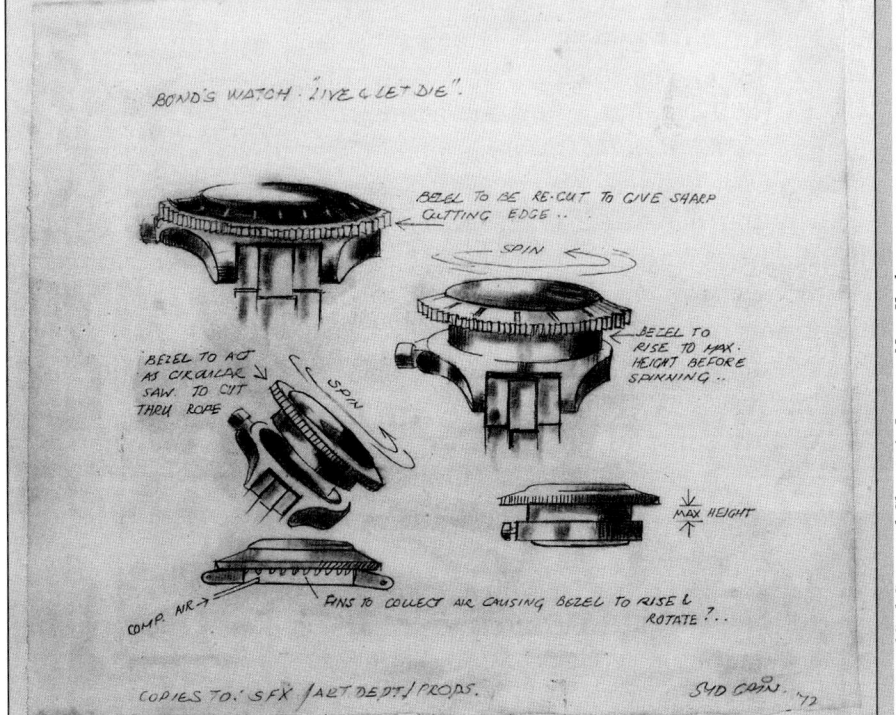

RIGHT: Production drawing by *Syd Cain* for the 'movie prop' Submariner (model 5513) used in the *James Bond* Film "Live And Let Die". Circa 1973

This drawing sold at a Christie's auction in 2001 for £7,233.

MILGAUSS

Year Introduced: 1954
First Model: 6541
First Movement: 1065M

All models
Case Size: 40mm
Lug Size: 20mm

Model 6541, Circa 1958

Introduced in 1954, the Milgauss (model 6541) was the first watch designed specifically for people working in power plants and research labs, where electromagnetic fields can play havoc with the accuracy of a watch. To protect the delicate balance workings, the movement contained anti-magnetic alloys, and was encased by an iron shield. The watch's magnetic intensity rating was to 1000 *oersted*[39], thus the name *Milgauss* is derived from the French word *mille* (meaning one thousand) and *gauss*[40] (unit of magnetic flux density).

Early on, the watch's appearance was similar to that of the Submariner, with an over-sized case and bezel, featuring a Twinlock crown, and riveted construction Oyster bracelet. While the watch only saw two models (6541 and 1019), they went through numerous configuration changes before finally being discontinued around 1988.

Probably some of the biggest changes were the evolution of the hands: from early leaf shaped, to the "Mercedes-style" with *lightning bolt* seconds, and subsequently the stick shaped hands that saw the watch to the end. Also notable was on model 1019, when the Submariner-style numbered bezel was replaced with a plain, smooth finished bezel. The earliest, and most desirable model for collectors, featured a Submariner bezel and dial, and the name 'Milgauss' positioned above the 6 rather than the subsequent position under the 12.

Milgauss (model 1019).
Circa 1969

GMT-MASTER

Year Introduced: 1954
First Model: 6542
First Movement: 1036

All models
Case Size: 40mm
Lug Size: 20mm

Courtesy of generalwar.com

Model 1675, Circa 1970s

In 1954, Rolex launched the GMT-Master (model 6542), after a request from Pan American Airlines for a watch that "could simultaneously display the exact time in two different time zones." The watch was an instant success, and was adopted by Pan AM, as well as numerous other airlines worldwide, as their official timepiece.

The earliest versions are easily identified because they are not marked 'GMT-Master' on the dial, but instead have the depth rating "50m = 165ft" printed in red above the 6. Early versions also featured an acrylic *Bakelite* bezel, which had a darker finish, so as not to be reflective into the pilot's eyes. This bezel was found to be inferior, because it had a tendency to fracture when in very warm environments. It was quickly replaced with a metal bezel, making these early models quite desirable for collectors.

Another rarity for the early GMT was the presence of a *white* dial. Apparently, Pan AM ordered a small number (probably less than 200) of watches with this configuration, "to differentiate between watches intended for air crew and for ground staff."—thus, black dials were issued to air crew, with white dials issued to ground staff.[41]

In the early 1960s, Rolex changed the color of lettering printed on the dial from gold to white, and with it the date wheel numbers changed from 'alternating' red/black to all

Courtesy of watchcommander.com

Early GMT (model 6542) with *Bakelite* bezel. Note the tiny arrow on the tip of the 24-hour hand. Circa 1950s

black.

By the mid 1960s, the extra function 24-hour hand switched from a small arrow on the tip, to a larger arrow. Around the same time Rolex changed the wording at the bottom of the dial from *Swiss* to *Swiss T<25*, signifying the switch from Radium to Tritium as the luminous material used on the dial and hands.

Like the Submariner, the early GMT models did not have crown guards to protect the winding stem—this feature was added in the early 1960s (on model 1675), and a more rounded version was outfitted in the late 1960s. Also on the 1675, the wording "Official Certified Chronometer" printed on the dial, was first changed to "Superlative Chronometer Officially Certified."

Another feature missing from early models was the cyclops lens, positioned over the date aperture. Apparently, this was an option until the early 1960s, but very few made it out of the factory without it, making this a bit of a rarity.

In the early 1970s, Rolex outfitted a special version of the 1675 with a Jubilee bracelet—making it the only sports model to be factory-fitted with this bracelet design. At this time, Rolex also began offering the bezel with a black insert.

GMT-Master II (model 16710). Circa 2002

Around 1976, the 'hack' feature was added, and in 1981 the 1675 was renumbered as the 16750 when it was fitted with the 3075 movement, and with it the 'Quick Set' feature and sapphire crystal upgrade. The 16750 was quickly replaced by the 16700 GMT-Master, and 16710 GMT-Master II, which utilizes the new 3085 movement.

The new GMT-Master II is now capable of one-hour jumps, forward or backwards (without affecting the minute or second hands), and allowing more flexibility in viewing any two time zones simultaneously.

DAY-DATE
"President"

Year Introduced: 1956
First Model: 6511
First Movement: 1055

All models
Case Size: 36mm
Lug Size: 20mm

Courtesy of generalwar.com

Model 118239, Circa 2002

The first Day-Date (model 6511) was introduced at the Basel fair in 1956. It was an instant success, featuring the numbered date at the 3 position (aided by a cyclops lens), and the day of the week spelled out at the 12 position. The watch was available in 18kt gold or Platinum, and featured a new "President" bracelet, said to be named for President Dwight D. Eisenhower after one of the watches was presented to him as a gift to celebrate his reelection.

The early models were quite large, to house the mechanics required to drive the extra day-date wheels. However, this didn't prove to be much of a problem, as it quickly became Rolex's 'flagship' model. After only a year, the 6511 was replaced by the 6611 featuring a new (and improved) movement (cal 1055), and with it the first to be marked "Superlative Chronometer Officially Certified". Over the years to follow, the watch saw very few changes, until 1972 when the 'hack' feature was added. This feature would stop the second hand when the winding stem was pulled out fully, thus allowing one to synchronize the time with another source.

In the late 1970s, Rolex introduced two new improvements to their line. First was the 'Quick Set' feature, which allowed the date function to be set quickly (via the winding stem), without having to advance the hour hand past the midnight position—by 1983, all Rolex models were fitted with the 'Quick Set' feature. At this same time, Rolex began outfitting their watches with the new sapphire crystal. This improvement aided in the appearance, as well as the durability of the watch. The new crystal had a slimmer profile, yet was more waterproof and scratch resistant. When Rolex completed these improvements, they began outfitting the watches with a new case reference number featuring five-digits, replacing the old four-digit number.

The next improvement to be made came in late 1990, when Rolex introduced the 'Double Quick Set' feature, which now allowed both the date *and* day of the week to be quickly set via the winding stem.

Though the name 'President' has never appeared on the dial (it was actually the *bracelet* that was named the 'President'), it has become common place to refer to the men's Day-Date as the 'President'. Furthermore, the Lady-Datejust featuring a *President bracelet* is also sometimes referred to as a 'Lady-President'.

In what is probably the most news worth event to occur within the Day-Date line in some years, Rolex recently (in 2000) released the watch with an *Oyster* bracelet option (model 11820/ series)—but still retains the *concealed clasp* we're accustomed to. The Oyster bracelet version is available in 18kt yellow, white or pink (rose) gold and is said to be the heaviest version ever offered—weighing in at around 30% more than other Day-Date models.

Courtesy of Michael J. Rosenman

Lady DateJust (model 79178) with President bracelet. Circa 2002

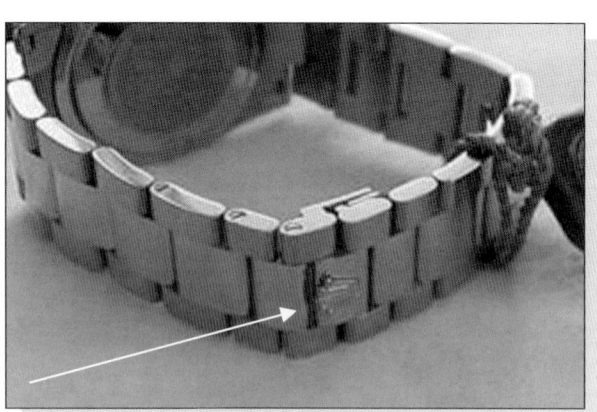

New Oyster bracelet with *concealed clasp,* outfitted to the Day-Date (model 11820/ series), available in 18kt yellow, white or pink (rose) gold. Circa 2000

Courtesy of generalwar.com

Day-Date (model 118205) featuring a domed bezel and new Oyster bracelet. Circa 2000

COSMOGRAPH
"Daytona"

Year Introduced: 1960
First Model: 6239
First Movement: 72B *(Valjoux)*

(Early models) **Gents**
Case Size: 37mm
Lug Size: 20mm
(Late models*)
Case Size: 40mm
Lug Size: 20mm

* Since model 16520

Courtesy of generalwar.com

Model 116528, Circa 2002

Chronograph: From the Greek words "chrons" and "graphis" which means "writing of time". A chronograph is a timepiece that, in addition to the normal time telling function, also performs a separate time *measuring* function such as a stop watch—with a separate seconds hand which can be started, stopped and reset to zero, via push-buttons on the side of the case.

Rolex released their first chronograph wristwatch around 1937. However, rather than designing the movement themselves, they decided to import movements from *Valjoux*—which proved useful for nearly 50 years. These "Anti-Magnetic" watches saw numerous styles with varying degrees of success.

In 1960, Rolex resurrected the faltering chronograph line with the introduction of the *Cosmograph* (model 6239). While a Cosmograph is in fact a chronograph by definition, the name "Cosmograph" was a creation of Rolex. The cosmetic difference being that a Cosmograph has the tachymeter scale engraved on the bezel, whereas chronograph models were printed on the dial.

The watch was powered by a *Valjoux* 72B movement, but was subsequently replaced with the 722/1. It is worth noting that these earliest Cosmograph versions had the tachymeter scale calibrated to 300 units per hour, but within a year was changed to only 200 units per hour.

In 1961, Rolex released a second version (model 6241), which like the 6239, was powered by the 72B movement. The difference between these two models was cosmetic, in

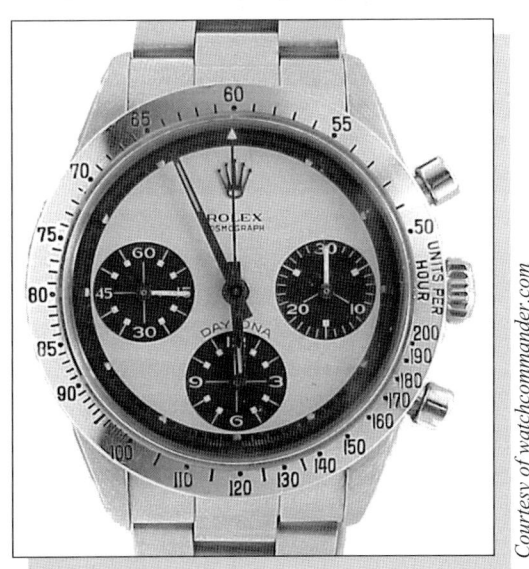

Courtesy of watchcommander.com

Daytona Cosmograph (model 6239) with exotic 'Paul Newman' dial. Circa 1960s that the 6239 featured a solid steel bezel, but the 6241 had a steel ring fitted with a clear acrylic insert.

These watches soon became known as the *Daytona*, so named after Daytona Beach, Florida, which is home to some of the biggest names in auto racing. The watches were very popular in the racing community, due to their usefulness when calculating average lap speed.

In this picture, Paul Newman is seen wearing the watch he made famous: the Rolex Daytona, with the exotic (contrasting register) dial.

(Please Note: The names "Cosmograph" and "Daytona" were not present on all dial through the years. Furthermore, examples have been seen with these names in different positions on the dial: below the name "Rolex", which is below the '12' position, as well as above the bottom register, in an arc fashion. This inconsistency has caused confusion over the years, with many collectors questioning the authenticity of their watches.)

From the start, the watches were available in two dials; the *standard* dials were either black (with silver registers), or silver (with black registers); and the *exotic* dials which were either black (with white registers), or cream white (with black registers). These exotic dials soon became simply known as the "Paul Newman", after he reportedly wore one in the racing film "Winning". Legend has it that Mr. Newman's picture (with the watch visible on his wrist) appeared on Italian movie posters to promote the film. Mr. Newman then subsequently appeared on the cover of a popular Italian magazine, thus sparking a love affair with the watch that has lasted over 30-years.[42]

After studying the film I can say that Mr. Newman does indeed wear a "stainless steel" watch in nearly every scene, however, the watch is never shown clear enough to positively identify the model. Furthermore, the face of the watch appears to be silver in color and the trademark *contrasting registers* are *not* identifiable. With that being said, I will offer another possible explanation. The 6239 was also available with an optional exotic *silver dial* featuring all *silver registers*. I believe this was the Daytona model worn in the film, with Mr. Newman subsequently donning the exotic (contrasting register) Daytona on the cover of the aforementioned Italian magazine. I must stress that there is no hard evidence to support this and at this point it is purely speculation and conjecture.

While all versions of the Daytona with *contrasting* registers have subsequently become known as Paul Newmans, some would argue that the only *true* Paul Newman models are described as follows: The 6239 and 6241 case numbers, manual wind, steel cases, with the two aforementioned 'exotic dial' configurations—featuring square markers within the registers.

Courtesy of watchcommander.com

Daytona Cosmograph (model 6263) with exotic dial. Circa 1970s

In 1965, the 6239 was replaced by the 6262, and the 6241 by the 6264, respectively. Both watches featured a new *Valjoux* 727 movement. Also in 1965, Rolex released a new watch to the line (model 6240). This was the first model to feature screw-down waterproof pushers and the name "Oyster" on the dial, thus it was now rated waterproof to 165 feet (50 meters).

In 1971, the 6264 was replaced by the 6265, and the 6262 by the 6263, respectively. Both new models now featured the new screw-down waterproof pushers, which were introduced on the 6240. These two models were also the first Cosmographs to receive the new larger Triplock winding crown. Both models continued in the Rolex catalog until being discontinued in 1987.

In 1988, Rolex released the new *Oyster Perpetual Cosmograph Daytona* (model 16520), which were powered by a modified Zenith *El Primero* movement (Cal. 4030). While the 16520 was stainless steel, it was also available in two-toned (stainless steel & 18kt yellow gold), as well as solid 18kt yellow gold models, as the 16523 and 16528, respectively. The first versions were calibrated to a 200 units per hour scale, but were subsequently upped to 400 units per hour, as they are today.

In 1992, Rolex released a new *Oyster Perpetual Cosmograph Daytona* (model 16518), which was only available in 18kt yellow gold, with a leather strap and safety deployment clasp. The bezel featured small triangles pointing to the

Daytona Cosmograph (model 116518) with exotic dial. Circa 2002.

individual calibrated numbers, rather than the small dots present on earlier models. By 1997, Rolex finally released a white gold version of this watch as model 16519.

In 2000, Rolex updated the Daytona line once again, with the introduction of the first "in-house" Daytona movement (Cal. 4130), which features a 72 hour power reserve—or 66 hours when the stopwatch function is used. This new model was also fitted with a special proprietary deployant clasp. It was also at this time that Rolex fitted the Daytona with a new 6-digit model number.

Courtesy of Universal Pictures

Vintage *lobby card* movie poster for the 1969 film *Winning*, starring Paul Newman, Joanne Woodward and Robert Wagner. Notice the wristwatch visible on Mr. Newman's wrist. It is believed that a similar movie poster was used in Italy which sparked the popularity of the Rolex Daytona.

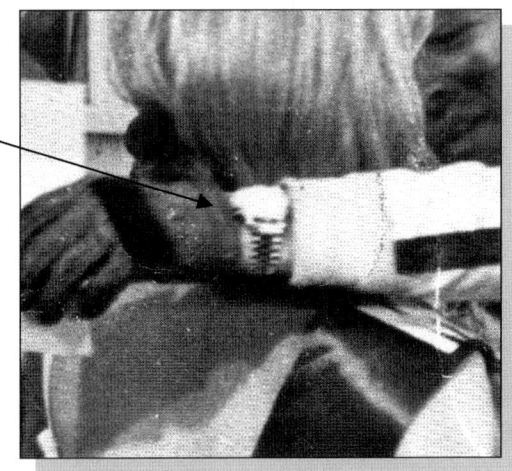

In this image we have enlarged the view of the aforementioned wristwatch. As you can see, the trademark "registers" can not be distinguished and therefore the wristwatch can not be positively identified as a Rolex *Daytona*.

SEA-DWELLER

Year Introduced: 1967
First Model: 1665
First Movement: 1575

All models

Case Size: 40mm
Lug Size: 20mm

Courtesy of generalwar.com

Model 16600, Circa 2002

Every Rolex model seems to have a story, but I feel none is more interesting than that of the Sea-Dweller. The explanation dates back to the 1960s, when the French commercial diving company, COMEX (**CO**mpagnie **M**aritime d'**EX**pertise) came to Rolex with an interesting technical problem.

With the growing demand for new oil sources, Comex began to service offshore oil and gas rigs. However, these new rigs were at such great depths that they required divers to be submerged for excessive lengths of time to perform the tasks at hand.

Unfortunately, the longer and deeper someone dives the more time they must spend decompressing between dives. This extra *decompression time* meant less time diving, and as the saying goes "time is money". Soon a new technique emerged that revolutionized the industry: *saturation diving.*

The conventional diving method utilizes a 'compressed air' mixture of nitrogen and oxygen. However, when underwater, a diver doesn't just *breathe* these gasses, but the body tissue also absorbs it to saturation. This can cause the alcohol-like effect of *Nitrogen Narcosis*, also known as "rapture of the deep", whereas the body absorbs a toxic level of nitrogen which in some cases can cause death.

Since nitrogen releases from the body rather slowly, it's necessary to ascend from a dive at a rate which allows the gas pressure to equalize as the diver resurfaces. Otherwise, the difference in pressure can cause DCI (decompression illness), a condition often referred to as "the bends".

With saturation diving, the gas mixture was switched to helium and oxygen. Since helium particles are smaller than nitrogen, they escape from the body much faster, therefore allowing the diver to stay down at depth longer without the fear of *Nitrogen Narcosis*. Furthermore, it was discovered that divers could spend their time between dives, actually *living* in special chambers, breathing the helium-oxygen mixture and remain pressurized to the depth they had been diving. This allowed them to fully decompress just once at the end of their shift to re-acclimate to the surface pressure. It was these *decompression chambers* which created the aforementioned technical problem.

Comex divers had been using the Rolex Submariner (model 5513) for years and it had served them well—actually, as it turns out, the watch performed too well. When divers spent long periods of time at the pressurized depth, the tiny helium particles would actually *penetrate* the watch's crystal and seal—this would equalize the pressure *inside* the watch to that of the depth. Therefore, when the diver would go through decompression, the helium particles could not escape the watch fast enough—due to the tight seal of the watch. This extremely high-pressure build up in the watch would cause the crystal (being the weakest link) to fail and literally explode from the case—not a fun thing to have happen, especially when you're in a small decompression chamber. Rolex had spent so much effort creating a watch that could withstand ridiculous amounts of pressure from the *outside*, they had never considered the possibility of pressure building up from the *inside*. When Rolex was approached with this problem they quickly went to work on a solution. What they came up with was ingenious, but yet very simple—a *one-way gas escape valve* on the side of the case, positioned opposite the winding crown.

The first prototypes were outfitted to special Submariner 5513 models issued to Comex divers. Some, but not all, bore the 'Comex' logo positioned above the depth rating "660ft = 200m", which was positioned above the 6. The watches also featured special Comex identification numbers engraved on the case back. Since these watches were exposed to harsher than normal conditions, they were sent back to Rolex every six months for a 'scheduled maintenance'—after all, these were utility watches in the truest sense of the word. During these overhauls, it was common for the watches to receive upgrades as well (i.e. new movements, dials or crystals). Therefore, prototypes in the original configuration are extremely rare.

In early 1967, Comex ordered another batch of the specially fitted Submariners. Rolex produced around 150, and officially designated the watch as the model 5514. These watches all bore the "Comex" logo on the dial, as well as the Comex identification numbers on back.

In late 1967, Rolex released the first Sea-Dweller to the general public as model 1665. This watch used the 1575 movement, featured the new Triplock crown, a thicker profile crystal (and later), a larger reinforced case—the depth rating was also increased to 2,000 feet (610 meters). Above the depth rating was now printed in red: *SEA-DWELLER SUBMARINER 2000*.

Also in late 1967, Comex divers were being issued a version of the 1665—these models did not bear the Sea-Dweller/Submariner name, but merely displayed the now standard "Comex" logo.

By the mid 1970s, the 1665 simply read *SEA-DWELLER* on the face (in white), and the tag *SUBMARINER 2000* was dropped. At this point, the watch stayed relatively unchanged until it was discontinued around 1981.

In the meantime, Rolex was busy with a new model, which they released in 1978, as the 16660. This new watch was fitted with the 3035 movement, featured a (flat profile) sapphire crystal, and newly improved, larger gas escape valve. The depth rating was now increased to a staggering 4,000 feet (1,220 meters).

Courtesy of bjsonline.com

ABOVE: Submariner (model 5514) with 'Comex' markings.

BELOW: Sea-Dweller (model 1665) with 'Comex' markings.

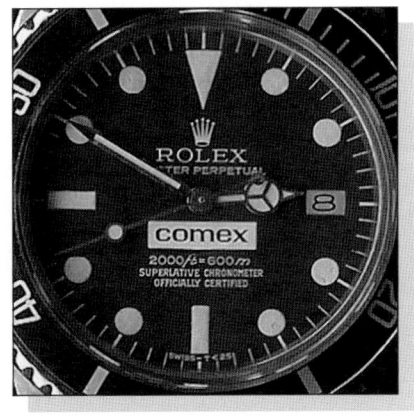

Courtesy of bjsonline.com

OYSTERQUARTZ

Year Introduced: 1970
First Model: 5100
First Movement: Beta 21

All models
Case Size: 36mm
Lug Size: Integral

Model 17000, Circa 1980s

Rolex entered the quartz watch market in 1970—quite reluctantly I might add. They had been a contributing member of the *Centre Électronique Horloger* (Electronic Watch Center) or C.E.H. in Neuchâtel, since its inception around 1960. This consortium was created to develop technology in the field of electronic timekeeping. During a highly publicized event, the C.E.H. released their quartz movement, the *Beta 21*, on April 10, 1970. However, Rolex declined to partake in this unveiling, but instead decided to release their own model a few months later. One can only speculate as to the reason for Rolex backing out of this event in the 'eleventh hour', after being involved in its development for a decade. It has been suggested that Rolex may not have agreed with the C.E.H. on certain key topics. Other suggest it was just another example of Rolex's reputation for "over-engineering", thus refusing to place their name and reputation behind a product they did not fully support.

With that being said, Rolex released their own quartz watch, simply called the *Rolex Quartz Date* (model 5100), at the Basel fair on June 5, 1970. The watch was an instant success—much to Rolex's surprise. In fact, the opening orders were so far beyond their expectations, the initial in-

Courtesy of watchcommander.com

The first Rolex Quartz Date (model 5100). Circa 1970

ventory was sold out almost immediately. This was probably due to the newness of the technology, with consumers of the time craving anything 'modern'. The design was in fact very modern and featured an angular-shaped case, which some have described as "clunky". The watch was the first to feature the new sapphire crystal, which would subsequently be added to the entire Rolex line. Another distinction for the Rolex Quartz was that it was the first Rolex model in many years *not* to feature an Oyster case.

The newness quickly wore off and sales of the Rolex Quartz dropped, as did the *Beta 21*. Rolex soon pulled out of the C.E.H. in favor of continuing their own research—which they had started some twenty years before. The Rolex Quartz was subsequently discontinued in 1972.

Rolex resurrected their quartz line with the introduction of the *Oysterquartz* in 1977. This new 11 jewel quartz movement (calibre 5055), led to the Quartz Datejust (model 17000), and Quartz Day-Date (model 19018), respectively. These new watches noted numerous improvements over their predecessor, including a new slimmer case which now offered the protection of the Oyster's screwed back and crown. Accuracy of the Quartz was improved as well. The heart of the movement, oscillating at a frequency of 32,768 Hz, could now be guaranteed to err by less than one minute per year.

Unfortunately, this has not been enough to save the Oysterquartz, as it has enjoyed only limited success. This is largely due to the rash of counterfeit Rolexes to hit the market since the 1980s. Not to mention the misconception by the general public that quartz watches are in some way 'cheap'. In fact, many Rolex neophytes are surprised to hear that Rolex even makes a quartz watch. It seems to most that quartz watches are in someway inferior in quality to a mechanical watch, when the opposite is actually true (with respect to accuracy).

While Rolex has set limits on the Oysterquartz, with current production comprising only 2% of their line, they have continued to conduct extensive research into electro-mechanical timekeeping. It has even been suggested that Rolex could be developing a perpetual rotor that in some way acts as a tiny generator to continually charge the quartz battery—thus a perfect marriage of mechanical and electronic timekeeping. However, since Rolex is so secretive about their actions (and rightly so), we will not likely hear of any new technologies until they are displayed in the shop-owners' cases.

YACHT-MASTER

Year Introduced: 1992
First Model: 16628
First Movement: 3135

	Gents	Mid-Size	Ladies
Case Size:	40mm	34mm	29mm
Lug Size:	20mm	17mm	13mm

Courtesy of generalwar.com

Model 16622, Circa 2002

In 1992, the Yacht-Master (model 16628) was first introduced, available in 18kt yellow gold, exclusively. Then in 1994, Rolex added two new models to the line: a ladies (model 69628), and mid-size (model 68628), respectively—marking the first time a *Professional* series watch was released in the smaller sizes. Originally, these models were only available in 18kt yellow gold as well. However, in 1996 Rolex released two-toned (steel & 18kt yellow gold) models as the ladies' (model 69623), and mid-sized (model 68623), respectively. Today, an all-stainless steel version is also available, but only in mid-sized models.

In 1997, Rolex released the Yacht-Master in *Rolesium*, a term patented by Rolex in 1932, signifying a stainless steel and platinum finish. The success of this configuration has been likened to that of the stainless steel Daytona, with sales in the secondary market exceeding that of the initial retail price. This of course was due to the limited availability of the watch, which Rolex will likely continue to cash in on for years to come. The Yacht-Master line as a whole has grown to become one of the more popular models of recent years, especially with the younger group of buyers hitting the market.

QUICK REFERENCE FOR
ROLEX MODEL EVOLUTIONS

Illumination Material: *Radium* was introduced around 1913 (with the "SWISS MADE" designation at the bottom of the dial), then replaced with *Tritium* around 1950 (designated by "T SWISS MADE T" or "SWISS—T < 25"), then subsequently replaced by *LumiNova* around 1998 (now again designated by "SWISS MADE").

Crystal Material: *Synthetic (plastic) crystals* were introduced around 1927, with the introduction of the *Oyster* waterproof watch. While the *Synthetic Sapphire crystal* was first introduced on the Quartz Date (model 5100) in 1970, it was subsequently introduced to the rest of the line by the late 1970s/early 1980s. 'Plastic' crystals were discontinued around 1987 on date models, and 1991 on non-date models.

Cyclops: First introduced at the Basel fair in 1954, on the Datejust (model 6605).

Winding Crowns: The first screw-down crown, known as the *onion,* was introduced in 1927, and continued until around 1929 when it was replaced with the *drum-shaped* crown which continued into the early 1940s. *Dimple* crowns were used from the late 1930s to early 1940s, while *Oyster Patent & Rolex Oyster* (Bubbleback) crowns were used from the mid 1930s through the late 1940s. *Super Oyster* crowns were introduced in the late 1950s, but used for only a few years. The *Twinlock* crown was first introduced in the early 1950s. At this same time, the larger *Brevet* crown was introduced on divers' models, and subsequently evolved into the modern *Triplock* crown in the early 1970s.

Hands: The *Mercedes hands* were fitted to sports models, starting in the mid 1950s. Also around this same time, all sports models featured seconds hands which were painted white. However, this 'phase' lasted only a few years.

Bezels: First *Rotating bezel* introduced on the T-O-G in 1953. First *Uni-directional (one way) rotating bezel* introduced on the Submariner by the early 1980s.

Tachymeter Bezel Scale: Early chronographs were calibrated to *1000 units per hour.* However, when the Daytona (model 6239) was introduced in 1960, it was first calibrated to *300 units,* but within a year was changed to *200.* In 1988, Rolex released the Daytona (model 16520) which was also calibrated to *200 units,* but was soon changed to *400,* as it remains to this day.

Crown Guards: First introduced around 1959 on the Submariner (model 5512), with a *square* profile. However, by the early 1960s, their appearance was more *pointed*, and then by the mid 1960s they shifted to the *rounded* appearance as they are today.

One-Way Gas Escape Valve: First introduced in 1967 on the Submariner (model 5513).

Bracelets: *Jubilee* bracelet introduced in 1945 (on the Datejust). *Oyster* bracelet introduced in 1947-48. (*Rivetted link:* Produced from the late 1940s to early 1970s. *Folded link:* Early 1960s to early 1970s. *Solid link:* Early 1970s to present.) *President* bracelet introduced in 1956 (on the Day-Date). *'Flush-fit' end pieces* introduced in 1954.

Bracelet Buckles: *Flip-lock clasp* introduced in the late 1960s. *Concealed Clasp* (President bracelet) introduced in the early 1970s.

Case Reference Numbers (AKA model numbers): Vintage Rolex *model numbers* featured three or four digits until the mid 1980s when they were changed to a five-digit number—This renumbering often coincided with the introduction of the *sapphire crystal* and *quick set* feature. In 2000, the number again changed, this time to a six-digit number.

Hacking Feature: While a primitive hacking feature was present on some examples during WWII, it was widely introduced to Rolex models around 1972.

Quick Set Feature: While this feature was first introduced in the late 1970s, it was fitted to all date models by around 1983.

Double Quick Set Feature: First introduced in late 1980s/early 1990s.

Beats: Rolex movements were rated at 18,000 BPH in 1957, 19,800 BPH by 1964, and 28,800 BPH by 1977.

Rolex Dial Markings: Coronet (or crown) logo was first introduced on the dial in 1939.

Chronometer Markings: The chronometer designation first appeared on the dial around 1935 as *"Chronomètre"* (French), then was replaced with the English version *"Chronometer"* around 1947. By 1948, it was changed to *"Certified Chronometer"*, then around 1949 it was again changed to read *"Officially Certified Chronometer"*. Finally around 1957, it changed to its current designation *"Superlative Chronometer Officially Certified"*.

Hallmarks: While the *lady's head* (or "queen's head") is still in use, the *St. Bernard dog's head* hallmarks were introduced on some models in the mid 1990s.

[34] According to *The Best of Time, Rolex Wristwatches*, by Dowling & Hess: The fake Sporting Prince models can be identified by the back of the case. *"...the correct wristwatch case is curved to the wrist while the pocket watch back is bowed outward..."*

[35] It has been rumored that the Rolex Watch Company was the winning bidder of the Deep Sea Special #5, which means of the seven watches made, Rolex is in possession of six, with the remaining model on display at the Smithsonian Institute in Washington D.C.

[36] While the *Trieste* was 'officially' captained by Professor Auguste Piccard's son Jacques Piccard, US Navy Lt. Donald Walsh was near the helm since the US Navy had purchased the bathyscaphe from Mr. Piccard two years earlier, in 1958. Thus, the Trieste was sailing under the American flag during its voyage to the *Marianas Trench*.

[37] The fact that the 6200 was powered by the early A.296 movement is further support to the theory of the 6200 being the *first* Rolex 'prototype' diving watch. The A.260 movement present in the 6204, and 6205, was an improved version of the A.296. Furthermore, other early 'prototype' models released in 1953 featured the A.296, including: the Explorer (model 6098) and Turn-O-Graph (model 6202), respectively.

[38] According to *Vintage Rolex Sports Models*, by Skeet & Urul: *"...the black band is always the same size and in the same place, suggesting that it was done at the time of manufacture."* Again, lending credibility to the theory that Rolex had not yet secured the rights to the "Submariner" name.

[39] *Oersted:* The centimeter-gram-second electromagnetic unit of magnetic intensity, equal to the magnetic intensity one centimeter from a unit magnetic pole. [After Hans Christian *Oersted* (1777-1851).] - *The American Heritage Dictonary*, Second Colege Edition. Copyright © 1985 by Houghton Mifflin Company. All rights reserved.

[40] *Gauss:* The centimeter-gram-second electromagnetic unit of magnetic flux density, equal to one maxwell per square centimeter. [After Karl F. *Gauss* (1777-1855).] - *The American Heritage Dictonary*, Second Colege Edition. Copyright © 1985 by Houghton Mifflin Company. All rights reserved.

[41] Quoted from *Vintage Rolex Sports Models*, by Skeet & Urul.

[42] Source: *The Best of Time, Rolex Wristwatches*, by Dowling & Hess.

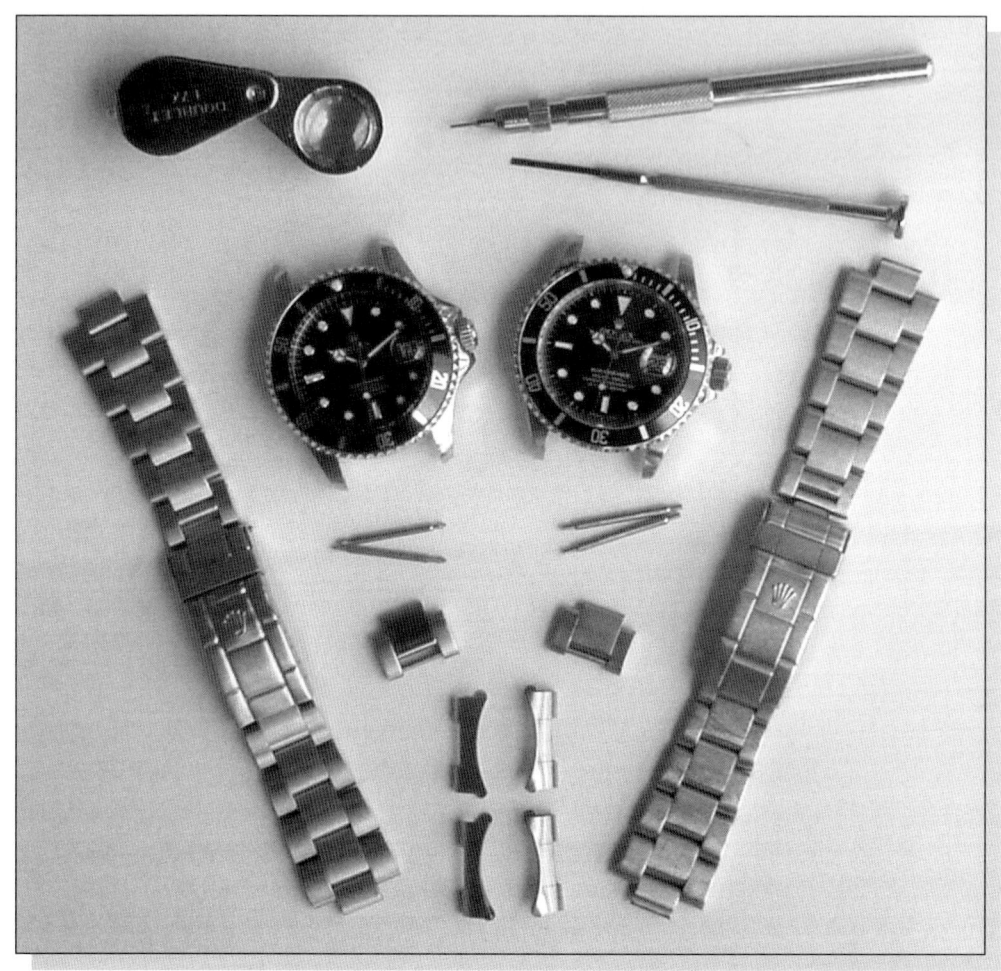

*I hardly know so true a mark of a little mind
as the servile imitation of others.*
— Fulke Greville

PART II

Rolex or Replica?
DON'T GET E-SCREWED!

HOW TO USE THIS SECTION

Rolex was there when Hillary and Tenzing conquered the summit of Mt. Everest, they accompanied Jacques Piccard on his journey to the deepest ocean floor in the world, the Challenger Deep of the *Marianas Trench*. Chuck Yeager strapped one to his wrist when he broke the sound barrier in 1947, as did Sean Connery when he portrayed James Bond in the spy films of the 1960s.

They've gone higher, deeper and faster than any other watch in the world, but it appears they're now facing their most difficult challenge yet… *Counterfeit watches*. With the every-growing popularity of online auctions like eBay and Yahoo, unscrupulous sellers are passing off *counterfeits* as the real thing—and doing so with alarming success.

We're not talking about the cheap fakes from the 70s & 80s, with second hands that 'tick', or dials featuring misspelled words. No, these are incredibly sophisticated replicas with sweep movements, laser-printed dials and (in many cases) counterfeit boxes with warranty papers. What was once a business operated from the street corners of Taiwan, has turned into a multi-billion dollar industry.

Let's face it, we've all seen them… a seller on eBay is listing a Rolex Daytona for $200 bucks—with no reserve. The auction ends in 22 minutes and you're ready to make a killing! That's when it happens. You notice in the item's description that the seller *claims* to have bought the watch at some "estate sale" and therefore he "cannot guarantee authenticity".

You start to sweat… should I, or shouldn't I? After all, the picture *looks* real and the story sounds believable—maybe it is real? The truth is, the seller probably bought this FAKE from his supplier for $50 bucks and runs the same ad each week. It's very easy to get taken like this. You get caught up in the excitement of bidding and end up buying something you really don't want.

Now here's the good news. By taking a few simple precautions and knowing what to look for, you can keep from making this costly mistake. To help walk you through this process, I have divided this part of the book into the following 9 detailed topics:

Watch Parts, Tools and Terminology
The Cursory Inspection
Watch Disassembly
The Detailed Examination (Exterior & Interior)
Replica Categories
Accessories
Vintage Counterfeits
Common Counterfeit Mistakes
Shopping Online... *Caveat Emptor:* Buyer Beware

Each of these topics are designed to help further your knowledge of Rolex wristwatches, how they're made and how counterfeiters try to copy them. The inspections cover a wide range of details concerning the watch's appearance and functions.

However, since counterfeits are made with a wide range of sophistication and are probably even being updated as I write this book, I must stress that the topics covered in *The Cursory Inspection* and *The Detailed Examination* should never be taken as gospel. These topics are merely designed to help you identify those features which indicate a *possibility* that the watch is counterfeit. Furthermore, the only way to be completely certain that a Rolex is in fact 100% genuine is by taking it to an authorized Rolex dealer for an inspection and appraisal.

With that being said, I suggest you read the following topics several times, thus familiarizing yourself with the material before attempting to identify a watch as genuine or counterfeit.

WATCH PARTS, TOOLS and TERMINOLOGY

Dial: This is the face of the watch, on which the hour markers (or indices) and hands are attached. On date and day-date models, an aperture is cut in the dial to allow the date wheels to be read.

Hands: The hour hand, minute hand and second hand are used to display the time.

Crown: The round-shaped "winding stem" by which the time is set and the movement can be hand wound.

Crystal: The clear "glass" that covers the dial of the watch. They are available in two varieties: *sapphire* and *plastic*. Also, on most date models, a bubble (or "cyclops") will be attached to the face of the crystal, thus magnifying the date wheel indicator.

Bezel: The round outer-ring fitted around the crystal to hold it pressure-proof to the case. On some sports models, the bezel will turn and/or perform some function on the watch (ie. elapse time indicator, 24-hour marker, etc...)

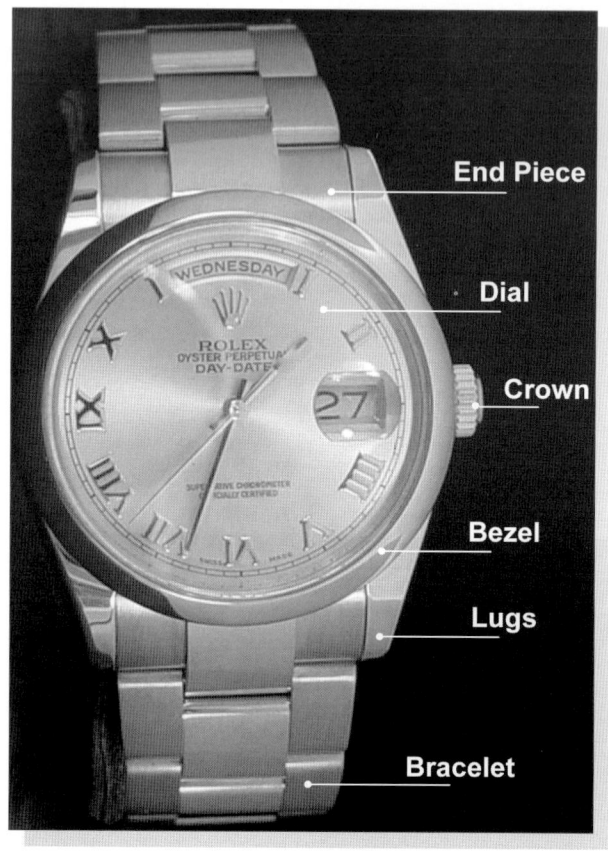

Lugs: The two pointed edges on either end of the case, by which the bracelet is attached to the case via the end pieces—these are sometimes called the "horns".

End Piece: The small (usually hollow) piece of metal, crafted to look like a bracelet link, which allows the bracelet to be attached to the case via tiny spring bars.

Spring Bar: A small spring-loaded pushpin, which passes through the end piece into either side of the lugs, thus, holding the bracelet onto the case.

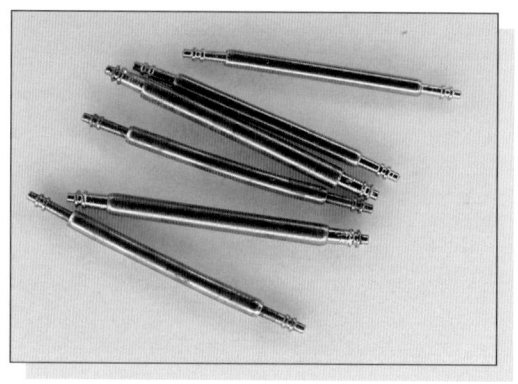

Assorted spring bars.

Case: The "body" or "head" of the watch. This is what houses the movement and on which the dial and bracelet are attached. On *Rolex Oyster* models, the case is hewn from a solid piece of stainless steel, gold or platinum. There are two types of cases as follows:

Spring Bar Hole Cases: These cases have tiny holes that extend all the way through the watch's lugs, allowing the spring bar ends to be visible inside the holes. The spring bars are removed by inserting the spring bar removal tool through these holes. Most Rolex cases had spring bar holes until around the 2000 model year, when they switched to no-hole cases.

No-Hole Cases: These cases still use spring bars, but they are not visible through the lugs. The spring bars are removed by inserting the spring bar removal tool via tiny slots on either end of the end piece on the bottom side.

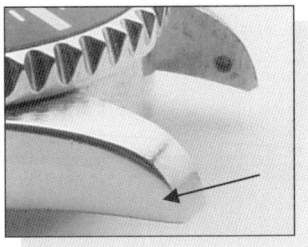

(It is worth mentioning that some *vintage* models featured a single spring bar hole on one lug, while the opposite lug did not.)

Bracelet: Also called the band, it is usually made of stainless steel and/or gold, and is tightened by some type of clasp.

Spring Bar Removing Tool: This tool is used to remove the spring bars (located between the lugs), and thus removing the bracelet from the watch's case. They come in a number of shapes and sizes, but if you're in a pinch a paperclip can sometimes suffice.

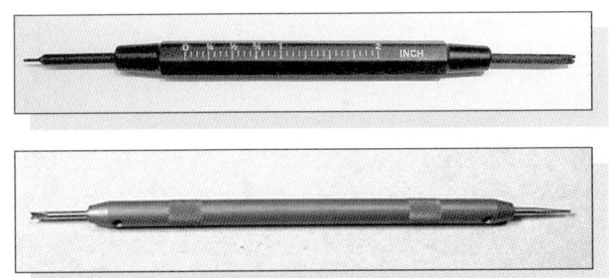

Jeweler's Screwdriver set: These are used to remove the bracelet's links. It is important to use a good quality screwdriver of the proper size, as using the wrong tool can scratch or damage the bracelet.

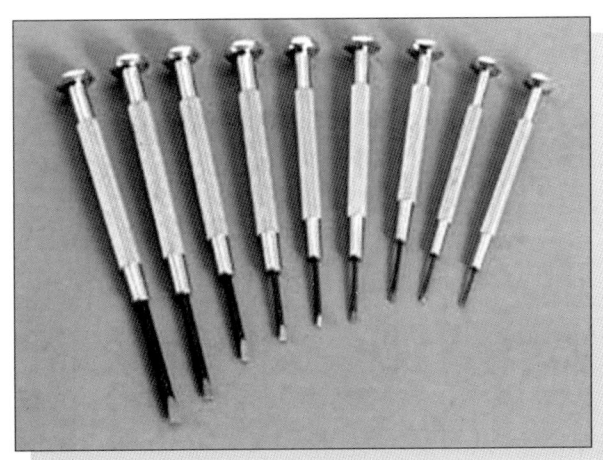

Jewelers' loupe: Often called a magnifier loupe, it is used to inspect fine detailed markings and very small parts. At least a 10x power magnification is recommended for a full detailed inspection.

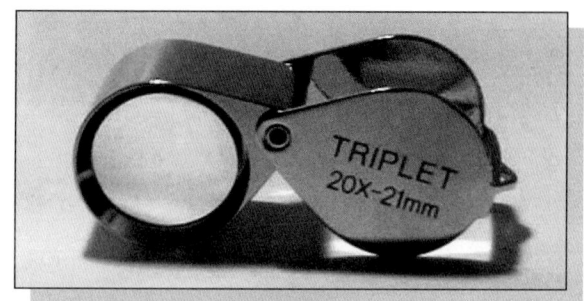

Case Back Openers: These can also be called *case back wrenches*, or *blocking tools*. They're used to unscrew the case backs to gain access to the movement. The standard Rolex socket sizes are as follows: 18.5mm, 20.2mm, 22.5mm, 26.5mm, 28.3mm and 29.5mm.

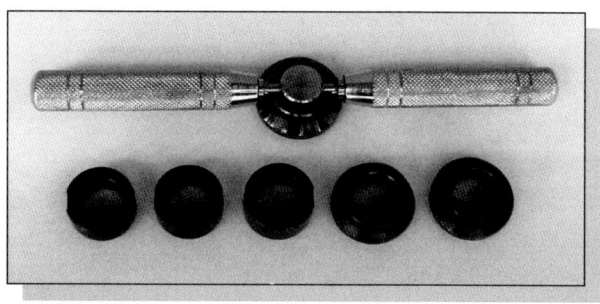

Non-genuine Rolex parts are categorized into the following 2-types:

Aftermarket: Any non-genuine, or non-Rolex made parts that DO NOT bear counterfeit Rolex trademarks, logos or hallmarks.

These parts may be used to replace parts that were damaged (e.g. broken crystals, bracelets, etc…), or upgrades done to the watch (e.g. upgrade diamond dials, bezels, or bracelets) because they are generally less expensive than genuine Rolex parts.

Counterfeit: Any aftermarket parts that DO bear illegal, fake or otherwise non-authentic Rolex trademarks, logos or hallmarks.

These parts are created with the sole intention of deceiving someone by misrepresenting the watch/parts as authentic Rolex made and should be avoided.

PLEASE NOTE: Throughout this book I may refer to Rolex stamping or engraving as "Hallmarks". While a *true* hallmark is technically described as "a mark or stamp indicating the purity of a metal, or the date and/or country of import", and does not include that of a company's identification stamp or trademark, I have taken certain liberties with the term *Hallmark* and use it in the generic sense for lack of a better word.

THE CURSORY INSPECTION

When inspecting a Rolex you want to keep one very important thing in mind…

Rolex watches are PERFECT, or as close to perfect as you can get.

Rolex has the reputation for over-engineering everything in their watches, from the movements right down to the detail they put into a screw—nothing is done half way. When inspecting a would-be Rolex, look for the most minute of details in quality and workmanship—if the detail looks questionable, then chances are it's probably a fake.

I suggest taking a trip to your local Rolex dealer and get some "hands on" time with as many authentic Rolexes as you can. Hold them, feel them—do everything but taste them. You want to feel very comfortable with the way they look and move. Turn the crown and bezel, and inspect how the bracelet's clasp operates. This will give you more confidence when trying to detect a counterfeit.

Most of the topics covered in this section can be done without any disassembly of the watch and with a little practice can be completed in just a few minutes.

While performing the Cursory Inspection we will look for the more obvious errors, which are listed below:

1) Weight: When you hold the watch it should feel heavy—*exceptionally heavy*. Rolex Oyster cases are hewn from a solid ingot of stainless steel, gold or platinum and are considerably heavier than that of an average watch. The gold model fakes are easier to detect since they are actually not gold at all, but rather are just artificial plating over a cheap steel case. However, some high-end fakes and conversions may use solid gold cases.

2) Finish: Again, this refers to the fact that most fake models use artificial gold plating over steel. This can make the watch look very "brassy" (almost like 24 karat) instead of the 18kt gold tone seen on current genuine Rolex watches—Stainless steel models can be more difficult to detect. (*Please Note: Vintage Rolex watches were also available in 9kt and 14kt gold, respectively.*)

3) Sweeping Movement: Also known as the "step" or "action", sweep refers to the movement of the second hand quickly *ticking* at approximately 5-8 times per second—giving the illusion of sweeping. (For more info on this, see the FAQ section at the end of this book). The exceptions to this are the Rolex *Oysterquartz* and often forgotten *Tru-beat* models which tick once per second.

It is worth noting that older fakes used a cheap quartz movement, which also tick only one time per second. Newer fakes may sweep, but they usually have a 'choppy' step. This is because the cheaper movements only tick at around 3-4 times per second. While this may not sound like much of a difference, if you look closely it *is* visible to the naked eye.

4) Clear Case Backs: This refers to some fakes which will have a clear window in the case back, giving you a view of the watch movement. This is probably the easiest way to detect a fake, as Rolex has to this day NEVER made a watch with a clear case back. Again, this is just a way for the counterfeiters to be creative.

5) Case Back Markings: This can be another easy giveaway on low-end fakes. Authentic Rolex watches (in most cases) will not have any logos or engraving on the case backs. The few exceptions are as follows:

Some ladies models (prior to the mid 1990's) had "Original Rolex Design", or a similar variation thereof, engraved on the case back in an arc fashion. This engraving was not very deep, and is easily removed during refinishing. Thus, it may not be present on all ladies models.

Current Sea-Dweller case backs will have "ROLEX OYSTER ORIGINAL GAS ESCAPE VALVE" engraved around the outside of the case back in an arc fashion. Earlier models had similar engraving, but may also include "Patent Pending", or "Rolex Patent".

In addition, Rolex Submariner & Sea-Dweller Comex models will be engraved with both the *Rolex* and *Comex* names along with a two, three or four-digit identification number used by Comex. COMEX (**Co**mpagnie **Ma**ratime d'**Ex**pertise) is a French commercial diving company that has had a business relationship with Rolex since the 1960's. (Warning: These are highly desirable models and thus are often counterfeited, so be careful.)

Counterfeits may also have large Rolex crown logos, model numbers, serial numbers or hallmarks engraved or even molded into the case back. Again, Rolex does not do this, so it is a sure sign of a fake.

Counterfeit Rolex Yacht-Master with clear back. Circa 2000

Counterfeit Rolex case back with fake reference number stamp. Circa 1993

Counterfeit Rolex case back with fabricated hallmarks. Circa 2000

Counterfeit Rolex Daytona case back. Circa 2002

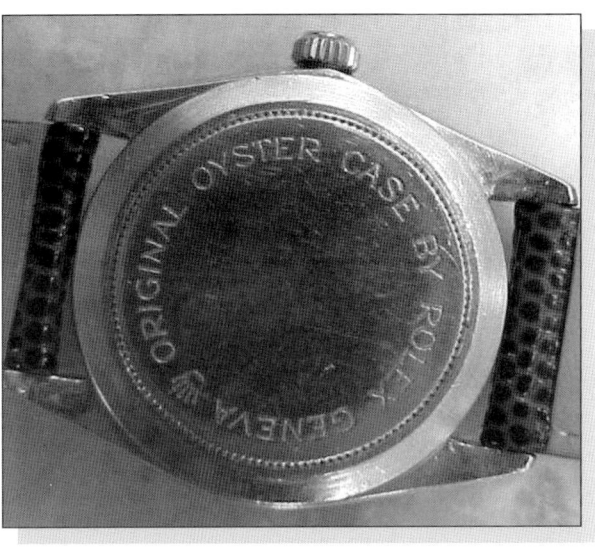

Genuine ladies Rolex case back. Circa 1940s

Genuine Rolex Sea-Dweller case back. Circa 2000

Genuine Rolex Sea-Dweller case back. Circa 1970s

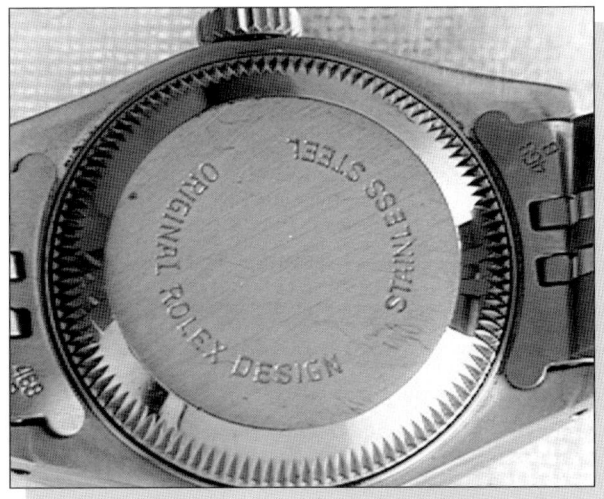

Genuine ladies Rolex case back
(stainless steel). Circa 1980s

Genuine Rolex Submariner case back with
Comex markings. Circa 1982

6) Case Back Stickers: Authentic Rolexes currently have a hologram encoded sticker (on the case back) featuring the Rolex crown centered over the watch's model reference number. Counterfeiters have started faking these stickers, but (so far) they are unable to effectively duplicate the hologram.

It is common for the sticker to be removed by the wearer after a period of time, so if the watch doesn't have this sticker it doesn't mean it's fake.

The hologram part of the sticker is actually the outer layer. Therefore, it's common for this coating to be worn down over time, leaving just a pale green sticker with a faint outline of the Rolex crown, with no hologram.

It is also worth mentioning that many counterfeit stickers will bear the same reference number on different watch models. The example above is a counterfeit Day-Date, but features the case reference number *16233* (which is actually the designation for a Datejust). I have witnessed this same numbered sticker (16233) incorrectly featured on a Daytona and Yacht-Master as well. For information on correct numbers, you can review the *Case Reference Numbers* section of this book.

7) Crystal: Rolex uses laboratory grade, synthetic sapphire crystals which will actually feel cool to the touch. Whereas, counterfeits will often feature a glass, or acrylic (plastic) crystal, which will not have the cool-touch feel. (Note: Rolex totally discontinued using acrylic crystals by 1991.)

Glass crystals may also give a greenish tint when viewed across the top angle, into the beveled edge. Whereas, sapphire crystals will give a clear/white appearance. It is worth noting that some newer fakes have tried to hide this appearance by 'frosting' the edges of the crystal, therefore giving it a milky white appearance.

Counterfeit Rolex sticker—note the crown and background pattern are stamped and are not a hologram.

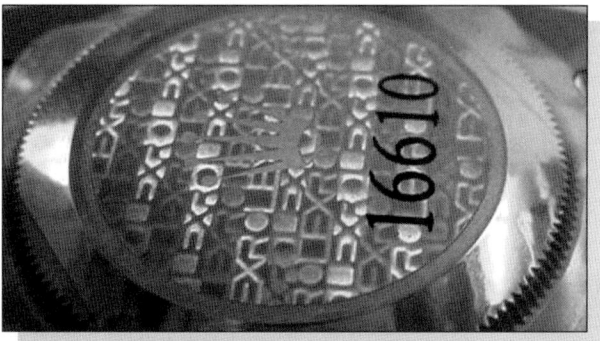

Genuine Rolex hologram sticker.

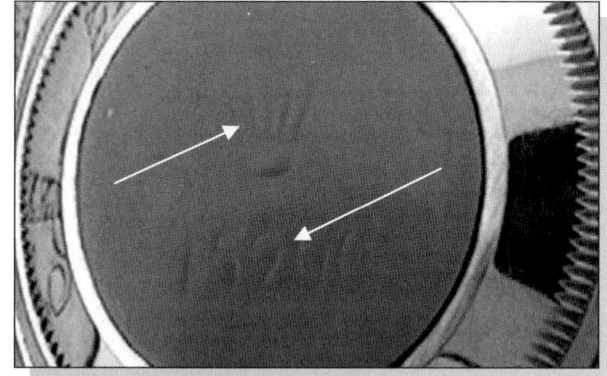

Genuine 'worn out' Rolex sticker, with just a faint outline of the 'crown' and model # 15200 visible.

Genuine Rolex sapphire crystal with beveled edge.

8) Cyclops: For authentic Rolexes, the crystal (on all current date models—excluding Sea-Dweller) will have a glass bubble, or "cyclops" attached to the crystal, placed over the date. Its purpose is to magnify the tiny date aperture and does so at 2.5 times magnification. If you look at the date at an angle (without looking through the cyclops) you will see that the date aperture window is actually very tiny and the cyclops magnifies it considerably.

However, on MOST counterfeit models the date magnification is more like 1.5 times, at best. This may not sound like much of a difference, but when looking at the dates side-by-side it's obvious. The date window should practically "fill-up" the cyclops—the fakes don't even come close.

The date wheel should be one of the first things you look for and is probably one of the easiest ways to detect a low or mid-level fake. Do keep in mind however, upper-level, or conversion fakes may very well have the full magnification. It's also worth noting that on some fakes the cyclops will be crooked on the crystal—Genuine Rolexes will be perfectly positioned.

Rolex Submariner cyclops magnification comparison.
Genuine Rolex on the left with a counterfeit Rolex on the right.
Note the counterfeit cyclops is also positioned a bit low on the crystal.

Rolex Datejust cyclops magnification comparison.
Genuine Rolex on the left with a counterfeit Rolex on the right.
Note the counterfeit cyclops is also positioned a bit high on the crystal

(Please Note: It's common for counterfeit sellers to hide the magnification on their watches. They photograph them in a way as not to give a clear view through the cyclops. Or, they position the minute hand to pass over the date window so as to obscure the view. Many counterfeit dealers will make outright claims that their watch has 2.5 times magnification when it does not.)

Also, dealers will sometimes display a picture that is so poor in quality that you can't identify details on the watch (see the example below). They will often claim the camera is new or they just don't know how to operate it correctly.

Genuine Rolex Submariner—Note how tiny the date aperture is without viewing thru the Cyclops.

The seller of this counterfeit has positioned the watch so the date magnification can not be determined.

In this example, the seller has displayed a picture that is completely useless. He claims the watch to be a genuine Rolex Datejust (which it may actually be). Unfortunately, the picture is so blurry there is no way of telling if it is authentic.

9) Illumination Markings: On authentic Rolex watches, the hands and hour markers are coated with a chemical that, when "charged" with direct light for a short period of time, will then glow in the dark. Please keep in mind that the effectiveness of this chemical will deteriorate over time, and if the watch is older it may not glow at all. Also, fakes may only glow for a few minutes after charging, whereas genuine Rolexes should hold the charge much longer.

The illumination coating should be fairly smooth looking, particularly on late models. However, counterfeits *may* appear very pitted under a loupe. (as seen in the image comparison below.)

Genuine Rolex Submariner with illuminated hands/hour markers.

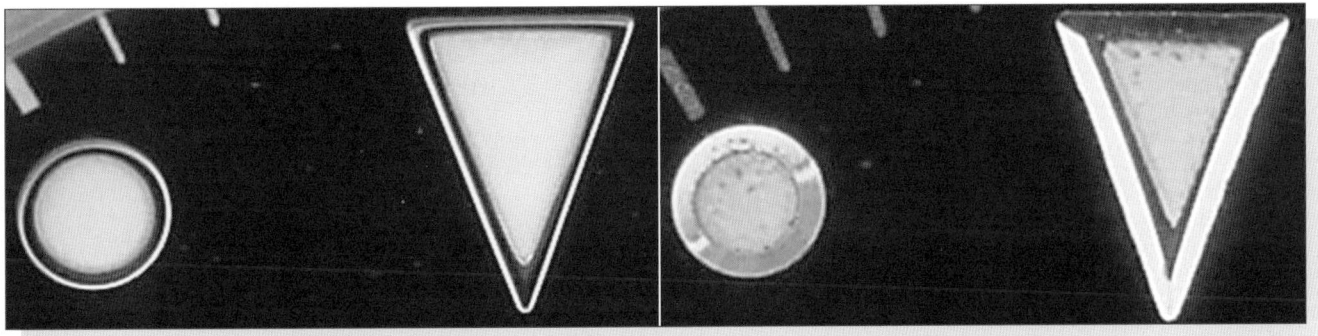

Extreme close-up comparison of the illumination markers on a Submariner. (viewed with a 10x loupe)
Genuine Rolex on the left with a counterfeit Rolex on the right.
Notice how 'pitted' the luminous material is on the counterfeit.

10) Crown Seal: Rolex models featuring the *Triplock* crown (i.e. Submariner, Sea-Dweller and Daytona) utilize an extra seal within the threads of the winding crown's tube. This gasket resembles a black rubber o-ring and can be visible when the winding crown is unscrewed fully. I have never seen a full counterfeit with this seal. Of course conversion fakes, being made with some genuine Rolex parts, could still have this seal.

Genuine Rolex
Triplock crown.

Counterfeit Rolex Submariner with
a basic screw crown (no seal).

Genuine Rolex Submariner with
a *Triplock* crown (rubber seal).

11) The Winding Crown: First, unscrew the crown. Is it tight and smooth as it unscrews, or is it rough and hang up as you turn it? Now wind the watch. Again, is it smooth—or is it noisy? Cheap fakes may have a "tinny" sound, while genuine Rolexes (particularly newer ones) will be smooth and relatively quiet.

When you set the time, slowly turn the hands back and forth. Does the second hand jump around wildly? On higher quality movement (that are properly adjusted) the second hand will move very little—no more than a couple second markers. However, cheaper (or poorly adjusted) movements can jump past five to ten second markers.

When inspecting the winding crown, check the quality of the 'coronet' logo marking on the end. A genuine Rolex is a solid piece with the logo engraved, whereas most (earlier) fakes have the logo glued on the end (as is the case with the example on the right).

Also, check the size and shape of the crown. Since counterfeit parts are usually just converted generic parts, they will often be of the wrong size or shape. In the example at the bottom right, there are two counterfeit Rolex Daytonas—note the different thicknesses of the Triplock crowns.

Glued-on crown

Counterfeit Rolex Datejust with glued-on 'coronet' logo.

12) Hacking Feature: In the early 1970's, Rolex introduced the hacking feature. This simply means when you unscrew the crown and pull it out to the second click (to set the time), the second hand STOPS. This is done to simplify the time setting procedure. On lower end fakes the second hand may continue ticking. On the other hand, if you're looking at a vintage watch and it has a newer movement with a hacking feature, you can assume it is fake or has been altered from its original movement.

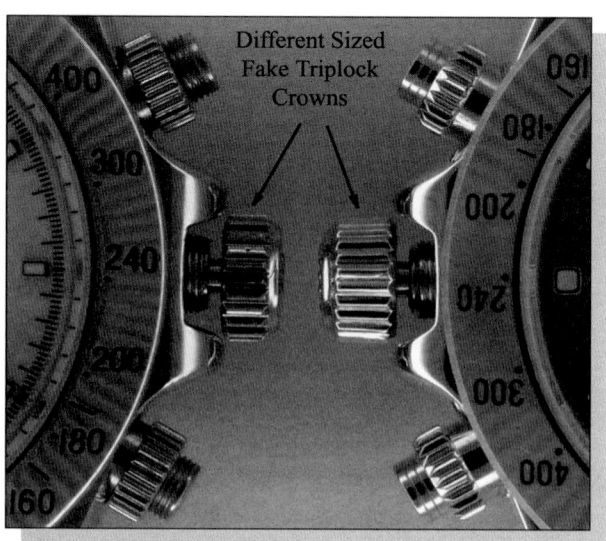

Different Sized Fake Triplock Crowns

Two counterfeit Rolex Daytonas with different sized Triplock crowns—note the difference in thickness and shape.

13) Date Wheels: The numbers in these wheels should appear clear and perfectly centered in the opening.   Counterfeits will often be misaligned or crooked in the window.   Be sure to check every number in the wheel, as sellers may position the date so as to show the best looking number on the wheel.   Also, check the background color of the wheel.   Often counterfeits will have a rough, off-white shade.

Various examples of counterfeit Rolexes featuring date apertures with misaligned date wheels.

14) Quick Set & Double Quick Set Feature:

The *Quick Set* feature was first introduced in the late 1970s and was fitted to all date models by 1983. This feature allows the date to be rapidly set via the winding crown, without having the hour hand pass over the 'midnight' position.

The *Double Quick Set* feature was introduced to Day-Date models by late 1990. Similar to the *Quick Set*, this feature allows both the *day* and the *date* to be rapidly set via the winding crown.

It is important to check these features and make sure they are operating smoothly throughout the function. If it feels choppy, or the date wheel drags, it may indicate a counterfeit or a genuine Rolex that has been poorly maintained.

(*Please Note: Even though the date feature is described in Rolex literature as changing "automatically at midnight", the actual switch may occur anywhere from 15-20 minutes before or after midnight. This is usually just a matter of adjustment of the date wheel mechanism—the important thing to note is that when the date changes, it does so in a quick shutter-like action.*)

15) Extra Functions: Daytona Cosmograph models have small subsidiary dials on the face of the watch to aid in performing additional functions. Fakes will either have non-working dials, meaning that they are just for show, or they are the wrong functions. (e.g. they will have calendars showing day and date, etc…) Also, the 4th hand on GMT or Explorer II may not be functional, again they are often just for show. An explanation of these functions is detailed in the 'Basic Operation' section of this book.

It is worth mentioning that the large 'sweep' hand on the Daytona is part of the *stop watch function* and is not the primary second hand (the second hand for the watch is the bottom *20/40/60* register). Therefore, this large sweep hand should not move until the stop watch function is activated.

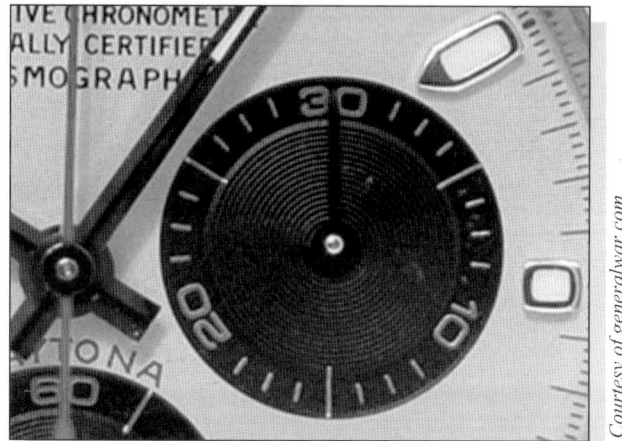

Genuine Rolex Daytona. Notice the tight concentric circles inside the registers. Fakes will rarely have these circles.

Courtesy of generalwar.com

Genuine Rolex GMT with 24-hour hand and bezel.

Comparison of the extra-function registers on a Daytona Cosmograph.
Genuine Rolex on the left, with a counterfeit Rolex on the right.
Note the incorrectly marked registers on the counterfeit, as well as the incorrect spacing.
Genuine Rolex will have these dials spaced farther 'outside' on the dial, as shown in the example on the left.

16) Dial Markings: We'll now take a look at the dial (or face) of the watch. For the most part, counterfeits will have "proper markings"—meaning they will have the correct words printed on the face. What we will look at is the detail and quality of the printing. Counterfeit markings will often appear fuzzy, or of the wrong size, shape or type font.

You may also want to look for any imperfections such as scratches or chips in the painted letters, as well as dust particles trapped under the crystal. It is important to check the detail with a loupe and again remember the detail on Rolex watches should be flawless.

Detailed dial comparison of a Submariner—Genuine Rolex on the left, with a counterfeit on the right. Notice how the counterfeit markings lose detail when viewed under a 10x loupe.

In the comparison photos below, imperfections can be seen on the counterfeit Daytona, in the form of tiny scratches and dust (on the dial) under the crystal. Also, under closer inspection it is revealed that the hour indices are misshaped (too fat) and the registers, while they are marked somewhat accurately in this example, are still not of the correct size or position—notice how they are smaller and positioned too far inward on the dial.

Furthermore, when inspecting the name "DAYTONA" (positioned between the bottom register and the center post), you will notice that the type font is incorrect. The genuine Daytona features the letter "A" with a flatter top, whereas the counterfeit has more of a point.

This is a good example of how counterfeits have been improving in recent years. Compare these pictures with the counterfeit Daytona featured under topic 15: *Extra Functions,* on page 92. However, while the markings on the registers are (more) correct on the newer fake (shown below), the spacing on these registers are still incorrect, thus easily detected.

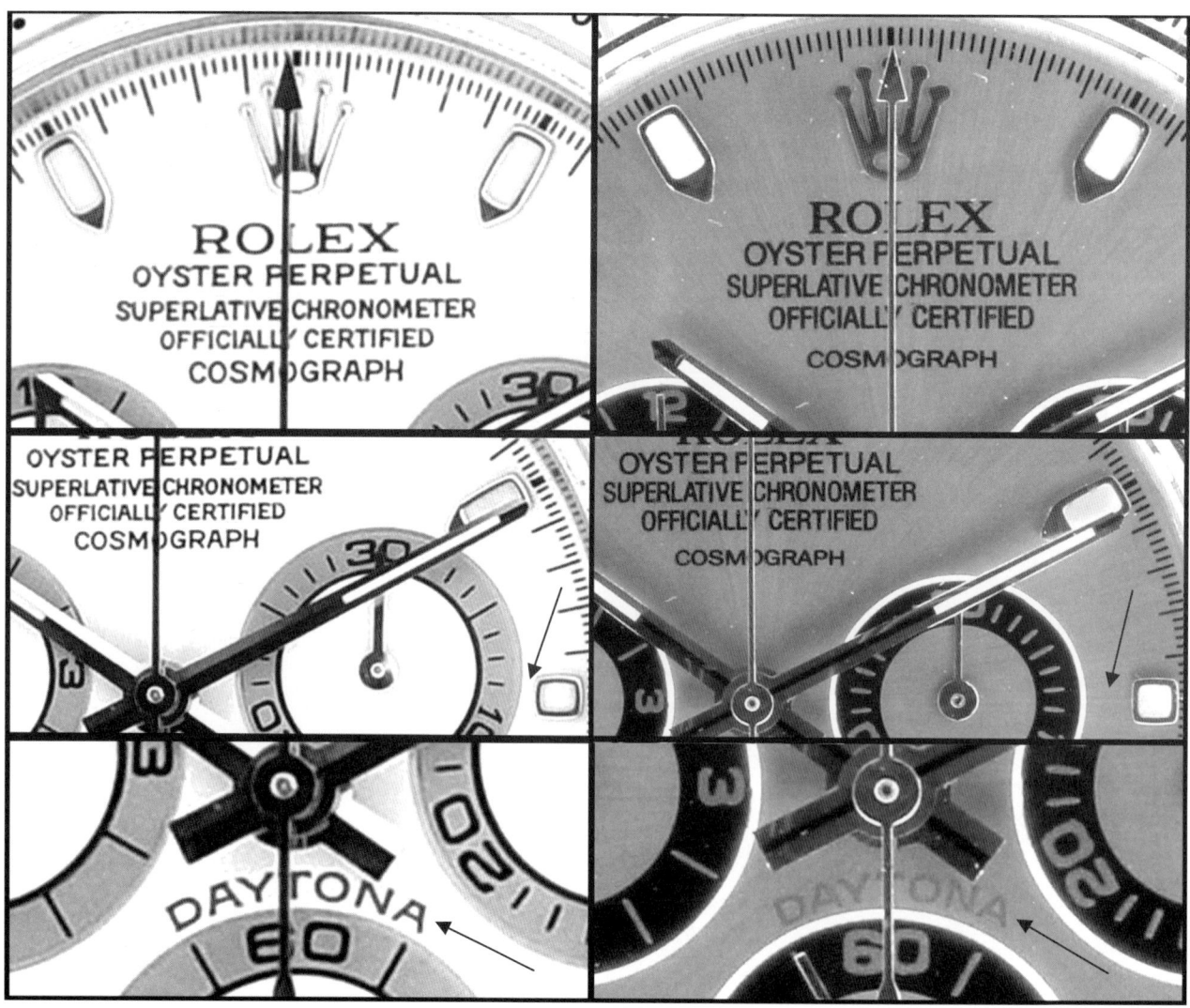

Detailed dial comparison of a Daytona, as viewed with a 10x loupe.
Genuine Rolex on the left, with a counterfeit on the right.
Notice the imperfections on the counterfeit, as well as the font and incorrectly positioned registers.

'SWISS MADE' Dial Markings: In the past, most Rolex models displayed the following in tiny print (at the bottom of the dial): "T SWISS MADE T", or on divers' models: "SWISS T < 25".

This referred to the type and amount of radioactive chemical used on the hour indices and hands to allow them to illuminate in the dark. However, around 1998 Rolex started converting to a different (safer) chemical and thus the marking should now simply read: "SWISS MADE". (For more info on this, see the FAQ section at the end of this book.)

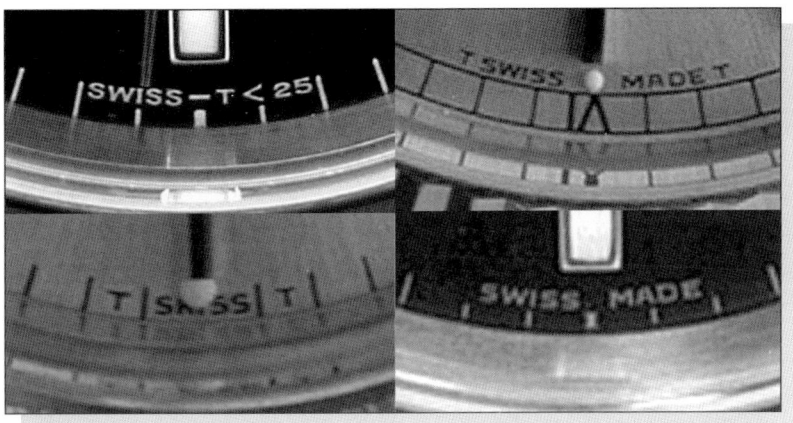

Genuine 'Swiss' markings, located at the bottom of the dial.

One last note on the dial's appearance is the outer edge of the dial, where it angles upward toward the bezel. On genuine Rolexes, this outer edge (which is actually part of the case) will appear to have a satin-like finish (matching the color of the case). Fakes however, *may* give a glass-like mirror reflection of the dial (as seen in the image comparison below).

Genuine Rolex Submariner with 'satin finish' outer edge.

Counterfeit Rolex Submariner with 'mirror finish' outer edge. Note reflection of the hour indices visible in the mirrored edge.

17) Hour/Minute/Second Hands: This is a common mistake for many (but not all) counterfeits. Since they often use converted hands from other watches, they may often be of the wrong size (too short). Also, when checking the minute hand on a Yacht-Master you will notice that it's a bit thicker than that of a Submariner. However, to cut costs, counterfeits often use the same hands on these watches! You may also notice that in the Daytona comparison below, the hands on the fake are actually flat-tipped (like on a Day-Date), rather than the pointed-tip hands seen on a genuine Daytona.

Check the color of the hands as well, Rolex hands will match the color of the bezel. Therefore, a SS Submariner will have *irodium* plated white gold hands, whereas a two-Tone Submariner will use yellow gold hands.

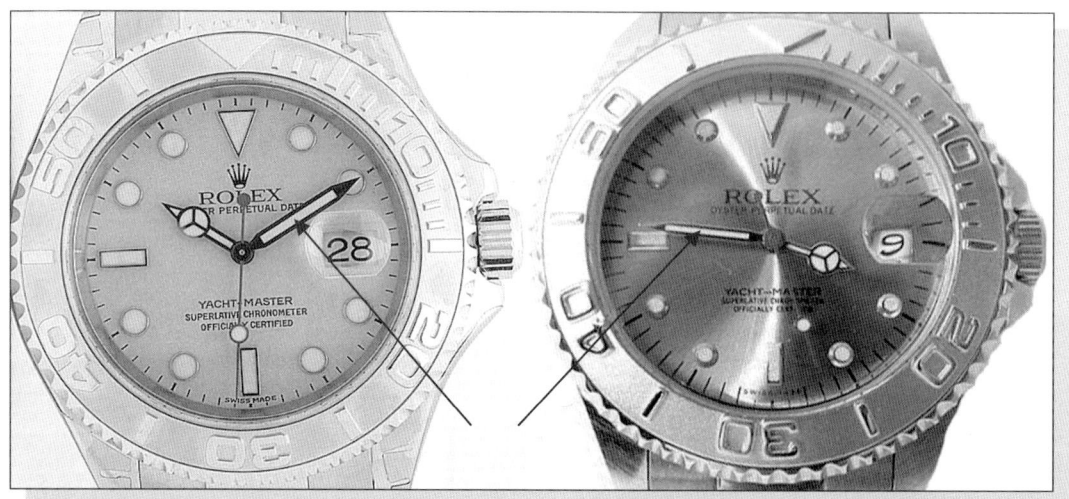

Comparison of Rolex Yacht-Master minute-hands—note the difference in thickness.
Genuine Rolex on the left (with thick minute hand).
Counterfeit Rolex on the right (with thinner minute hand).

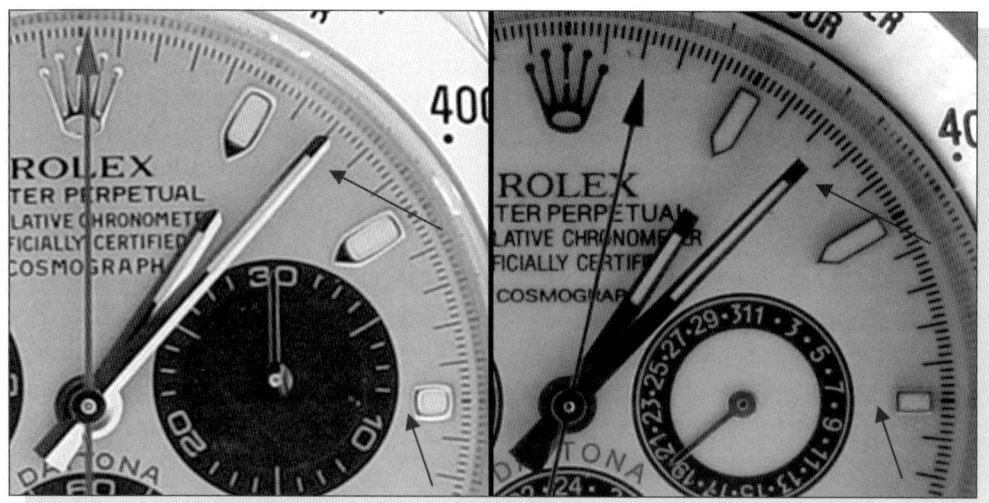

Comparison of Rolex Daytona hands—note the difference in length and shape.
Genuine Rolex on left (with longer hands—pointed on the end).
Counterfeit Rolex on the right (with shorter hands—squared on the end).

18) Hour/Minute Indices: The hour markers should be positioned perfectly. Fakes will often be misaligned, or positioned too far outward on the dial.

On newer sport models, the illuminated round hour markers are surrounded with a thin metal border matching the color of the bezel. Again, a SS Submariner will have hour indices trimmed in *irodium* plated white gold, and a 2-Tone Submariner will use yellow gold. The exception to this is vintage models like the Submariners and Sea-Dweller which did not have this border.

Comparison of new versus old style genuine Rolex Submariners.
New-style Submariner on left, with borders around the hour markers.
Old-style Submariner on right, with no borders around the hour markers.

19) The Rotating Bezel: On sport models with *Rotating Bezels* (i.e. Submariner, Sea-Dweller and GMT-Master) the bezel should be tight and have (about) 120 quiet 'clicks' when turned (2 per minute marker). Whereas, fakes are usually loose, sloppy and often get hung up as they turn. Again, fakes usually give a loud 'tinny' sound when turned and only around 60 clicks.

Submariner rotating bezel.

20) One-Way Gas Escape Valve: The Rolex Sea-Dweller is equipped with a *one-way gas escape valve* on the side of the case—opposite the winding crown. This tiny round opening is used during de-compression to allow the case to depressurize after lengthy *saturation dives*. Counterfeiters have re-cently begun copying the Sea-Dweller, particularly the 'Red' *Sea-Dweller Submariner 2000*.

(*Please Note: ALL Sea-Dwellers will be equipped with this tiny valve. While it is unlikely that coun-terfeiters will ever be able to duplicate this feature, they will no doubt eventually fabricate their cases to 'cosmetically" replicate this appearance.*)

Rolex Sea-Dweller with *one-way gas escape valve*, positioned on the side of the case—opposite the winding crown.

21) Heavily Encrusted Watches: This refers to the excessive use of diamonds (usually fake) or other precious stones on the watch's case and/or bracelet. While Rolex does offer some of their high-end watches ("Crown Collection" series) with precious stones, it is unlikely to find a Datejust so equipped like in the pic-ture on the right. This configuration is often referred to as an 'iced' watch, with the reference being to ice (or diamonds). With that being said, it's probably one of the ugliest watches ever made.

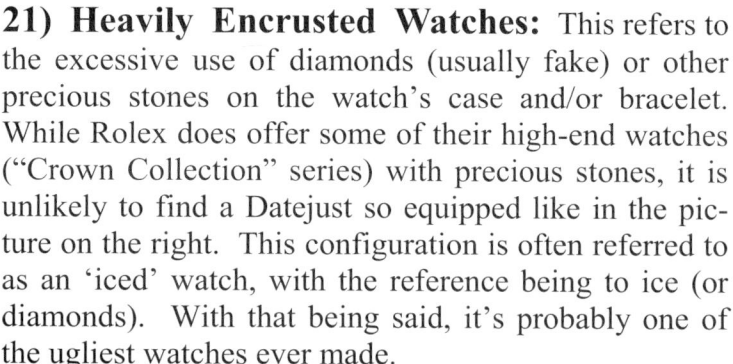

22) Case Ref. & Serial Numbers: Rolex Oyster cased watches have a *Serial Number* engraved between the lugs (6 o'clock position), and a *Case Reference Number* (12 o'clock position). A full detailed descrip-tion of these numbers is located in *Part III: Rolex Parts Identification* section of this book.

Counterfeit Rolex Datejust with excessive (fake) diamonds and other precious stones on the dial, case and bracelet.

The example below is of a counterfeit two-toned Submariner with engraved numbers. While these numbers are very convincing, apparently all examples from this source appear with the SAME num-bers: *Case Reference Number* 16613, which correctly indicates a two-toned Submariner, and *Serial Number* W860168, which indicates approximately a 1994/95 production date.

Courtesy of rarerolex.com

Very convincing counterfeit Submariner with engraved *Serial Number* (left) and *Case Reference Number* (right).

23) Micro-Etched Crystals: Brand new for 2002, Rolex has started *micro-etching* a tiny 'coronet' (or crown) logo into the crystal, at the 6 o'clock position. This mark is quite small, so it's difficult to see with the naked eye. However, when viewed under a loupe, the faint outline can be distinguished, as seen in the examples below.

Courtesy of generalwar.com

RIGHT: 2002 Rolex Day-Date, with an arrow indicating the position of the *micro-etching*.

BELOW LEFT & RIGHT: *Micro-etched* crown in the crystal of the watch shown above. Please Note: In the image on the left, we have *outlined* the etching so it is easier to identify, while the image on the right is unaltered.

Courtesy of generalwar.com

RIGHT: 2002 Rolex Lady Datejust, with an arrow indicating the position of the *micro-etching*.

FAR RIGHT: Enlarged view of the *micro-etched* crown in the crystal of the watch shown on the right. In this image we have *circled* the etching to help you identify it.

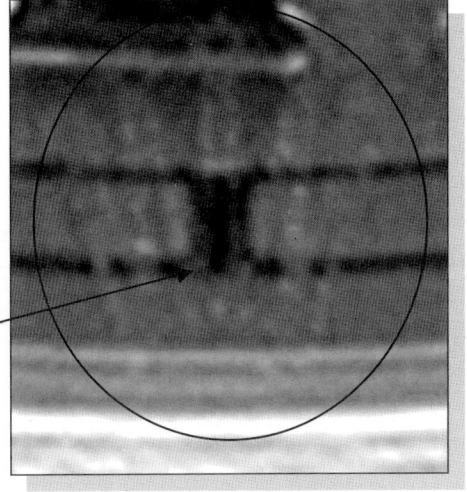

Courtesy of Michael J. Rosenman

WATCH DISASSEMBLY

There are two main disassembly steps: **Bracelet Removal** and **Case Back Removal** which are explained below.

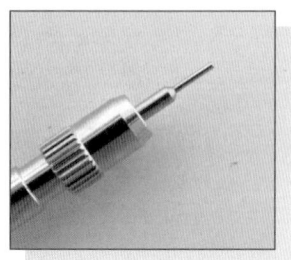 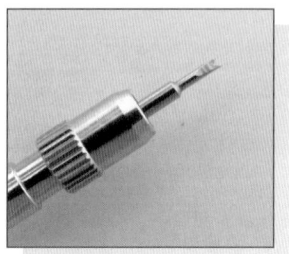

Spring bar tool tips.
LEFT: For cases with 'Spring Bar Holes'.
RIGHT: For cases with 'No-Holes'.

Step 1 - Bracelet Removal

Spring Bar Hole Cases: Insert the pointed end of the spring bar removal tool into the hole. Now push in on the spring bar, while at the same time pushing to the side. This will catch the spring bar tip onto the inside of the lug, and it will not come back through the hole. These spring bars can be tight and it may take a while so be patient. Once you have one side done, repeat these steps on the other three lugs, until the bracelet is completely removed from the case.

Spring bar hole case.

No-Hole Cases: Insert the flat end of the spring bar removal tool into the tiny slot on either end of the end piece, hooking it onto the spring bar. Now push down, while at the same time pushing to the side. This will catch the spring bar tip onto the inside of the lug. These spring bars can be tight and it may take a while so be patient. Once you have one side done, repeat these steps on the other three lugs, until the bracelet is completely removed from the case.

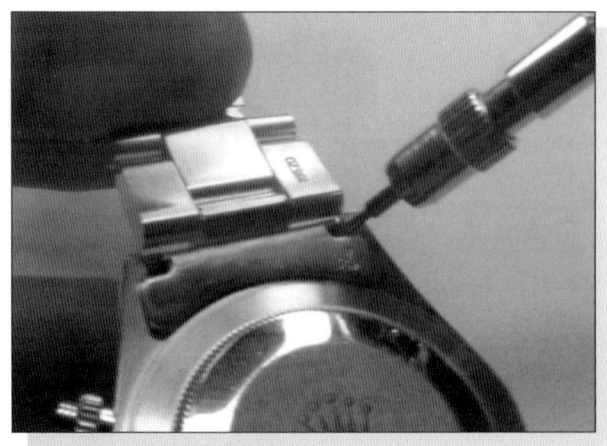

No-hole case.

Case back wrench (socket-style).

LEFT: Notice the matching tooth edge grooves on the socket.
RIGHT Wrench is in position to remove case back.

Step 2 - Case Back Removal

Case back removal is only necessary to inspect the movement and markings INSIDE the case back, and can be skipped if this step is not possible (by you) or is not necessary.

Rolex case backs are actually screwed together giving it a hermetic seal. The case back will have a grooved, or coined edge which are actually tiny "teeth". These teeth fit into a socket-like tool, which is then turned counter-clockwise to remove the case back.

Counterfeits will often have screw-on case backs and in most cases will use the same size Rolex tools.

WARNING: Be careful when attempting this step. It is easy to scratch or mar the case back if you don't know what you're doing. Rolex uses a seal (or gasket) inside the case back and it is possible to damage this seal by improper removal and/or replacement of the case back. These seals are not cheap to replace, so if you question your ability in this step I suggest taking the watch to jeweler who is more familiar with the procedure. Furthermore, failure to correctly replace the case back can result in compromising the hermetic seal of the watch and thus affecting its pressure-proof seal.

I am not responsible for any damage which may occur during the disassembly of your watch.

THE DETAILED EXAMINATION

(Exterior)

For a description of identification numbers including: *End Piece Numbers*, *Bracelet Numbers*, *Serial Numbers* and *Case Reference Numbers*, see *Part IV: Rolex Parts Identification*, later in this book.

Bracelet End Piece: As described earlier, an end piece is a small piece of metal which is crafted to look like a bracelet link and by which the bracelet is attached to the watch's case. These end pieces come in a few different styles, depending on the case style. That is to say that cases with spring bar holes will have one style, and no-hole cases will have another. Furthermore, Rolex has started using a new style of SEL (solid end link), whereas this piece is actually attached to the bracelet as the final link.

Courtesy of bjsonline.com

Courtesy of bjsonline.com

TOP LEFT: New-style Solid End Link (SEL).

LEFT: Old-style 2-part End Piece.

ABOVE: Old-style End Piece featuring the number "501B" stamped on the reverse side.

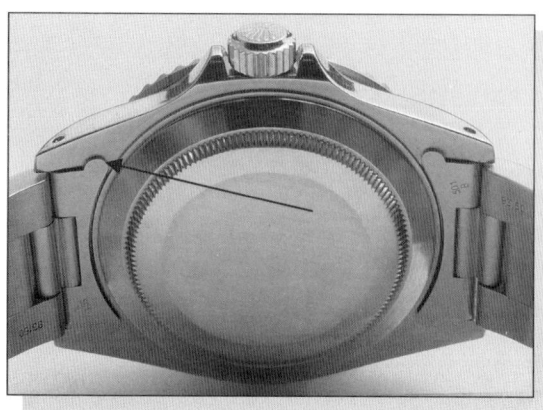

LEFT: Daytona featuring the new Solid End Links (SEL) configuration, whereas the end pieces are actually 'links' permanently attached to the ends of the bracelet.

RIGHT: Submariner featuring the conventional (separate) end pieces.

Bracelet Links: The links on modern Oyster bracelets are tapered in thickness around the bracelet. That is to say that the links closer to the case are thicker than the links toward the buckle, as seen in the image below. However, cheaper (counterfeit) bracelets will often be of the same thickness all the way around.

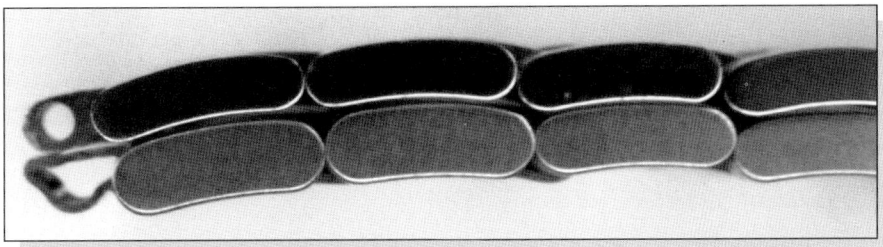

Comparison photo of bracelet links, with a genuine Rolex Oyster on bottom and a counterfeit on top. Notice how the genuine Rolex links are thicker on the left, whereas the counterfeit's are the same thickness all the way across.

Next, look at how the bracelet functions. Genuine Rolex bracelets are smooth and operate perfectly. Whereas, a counterfeit may be tight or even get 'kinks' when folded, due to the poorly fitted links.

To check this, fold the bracelet's links in an accordion-like fashion, then pick the bracelet up by the buckle. The weight of the case should flatten the links out smoothly, but a counterfeit will often remain tightly kinked, as seen in the comparison on the right.

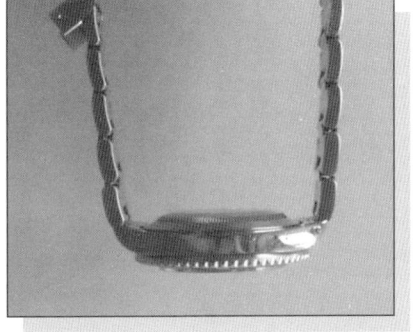 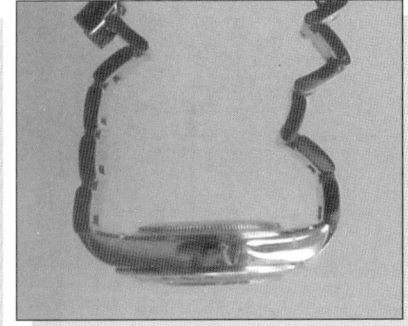

LEFT: Genuine Oyster bracelet, note how the links straighten out smoothly when picked up.

RIGHT: Counterfeit Oyster bracelet, note how the links remain tightly 'kinked' when picked up.

Be careful not to confuse this smoothness of the bracelet with 'stretch', which is when the bracelet's links become worn out (or stretched out) over time, and therefore do not hold their shape—as seen in the comparison photos on the right. While this does not give the indication of a fake, it does mean that the bracelet is worn out and therefore should be replaced.

It is also worth mentioning that *early* "US Bands" were characteristically loose and may not indicate a need to replace.

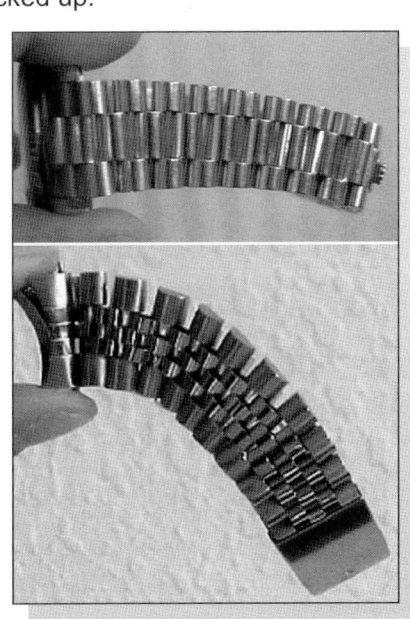

The comparison on the right shows a properly functioning bracelet on top, with an older 'stretched' bracelet on the bottom.

Jubilee Bracelet Links: The center links of a *Jubilee* bracelet are actually *molded* into the 'half-moon' shape, rather than *bent* into shape. To add additional stability, they are made with thicker corner walls, like in the example on the right. However, counterfeits are simply 'bent' into shape and will not have this thick appearance in the corners.

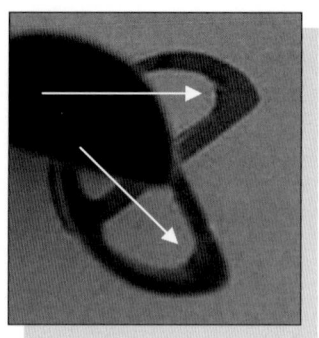

Genuine Rolex Jubilee link, with molded center links.

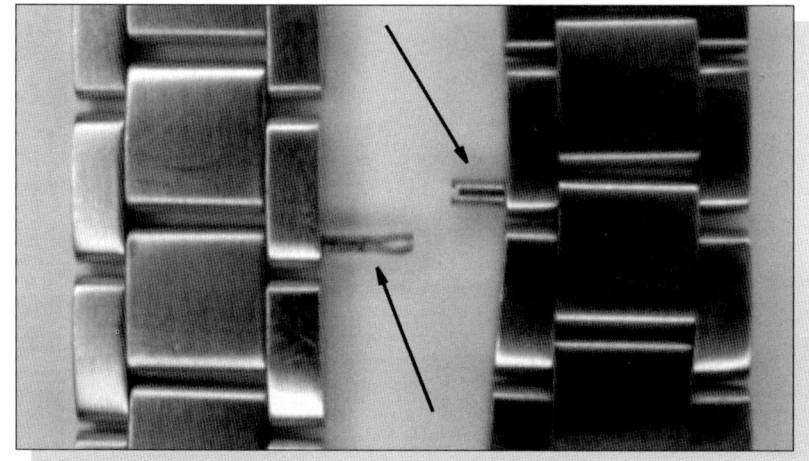

Bracelet Link Screws: The bracelet's links are held together with tiny machined screws. However, fakes (particularly older ones) will often use push-pins like in the comparison photo on the right.

Comparison photo of bracelet links.
Fake 'push-pin' on the left, and genuine 'screw' on the right.

While most counterfeits will use push-pins as described above, recently a series of Oyster bracelets have been surfacing with 'screw' links. However, by inspecting these screws under a loupe you are able to identify flaws like in the following comparison images:

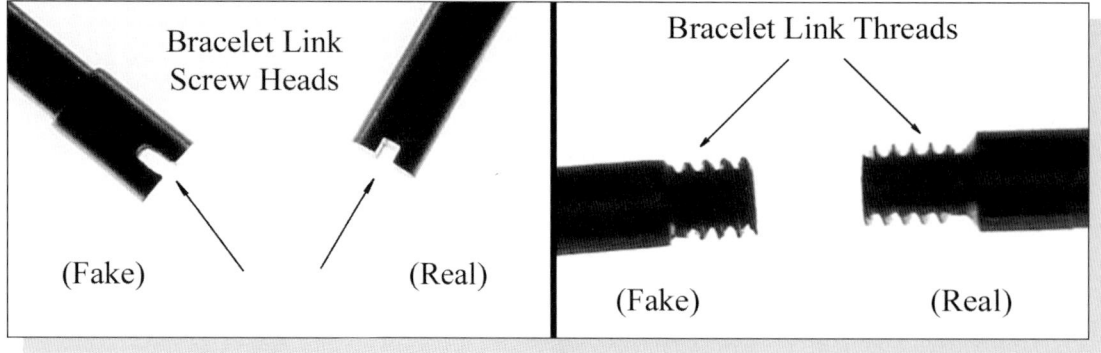

Detailed comparison photos of link screws, as viewed under a 5x loupe.

LEFT: Comparison of screw heads, with a fake on the left and genuine on the right.
Genuine screws have 'square' shaped slots, while fakes often have a 'V' or 'U' shaped slot.

RIGHT: Comparison of screw threads, with a fake on the left, and genuine on the right.
Genuine threads have a 'tapered gap' or 'shoulders' at the end where the threads finish into the screw's shaft, while fake threads will often not have this 'tapered gap' finish.

A more detailed comparison of the screw threads, as viewed under a 17x loupe.
In this comparison, the 'tapered gap' or 'shoulders' are more easily identified, where
on the counterfeit the threads just abruptly end into the screw's shaft.

It is also worth mentioning that the tips of the screws will have a concaved dimple or
'doughnut' shape.

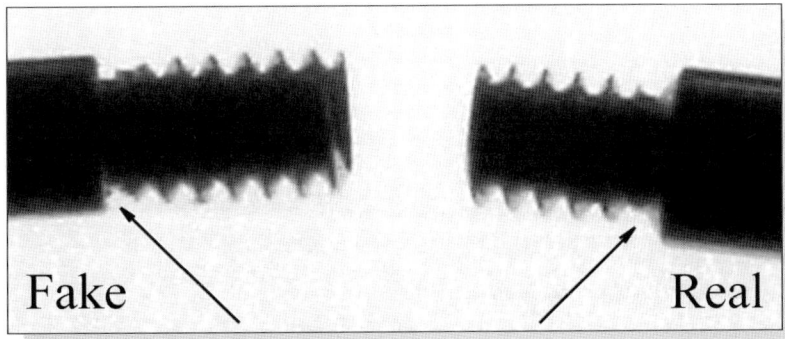

Detailed comparison of screw threads, as viewed under a 10x loupe.
In this comparison, the fake screw threads have a 'flattened gap' at the
end, instead of the 'tapered gap' or 'shoulders' on the genuine screw.

Bracelet Clasp 'Hallmarks': Rolex Oyster & Jubilee bracelets are stamped with a logo (or 'hallmark' for lack of a better word) on the inside of the folding clasp. The stamping includes the name "ROLEX" surrounded with a series of scrolled lines and is topped with the *coronet* (or crown). Counterfeit stamping is poor in quality and can be identified under a loupe. Furthermore, the Rolex crown is often misrepresented with a very *round* "O" shape at the base. The genuine Rolex crown features a flatter *oval* shape on the base, as represented in the images below.

Please Note: Over the years, this stamping has varied and the representation below is just an example with respect to the 'quality' of this stamping.

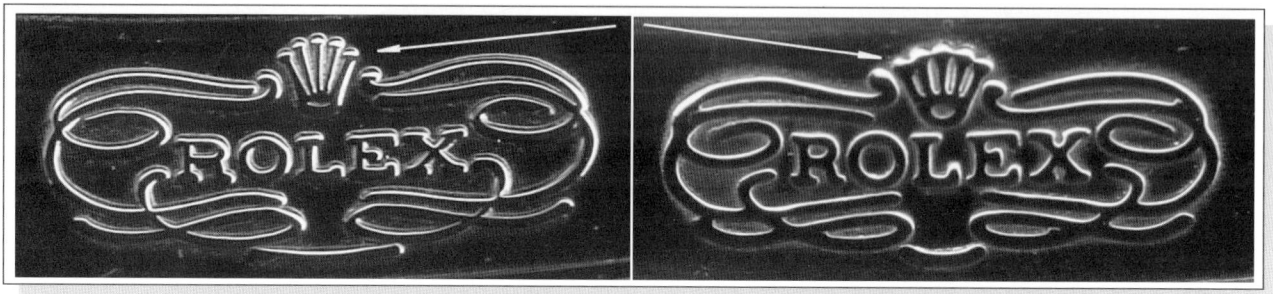

Comparison photo of bracelet hallmarks, with genuine on the left and fake on the right. Note the symmetrical scrolled spacing and shape of the Rolex crown at the top. Fake logos tend to have a very fanned out appearance at the points of the crown.

RIGHT: Counterfeit Oyster bracelet stamping. Note the poor spacing on the scroll work and misshaped base of crown.

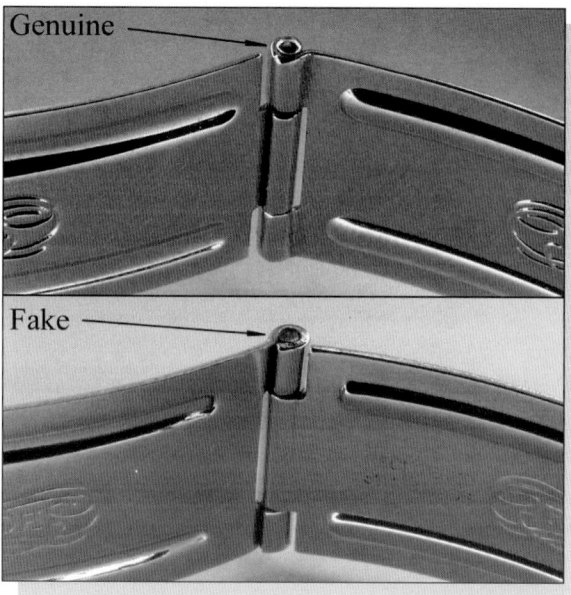

Genuine

Fake

Bracelet Clasp Hinge: Rolex bracelet clasps are hinged with a tiny pin. On genuine models, this pin will be finished on both ends, as seen in the comparison photo.

RIGHT: Comparison photo of the bracelet clasp hinge. Note how the genuine hinge is finished, whereas the fake is simply a cut piece of metal.

Divers' Extension Clasp: Rolex divers' models (i.e. Submariner and Sea-Dweller) will be equipped with a folding extension link which is hinged from underneath the bracelet's clasp. Counterfeiters have recently begun copying this, but under closer examination a number of flaws can be detected.

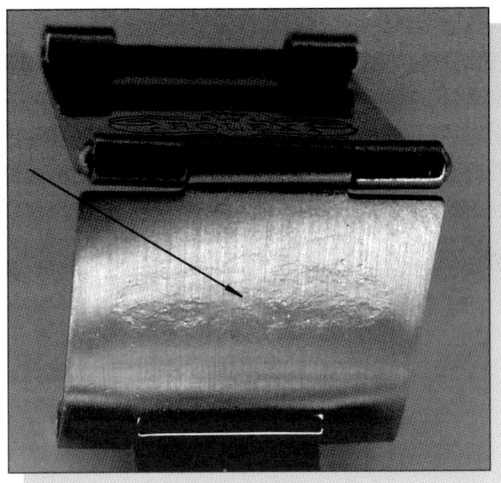

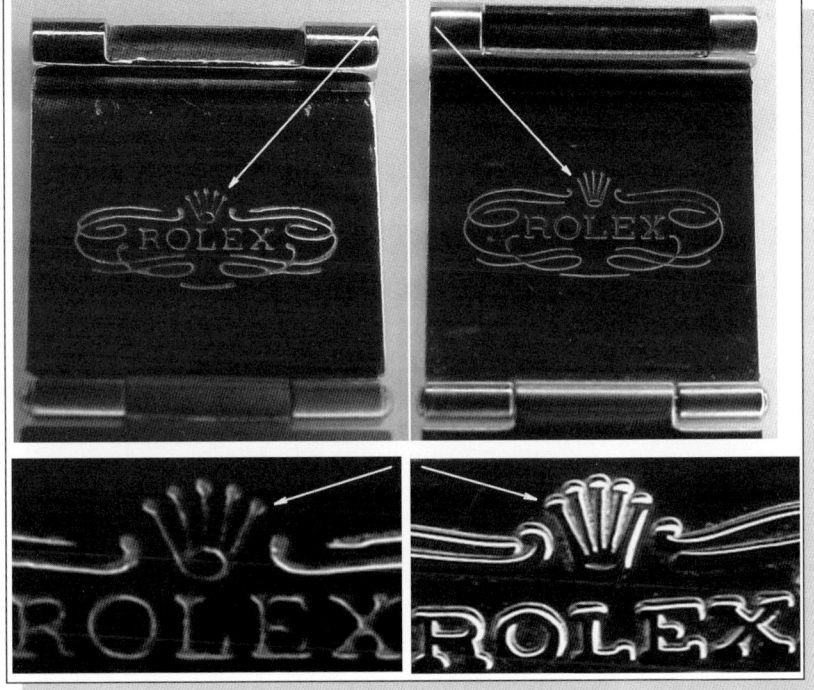

ABOVE: Reverse side of a counterfeit divers' extension. Note the faint metal disfiguration where the 'Rolex' stamping shows thru. This is due to the inferior quality of the metal used on many fakes.

Divers' extension comparison photos, as viewed under a 5x and 10x loupe, respectively.

RIGHT: Genuine—Note the quality of printing, including the Rolex *crown* with PERFECT spacing.
LEFT: Fake—Note the shape of the *crown*, with the 5-points fanned out, as well as the incorrectly shaped base of the crown, with an "O" appearance, instead of the flatter *oval* on genuine Rolex.

Bracelet Clasp Stamping: Rolex Oyster and Jubilee bracelets are stamped with the crown logo on the outside of the clasp. When viewed under a loupe, the counterfeits can be detected by their inferior quality stamping, as seen in the comparison photos below.

Comparison photo of bracelet clasp stamping, as viewed under a 10x loupe.

RIGHT: Genuine, with perfect quality and spacing.
LEFT: Counterfeit, with slightly fanned-out spacing of the points. Also, note the metal disfiguration *between* the point, due to the poor stamping quality.

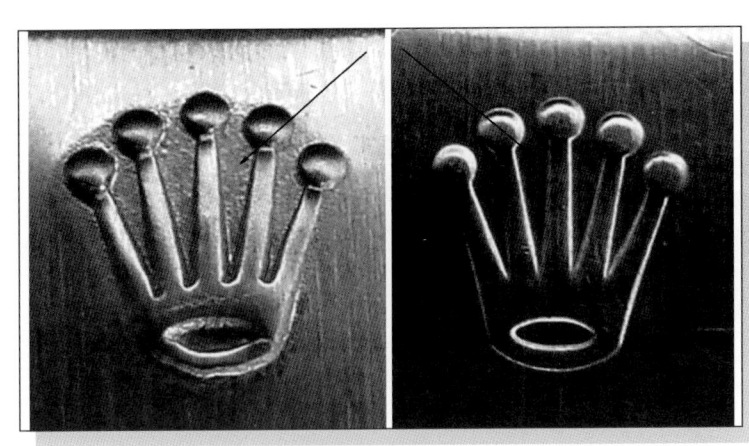

President Clasp Hallmarks: Rolex President bracelets are stamped with hallmarks on the inside of the folding clasp, as shown below. On the *Counterfeit* bracelet at the bottom, you will notice how these hallmarks lose their detail when viewed under a loupe. Please Note: This example is of a men's bracelet—ladies' models have the same hallmarks, but with a slightly different layout.

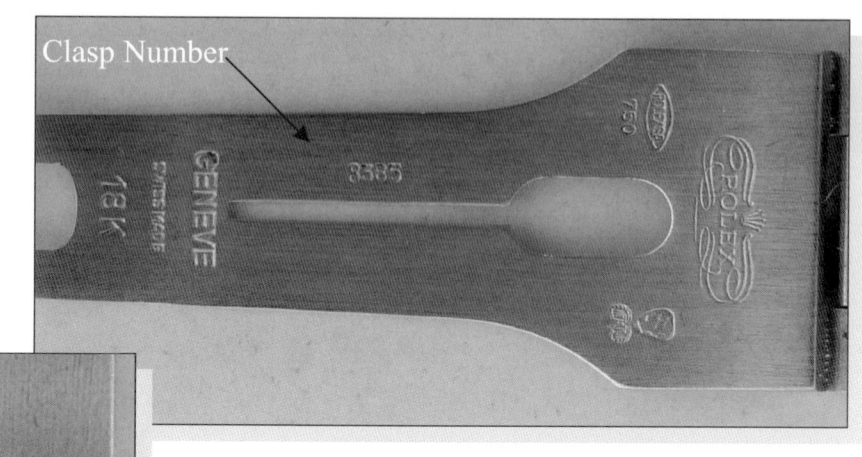

Clasp Number

Genuine President bracelet clasp *hallmark* stamping. Notice how the stamping is perfect in detail and quality. The *only* exception being the *scrolled* Rolex markings at the top, which will be perfect *except* for the tips of the crown which will NOT have finished 'balls' on the ends. The reason for this is the curvature of the clasp at the top, making it difficult to stamp.

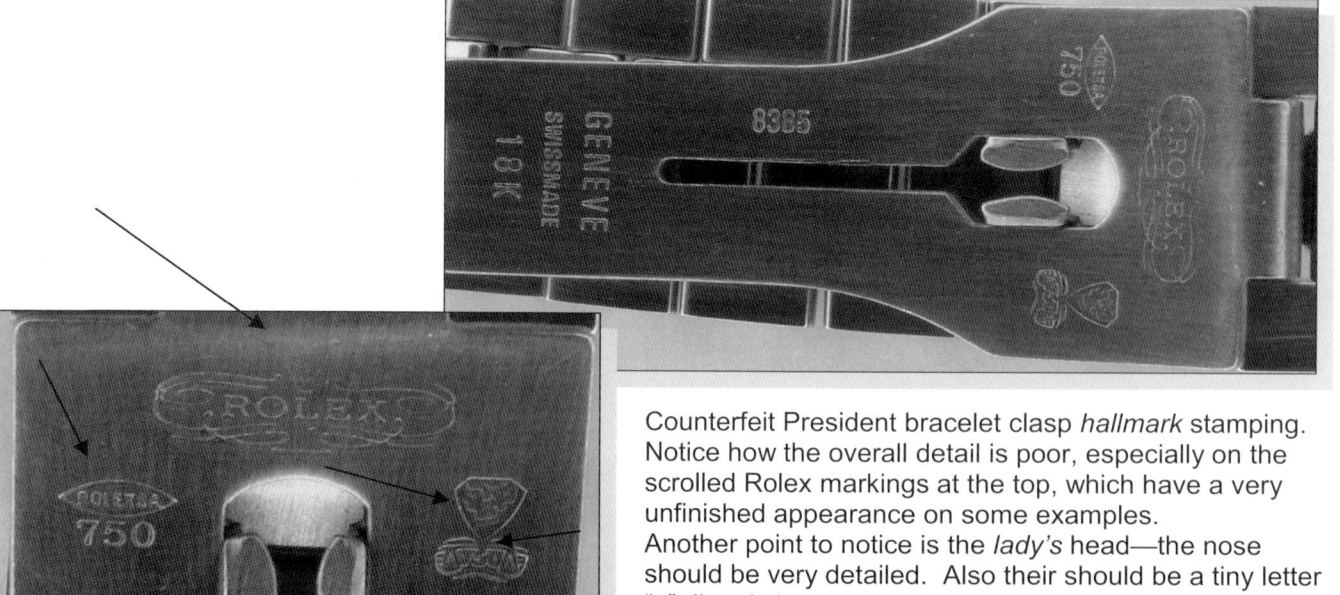

Counterfeit President bracelet clasp *hallmark* stamping. Notice how the overall detail is poor, especially on the scrolled Rolex markings at the top, which have a very unfinished appearance on some examples.
Another point to notice is the *lady's* head—the nose should be very detailed. Also their should be a tiny letter "g" directly below the head—not present on the counterfeit shown here.
On newer models, the clasp may feature a *St. Bernard* dog's head instead of the lady's head shown here. In that case you should check the nose, as well as the ear, which should feature the aforementioned tiny letter "g".

Case Lug Hallmarks: As with gold bracelets, gold Oyster cases will have similar hallmarks located on the lug tips, as shown in the examples below. These hallmarks will include: *"18K"*, the *Balance Scales* (with *"750"* through the center) , and the *ladies' head—or St. Bernard dog's head* on some models since the mid 1990s.

'Stainless Steel' (on stainless steel models) Hallmarks (on gold models)

'Registered Design'

Case Reference Number

Serial Number

RIGHT: On gold-cased Oysterquartz models, all of the hallmarks will be located on the back of a single lug tip, as detailed in the image on the right.

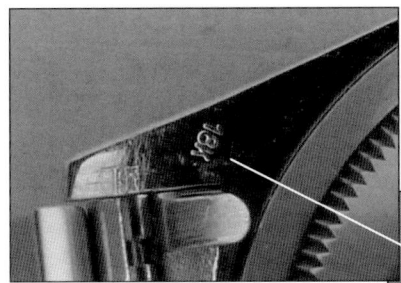

BELOW: On all other gold-cased Oyster models, the hallmarks will be located on the back of three of the lug tips, as detailed in the images below.

ABOVE: *"18K"* hallmark.

BELOW: *Ladies'* (or St. Bernard dog's) *head* hallmark.

ABOVE: *Balance Scale* hallmark featuring *"750"* through the center.

Please Note: The final lug tip is left blank and does not feature a hallmark.

THE DETAILED EXAMINATION

(Interior)

Movements: Counterfeit movements are (in most cases) very easily identified. They are often just generic movements (like Miyota) and have no 'Rolex' markings or hallmarks. However, some counterfeits will have obvious counterfeit Rolex markings, as seen in the images below.

(*Please Note: These images are just a brief example and should not be considered a complete representation of counterfeit movements used.*)

TOP LEFT: 'Generic' Miyota movement, used in many counterfeit Rolex models.

TOP RIGHT: Counterfeit Rolex movement with *hallmarked* rotor, seen in numerous 'clear-back' counterfeit Rolex models.

RIGHT: Counterfeit Rolex movement with *hallmarked* rotor, as seen in a vintage counterfeit Bubbleback.

Rather than try to describe every aspect of a *genuine* Rolex movement, I will simply say that the sophistication and quality is very easy to distinguish. When viewing the genuine Rolex movements on this page, as opposed to the *generic* counterfeits on the previous page, it is easy to see the difference. Mass produced counterfeits will not even come close to the quality and detail put into a genuine Rolex movement. One feature to note is the presence of 'colored' dials on late model movements. These dials (red and gold) are identified in the image on the bottom right (movement Cal. 3135).

Inside Case Back Markings: Over the years, Rolex has changed the engraving located inside the case back of the watch. However, the one thing that hasn't changed is the quality and attention to detail, with respect to these markings. Rather than try to explain every generation of markings, I will focus on the quality and detail.

In the example on the right, you will notice that the counterfeit markings are very similar to the genuine case backs shown below. However, the stamping on the counterfeit is 'off center', as well as incorrectly proportioned around the *coronet* logo—meaning it is fanned-out too far.

It is worth mentioning that gold-cased Rolexes will have hallmark stamps inside the case backs, in addition to the standard Rolex logos, as seen in the example below (bottom center).

Counterfeit markings (inside case back). Note the inferior quality and positioning of the stamping.

REPLICA CATEGORIES

All replicas are not made in the same place, nor are they all made by the same people. There are numerous levels of sophistication and features, and therefore not every replica series will be exactly the same. With that being said, for simplicity sake, I have grouped Counterfeit Rolex watches into 5-categories as follows:

Category I   "Low Level" Replica
Category II   "Mid Level" Replica
Category III   "High Level" Replica
Category IV   "Swap-Job" or "Mix & Match" Rolexes
Category V   "Converted" Rolexes

(Please Note: Category I, II and III listed above are "mass produced" counterfeit watches, while Cat IV and V are produced (or faked) on an individual basis.)

Category I – "Low Level" Replica:

These are the cheap copies from years past and were usually made in Taiwan or China.

Price Range: $25-$50.

Movement: Usually quartz, which means the second hand *ticks,* and the watch requires a battery – very obvious.

Inside: The cases often have flip-open cases (not screw-in like genuine Rolex). Again, the movements will be quartz and thus will not even look close to that of an authentic Rolex. No Rolex markings on movement or inside case back.

Finish: Very thin (artificial) gold plating and wears off in just a couple months. Color is very "brassy" and not convincing.

Weight: Very lightweight!! No where near that of an authentic Rolex, especially on gold models.

Case Seal: Not waterproof and hardly even water-resistant — No crown seal.

Watch Dial: Markings are poor quality (fuzzy when inspected with a loupe), and often incorrect. Hands are usually wrong size, and *illumination* (if any) is poor and only lasts a short time. The cyclops is poor quality with very little magnification (not 2.5 magnification like a genuine Rolex).

Overall Markings: Poor quality, with incorrect or even missing markings on case back and bracelet.

Bracelet: Again, cheap plating and even *hollow* links in most cases. "Push pins" instead of "screws" in bracelet links.

Case Backs: Incorrect stamps and/or stickers. Some will have "clear backs" (AKA. skeleton cases), or engravings of model number/hallmarks on case back.

Serial/Model Numbers: Non-existent or WRONG numbers and/or location.

Form and Function: Overall the watch performs poorly. Crowns and Bezels will be loose or sloppy. Extra function dials (i.e. Daytona registers) will NOT be functional (just for show). The life expectancy is rarely over a couple months.

Conclusion: There is a reason you don't see these fakes anymore. Anyone with an IQ over 12 should detect them.

Category II – "Mid Level" Replica:

These are the most common models currently seen in numerous online auctions.

Price Range: $75-$200 depending on the model.

Movement: Perpetual movement (no battery). However, the sweep second hand is sometimes *choppy* and thus not as convincing.

Inside: The cases usually have screw-in case back (like Rolex) and can only be opened with Rolex-style tools. Movements and inside case backs are marked wrong or not at all.

Finish: Artificial gold plating is of moderate quality and will show wear after a few months if worn often. Color (on gold models) still looks a bit brassy. Therefore, Cat. II replicas are more convincing in stainless steel models.

Weight: Heavier than Cat. I, but still far from that of an authentic Rolex (especially on gold models). Again, stainless steel models are a bit more convincing.

Case Seal: Watch is water-resistant, but NOT waterproof. This means you can probably shower with it, but don't take it for a swim — No crown seal.

Watch Dial: Usually have proper markings, but the detail and quality is moderate at best (fuzzy when inspected with a loupe). Hands can be the wrong size on some models. Illumination markers are suspect and usually doesn't last beyond a couple years. Cyclops is often crooked and does not magnify a full 2.5 times.

Overall Markings: May have what appears to be correct markings, but closer examination will often show wrong or missing numbers on bracelet, clasp, etc… Also, hallmarks will have errors.

Bracelet: May have "solid" links, with "screws", but closer examination will detect poor quality (especially in threading).

Case Backs: Some will still have "clear backs" (AKA. skeleton cases), or engravings of model number/hallmarks on case back. Please Note: Cat. II models are getting better about leaving the case backs blank. However, most will include incorrect stickers.

Serial/Model Numbers: Non-existent or WRONG numbers and/or location.

Form and Function: Overall the watch performs like a low-end watch. Crowns and bezels will not be very tight. Extra function dials (i.e. Daytona registers) will usually not be functional. Most are just for show, however recently they are showing up with somewhat functional dials. The life expectancy is a few years (if you don't ride it hard).

Conclusion: These watches can convince SOME people, but upon routine examination you should detect a number of problems.

Category III – "High Level" Replica:

These models are commonly referred to as "Italian" or "Swiss" made replicas with 17 or 21 Jewel movements. However, this is just a sales tactic and they are not much better than Cat. II.

Price Range: They sell for $500-$1500 depending on the model. Gold or high demand models (i.e. Daytona, etc…) usually sell for more.

Movement: Perpetual movement (no battery). Claimed to use Swiss-made ETA movement, but this is often just hype. Second hands will sweep and may appear convincing.

Inside: The cases have screw-in case back (like Rolex) and can be opened with Rolex-style tools. Movements will usually be marked incorrectly. Also, the case back will rarely have any markings. Even though this may be a fairly convincing replica, the inside inspection will be conclusive.

Finish: Gold plating is said to be thicker, but overall color will not be quite convincing. The thicker plating will not show wear as easily. Stainless steel models are much more convincing.

Weight: Heavier, but still not quite that of an authentic Rolex—Especially on gold models.

Case Seal: Watch is water-resistant and said to be waterproof to a few feet. No crown seal, so don't go diving with it.

Watch Dial: In most cases will have proper markings, but the detail and quality can still be detected with a 10x loupe. Hands can still be the wrong size on some models. Illumination markers are okay, but usually won't last beyond a few years. Cyclops is said to be 2.5 times magnification on some models, so be careful of these watches on your cursory inspection.

Overall Markings: Markings are pretty good, but may still have wrong or missing numbers on bracelet, clasp, etc…

Bracelet: "Solid" links, with "screws", but closer examination may detect poor quality (in threads).

Case Backs: Solid backs with fairly convincing sticker, so be careful.

Serial/Model Numbers: Some have been seen with authentic looking serial/model numbers between the lugs. However, closer examination will show incorrect engraving and many will have the *same* numbers. Be careful of watches with these numbers, they can be very convincing.

Form and Function: Overall the watch performs like a average watch and can pass a cursory inspection so be careful. Crowns and bezels will be tighter than lower level fakes. Extra function dials (i.e. Daytona registers) will usually be functional to some degree. The life expectancy is okay if they are taken care of, but again no where near that of an authentic Rolex.

Conclusion: These watches can be VERY convincing if you are not careful. However, If you do a FULL inspection, you should be able to detect these fakes.

Category IV – "Swap-Job" or "Mix & Match" Rolexes:

Swap-Job or *Mix & Match* refers to any watch that contains BOTH authentic Rolex parts AND aftermarket and/or counterfeit parts. Thus "swapping" or "mixing" the genuine with non-genuine parts. Keep in mind that the parts could have been replaced PRIOR to the seller owning the watch, thus he/she may not even be aware of the replacement.

Needless to say, the presence of aftermarket or counterfeit parts will greatly reduce the value of the watch. (e.g. A genuine Rolex SS Oyster bracelet may retail for over $600, whereas an aftermarket SS model could be purchased for less than $100. These Scenarios make "swap-job" or "mix and match" watches very dangerous in the secondary market and is why you should fully inspect watches BEFORE you buy.

Furthermore, by having these aftermarket/counterfeit parts on the watch, it may void your factory Rolex warranty. That's right, Rolex may not warranty a watch if it contains non-genuine Rolex parts (whether they are aftermarket OR counterfeit). If you send in the watch for warranty work, Rolex may REQUIRE you to replace the non-genuine parts with genuine Rolex parts PRIOR to them performing the warranty work. This is due to the fact that aftermarket parts are inferior in quality and may cause the watch to perform incorrectly. Also, if your watch contains counterfeit parts, Rolex will confiscate the illegal parts and again you will have to replace them PRIOR to Rolex performing the warranty work.

Category V – "Converted" Rolexes:

Converted Rolexes are a very dangerous form of *Swap-Job / Mix & Match*. This refers to any watch that has been "converted" from one model to another with the use of aftermarket or counterfeit parts. Let me explain...

Lets assume you have a late model SS Submariner, which you purchased used for around $2,500. Now lets say your replace the SS "center links" of the bracelet with aftermarket gold-tone links, but retain the original genuine clasp (or you even replaced it with an authentic 2-tone clasp). Next you replace the SS bezel, crown, dial, end pieces and hands with aftermarket gold-tone pieces. You may have spent $500 for the replacement parts, but you sell this "converted" watch for upwards of $5,000 as a 2-tone SS & 18kt Submariner. You now have made a $2,000 profit! Not to mention you have the genuine SS parts you removed from the watch.

These are VERY difficult to detect because the watch is basically a GENUINE Rolex, but has been "cosmetically" converted to appear as another. While you're busy looking at the movement and operation of the watch, you may overlook the cosmetic features. This is why it is important to inspect the entire watch before accepting it as authentic—I just can't stress this enough!

ACCESSORIES

Sellers may include various accessories with their watch, in hopes that the mere presence of these items would in some way lend credibility as to the authenticity of their watch.

**DO NOT TAKE A WATCH AS AUTHENTIC
JUST BECAUSE IT HAS VARIOUS WOULD-BE ROLEX ACCESSORIES!**

The fact is you can buy these accessories on eBay and other online auctions with prices ranging from $5 to $50. Some are real, while others are just clever fakes. These accessories can range from: *hologram hang tags, Rolex boxes* (both inner and outer), *anchors, spoons, price tags, polishing cloths, leather wallets, owner's manuals, chronometer certificates*, etc…

The following pages will discuss some of these accessories and how the counterfeits have tried to copy them.

Paperwork: Rolex watches will often include 'paperwork'. These papers are often counterfeited with the aid of high-quality color copiers. To identify the papers as original you should check the *Seal* (located at the bottom of the certificate), as well as the headings: *"Full One Year Warranty"* and *"Official Chronometer Certification"*, which will be embossed— meaning they are stamped into the paper and can be read from the reverse side.

Also, (on newer issued paperwork) the paper will be printed with a 'crown' watermark across the page. To view this watermark, hold the paper up to the light.

Again, you should never base a watch's authenticity on the presence of such paperwork.

Please Note: The red letters printed on the warranty card is a code used by Rolex to identify when the watch was shipped from them to the authorized Rolex dealer. This code is as follows:

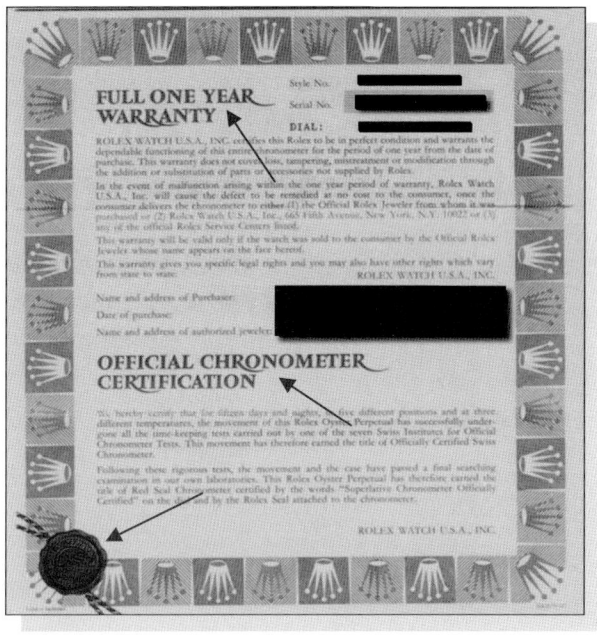

Rolex *Warranty* & *Official Chronometer Certification* Paperwork. The 'arrows' indicate location of the *Seal*, and *Headings* which should be 'embossed' into the paper.

R O L E X W A T C H
1 2 3 4 5 6 7 8 9 0

Therefore, if the code is "X CE", then the shipping date was May of 1994.

Hang Tags: Rolex watches are accompanied with a 'hang tag' which represents the rating of chronometer. These are often referred to as *hologram hang tags,* since one side of the tag features a hologram of the Rolex crown, as seen in the comparison photos below.

Rolex hang tag comparison. In each case above, the left tag is genuine, while the right tag is fake.

LEFT: Front view of the hang tag-Note the lettering on fake tags will often be of poor quality.

RIGHT: Rear view of the hang tag-Note the counterfeit does NOT feature the genuine Rolex hologram.

Rolex watches are packaged inside two boxes. The **outer box** is cardboard, while the **inner box** is leather.

(*Please Note: Rolex has just released a new box scheme for 2002. However, the design shown below—used throughout the 1990s—is by far the style most copied by counterfeiters.*)

Cardboard Boxes (outer): These boxes have changed over the years, featuring various colorful motifs. However, the quality and construction has not changed. Counterfeits can be identified by their inferior printing and color, which is usually too dark since they're often 2nd generation photocopies of the original. I suggest inspecting some genuine boxes so you will be able to identify their color schemes.

Comparison photos of Rolex (outer) cardboard boxes, with counterfeit on the left and genuine on the right.

Close-up comparison photos of the outer box markings.
Counterfeit box on the left, and genuine Rolex box on the right.
Note the counterfeit is darker and a bit fuzzy.

Leather Boxes (inner): These boxes have changed over the years as well. The box used throughout the 1990s features a green stitched leather (outer), with a varnished wood lining (inner). Counterfeits will be a cheap vinyl (outer), with an unfinished wood lining (inner).

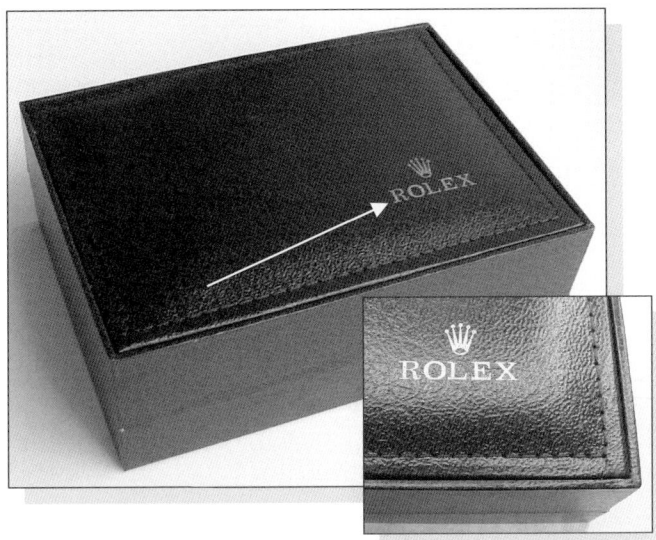

Comparison photos of Rolex (inner) leather boxes, with counterfeit on the left and genuine on the right. Please Note: The counterfeit features a fake "Rolex" and *crown* logo stamped on the cover, while the genuine box features an embossed *crown* logo pressed into the leather.

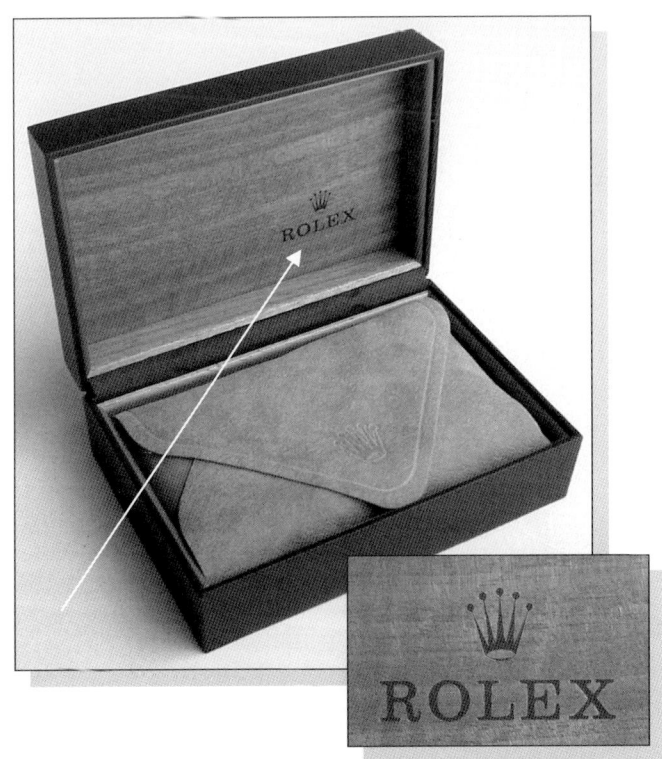

Comparison photos of the *inside* of Rolex leather boxes, with counterfeit on the left and genuine on the right. Note the difference in wood finish and printing locations.

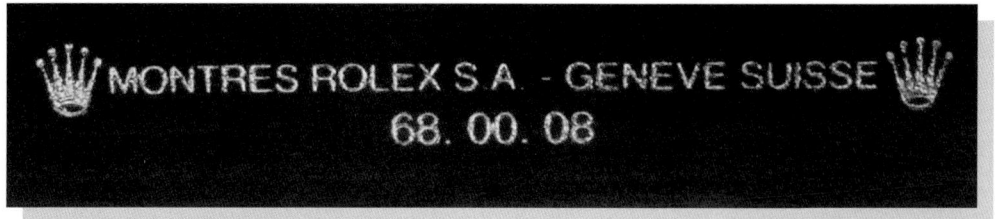

Rolex markings located on the bottom of the (inner) leather box.
Please note: Not all boxes will have these exact numbers, but they will be similar.

Inner Box Pillow Cushions: Rolex inner boxes feature a pillow cushion which the watch is wrapped around. These pillows look like suede leather, but are a very soft material. The counterfeits however, are very cheap in appearance and quality, and even feel rough to the touch.

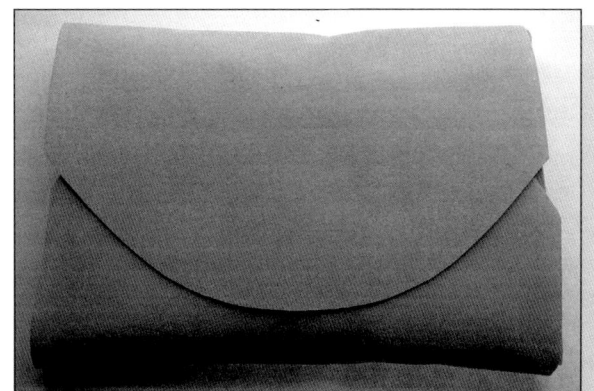
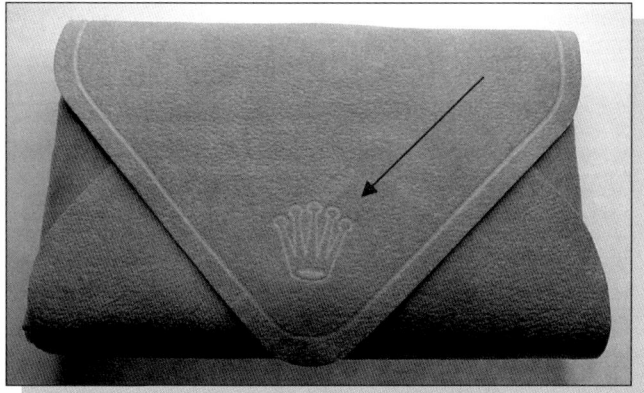

Comparison photos of the inner pillow cushion, with fake on the left and genuine on the right.
Note the shape of the pillows, as well as the trimmed edge and Rolex *crown* logo embossed in
the material of the genuine pillow.

VINTAGE COUNTERFEITS

Counterfeiters have been copying wristwatches for over a century. Ever since companies began distinguishing their watches with a name, counterfeiters were there copying it to make a quick buck. In fact, the more of a public demand there is for a particular brand, the more counterfeits there will be—It's the basic principle of supply and demand, and is very evident with the recent surge of *vintage counterfeits*. As the popularity of mechanical wristwatches has increased over the past few years, with new collectors looking for early Bubblebacks, Explorers and Sea-Dwellers, the counterfeiters have come up with some *new* vintage copies to fool the unsuspecting victim

A disturbing feature on some fake Bubblebacks is the presence of *reference* and *serial numbers* between the lugs. However, while these numbers may appear to be correct for the model and year of the watch, many will display the *same* numbers (Ref# 5015 and Serial# 545383), as seen in the images below. Furthermore, these fakes are showing up with a varying degree of sophistication, which supports the fact that they are produced by different sources. A similar counterfeit Bubbleback was identified in *The Best of Time Rolex Wristwatches,* by James M. Dowling & Jeffrey P. Hess, with the same identification numbers. However, that particular counterfeit was of a much higher sophistication and featured a highly detailed counterfeit movement.

The following pages display a number of vintage counterfeits, along with a brief description of points to inspect. Please keep in mind however, these are just a small example of what is in circulation, therefore you should always exercise extreme caution when purchasing watches from an unknown source. Furthermore, all of the watches featured in this section are 'mass produced' counterfeits, which are much easier to detect than *Swap-Job* or *Mix & Match* counterfeits.

 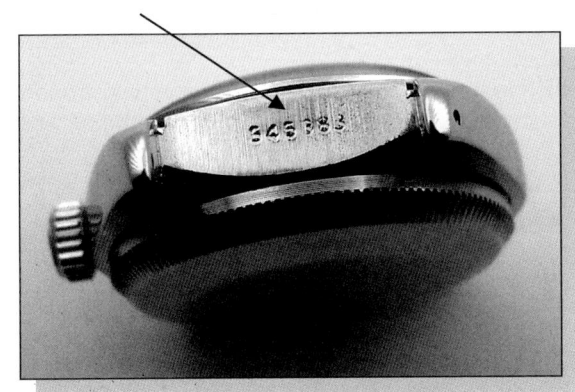

Counterfeit Rolex Bubbleback identification markings.

LEFT: Counterfeit *Case Reference Number* "5015" located between lugs at the 6 o'clock position.
RIGHT: Counterfeit *Serial Number* "545383" located between the lugs at the 12 o'clock position.

Notice the poor quality in the stamping of these numbers. In fact, the numbers actually appear to be *molded* into the case before being finished.

TOP LEFT: Arabic numeral dial with arrow-shaped hour indices, marked *Rolex Oyster Perpetual Explorer*, featuring subsidiary seconds and shaped hands.

TOP RIGHT: "Honeycomb" Arabic numeral dial with arrow-shaped indices, marked *Rolex Oyster Perpetual*, featuring subsidiary seconds and leaf shaped hands.

BOTTOM LEFT: Arabic numeral dial, marked *Rolex Oyster Perpetual*, featuring center seconds and *Dauphine* style hands

BOTTOM RIGHT: Roman/Arabic (California) dial marked *Rolex Oyster Perpetual Explorer*, featuring subsidiary seconds and shaped hands.

Please Note: Rolex did not mark the Bubbleback dials with *Explorer*, as seen in two of the examples above. Also, the winding crowns featured on three of these watches (excluding the TOP RIGHT) is the *Twinlock*, which was not available when these versions of the Bubbleback (model 5015) were in production.—the *Twinlock* was not patented until 1953, and while some 'claim' to have seen some late model Bubblebacks fitted with the *Twinlock*, it has not been confirmed and they were likely not so equipped from the factory.

All four of the examples above feature the same stainless steel case and bezel. Upon closer examination of these watches will show the cases are in 'perfect' condition. The Bubbleback these counterfeits are attempting to represent was produced over 60 years ago! However, since these watches are basically *new,* they will not likely have the wear of a 60+ year old watch, and thus are quite easy to distinguish.

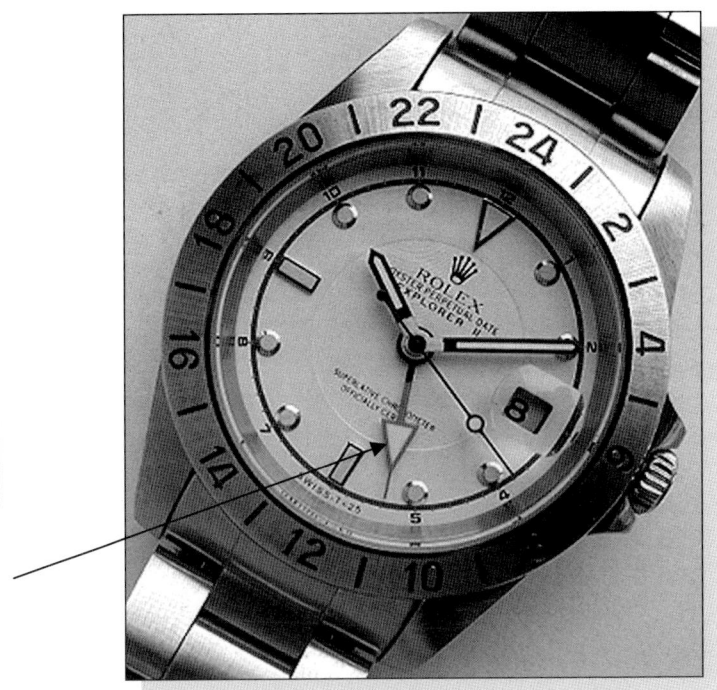

TOP LEFT: Counterfeit black dial *Explorer II* (early model) featuring the larger orange 24-hour hand.

TOP RIGHT: Counterfeit white dial *Explorer II* (early model) featuring the larger orange 24-hour hand.

BOTTOM LEFT: Counterfeit *Explorer* (early model) featuring 3-6-9 Arabic dial with baton indices.

BOTTOM RIGHT: Counterfeit (red) *"Sea-Dweller Submariner 2000"*, featuring early style hour indices *without* metal trim. Please Note: 'Mass produced' counterfeit Sea-Dwellers are easy to identify since they will not have the *one-way gas escape valve*, positioned on the side of the case, opposite the winding crown.

COMMON COUNTERFEIT MISTAKES

In addition to the topics discussed in the previous sections, counterfeiters often make obvious configuration mistakes. That is to say, they manufacture watches with a bracelet, bezel, or color that has never been offered by Rolex. Here are just a few of the more common mistakes that have been witnessed:

1) Bezels: Submariners have been spotted featuring a GMT style bezel (as seen in the image on the right), or vise versa with GMTs fitted with Submariner bezels.

2) Metal Configurations: Some counterfeit Day-Date (or 'President') models will feature a two-tone (stainless steel & gold) case and bracelets. Please note: Day-Date models are not available in any stainless steel configuration—they are only available in solid 18kt yellow, white or pink (rose) gold, as well as platinum.

The counterfeit *Submariner* shown above is (incorrectly) fitted with a *GMT* 24-hour bezel.

3) Divers' Extensions: Counterfeiters have begun to create a very convincing heavy Oyster bracelet with screw links and divers' extension. However, they tend to get carried away and feature the divers' extension feature on models which do not use it. Rolex only offers the divers' extension on the diving watches (ie. Submariner and Sea-Dweller), but the counterfeiters will feature it on models such as the Daytona, Yacht-Master and sometimes even the Datejust.

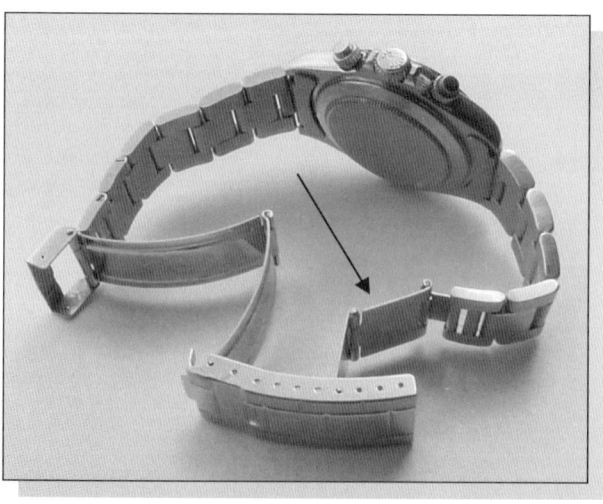

The counterfeit *Daytona* shown above is fitted with an *Oyster-style* bracelet (incorrectly) featuring a divers' extension.

4) Daytona Bracelet Buckles: Counterfeiters will sometimes use the wrong bracelet buckle on the Daytona—meaning they will simply use an Oyster buckle that has been converted cosmetically.

Late model Daytonas (until 2002) used an Oyster-style folding clasp fitted with a *shorter* Oyster-style buckle—with the Rolex crown placed on the flip-lock instead of the buckle body. However, in 2002, the Daytona received a new proprietary clasp and buckle. The new design features a shaped deployant clasp, with a new smooth buckle design (as seen in the images below).

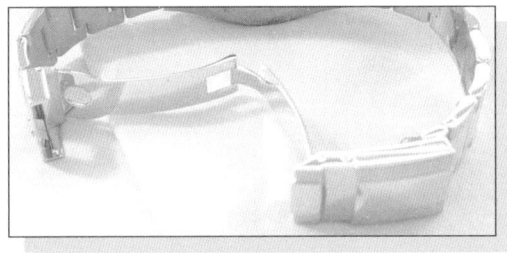
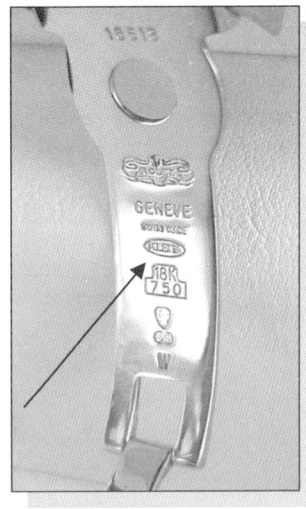
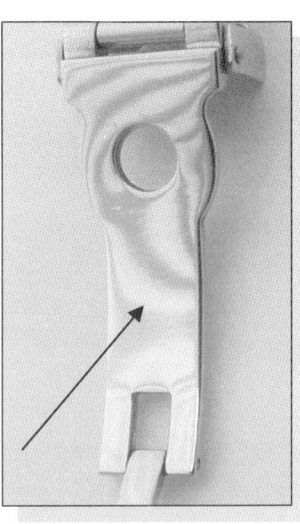

LEFT (top): Old-style Daytona bracelet featuring standard Oyster buckle. (used prior to 2002).
LEFT (bottom): New-style Daytona bracelet featuring the new deployant clasp. (used since 2002).

RIGHT: New-style Daytona clasp (on left) featuring 18kt gold hallmarks, compared with new counterfeit clasp (on right) with no hallmarks.

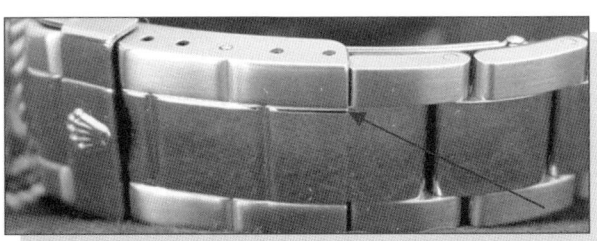
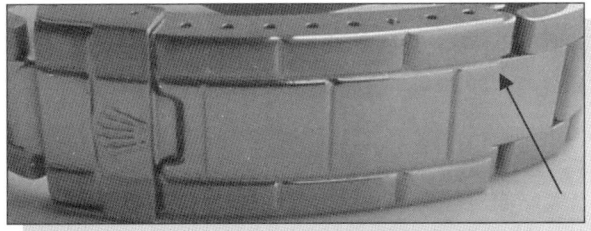

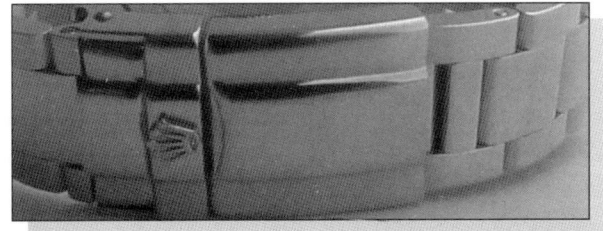

Daytona buckles—genuine on the left, fake on the right.—old style on the top, new design on bottom.

TOP: Notice how the genuine buckle is shorter, while the fake is just a standard Oyster buckle which has been cosmetically fitted with the Rolex crown on the flip-lock clasp rather than the buckle body.

BOTTOM: While the fake is of the proper (shorter size), it has poor finishing around the flip-lock clasp.

5) President Bracelet Buckles: Rolex President bracelets are attached to the concealed clasp via a final link which is attached to the clasp. However, counterfeits will often simply attach the bracelet via a push-pin, as seen in the examples on the right.

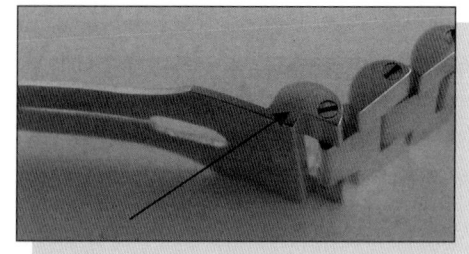

TOP RIGHT: Genuine *President* bracelet clasp, featuring a final link which is physically attached to the clasp.

BOTTOM RIGHT: Counterfeit *President* bracelet clasp, featuring a simple push-pin to attach it to the bracelet.

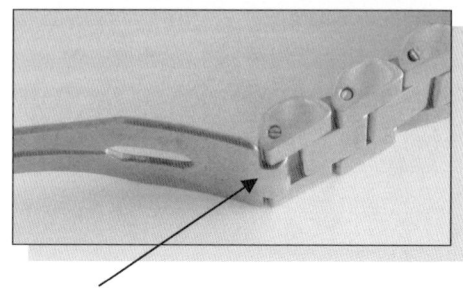

6) Winding Crowns: Rolex only offers the *Triplock* crown on the Submariner, Sea-Dweller or Daytona. However, counterfeiters sometimes fit this crown to other watches like the GMT, or Yacht-Master.

Furthermore, counterfeiters will often use modern crowns like the *Twinlock* on vintage replicas. These older watches like the early *Bubbleback* used a different crown design, as seen in the images below.

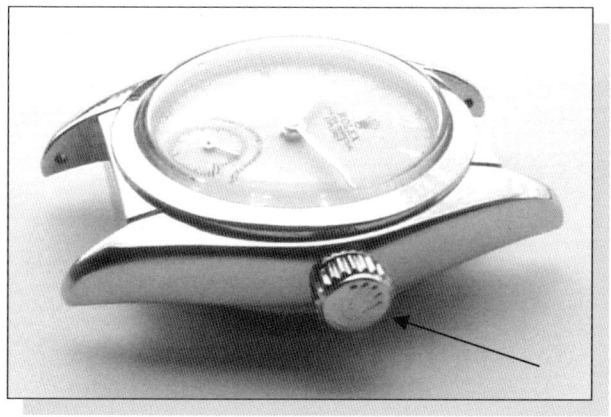

In this example, a counterfeit 1940s *Bubbleback* is seen fitted with a modern *Twinlock* crown.

TOP LEFT: *Twinlock* winding crown features the Rolex coronet underscored with a single line.

TOP RIGHT: *Triplock* winding crown features the Rolex coronet underscored with 3-dots.

BOTTOM LEFT: *Brevet* winding crown was the predecessor to the *Triplock*, and features the Rolex coronet underscored with the word "BREVET" meaning 'patented'.

BOTTOM RIGHT: *Vintage* style crowns, dimple style (on left) and "Rolex Oyster" (on right).

SHOPPING ONLINE...
Caveat Emptor: Buyer Beware

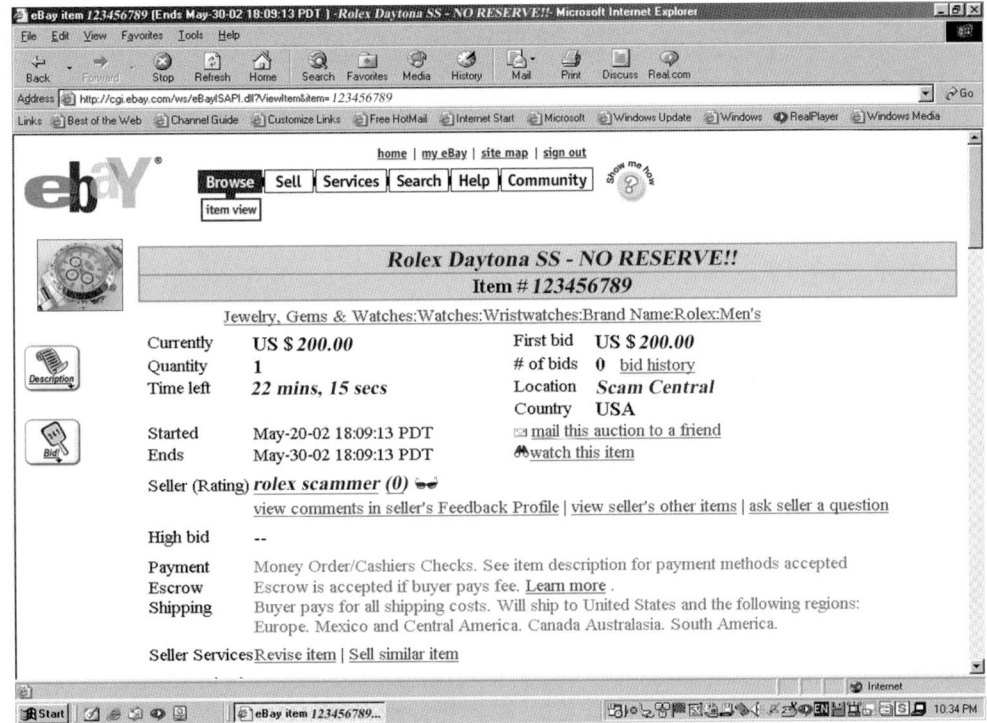

Many people are buying and selling Rolex and other fine timepieces over the internet. Most are honest people representing their product correctly, however, some are either intentionally or unintentionally representing their watches as something they are not. Replicas, Fakes, Copies, Knock-Offs or Counterfeits... whatever you call them, it means the same thing and if you're not careful you might get stuck with one. Therefore, it's very important to know *who* you're buying from.

Unfortunately, this can be very difficult when you're buying online and the auction ends in twenty-two minutes!—and that's exactly what these sellers are counting on. They list just enough information to peak your interest, but not enough to make an informed decision. The following pages give a few tips on investigating the online seller for potential scams.

Seller's Feedback: This may sound like a no-brainer, but there are a few things to consider when investigating someone's feedback before making a 'big ticket' purchase. You should look, not only at the feedback rating, but also at whether they were the 'buyer' or 'seller' for those feedback related transactions. Sellers will sometimes inflate their own feedback by buying (or selling) numerous inexpensive items just to increase their rating and appear legitimate. Therefore, they may have a good feedback rating for multiple items, but they may never have sold a high-dollar item such as a Rolex.

It is also worth mentioning that just because someone has a couple negatives doesn't mean they're a high-risk. Often negative feedback is a mistake or just the result of a hot-headed individual, not to mention it could be retaliation for a justified negative left for the other party. Furthermore, negative feedback should always be considered on an individual, or even on a *percentage* basis—eBay's requirements for Power Sellers is a positive feedback of at least 98%. I would consider this a good rule of thumb.

Seller's Other Listings and Previous Sales: This refers to the seller's 'track record' and should be considered before making a purchase. If their past sales were for *Beannie Babies* and *Pokemon Cards*, then you probably want to think twice before purchasing a $5,000 Rolex from them. I would also suggest looking for other products which *could* raise a 'red flag' with respect to their credibility.

These items include excessive amounts of Rolex parts and aftermarket accessories—remember 'aftermarket' parts are merely a step away from being counterfeit and could be used in 'swap-job' or 'converted' Rolex counterfeits. These parts could include bezels, bracelet links, buckles and end pieces, as well as accessory boxes, hang tags, etc... To search a seller's previous sales, click the "SEARCH" button at the top of eBay's home page, then select "SELLER"—It is important that you select "Include completed items" to view auctions that have ended.

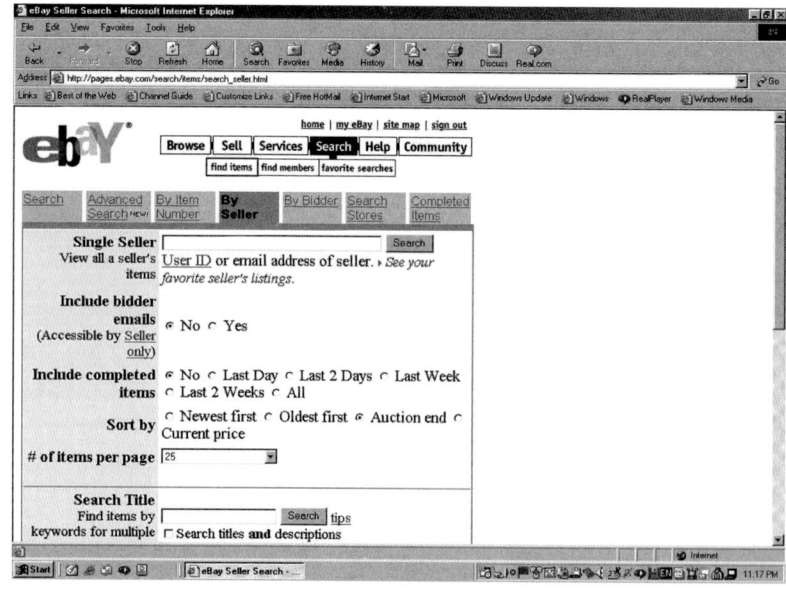

Ebay's Search Page (seller).

Seller's Previous Purchases: If the seller has recently purchased a number of questionable watches, parts or accessories (i.e. hang tags, boxes or warranty papers), then you may want to question the authenticity of the watch. Sellers will often buy these accessories (genuine or counterfeit) to add to the credibility of their watch. You can check a seller's previous purchases by clicking the "SEARCH" button at the top of eBay's home page, then select "BIDDER"—It is important that you select "Include completed items" to view auctions that have ended.

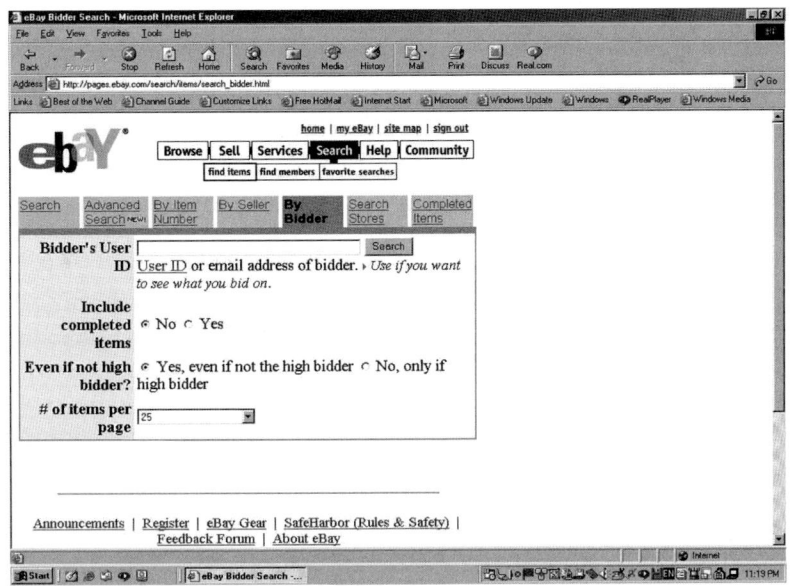

Ebay's Search Page (bidder).

Item's Description: Always check the item's description for details which may raise questions. These may include questionable pictures, which they may have stolen from Rolex's website (or other EBAY sellers). This means the seller claims the "picture is of the actual watch for sale", but you recognize it as a picture used in another seller's auction. Sellers may also take pictures at a poor angle or slightly out of focus to hide some imperfection with the watch. They will often explain this by stating that the camera is cheap, or they just don't know how to use it.

Get a Guarantee: Always make sure the seller is willing to offer a guarantee on the watch—both on its authenticity and your overall satisfaction with the item. Counterfeit sellers will often claim they purchased the watch from a third-party, and therefore they "can't (or won't) guarantee its authenticity". This is merely another way of saying that the watch is in fact counterfeit. A legitimate seller should always give a guarantee on their watch. In fact, many sellers will even warranty the watch for a short period of time, particularly if the watch was recently serviced.

Payment Options: What payment options does the seller accept? Does he insist on a *wire transfer* or a *cashier's check,* or will he allow you to send funds via a credit card? You should try to pay via credit card or a third-party service (i.e. eBay Payments, BidPay, etc…) since you can always dispute the charge if there is a problem with the authenticity.

Using Escrow: With a third-party escrow service the buyer sends funds to the service, which then notifies the seller that funds have arrived and it is okay to send the product. When the product arrives, the buyer notifies the service that it is okay to forward the funds to the seller. Escrow services are basically a middle-man or go-between, and can protect the buyer from potential scams. However, these services are not cheap and the seller will usually require the buyer to pay the escrow service fee, which is usually upwards of 10%.

Deposits: Sometimes a seller will offer to use escrow, but requires a deposit up front. If a seller is trying to represent a $50 counterfeit as a $5,000 Rolex, he may require a $500 deposit (10%) and then offer to use escrow for the $4,500 balance. The fact is if he gets $500 for this $50 counterfeit, then he has made a successful profit.

Ending the Auction Early: Beware of any seller who states in the auction that they "reserve the right to end the auction early". This basically means that once the auction receives a bid, they will end the auction early and the high bidder would be required to buy the item at that price. This is often done when the seller is afraid the auction will be identified as a counterfeit by the auction service (i.e. EBAY) and therefore canceled by them. In my opinion, no legitimate seller would ever want to end an auction early, because they're losing money by not allowing the auction to receive additional bids.

Private Auction: Sellers will often take advantage of the eBay option 'Private Auction', whereby the bidders identities are kept secret (from everyone but the seller). While many sellers have good reason for this, sometimes it's done so they can "shill" bid their own auction up by bidding on it himself. This also protects them from others e-mailing his bidders to inform them of his items being counterfeit. Again, many legitimate seller will use the 'Private Auction' feature to protect the identity of their bidders. Just use common sense and consider it on an individual basis.

Selling Price—Too High or Too Low: You *may* want to be cautious of *some* sellers who list an auction with a very low opening bid price and no reserve price. No legitimate seller would sell an authentic Rolex for $300 when it's worth $3,000—it's just common sense. On the other hand, a seller may intentionally set the reserve price *above* the value of the watch so the auction will never be successfully won—then when the auction ends the seller contacts each of the bidders offering to sell them the watch at a reduced price, thereby circumventing eBay's fees. Please Note: By purchasing the watch without a completed auction, the bidder is unable to leave negative feedback when the transaction goes south.

Bait and Switch: This refers to a seller who displays the picture of a genuine Rolex, but actually ships a counterfeit copy. By the time the bidder realizes it's fake, the seller has registered a new user ID and moved on to the next victim. Again, you need to know who you're buying from and make sure the photo is of the actual watch for sale.

Buying from 'Overseas': I suggest exercising extreme caution when bidding on items from 'overseas' sellers, particularly those whom are unknown. That's not to say that they can't be trusted, but if something was to go wrong with the transaction, then it would be very difficult to do anything about it. There is also the issue of dealing with customs and international shipping. I'm not saying it can't be done, but you should take precautions and only deal with reputable international dealers after investigating them fully.

In addition to these topics, there are a few questions you should always ask before purchasing via the internet. They may sound very basic, but they should always be verified before making the purchase.

What is the case reference (or model) number?

What is the serial number?

What is the year of the watch?

Where did the seller acquire the watch?

Why is the seller selling the watch?

Is the watch all original, or has it been modified?

Does it come with box, papers, etc..?

Does the watch operate properly?

When was the watch serviced last?

Is there a guarantee or warranty on the watch? And if so by whom?

You should also verify the features of the watch you are buying (i.e. quick set, sapphire crystal, etc...) This is important so you can verify the watch you purchased is the one you receive. I recently spoke with an individual who purchased a Day-Date (Circa mid 1980s, single quick set, sapphire crystal) on eBay from a "legitimate" dealer in California. However, due to a shipping error, he received the wrong watch—a very similar looking Day-Date (Circa late 1970s, no quick set, plastic crystal). Unfortunately, since he never asked the questions listed above, it is merely his word against the seller. He did in fact receive a Rolex Day-Date, but its value is considerable less than what he paid for. The last I heard, the bidder was still trying to get this mistake cleared up.

Hopefully, these tips will give you a little more confidence when making your next online purchase. The best advice I can give is to do your homework and only deal with reputable sellers. So the next time you're online and the deal looks too good to be true, guess what... it probably is.

*Anything of true quality is worth more
than the sum of its parts.*
—Anonymous

PART III

ROLEX PARTS IDENTIFICATION

Case Identification Numbers
End Pieces
Bracelets
Oyster Crowns
Oyster Tubes
"Standard" Dials
"Additional Cost" Dials
"Trade-In" Dials & Bezels
Movements

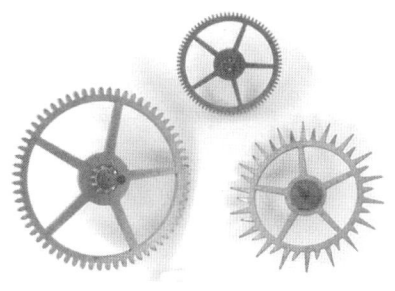

CASE IDENTIFICATION NUMBERS

Rolex wristwatches feature two sets of numbers for identification: a *Serial Number* and a *Case Reference Number*. On modern (Oyster) cases, these numbers are engraved between the lugs, hidden behind the end pieces. The *Serial Number* is located at the 6 o'clock position, while the *Case Reference Number* is at the 12 o'clock position. Additionally, the *Case Reference Number* is engraved inside the case back. On older cases, the *Serial Number* and/or *Case Reference Number* was engraved along the edge of the case back. On OysterQuartz models, the *Case Reference* and *Serial Numbers* are located on the back side of the case lugs, as seen in the illustration below.

Case Reference Number engraved between lugs (12 0'clock position)

Serial Number engraved between lugs (6 0'clock position)

Diagram of Rolex Oyster *Case Reference* and *Serial Number* locations.

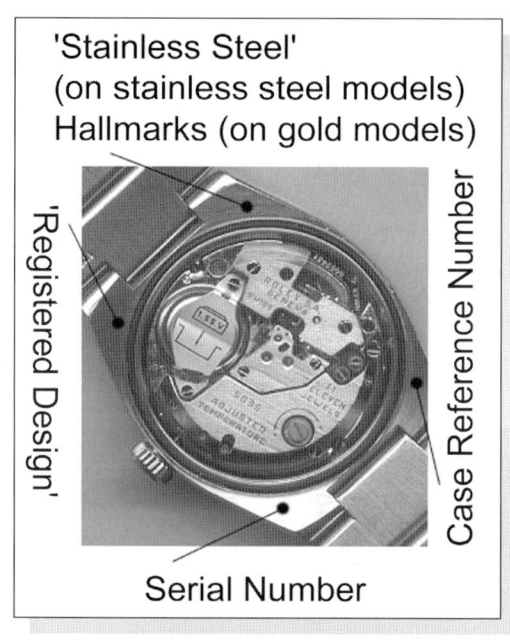

'Stainless Steel'
(on stainless steel models)
Hallmarks (on gold models)

'Registered Design'

Case Reference Number

Serial Number

Diagram of Rolex OysterQuartz *Case Reference* and *Serial Number* locations

Roman Numeral Dating 'IV 56'

Case Reference Number 6536-1

Inside Rolex case back featuring *Roman Numeral Dating* 'IV 56' & *Case Reference Number* '6536-1'

Vintage Rolex case back featuring the *Serial Number* engraved along the edge. c.1938

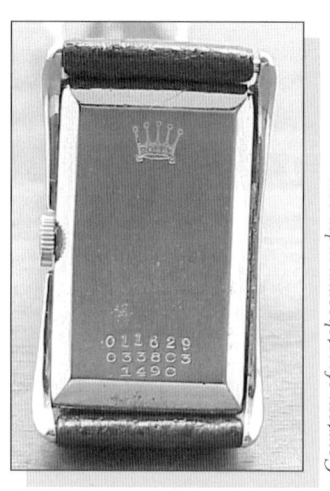

Courtesy of watchcommander.com

Rolex Prince (model 1490) case back featuring engraved *model* and *serial number*.

Serial Number between the lugs (6 o'clock position).
The heading "STAINLESS STEEL" will only appear on
steel cased watches. Gold or platinum cases will NOT
have a heading above the *Serial Number*. Older models may have *"DEPOSE"* or some variation thereof.

Serial Numbers:

In 1927, Rolex began issuing every Rolex Oyster case a unique serial number to distinguish them from one another. Around 1953, the numbers reached the 999,999 mark, at which time Rolex decided against adding a 7th digit, thus continuing into the "millions"—Instead, they started the sequence over at 100,001.

Around this same time, Rolex had initiated another dating system—They stamped the inside of the case back with a code consisting of a Roman numeral and two numbers. The Roman numerals were I, II, III and IV, which represented which quarter of the year the watch was produced. The numbers simply represented the two-digit year in which the watch was produced. Therefore, the code IV 53 would represent the 3rd quarter (i.e. July-September) of 1953—this code system continued until around 1970.

In the early 1960s, Rolex once again reached the 999,999 mark, but this time added a 7th digit and continued until mid 1987, when the numbering reached 9,999,999. At this time Rolex elected to start numbering with a letter prefix (e.g. R000001).

The system started with the letter "R", which was then subsequently followed by L-E-X. Thus, spelling out the word "ROLEX" with the "O" being omitted, to help avert any possible confusion with the number "0". This sequence continued through November 1991, when a *new* numbering system was introduced utilizing the letters N, C and S, which took them through 1993. In 1994, Rolex started yet another sequence with the letters: W, T and U, then A, P, and K in subsequent years.

To add to the confusion, many of these prefixes have run concurrently over the past few years, giving the appearance of a *random* numbering system. Therefore, only Rolex knows *exactly* when any particular watch was made and they aren't talking.

Serial Numbers by Date of Manufacture

The following list is comprised of known serial numbers for the years listed. By checking a particular serial number against this list you should be able to date a watch with reasonable accuracy. However, it is no guarantee as to when your watch was shipped from the factory. Furthermore, this list only applies to Rolex Oyster-cased watches.

(Please Note: According to Jeffrey P. Hess, co-author of The Best of Time Rolex Wristwatches, there are a number of books in print which list 'incorrect' serial number dates. Mr. Hess, along with the co-author James M. Dowling have done extensive research with respect to Rolex production dates. The list below was reprinted, with permission, directly from their aforementioned book.)

Serial #	Date	Serial #	Date	Serial #	Date	Serial #	Date
21691	1927	937170	I 1954	1041729	II 1964	9290000	1986
23969	1928	941699	I 1953	1182076	III 1964	9766000	1987
24747	1928	952892	I 1954	1259699	II 1965	9999999	1987 ½
28290	1930	955466	IV 1953	1345681	IV 1965	R000001	1987 ½
29312	1932	964789	IV 1953	1871000	1966	R999999	1988
29933	1933	973697	IV 1953	1994956	III 1966	L000001	1989
30823	1934	973930	III 1953	2163900	1967	L999999	1990½
35365	1935	116578	IV 1953	2426800	1968	E000001	1990½
37596	1936	132562	III 1953	2555384	II 1970	E999999	1991½
40920	1937	139400	I 1956	2689700	1969	X000001	1991½
43739	1938	139477	I 1956	2952600	1970	N000001	Nov 1991
71224	1939	282632	III 1955	3215500	1971	C000001	1992
99775	1940	321884	IV 1957	3478400	1972	S000001	1993
106047	1941	345500	II 1957	3741300	1973	W000001	1994/5
143509	1942	360171	I 1958	4004200	1974	T000001	1996
230878	1943	383893	I 1958	4267100	1975	U000001	Aug 1997
269561	1944	362214	I 1958	4538000	1976	A000001	Nov/Dec 1998
302459	1945	385893	II 1958	5008000	1977	P000001	Jan 2000
387216	1946	391528	III 1958	5482000	1978	K000001	Mid 2001
529163	1947	426074	IV 1958	5958000	1979	Y000001	*2002
628840	1948	412128	IV 1958	6434000	1980		
710776	1951	693808	II 1960	6910000	1981		
840396	1952	763663	II 1962	7386000	1982		
929426	IV 1953	764754	I 1962	7862000	1983		
930879	I 1953	869868	IV 1962	8338000	1984		
931080	II 1953	985015	I 1964	8614000	1985		

* New for 2002, Rolex models have now been identified with a new "Y" prefix designation.

Ref. Number between the lugs (12 o'clock position).
The heading will be either "ORIG ROLEX DESIGN" or
"ORIG. ROLEX DESIGN" - However, this heading did
NOT appear on ladies' cases until the mid 1990s. Older
models may have *"BREVET"* or some variation thereof.

Case Reference Numbers:

For the most part, vintage Rolex wristwatches utilized a 4-digit *Case Reference Number* (commonly called the 'model number'). Then in the mid 1980s, Rolex switched to a 5-digit number, which for the first time signified the bezel and case material configuration. This renumbering often coincided with the introduction of the *sapphire crystal* and *quick set* feature.

An explanation of the 5-digit *Case Reference Number* is as follows: The first three-digits describe the **Watch Type**. The second from the last describes the **Bezel Type** (with some exceptions, especially on more recent models), and the last number describes the **Case Material Configuration** of the watch. Thus, by using the *Case Number Quick Reference* listed on the following pages, the *Case Reference Number:* 16233 designates a Stainless Steel & Yellow Gold (two-tone) Oyster Perpetual Datejust, with fluted bezel.

Finally in 2000, Rolex once again changed the *Reference Number*, this time increasing it to a 6-digit number by adding an extra "1" before the previous number (e.g. The Daytona 16523 was renumbered as 116523). These numbers, as discussed earlier, are engraved between the lugs at the 12 o'clock position and again inside the case back.

CASE NUMBER QUICK REFERENCE

The following charts give a quick reference for identifying common Rolex Oyster Case Reference Numbers. A more comprehensive detailed list, *Appendix II: ROLEX Case Reference Numbers*, is located in the back of this book.

Watch Type...

Oyster 'Manual-Wind': 106, 107, 114, 157, 208, 213, 231, 241, 242, 251, 257, 259, 270, 284, 289, 300, 309, 313, 327, 335, 347, 349, 364, 376, 388, 397, 406, 407, 412, 436, 446, 449, 462, 464, 500, 502, 505, 602, 604, 614, 624, 641, 642, 644, 648, 678, 801, 802.

Oyster 'Manual-Wind' (Mid-Size): 123, 228, 259, 311, 312, 422, 444, 502, 602, 642, 643, 802.

Oyster 'Perpetual': 100, 101, 102, 103, 142, 306, 327, 335, 345, 368, 369, 371, 379, 387, 402, 436, 440, 468, 498, 501, 502, 505, 506, 555, 601, 602, 605, 607, 608, 609, 610, 611, 620, 621, 628, 629, 630, 633, 650, 651, 653, 655, 656, 658, 659, 661, 662, 663, 671, 672, 760, 761, 762, 805, 807, 808.

Oyster 'Perpetual' (Mid-Size): 427, 430, 485, 517, 634, 654, 655, 674, 675, 770, 774, 775.

Oyster 'Perpetual' *Airking*: 100, 140, 141, 550, 552, 570.

Date: 150, 151, 152, 153, 155, 651, 653, 686, 694.

Date (Lady): 651, 654, 690, 691, 692, 693, 696, 790, 791, 792, 802, 803.

Date (Mid-Size): 662, 674, 682, 686.

Date 'Manual-Wind': 454, 626, 649, 666, 669, 965.

Date 'Manual-Wind' (Mid-Size): 505, 606, 646.

Datejust: 160, 161, 162, 163, 446, 503, 603, 607, 610, 615, 630, 660.

Datejust (Mid-Size): 662, 680, 681, 682, 781, 782, 806.

Datejust (Lady): 625, 651, 690, 691, 692, 790, 791, 792, 802, 803.

Datejust *Thunderbird Bezel*: 162, 630, 660.

Day-Date *President*: 180, 181, 182, 183, 651, 661, 1182, 1183.

Gent's Masterpiece: 189.

Ladies' Masterpiece: 692, 693, 802, 803.

Chronograph: 107, 122, 202, 205, 230, 250, 270, 273, 281, 291, 292, 303, 305, 308, 318, 323, 333, 334, 346, 348, 352, 363, 364, 366, 369, 373, 382, 383, 399, 406, 409, 410, 411, 431, 435, 450, 453, 476, 503, 603, 606, 623, 817, 818, 820, 823, 916.

Cosmograph *Daytona* 'Manual-Wind': 623, 624, 626.

Cosmograph *Daytona* 'Perpetual': 165, 1165.

Yacht-Master: 166, 686, 696, 1662.

Yacht-Master (Mid-Size): 686, 1682, 1686.

Yacht-Master (Lady): 692, 693, 696, 1692, 1696.

Explorer: 101, 142, 550, 570, 615, 629, 635, 661, 804.

Explorer II: 165.	**GMT Master II:** 167.
Turn-O-Graph: 620.	**Milgauss:** 101, 654.
Submariner: 140, 550, 551, 620, 653.	**Tru-Beat:** 655.
Submariner (Date): 166 & 168.	**OysterQuartz Datejust:** 170.
Sea Dweller: 166, 551.	**OysterQuartz Day-Date:** 190.
GMT Master: 167, 654.	

Bezel Type...

0 = Polished
1 = Finely Engine Turned
2 = Engine Turned
3 = Fluted
4 = Hand Crafted
5 = Pyramid
6 = Rotating Bezel

Material...

0 = Stainless Steel
1 = Yellow Gold Filled
2 = White Gold Filled (or) SS & Platinum
3 = Stainless Steel & Yellow Gold
4 = Stainless Steel & White Gold
5 = Gold Shell (or) 18k Pink Gold (or) Rose Gold
6 = Platinum
7 = 14k Yellow Gold
8 = 18k Yellow Gold
9 = 18k White Gold

BRACELET, DIAL & BEZEL METAL CODE CHART:

00 = Stainless Steel
0A = Stainless Steel
01 = Placor
10 = Yellow Gold Filled
11 = Placor
13 = Gold Filled Case &
       14KT Yellow Gold Bezel
31 = Stainless Steel & 14KT Yellow Gold
33 = Stainless Steel & 18KT Yellow old
41 = Stainless Steel & 14KT White Gold
44 = Stainless Steel & 18KT White Gold
66 = Platinum
70 = 14KT Yellow Gold
77 = 14KT Yellow Gold

79 = 14KT White Gold
80 = 18KT Yellow Gold
82 = 22KT Yellow Gold
88 = 18KT Yellow Gold
89 = Bicolor Combination 18KT Yellow &
       White Gold
90 = 18KT White Gold
98 = Tridor Combination 18KT Yellow,
       White & Pink Gold
99 = 18KT White Gold

These numbers are used when ordering
Diamond Dials & Bezels.

END PIECES

End Piece Reference Numbers: On most models, there should be a part number (usually) stamped on the bottom right corner of the end piece. It should be a three-digit number sometimes followed by a letter.

All stainless steel bands will have a number starting with the number "5". Whereas, on two-toned (i.e. stainless steel and 18kt yellow gold) the number will start with the number "4". This is important to note and may identify a stainless steel model that has been converted to a two-toned model, while altering the original end pieces.

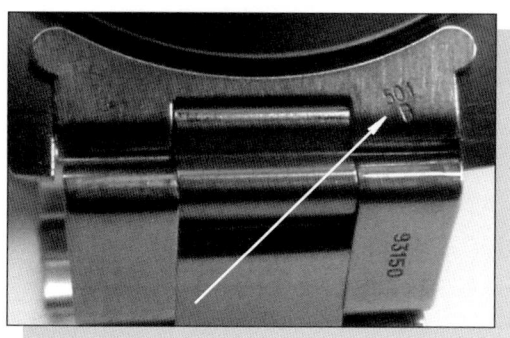

Oyster bracelet End Piece, featuring the number 501B.

Some of the exception to these numbers are as follows:

The Sea-Dweller will have the number configuration listed above, but it will be stamped *inside* the face of the end piece.

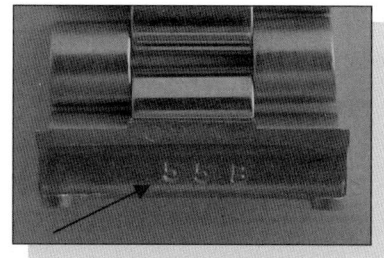

President Bracelet (SEL) Solid End Link, with the number '55B' engraved *inside* the face.

Gents *President* models will have the number "55" stamped *inside* the face of the end piece until around 1988, when the number was changed to "55B". The ladies models will have the number "68B"

New for 2001, the Oyster bracelet for some of the sport models (i.e. Submariner, Sea-Dweller, Daytona and Yacht-Master) started using solid end links (SEL). These models have a three-digit number stamped *inside* the face of the end piece with a tiny Rolex coronet hallmark on either side. The first digit will indicate the bracelet's metal (i.e. 7= Stainless/18K, 8= Stainless Steel)

Also new for 2001, the gents President models changed the end piece entirely. On these models, the end piece will use the same five-digit number stamped on the bracelet clasp. It will also have a tiny Rolex coronet hallmark on either side.

This list may not be all-inclusive, as Rolex is starting to make some changes to their watch configurations. If you find exceptions I missed, please let me know.

A partial list of known end pieces numbers are available in the *Rolex Bracelet Identification* section of this book.

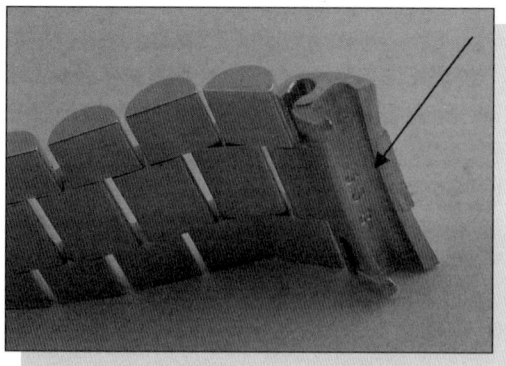

Alternate view of the *President* Bracelet (SEL) Solid End Link, with the number '55B' engraved *inside* the face.

BRACELETS

Bracelet Reference Numbers: On Oyster model bracelets, there should be a bracelet number stamped on the clasp, as well as on the final link next to the end piece. The numbers will vary, but the final digit (like in the *Case Reference Number*) will indicate the bracelet's material as follows:

0 = Stainless Steel
1 = Yellow Gold Filled
2 = White Gold Filled (or) SS & Platinum
3 = Stainless Steel & Yellow Gold
4 = Stainless Steel & White Gold
5 = Gold Shell (or) 18k Pink Gold (or) Rose Gold
6 = Platinum
7 = 14k Yellow Gold
8 = 18k Yellow Gold
9 = 18k White Gold

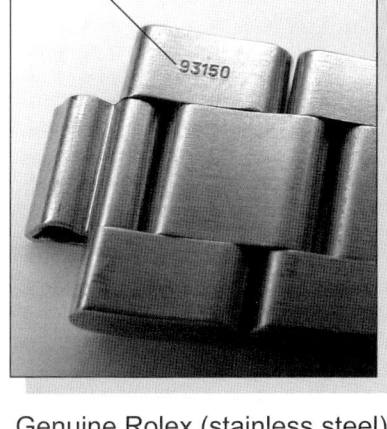

Rolex bracelet reference number

Genuine Rolex (stainless steel) Oyster bracelet.

LADIES' GOLD BRACELET CLASP. Note the bracelet number (6251) on the left. Also, *gold* clasps will feature hallmarks in the positions shown on the right.

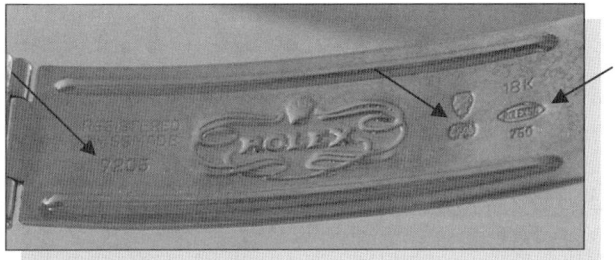

MID-SIZE GOLD BRACELET CLASP. Note the bracelet number (7205) on the left. Also, gold clasps will feature hallmarks in the positions shown on the right.

MEN'S 2-TONE BRACELET CLASP. Note the bracelet number (62523) on the right. Also, on 2-tone models the bracelet number will be followed by "D18", "H18", "HD18" or "18". The 'alpha-numeric' code (shown here as J12) is a manufacturing code and varies by model. 2-tone models will also be stamped "Steelinox"

MEN'S STEEL BRACELET CLASP. Note the bracelet number (93150) on the right. Also, the 'alpha-numeric' code (shown here as R2) is a manufacturing code and varies by model. Stainless Steel models will be stamped "Steelinox".

It is worth mentioning that older bracelets (until around 1970) also featured a 3-digit number, signifying the date of manufacture—a single-digit above a double-digit (i.e. 3 over 58 signifies the 3rd quarter of 1958). This system is much the same as the dating code used inside case backs (1950s-1970s).

Oyster (Men's)
(12 links)

Oyster (Ladies')
(13 links)

 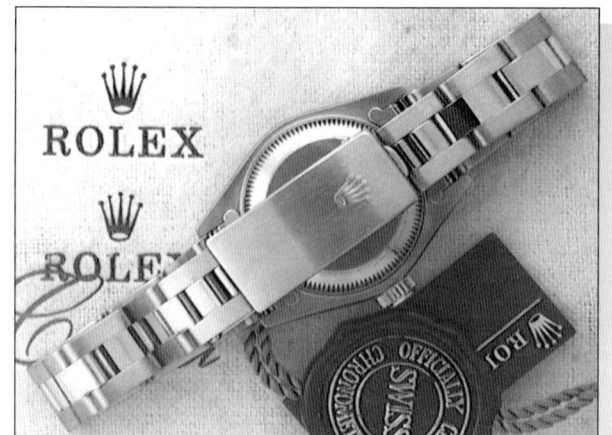

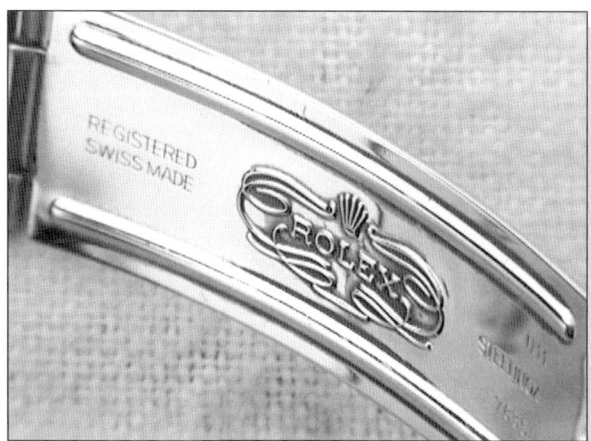 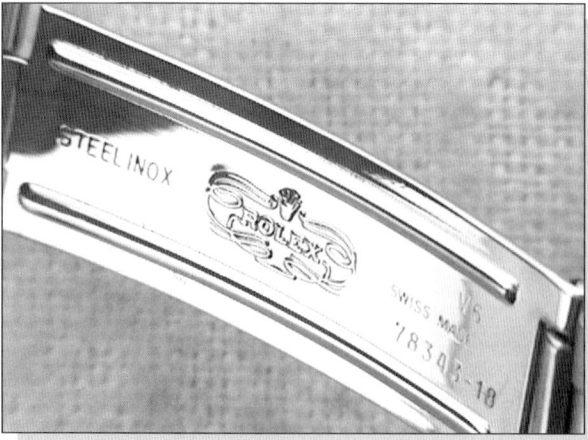

All images on this page courtesy of Masterpiece Jewelry

Oyster-Lock
(12 links)

Yacht-Master (Oyster-Lock)
(12 links)

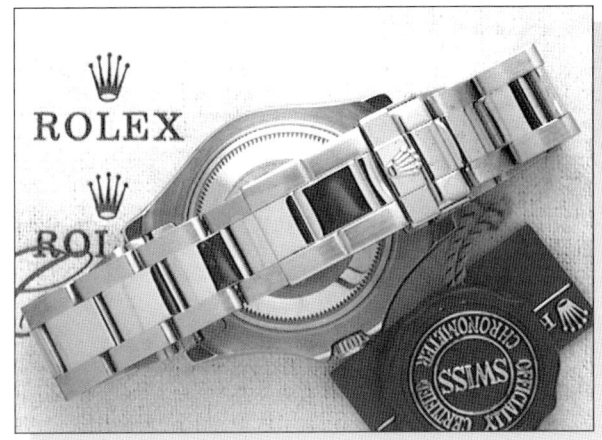

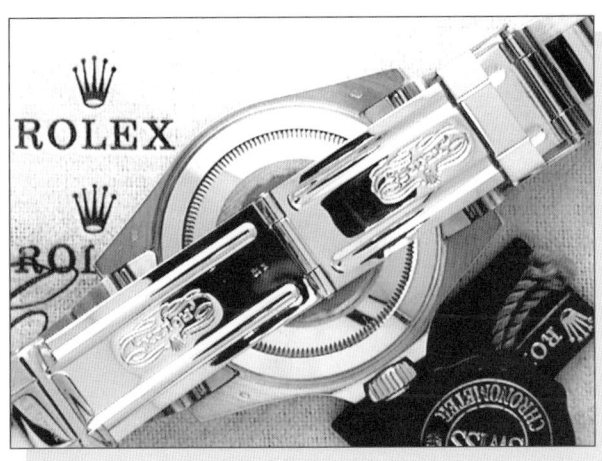

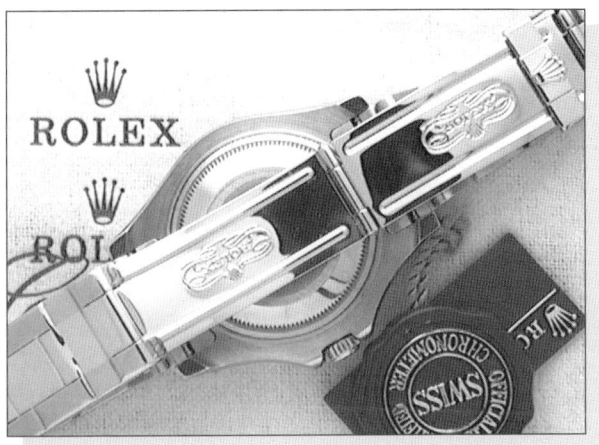

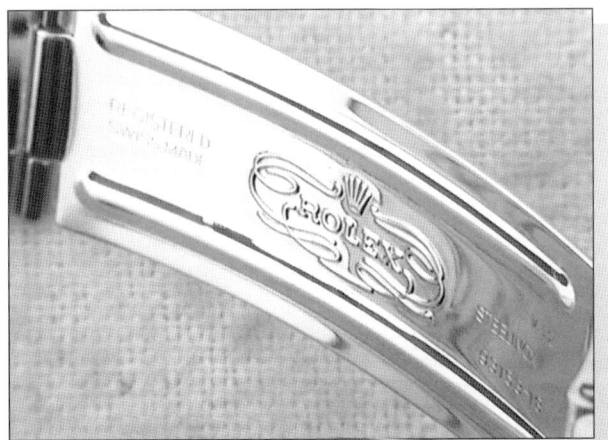

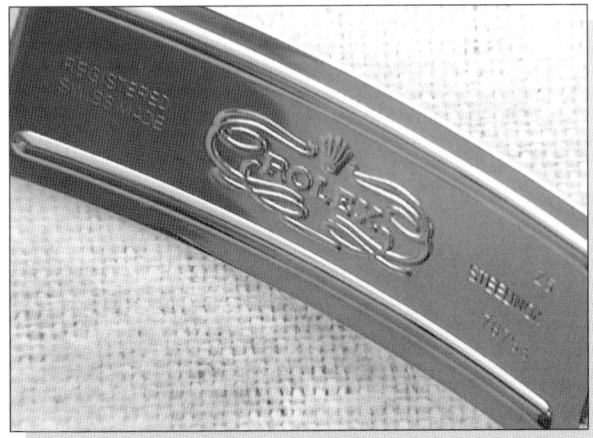

Jubilee (Men's)
(21 old **or** 22 new **links**)

Jubilee (Ladies')
(21 links)

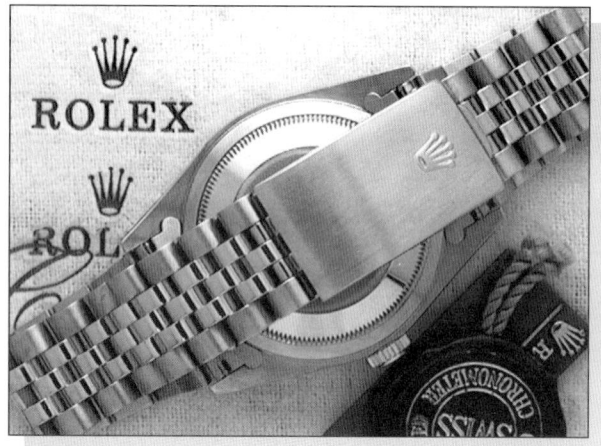

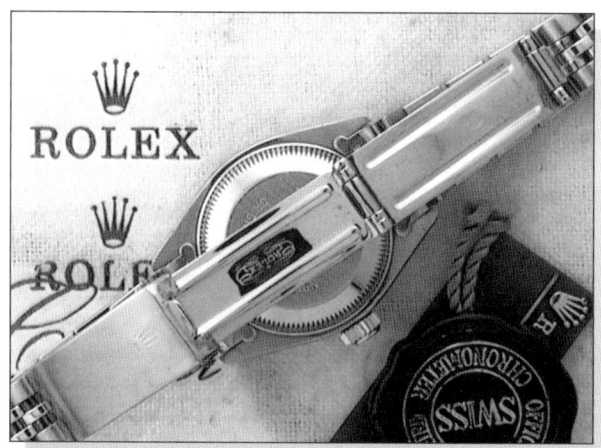

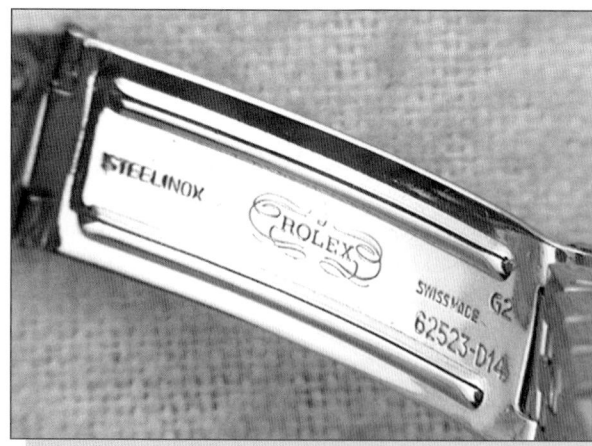

Daytona—Old (Oyster-Lock) (12 links)

Daytona—New Style (Steel) (12 links)

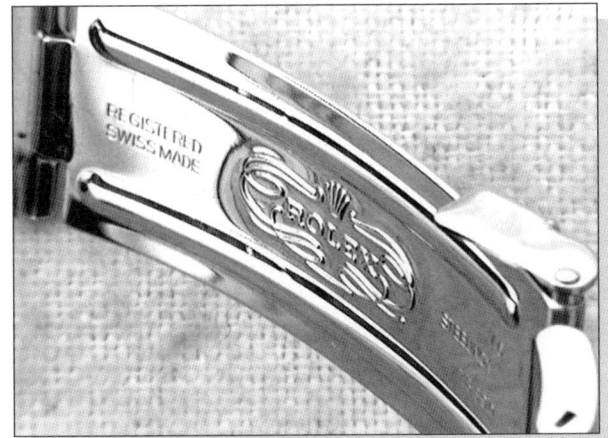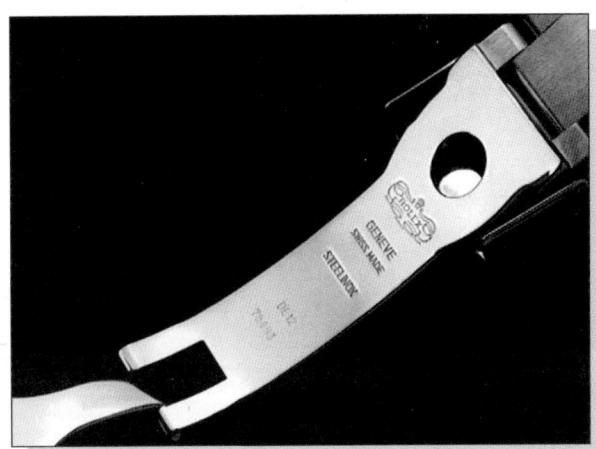

President (Men's)
(23 old or 24 new links)

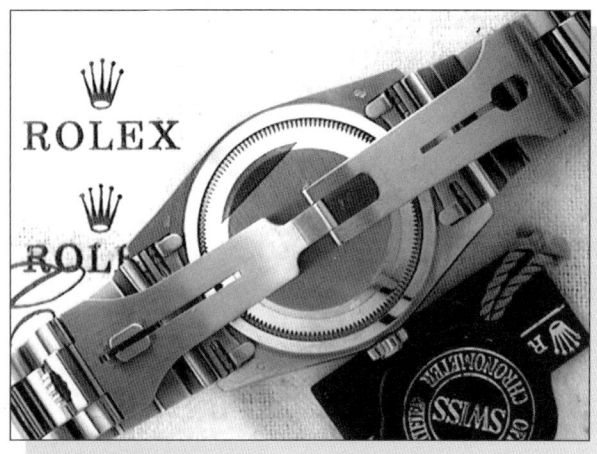

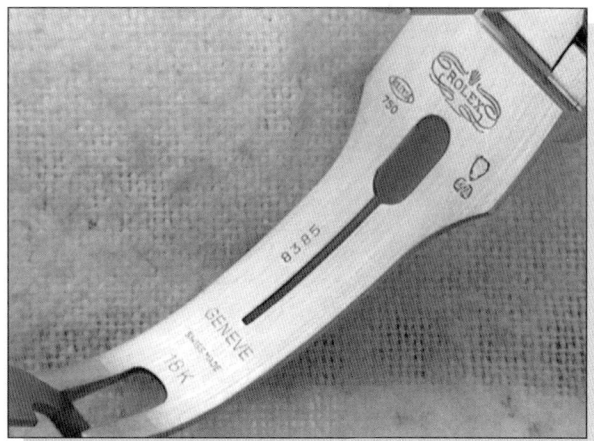

President (Ladies')
(36 links)

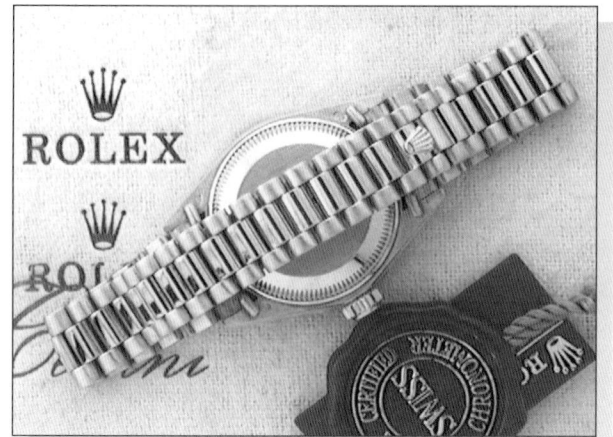

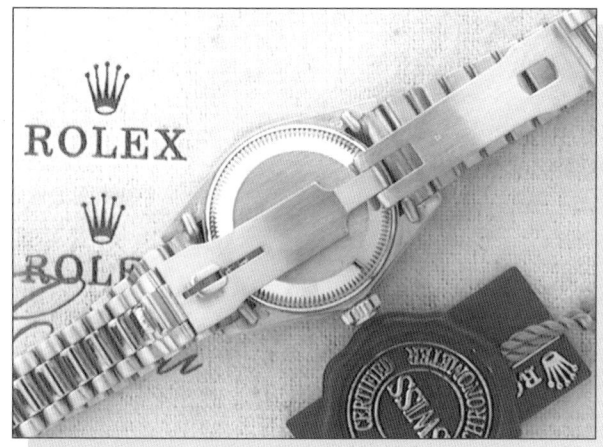

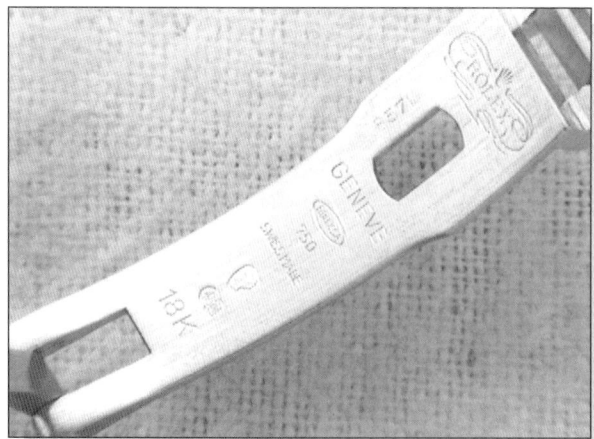

All images on this page courtesy of Masterpiece Jewelry

Daytona—New Style (18KT) (Leather Strap)

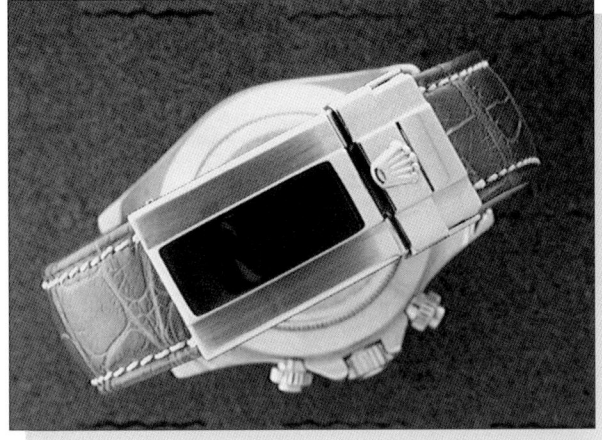

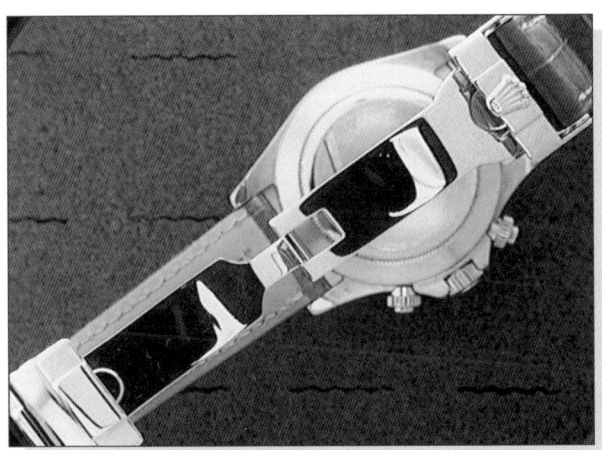

The following pages provide a resource for identifying *some* Rolex bracelets. They are listed in numeric order by the *Bracelet Reference Number*—this is not a complete list.

METAL: Lists the material from which the bracelet is made.

SIZE mm: Lists the size of the bracelet in millimeters, as follows:

13mm/14mm = Ladies.
17mm = Mid-sized.
19mm/20mm = Men's.

BRACELET STYLE: Lists the style of the bracelet. (i.e. Jubilee, Oyster, etc…)

CLASP NOTES: Lists the type of clasp used. (i.e. Concealed, Oyster-Lock, etc…)

END PIECE REFERENCE NUMBER: Lists *End Pieces* that have been identified for those particular bracelets—this is not a complete list.

MISCELLANEOUS NOTES: Lists known watch models that have featured these particular bracelets.—this is not a complete list.

Abbreviations: While most of the abbreviations listed are self-explanatory, here are a few others: OP, Oyster Perpetual; AK, Air King; T-O-G, Turn-O-Graph; EXP, Explorer; O-Lock, Oyster Lock; 18KY, 18Kt Yellow Gold; 18KW, 18Kt White Gold; YGF, Yellow Gold Filled.

When ordering a bracelet separately, the following 9 character code number is used:

B	**7286**	**88**	**B6**
Bracelet	**Style Number** (AKA *Bracelet Ref Number)*	**Metal Code** a complete list is found on page 141.	**End Piece Code**

ROLEX BRACELET IDENTIFICATION

Bracelet Ref #	Metal	Size mm	Bracelet Style	Clasp Notes	End Piece Ref #	Misc Notes.
24/8	18KY	17	Mesh (Flat)	Regular		
100/8	18KY	13	Bark	Regular		
100/9	18KW	13	Bark	Regular		
101/8	18KY	13		Regular		
101/8	18KY	17		Regular		
101/9	18KW	17		Regular		
102/8	18KY	13		Regular		
102/8	18KY	17		Regular		
102/8	18KY	19	Moire	Regular		
102/9	18KW	13		Regular		
109/1	YGF	20	Jubilee	Regular		
114/0	SS	13	Oyster	Regular		
115/0	SS	13	Oyster	Regular		
200/0	SS	20	Jubilee	Regular		
200/0	SS	20	Jubilee	Regular		
201/0	SS	13	Jubilee	Regular		
201/0	SS	19	Oyster	Regular		
202/0	SS	17	Oyster	Regular		
202/0	SS	19	Oyster	Regular		
203/0	SS	20	Oyster	Regular		
204/0	SS	17	Oyster	Regular		
206/0	SS	17	Oyster	Regular		
206/0	SS	19	Oyster	Regular		
207/0	SS	20	Oyster	Regular		
208/0	SS	20	Jubilee	Regular		
209/0	SS	19	Jubilee	Regular		
210/0	SS	13	Jubilee	Regular		
211/0	SS	17	Oyster	Regular		OP Date (Older)
211/8	18KY	13	Damier	Regular		OP Date (Older)
212/8	18KY	13	Damier	Regular		OP Date (Older)
213/8	18KY	17	Milanese	Regular		OP Date (Older)
216/0	SS	17	Oyster	Regular		
218/0	SS	20	Jubilee	Regular		Datejust
219/0	SS	17	Jubilee	Regular		
219/0	SS	19	Oyster	Regular		
221/8	18KY	17	Damier	Regular		OP Date (Older)
222/8	18KY	17	Damier	Regular		OP Date (Older)
223/8	18KY	17	Milanese	Regular		OP Date (Older)
224/8	18KY	17	Milanese	Regular		OP Date (Older)
231/8	18KY	17	Damier	Regular		OP Date (Older)
233/8	18KY	17	Milanese	Regular		OP Date (Older)
264/8	18KY/W	~	Chevrons	Regular		OP Date (Older)
264/8 Bic	18KY/W	~	Chevrons	Regular		OP Date (Older)
301/3	SS/14KY	19	Oyster	Regular		
302/3	SS/14KY	17	Oyster	Regular		
302/3	SS/14KY	19	Oyster	Regular		
303/3	SS/14KY	20	Jubilee	Regular		
304/3	SS/14KY	19	Jubilee	Regular		
306/3	SS/14KY	17	Oyster	Regular		
306/3	SS/14KY	19	Oyster	Regular		
308/3	SS/14KY	20	Oyster	Regular		Datejust; GMT

ROLEX BRACELETS (continued)

Bracelet Ref #	Metal	Size mm	Bracelet Style	Clasp Notes	End Piece Ref #	Misc Notes.
310/3	SS/14KY	13	Jubilee	Regular		
310/7	14KY	13	Jubilee	Regular		
311/3	SS/14KY	17	Oyster	Regular		
313/3	SS/14KY	20	Jubilee	Regular		
313/8	18KY	13	Jubilee	Regular		OP; Date (Older)
314/3	SS/14KY	17	Jubilee	Regular		
314/3	SS/14KY	19	Jubilee	Regular		
314/3	SS/14KY	19	Oyster	Regular		OP; Date
320/3	SS/14KY	13	Oyster	Regular		
323/8	18KY	~	Milanese	Regular		OP; Date (Older)
324/8	18KY	~	Milanese	Regular		OP; Date (Older)
333/8	18KY		Milanese	Regular		OP; Date (Older)
401/7	14KY	19	Oyster	Regular		
402/7	14KY	17	Oyster	Regular		
402/7	14KY	19	Oyster	Regular		
403/7	14KY	19	Jubilee	Regular		
405/7	14KY	17	Jubilee	Regular		
405/7	14KY	19	Jubilee	Regular		OP; Date
405/7	14KY	19	Oyster	Regular		
406/7	14KY	17	Oyster	Regular		
406/7	14KY	19	Oyster	Regular		
410/7	14KW	13	Jubilee	Regular		
410/7	14KY	13	Jubilee	Regular		
411/7	14KY	17	Oyster	Regular		
411/7	14KY	19	Oyster			
420/7	14KY	13	Oyster	Regular		
420/8	18KY	13	Oyster	Regular		
501/1	YGF	19	Oyster	Regular		
502/1	YGF	19	Oyster	Regular		
506/1	YGF	19	Oyster	Regular		
514/1	YGF	19	Oyster	Regular		
515/1	YGF	13	Oyster	Regular		
516/1	YGF	13	Oyster	Regular		
704/7	14KY	13	Mesh Flat	Regular		
705/7	14KY	13	Chameleon (Brick)	Regular		
706/9	18KW	13	Chameleon (Brick)	Regular		
715/8	18KY	20	Mesh Flat	Regular		
716/8	18KY	19	Mesh Flat	Regular		
725/8	18KY	19	Mesh Flat	Regular		
732/8	18KY	13	Chameleon (Mesh)	Regular		
1700/0	SS	~	Oyster	Regular		Oysterquartz; Datejust
1701/0	SS	~	Jubilee	Regular		Oysterquartz; Datejust
1701/3	SS/18KY	~	Jubilee	Regular		Oysterquartz; Datejust
1901/8	18KY	~	President	Concealed		Oysterquartz; Day-Date
1901/9	18KW	~	President	Concealed		Oysterquartz; Day-Date

ROLEX BRACELETS (continued)

Bracelet Ref #	Metal	Size mm	Bracelet Style	Clasp Notes	End Piece Ref #	Misc Notes.
1902/8	18KY	~	President "Pyramid"	Concealed		Oysterquartz Day-Date
1914/8	18KY	~	President "Karat"	Concealed		Oysterquartz Day-Date
6251/0	SS	13	Jubilee	Regular	568, 568B, 587, 591, 591B	Perpetual; Date; Datejust
6251/0	SS	17	Jubilee	Regular	587B	Datejust
6251/0	SS	19	Jubilee	Regular	574, 574B	AK; OP; OP Date
6251/0	SS	20	Jubilee	Regular	502, 502B, 550, 555, 555B	Datejust; T-O-G; GMT; Milgauss
6251/3	SS/14KY	13	Jubilee	Regular		
6251/3	SS/14KP	13	Jubilee	Regular		
6251/3	SS/18KY	13	Jubilee	Regular		
6251/3	SS/14KY	17	Jubilee	Regular		
6251/3	SS/14KY	19	Jubilee	Regular		
6251/3	SS/14KP	19	Jubilee	Regular		
6251/3	SS/18KY	19	Jubilee	Regular		
6251/3	SS/14KY	20	Jubilee	Regular		
6251/3	SS/14KP	20	Jubilee	Regular		
6251/3	SS/18KY	20	Jubilee	Regular		
6251/7	14KY	13	Jubilee	Regular		Datejust
6251/8	18KY	13	Jubilee	Regular		Datejust
6251/8	18KY	17	Jubilee	Regular		Datejust
6251/9	18KY	13	Jubilee	Regular		Datejust
6251/9	18KW	17	Jubilee	Regular		Datejust
6252/3	SS/14KY	13	Jubilee	Regular		OP; Datejust
6252/3	SS/18KY	13	Jubilee	Regular	468, 468B, 487, 491, 491B	OP; Datejust
6252/3	SS/18KY	17	Jubilee	Regular	487B	OP; Datejust
6252/3	SS/14KY	19	Jubilee	Regular		OP; Date
6252/3	SS/18KY	19	Jubilee	Regular	474, 474B	OP; Date; AK
6252/3	SS/14KY	20	Jubilee	Regular		Datejust; T-O-G
6252/3	SS/18KY	20	Jubilee	Regular	402B, 450, 455, 455B	Datejust; T-O-G
6311/0	SS	17	Jubilee	Regular	587, 587B	Datejust
6311/0	SS	20	Jubilee	Regular		Datejust
6311/3	SS/18KY	17	Jubilee	Regular	487, 487B	Datejust
6311/3	SS/18KY	20	Jubilee	Regular		Datejust
6311/7	14KY	20	Jubilee	Regular		Datejust
6311/8	18KY	17	Jubilee	Regular		Datejust
6311/8	18KY	19	Jubilee	Regular		OP; Date
6311/8	18KY	20	Jubilee	Regular		Datejust; GMT; T-O-G
6311/9	18KW	17	Jubilee	Regular		Datejust
6311/9	18KW	20	Jubilee	Regular		Datejust
6411/8	18KY	17	"Super Jubilee Karat" w/ 263 brilliants	Concealed		Datejust

ROLEX BRACELETS (continued)

Bracelet Ref #	Metal	Size mm	Bracelet Style	Clasp Notes	End Piece Ref #	Misc Notes.
6411/9	18KW	17	"Super Jubilee Karat" w/ 263 brilliants	Concealed		Datejust
6411/9 Bic	18KBIC	17	"Bicolor Super Jubilee Karat" w/ 263 brilliants	Concealed		Datejust
6451/8	18KY	13	"Super Jubilee Karat" w/ 344 brilliants	Concealed		Datejust
6451/9	18KW	13	"Super Jubilee Karat" w/ 344 brilliants	Concealed		Datejust
6451/9 Bic	18KBIC	13	"Bicolor Super Jubilee Karat" w/ 344 brilliants	Concealed		Datejust
6453/8	18KY	13	"Super Jubilee Karat" w/ 351 brilliants	Concealed		Datejust
6453/9	18KW	13	"Super Jubilee Karat" w/ 351 brilliants	Concealed		Datejust
6454/8	18KY	13	"Super Karat" (Jubilee) w/ 89 lg brilliants	Concealed		Datejust
6454/9	18KW	13	"Super Karat" (Jubilee) w/ 89 lg brilliants	Concealed		Datejust
6490/8	18KY	14	"Super Karat" (Oyster) w/ 100 lg brilliants	Concealed		Datejust
6490/8P	18KY	14	"Super Karat" (Oyster) w/ 100 pink sapphires	Concealed		Datejust
6490/9	18KW	14	"Super Karat" (Oyster) w/ 100 lg brilliants	Concealed		Datejust
6490/9S	18KW	14	"Super Karat" (Oyster) w/ 100 sky-blue sapphires	Concealed		Datejust
6634/0	SS	11	Oyster	Regular		
6634/0	SS	13	Oyster	Regular		
6634	GP	13	Oyster	Regular		
6634/7	9KY	13	Oyster	Regular		
6634/8	18KY	13	Oyster	Regular		
6635/0	SS	15	Oyster	Regular		
6635/0	SS	17	Oyster	Regular		
6635/0	SS	19	Oyster	Regular		
6635/0	SS	20	Oyster	Regular		
6635	GP	20	Oyster	Regular		
6635/7	9KY	20	Oyster	Regular		
6636/0	SS	20	Oyster	Regular		
7177/9	18KW	13	Chameleon (Mesh)	Regular		
7204/7	14KY	13	Oyster	Regular		OP; Datejust
7204/8	18KY	11	Oyster	Regular		
7204/8	18KY	13	Oyster	Regular		OP; Datejust
7204/9	18KW	13	Oyster	Regular		OP; Datejust
7205/7	14KY	17	Oyster	Regular		OP; Datejust
7205/7	14KY	19	Oyster	Regular		OP
7205/8	18KY	17	Oyster	Regular		OP; Datejust
7205/8	18KY	19	Oyster	Regular		OP; Date

ROLEX BRACELETS (continued)

Bracelet Ref #	Metal	Size mm	Bracelet Style	Clasp Notes	End Piece Ref #	Misc Notes.
7205/9	18KW	20	Oyster	Regular		Datejust; GMT
7206/7	14KY	20	Oyster	Regular		Datejust; GMT
7206/8	18KY	19	Oyster	Regular		OP; Date
7206/8	18KY	20	Oyster	Regular		Datejust; GMT
7215/5	YGF	19	Oyster	Regular		Air King
7274/6	Platinum	20	"Super President"	Concealed		Day-Date
7274/8	18KY "Tridor"	20	"Super President"	Concealed Center links pink & white gold.		Day-Date
7286/8	18KY	20	President	Regular		Day-Date
7286/9	18KW	20	President	Regular		Day-Date
7294/8	18KY	14	Oyster	Concealed		Datejust
7294/8	18KY "Tridor"	14	Oyster	Concealed Center links pink & white gold.		Datejust
7294/9	18KW	14	Oyster	Concealed		Datejust
7295/8 Bic	18KY	14	Oyster	Concealed Center links white gold.		Datejust
7295/9	18KW	14	Oyster	Concealed		Datejust
7385/5	18KR	20	Oyster	Concealed		Day-Date
7385/8	18KY	20	Oyster	Concealed		Day-Date
7435/8	18KY	~	Mesh	Regular		
7435/9	18KW	~	Mesh	Regular		
7490/8	18KY	14	"Super Oyster Karat" w/ 174 brilliants & 14 lg brilliants.	Concealed		Datejust
7490/8E	18KY	14	"Super Oyster Karat" w/ 174 brilliants & 14 lg emeralds.	Concealed		Datejust
7490/8P	18KY	14	"Super Oyster Karat" w/ 174 brilliants & 14 lg pink sapphires.	Concealed		Datejust
7490/8R	18KY	14	"Super Oyster Karat" w/ 174 brilliants & 14 lg rubies.	Concealed		Datejust
7490/8S	18KY	14	"Super Oyster Karat" w/ 174 brilliants & 14 lg sapphires.	Concealed		Datejust
7490/9	18KW	14	"Super Oyster Karat" w/ 174 brilliants & 14 lg brilliants.	Concealed		Datejust
7490/9S	18KW	14	"Super Oyster Karat" w/ 174 brilliants & 14 lg sapphires.	Concealed		Datejust

ROLEX BRACELETS (continued)

Bracelet Ref #	Metal	Size mm	Bracelet Style	Clasp Notes	End Piece Ref #	Misc Notes.
7491/8	18KY	Mans	Mesh (Flat)	Regular		
7491/9	18KW	Mans	Mesh (Flat)	Regular		
7494/8	18KY	14	"Oyster Karat" w/ 174 brilliants	Concealed		Datejust
7494/9	18KW	14	"Oyster Karat" w/ 174 brilliants	Concealed		Datejust
7495/8	18KY "Tridor"	14	"Oyster Karat" Center links pink & white gold w/ 15 lg brilliants	Concealed		Datejust
7497/8	18KY	14	"Super Oyster Karat" w/ 270 brilliants	Concealed		Datejust
7497/9	18KW	14	"Super Oyster Karat" w/ 270 brilliants	Concealed		Datejust
7498/8	18KY	14	"Super Oyster Karat w/ 286 brilliants	Concealed		Datejust
7498/9	18KW	14	"Super Oyster Karat" w/ 286 brilliants	Concealed		Datejust
7805/0	SS	13	Oyster	Regular		OP; Datejust
7805/0	SS	17	Oyster	Regular	551B	OP; Datejust
7805/3	SS/18KY	13	Oyster	Regular		OP; Datejust
7805/3	SS/18KY	17	Oyster	Regular	451B	OP; Datejust
7824/0	SS	13	Oyster	Regular	566B, 590B	OP; Datejust
7824/3	SS/18KY	13	Oyster	Regular	466B, 490B	OP; Datejust
7834/0	SS	11	Oyster	Regular		
7834/0	SS	13	Oyster	Regular	566, 590	OP; Datejust
7834/0	SS	13	Jubilee (Bark)	Regular		OP; Datejust
7834/1	YGF	11	Oyster	Regular		
7834/1	YGF	13	Oyster	Regular		
7834/3	SS/14KY	11	Oyster	Regular		
7834/3	SS/14KY	13	Oyster	Regular		OP; Datejust
7834/3	SS/18KY	13	Oyster	Regular	466,490	OP; Datejust
7835/0	SS	17	Oyster	Regular	551, 557B, 562	OP; Datejust
7835/0	SS	19	Oyster	Regular	557, 557B, 571	OP; Datejust
7835/1	SS/YGF	19	Oyster	Regular		OP; Datejust
7835/3	SS/14KY	17	Oyster	Regular		OP; Datejust
7835/3	SS/18KY	17	Oyster	Regular	451, 451B	OP; Datejust
7835/3	SS/14KY	19	Oyster	Regular		OP; Datejust
7835/3	SS/18KY	19	Oyster	Regular	457, 457B	OP; Datejust
7836/0	SS	20	Oyster	Regular	501, 501B, 503, 558, 558B, 580	OP; Datejust, GMT; Milgauss

ROLEX BRACELETS (continued)

Bracelet Ref #	Metal	Size mm	Bracelet Style	Clasp Notes	End Piece Ref #	Misc Notes.
7836/3	SS/14KY	20	Oyster	Regular		Datejust; GMT
7836/3	SS/18KY	20	Oyster	Regular	401B, 403, 458, 458B, 480	Datejust; GMT
7839/0	SS	20	Oyster	O-Lock	803	Daytona
7839/3	SS/18KY	20	Oyster	O-Lock	703	Daytona
7839/3A	SS/18KY	20	Oyster	O-Lock		Daytona (SEL)
7839/8	18KY	20	Oyster	O-Lock		Daytona
7849/0	SS	20	Oyster	O-Lock		Daytona (SEL)
7866/8	18KY	20	Oyster	O-Lock		Daytona
7873/0	SS	14	Oyster	O-Lock	806	YM
7873/3	SS/18KY	14	Oyster	O-Lock	706	YM
7873/8	18KY	14	Oyster	O-Lock		YM
7874/0	SS	17	Oyster	O-Lock	807	YM
7874/3	SS/18KY	17	Oyster	O-Lock	707	YM
7874/8	18KY	17	Oyster	O-Lock		YM
7875/0	SS	17	Oyster	O-Lock	807	YM
7875/3	SS/18KY	17	Oyster	O-Lock	707	YM
7875/8	18KY	17	Oyster	O-Lock		YM
7876/0	SS	20	Oyster	O-Lock	808	YM
7876/8	18KY	20	Oyster	O-Lock		˙YM
7879/0	SS	20	Oyster	O-Lock	558B, 501B	EXP; GMT
7879/0A	SS	20	Oyster	O-Lock		Daytona (SEL)
7879/3	SS/18KY	20	Oyster	O-Lock	401B	GMT
7879/8	18KY	20	Oyster	O-Lock		GMT
7894/9	18KW	17	Oyster II	Concealed		
8153/8	18KY	13	President	Regular		Day-Date
8153/9	18KW	13	President	Regular		Day-Date
8209/8	18KY	20	President (Bark)	Regular		Day-Date
8209/9	18KW	20	President (Bark)	Regular		Day-Date
8210/7	14KY	20	Jubilee (Bark)	Regular		Datejust
8210/8	18KY	20	Jubilee (Bark)	Regular		Datejust
8211/7	14KY	13	Jubilee (Bark)	Regular		Datejust
8211/8	18KY	13	Jubilee (Bark)	Regular		Datejust
8211/8	18KY	13	President (Bark)	Concealed		
8211/9	19KW	13	Jubilee (Bark)	Regular		Datejust
8211/9	19KW	13	President (Bark)	Concealed		
8228/8	18KY	13	President (Bark)	Regular		Day-Date
8228/9	18KW	13	President (Bark)	Regular		Day-Date

ROLEX BRACELETS (continued)

Bracelet Ref #	Metal	Size mm	Bracelet Style	Clasp Notes	End Piece Ref #	Misc Notes.
8270/9	18KW "Tridor"	13	"Super President" Center links pink, yellow & white gold	Concealed		Day-Date
8285/9	18KW "Tridor"	17	"Super President" Center links pink, yellow & white gold	Concealed		Day-Date
8285/9	18KW "Tridor"	20	"Super President" Center links pink, yellow & white gold	Concealed		Day-Date
8289/8	18KY	20	President	Concealed		Day-Date
8289/9	18KW "Tridor"	17	"Super President" Center links pink, yellow & white gold	Concealed		Day-Date
8363/7	18KY	13	Mesh Florentine	Regular		
8363/7	18KY	17	Mesh Florentine	Regular		
8363/8	18KY	13	Mesh Florentine	Regular		
8363/8	18KY	17	Mesh Florentine	Regular		
8363/7	18KY	19	Mesh Florentine	Regular		
8363/8	18KY	19	Mesh Florentine	Regular		
8385/6	Platinum	20	"Super President"	Concealed		Day-Date
8385/8	18KY	20	"Super President"	Concealed		Day-Date
8385/8B	18KY	20	"Super President Baguette" w/ 50 brilliants & 23 baguettes	Concealed		Day-Date
8385/9	18KW	20	"Super President"	Concealed		Day-Date
8385/9B	18KW	20	"Super President Baguette" w/ 50 brilliants & 23 baguettes	Concealed		Day-Date
8386/7	14KY	20	"Super Jubilee"	Concealed		Datejust; GMT; T-O-G
8386/8	18KY	20	"Super Jubilee" (Bark)	Concealed		Datejust; GMT; T-O-G
8387/8	18KY	20	"Super Jubilee"	Concealed		Datejust
8389/6	Platinum	17	President	Concealed		Day-Date
8389/8	18KY	17	President	Concealed		Day-Date
8389/9	18KW	17	President	Concealed		Day-Date
8390/6	Platinum	13	President	Concealed		Day-Date

ROLEX BRACELETS (continued)

Bracelet Ref #	Metal	Size mm	Bracelet Style	Clasp Notes	End Piece Ref #	Misc Notes.
8390/8	18KY	13	President	Concealed		Day-Date
8390/9	18KW	13	President	Concealed		Day-Date
8391/8	18KY	17	"Super Jubilee" (Bark)	Concealed		Datejust
8470/6	Platinum	13	"Super President Karat" w/ 460 brilliants	Concealed		Day-Date
8470/8	18KY	13	"Super President Karat" w/ 460 brilliants	Concealed		Day-Date
8470/9	18KW	13	"Super President Karat" w/ 460 brilliants	Concealed		Day-Date
8472/8	18KY	13	"Super President Karat" w/ 204 brilliants	Concealed		Day-Date
8473/8	18KY	13	"Super President Karat" w/ 443 brilliants	Concealed		Day-Date
8485/6	Platinum	20	"Super President Karat" w/ 288 brilliants	Concealed		Day-Date
8485/8	18KY	20	"Super President Karat" w/ 288 brilliants	Concealed		Day-Date
8485/9	18KW	20	"Super President Karat" w/ 288 brilliants	Concealed		Day-Date
8486/8	18KY	20	"Super Jubilee Karat" w/ 222 brilliants	Concealed		Day-Date
8486/9	18KW	20	"Super Jubilee Karat" w/ 222 brilliants	Concealed		Day-Date
8486/9 Bic	18KW "Tridor"	20	"Bicolor Super Jubilee Karat" w/ 222 brilliants	Concealed		Day-Date
8489/6	Platinum	17	"Super President Karat" w/ 348 brilliants	Concealed		Day-Date
8489/8	18KY	17	"Super President Karat" w/ 348 brilliants	Concealed		Day-Date
8489/9	18KW	17	"Super President Karat" w/ 348 brilliants	Concealed		Day-Date
8552/8	18KY	20	Jubilee (Bark)	Regular		
8553/8	18KY	13	President (Moire')	Regular		Day-Date
8554/8	18KY	13	Jubilee (Moire')	Regular		
8554/9	18KW	13	Jubilee (Moire')	Regular		
8570/6	Platinum	13	President	Concealed		Day-Date
8570/8	18KY	13	President	Concealed		Day-Date

ROLEX BRACELETS (continued)

Bracelet Ref #	Metal	Size mm	Bracelet Style	Clasp Notes	End Piece Ref #	Misc Notes.
8570/8B	18KY	13	"Super President Baguette" w/ 74 brilliants & 35 baguettes	Concealed		Day-Date
8570/9	18KW	13	President	Concealed		Day-Date
8570/9B	18KW	13	"Super President Baguette" w/ 74 brilliants & 35 baguettes	Concealed		Day-Date
8571/8	18KY	13	"Super Jubilee" (Moire')	Concealed		
8606/8	18KY	13	Oyster	Regular		
8607/8	18KY	20	Mesh	Regular		
8723/8	18KY	20	President (Bark)	Concealed		Day-Date
8723/9	18KW	20	President (Bark)	Concealed		Day-Date
9235/8	18KY	13	President (Bark)	Concealed		Day-Date
9235/9	18KW	13	President (Bark)	Concealed		Day-Date
9290/8	18KY	20	Oyster	Flip-Lock		Submariner
9315/0	SS	20	Oyster	Flip-Lock w/ diver's extension	501B, 558B, 580, 593	EXP; Submariner
9315/3	SS/18KY	20	Oyster	Flip-Lock w/ diver's extension	401B, 493	Submariner
9316/0	SS	20	Oyster	Flip-Lock w/ diver's extension	892, 592, 592B	Sea-Dweller
9316A/0	SS	20	Oyster	Flip-Lock		Sea-Dweller
9325/0	SS	20	Oyster	Flip-Lock w/ diver's extension	801	Submariner
9325/3	SS/18KY	20	Oyster	Flip-Lock w/ diver's extension	701	Submariner
9351/0	SS	20	Oyster	Flip-Lock w/ diver's extension		Submariner
9486/8	SS/18KY	20	"Super Jubilee Karat" w/ 218 brilliants	Concealed		Day-Date
STO70	Leather	20	FlipLock	Oyster		

OYSTER CROWNS

No:	Description:	Designation:	Thread:	Metal:	Tube:
1	*"Rolex Oyster"*	6"	80	1-2-3	#201
2	*"Rolex Oyster"*	7"	80	Replaced by crown #19 Tube #202A	
3	*"Rolex Oyster"*	7" A	80	Replaced by crown #19 Tube #202A	
4	*"Rolex Oyster"*	7¾"	100	1-2-3	#203
5	*"Rolex Oyster"*	8"	100	1-2-3	#204
6	*"Rolex Oyster"*	8" A	100	Replaced by crown #8 Tube #205	
7	*"Rolex Oyster"*	8¾" 32 dents	100	1-2-3	#205
8	*"Rolex Oyster"*	8¾" 22 dents	90	1-2-3	#205
10	*"Rolex Oyster"*	9¾" et 10 ½"	110	1-2-3	#206
11	*"Brevet"*	10½" A	120	Discontinued—No replacement	
12	*"Rolex Oyster"*	13" Chrono	120	1-4-5	#204
13	*"Rolex Oyster"*	9¾" et 10½" Chrono	120	1-4-5	#206
18	*"Super Oyster Rolex"*	Replacement	90	1-4-5	#17
19	1-line under coronet	Special Crown	80	1-4-5	#202A
20	1-line under coronet	Twinlock 5,30	90	1-4-5-6	#208
21	1-line under coronet	Twinlock 6,00	90	1-4-5-6	#209
22	*"Brevet"* under coronet	Twinlock 8,00	110 Rolex	1	#207
23	Coronet	Twinlock Baby	90	Replaced by crown #20 Tube #208	
24	*"Brevet"* under coronet	Twinlock 8,00	120 Tudor	1	#207
25	Coronet	Twinlock 7,00	90	1-4	#210

METALS REFERENCE

1:	Steel	3:	Gold-filled, pink	5:	Gold, pink
2:	Gold-filled, yellow	4:	Gold, yellow	6:	Gold, white

OYSTER TUBES

No:	Description:	Crown:
17	Replacement	18
201	6"	1
202	7"	2
202	7" A	3
202A	Special Tube	19
203	7¾"	4
204	8"	5
204	8" A	6
204	13" Chrono	12
205	8¾" 32 dents	7
205	8¾" 22 dents	8
206	9¾" et 10 ½"	10
206	9¾" et 10 ½" Chrono	13
206	10½"	11
207	Twinlock 8,00 Rolex	22
207	Twinlock 8,00 Tudor	24
208	Twinlock 5,30	20
208	Twinlock Baby	23
209	Twinlock 6,00	21
210	Twinlock 7,00	25

"Standard" DIALS

No:		Description:
	SILVER	
10		Silver
11	*	Rhodium (Roman)
12	*	Silver Pyramide
13		Rhodium (Roman)
17	*	Silver Arabic
18		Silver Tapestry
	CHAMPAGNE	
20		Champagne
21		Champagne Roman
22		Champagne Pyramide (Roman)
23		Champagne Roman Shantung
25		Champagne Jubilee (Roman)
27		Champagne Arabic
28		Champagne Tapestry
	BLACK	
30		Black
31		Black Roman
32		Black Pyramide (Roman)
37		Black Arabic
38		Black Tapestry
	SLATE	
40		Slate
41		Slate Roman
42		Slate Mirror Roman
43		Steel Roman
45		Slate Jubilee (Roman)
46	*	Slate Jubilee Arabic
47		Slate Arabic
48	*	Slate Tapestry

No:		Description:
	WHITE	
50		White
51		White Roman
52		Ivory Pyramide (Roman)
53		White Roman Shantung
55		Ivory Jubilee (Roman)
56		Ivory Jubilee Arabic
57		White Arabic
	BLUE	
60		Blue
61		Blue Roman
63		Blue Roman
65		Blue Jubilee
66		Blue Jubilee Arabic
67		Blue Arabic
	BRONZE	
70		Bronze
72		Champ-Decorated Roman
73		Houndstooth (Roman)
	BORDEAUX	
80		Bordeaux
83		Pink Roman
87		Pink Arabic
	PLATINUM	
90		Platinum

* = Discontinued Dials

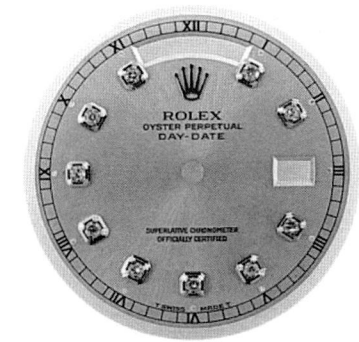

"Additional Cost" DIALS

No:		Description:
	SILVER	
1A		Silver w/ 8 Bril. & 2 Bag.
1B		Silver w/ 10 Bag.
1C		Silver w/ 11 Bril.
1G		Silver w/ 10 Bril.
1H		Cacholong Arabic w/ 2 Bril.
1J		Silver Jubilee Serti
1K		Rhodium Myriad Arabic
1L		Silver Diamond String & Bril.
1P		Silver Pleiade
1Q	*	Silver w/ 3 Diamonds
1R		Rhodium Serti
1S	*	Silver w/ 10 (bezel set) Bril.
1T		Pave w/ Green Enamel
1X		Pave w/ X-Large Diamonds
	CHAMPAGNE	
2A		Champ. w/ 8 Bril. & 2 Bag.
2B	*	Champ. w/ 10 Bag. Diamonds
2C		Champ. w/ 11 Bril.
2E		Engraved Pleiade Serti
2F		Champ. Arabic w/ 2 Bril.
2G		Champ. w/ 10 Bril.
2I		Champ. Ammonite Serti
2J		Champ. Jubilee Serti
2K		Champ. Myriad Arabic
2L		Champ. Diamond String & Bril.

No:		Description:
2M		Champ. Myriad
2N		Champ. Myriad Roman
2P		Champ. Pleiade
2Q		Champ. w/ 3 Diamonds
2R		Champ. Roman Serti
2S		Champ. w/ 10 (bezel set) Bril.
2T		Champ. Myriad Serti
2U		Champ. Shantung Serti
2Z		Pave w/ Diamonds
	BLACK	
3A		Blk. w/ 8 Bril. & 2 Bag.
3B		Blk. w/ 10 Bag. Diamonds
3C		Blk. w/ 11 Bril.
3G		Blk. w/ 10 Bril.
3H		Onyx Arabic w/ 2 Bril.
3I		Meteorite Arabic w/ 2 Bril.
3J	*	Blk. Jubilee Serti
3L		Blk. Diamonds String & Bril.
3Q		Blk. w/ 3 Diamonds
3S		Blk. w/ 10 (bezel set) Bril.
3T		Blk./Champ. w/ Bril.
3V	*	Blk. Vignette Serti
3Z		Pave Sapphires & Bril.

"Additional Cost" DIALS (continued)

No:		Description:
	SLATE	
4A	*	Slate w/ 8 Bril. & 2 Bag.
4B		Steel w/ 10 Bag. Diamonds
4G		Slate w/ 10 Bril.
4I		Slate Ammonite Serti
4J		Slate Jubilee Serti
4K		Slate Myriad Arabic
4M		Steel Myriad
4N		Slate Myriad Roman
4P		Slate Pleiade
4Q		Slate w/ 3 Diamonds
4S		Slate w/ 10 (bezel set) Bril.
4T		Steel Myriad Serti
4U		Steel Serti
4V	*	Slate Vignette Serti
4Z		Pave Rubies & Bril.
	WHITE/ EMERALDS	
5C		White w/ 11 Bril.
5D	*	Champ. Decorated Bril. & Emer.
5E	*	Engraved Pleiade w/ Emer.
5F		White Arabic w/ 2 Bril.
5I		Meteorite w/ 8 Bril. & 2 Bag.
5K		M-O-P Myriad w/ Emer.
5L		Champ. Diamond String & Bril.
5N		M-O-P w/ Emer.
5Q	*	White w/ 3 Diamonds
5R		White Roman Serti

No:		Description:
5S		White w/ 10 (bezel set) Bril.
5T		Pave w/ White Enamel
5U		White Serti
5X		Pave w/ XL Dia. set w/ Emer.
5Z		Pave w/ Emer.
	BLUE/ SAPPHIRES	
6A		Blue w/ 8 Bril. & 2 Bag.
6C		Blue w/ 11 Bril.
6D	*	Champ. Decorated Bril. & Sap.
6E	*	Engraved Pleiade w/ Sap.
6F		Silver w/ 2 Sap.
6G		Blue w/ 10 Bril.
6H		Blue Jadeite Arabic w/ 2 Bril.
6I		Azurite Serti
6K		M-O-P Myriad w/ Sap.
6L		Slvr./Champ. Dia. String & Sap.
6N		M-O-P w/ Sap.
6Q		Blue w/ 3 Dia.
6R	*	Slvr./Champ. Rainbow Sap.
6T		Pave w/ Blue Enamel
6U		Blue Serti
6V		Blue Vignette Serti
6X		Pave w/ XL Dia. set w/ Sap.
6Z		Pave w/ Sap.

"Additional Cost" DIALS (continued)

No:		Description:
	BRONZE/ RUBIES/ WOOD	
7A		Pink w/ 8 Bril & 2 Bag.
7B		Birch
7D	*	Champ. Decorated Bril. & Rubies
7E	*	Engraved Pleiade w/ Rubies
7F		Champ. w/ 2 Rubies
7I		Rubellite Serti
7K		Pave Arabic w/ Rubies
7L		Champ. Dia. String & Rubies
7M		African Mahogany
7N		M-O-P w/ Rubies
7Q		Brown w/ 3 Diamonds
7R		Houndstooth Roman Serti
7T	*	Pave w/ Red Enamel
7U		Champ. Mirror Serti
7V		Bronze Vignette Serti
7W		Walnut
7X		Pave w/ XL Dia. set w/ Rubies
7Y		Pave w/ 2 rows Rubies
7Z		Pave w/ Rubies
	STONE/ DIAMONDS	
8A		Aventurine Serti
8B		Pink w/ 10 Bag. Diamonds
8C		Coral Pyramide Serti
8D		Jade Serti
8E		Cornelian Serti

No:		Description:
8F		Ferrite Serti
8G		Grossular Serti
8H		Cacholong Serti
8I		Sodalite Serti
8J		M-O-P Jubilee Serti
8K		M-O-P Myriad Serti
8L		Lapis Lazuli Serti
8M		Champ. M-O-P w/ 2 Bril.
8N	*	Obsidian Serti
8P		Gold Lace Pleiade
8Q		Bordeaux w/ 3 Diamonds
8R		M-O-P Roman Serti
8S		Jasper Serti
8T		Pink Myriad Serti
8U		Pink Serti
8V		Bordeaux Vignette Serti
8W		Pink Mirror Serti
8X		Onyx Serti
8Y		Pyrite Serti
8Z		Pave Losange
	STONE	
9A		Adventurine Roman
9B		Black M-O-P w/ 10 Bag. Dia.
9C	*	Coral
9D		Champ. M-O-P Decorated Roman
9E		Cornelian Roman
9F		Ferrite Roman

"Additional Cost" DIALS (continued)

No:		Description:
9G	*	Grossular Roman
9H	*	Howlite Roman
9I		Rose MOP Decorated Roman
9J		M-O-P
9K		M-O-P Arabic
9L		Lapis Lazuli
9M		Malachite
9N		Obsidian Roman
9P	*	Opal
9Q	*	Turquoise
9R		M-O-P Roman
9S	*	Jasper Roman
9T		Tiger Eye
9U		White M-O-P Serti
9V		Rose M-O-P Serti
9W		Rose M-O-P Roman
9X		Onyx
9Y		Rose M-O-P Arabic
9Z	*	Pave Honeycomb
	STONE/ DIAMOND	
0C		Cellini Serti
0L		Lapis Lazuli Pyramide Serti
0P		Opal Serti
0Q		Turquoise Pyramide Serti
0R		White M-O-P Pave Roman
0S		Cellini Semi-Precious

No:		Description:
0U		Black M-O-P Serti
0W		Black M-O-P Roman
0X	*	Onyx Pyramide Serti
0Y		Black M-O-P Arabic

When ordering a **Diamond Dial** separately, the following 9 character code number is used:

MDA	10	88	1A
Diamond Dial Style: MD, MDA, MDD, MDR, MDG, MQG, MQA, MDB: Men's MSG, MSR: Mid-Size LD, LDD, LDC, LDG, LDR: Ladies'	**Number of Diamonds**	**Metal Code for Diamond Settings** a complete list is found on page 141.	**Dial Color Code** a complete list is found on pages 163-166

When ordering a **Diamond Bezel** separately, the following 7 character code number is used:

LBZ	40	88
Diamond Bezel Style: LBZ: Ladies' MSB: Mid-Size MBZ: Men's	**Number of Diamonds**	**Metal Code for Diamond Settings** a complete list is found on page 141.

* = Discontinued Dials; M-O-P = Mother of Pearl; Dia. = Diamonds; Bag. = Baguettes; Champ. = Champagne; Emer. = Emerald; Bril. = Brilliants; Sap. = Sapphires; Blk. = Black

"Trade-In" DIALS & BEZELS

DIALS   For Steel/Gold, 18kt. Gold or Platinum models only.

No:	Size:	Description/Notes:
LD102	Ladies'	10 baguettes on dial./ Datejust
LDD10	Ladies'	8 brilliants & 2 baguettes on dial. / Datejust
LDG/U10	Ladies'	10 brilliants on dial. / Datejust
LDR10	Ladies'	10 brilliants on Roman dial. / Datejust
LDC11	Ladies'	11 brilliants on dial. / Oyster Perpetual
LDD11	Ladies'	8 brilliants & 3 baguettes on dial. / Non-Date models
MSG/U10	Mid-size	10 brilliants on dial. / Datejust
MSR10	Mid-size	10 brilliants on Roman dial. / Datejust
MD102	Men's	10 baguettes on dial. / Day-Date
MDA10	Men's	8 brilliants & 2 baguettes on dial. / Day-Date
MDB10	Men's	10 baguettes on dial. / Day-Date
MDD08	Men's	8 brilliants on dial. / Date & Datejust
MDD10	Men's	8 brilliants & 2 baguettes on dial. / Date, DJ & D-D
MDD11	Men's	8 brilliants & 3 baguettes on dial. / Non-Date models
MDG/U10	Men's	10 brilliants on dial. / Datejust
MDR10	Men's	10 brilliants on Roman dial. / Date
MQA10	Men's	8 brilliants & 2 baguettes on dial. / Day-Date
MQG10	Men's	10 brilliants on dial. / Datejust

BEZELS   For 18kt. Gold or Platinum models only.

No:	Size:	Description/Notes:
LBZ3490	Ladies'	18KWG bezel w/ 34 brilliants. / Datejust
LBZ4066	Ladies'	Platinum bezel w/ 40 brilliants. / Datejust
LBZ4088	Ladies'	18KYG bezel w/ 40 brilliants. / Datejust
LBZ4099	Ladies'	18KWG bezel w/ 40 brilliants. / Datejust
MSB4488	Mid-size	18KYG bezel w/ 44 brilliants. / Datejust
MSB4499	Mid-size	18KWG bezel w/ 44 brilliants. / Datejust
MBZ4090	Men's	18KWG bezel w/ 40 brilliants. / Datejust
MBZ4460	Men's	Platinum bezel w/ 44 brilliants. / DJ & D-D
MBZ4466	Men's	Platinum bezel w/ 44 brilliants. / OP & O-Quartz D-D
MBZ4488	Men's	18KYG bezel w/ 44 brilliants. / OP & O-Quartz D-D
MBZ4490	Men's	18KWG bezel w/ 44 brilliants. / Date models
MBZ4690	Men's	18KWG bezel w/ 46 brilliants. / DJ & D-D

ROLEX MOVEMENTS

The following pages are designed to help you identify Rolex watch movements. The first three pages show (actual size) images of the movements, with a list of Ref/Cal numbers. You should be able to identify the movement by the basic wheel layout. It is important to note that different movements may look very similar, with the subtle differences being identification numbers and locations.

After identifying the closest match (or matches) to your movement, you should then proceed to the following pages where the movements are listed by Ref/Cal number. In this chart, various information is given for the movement which will help you further identify the movement, as follows:

Caliber (Size) [Old Ref]: This column lists the identifying number on the movement, expressed as a *Reference* or *Caliber* number. Also listed is the *Size* of the movement (in parenthesis), which is expressed in Lignes ''', and the *Old Ref* [in brackets], which is how the movement was identified in the past.

Movement Description: This column identifies features of the movement, such as the shape, type of seconds, manual or self winding, Chronometer status, as well as the presence of any shock protecting, calendar, date, hacking, or anti-magnetic devices, etc...

Base Caliber: This identifies the Caliber on which it was based. Meaning which was the first caliber designed in this series. If the indication is in fact "Basic Caliber", it means that that particular Caliber was the first in the series.

Engraved Info: This column details the presence of certain identification numbers, expressed in "quotes", as well as the location on the movement where they can be found.

Ø Size: This identifies the physical dimensions of the movement, expressed in millimeters.

 # Jewel: This column lists the number of jewels used on the movement. In most cases the movement was only available in one jewel configuration. However, some movements were available with different configurations and all known variations are listed. It is worth noting that, in most cases, the number of jewels are engraved on the movement.

Beats Per Hour: This identifies the step, or action of the movement. Older Rolex watches utilized 18,000 beats, but were subsequently upped to 19,800, 21,600 and 28,800 beats, respectively. It is also worth noting that Quartz movements are listed as 32,768 Hz, which is *cycles per second*.

Intro Year: This identifies the year the movement was first introduced, which can be helpful in further identifying the date of the watch.

ROLEX MOVEMENT DIAGRAMS

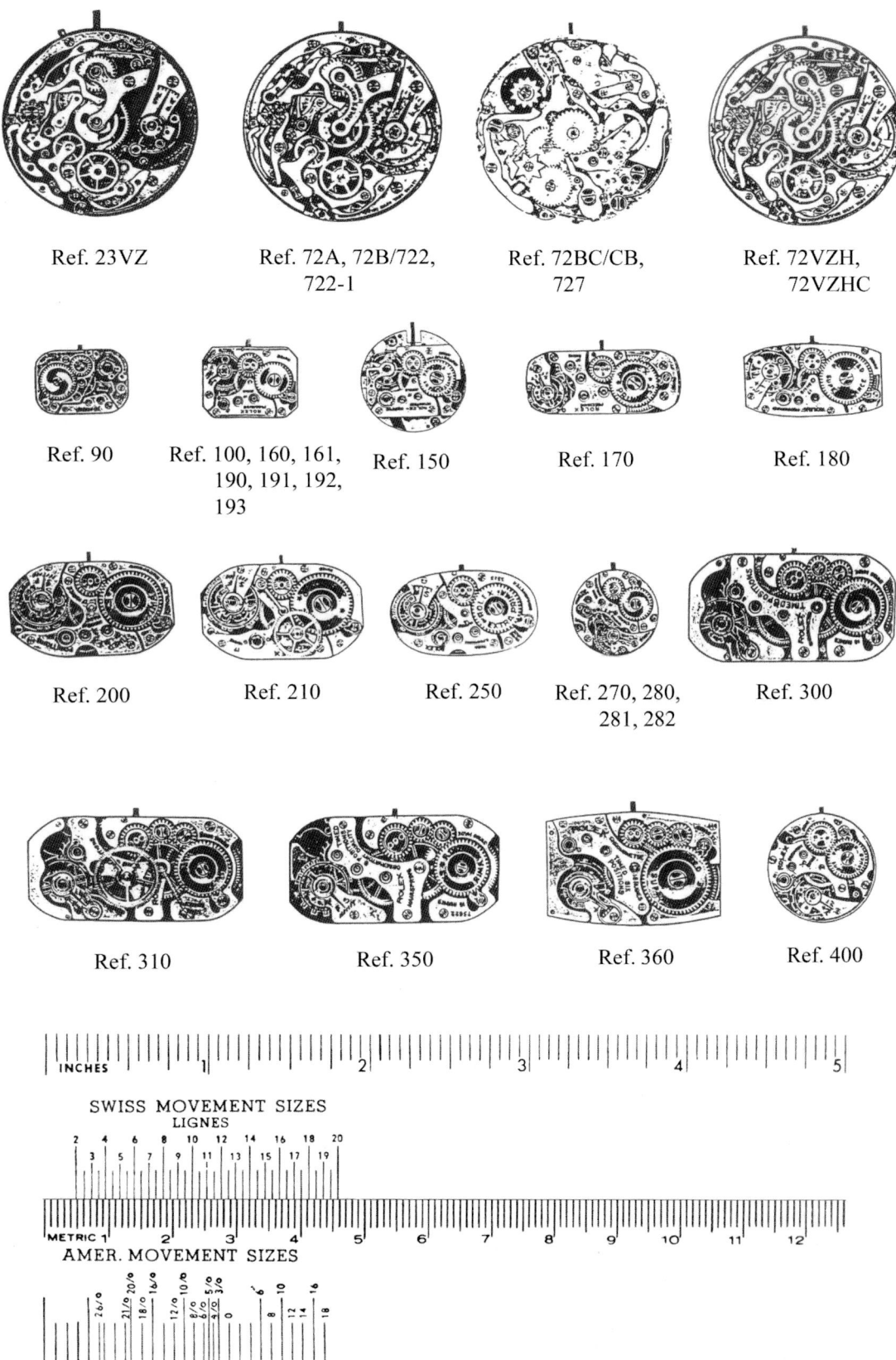

Ref. 23VZ

Ref. 72A, 72B/722, 722-1

Ref. 72BC/CB, 727

Ref. 72VZH, 72VZHC

Ref. 90

Ref. 100, 160, 161, 190, 191, 192, 193

Ref. 150

Ref. 170

Ref. 180

Ref. 200

Ref. 210

Ref. 250

Ref. 270, 280, 281, 282

Ref. 300

Ref. 310

Ref. 350

Ref. 360

Ref. 400

INCHES

SWISS MOVEMENT SIZES
LIGNES

METRIC

AMER. MOVEMENT SIZES

ROLEX MOVEMENT DIAGRAMS (continued)

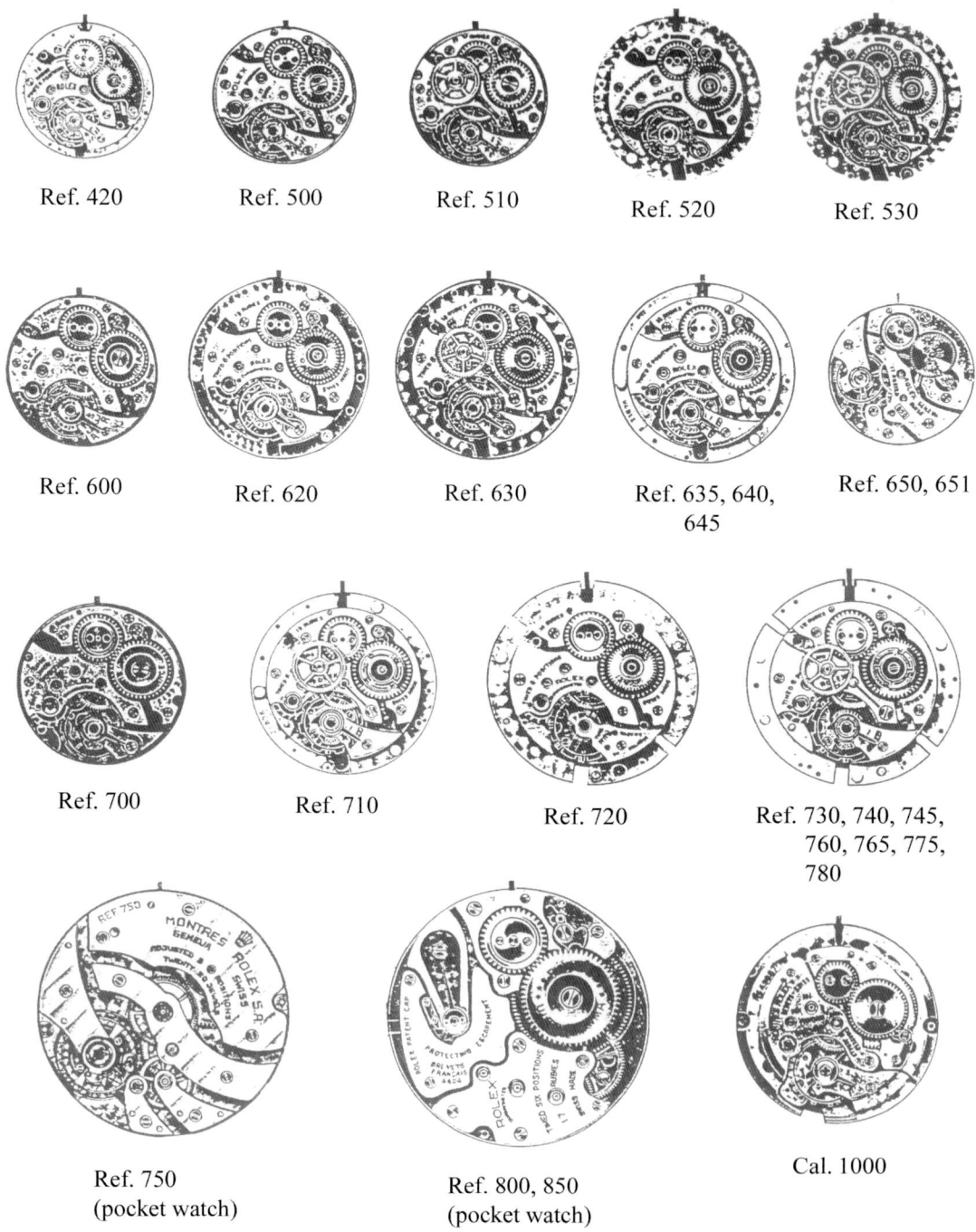

Ref. 420

Ref. 500

Ref. 510

Ref. 520

Ref. 530

Ref. 600

Ref. 620

Ref. 630

Ref. 635, 640, 645

Ref. 650, 651

Ref. 700

Ref. 710

Ref. 720

Ref. 730, 740, 745, 760, 765, 775, 780

Ref. 750 (pocket watch)

Ref. 800, 850 (pocket watch)

Cal. 1000

ROLEX MOVEMENT DIAGRAMS (continued)

Cal. 1030, 1035, 1036,
1036GMT, 1040,
1055, 1055B, 1065,
1065M/1080, 1065GMT,
1066, 1066GMT, 1066M

Cal. 1100

Cal. 1120, 1130,
1135

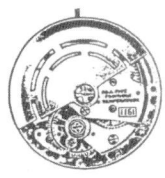

Cal. 1160, 1161,
1165, 1166

Cal. 1200

Cal. 1210, 1215,
1220, 1225

Cal. 1300

Cal. 1310, 1315

Cal. 1400, 1401

Cal. 1520, 1525,
1556, 1570,
1575GMT, 1580

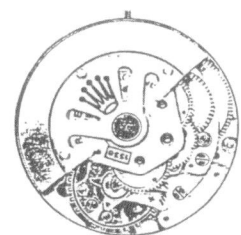

Cal. 1530, 1535, 1555,
1560, 1565, 1565GMT

Cal. 1600, 1601

Cal. 1800

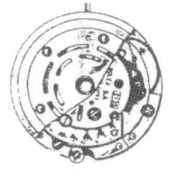

Cal. 2030, 2035,
2130, 2135

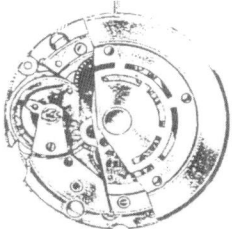

Cal. 3035, 3055, 3075,
3085

Cal. 5035, 5055

ROLEX MOVEMENTS IDENTIFICATION

Caliber (Size) [Old Ref]	Movement Description	Base Caliber	Engraved Info	Ø Size	# Jewel	Beats per hr	Intro Year
23VZ	*Manual wind, Chronograph w/ min. recorder, round-shaped, 2-dials.*	23	~	30mm x 5,85mm	17J	18,000	1947
13''' 72A (13''')	*Manual wind, Chronograph w/ hr. recorder, shock protecting, round-shaped, 3-dial.*	Basic Caliber	*"72A" on hub sinking of balance wheel.*	30mm x 6,95mm	17J	18,000	1961
13''' 72B (13''') Same as 722	*Manual wind, Chronograph w/ hr. recorder, shock protecting, round-shaped, 3-dial, (hairspring protection added to 72A).*	72A 13''	*"72B" on hub sinking of balance wheel.*	30mm x 6,95mm	17J	18,000	1962
13''' 72BC (13''')	*Manual wind, Chronograph w/ hr. recorder, calendar, shock protecting, round-shaped, 3-dial.*	72A 13''	*"72BC" or "72cB" on hub sinking of balance wheel.*	30mm x 6,95mm	17J	18,000	1962
13''' 72VZH (13''')	*Manual wind, Chronograph w/ hr. recorder, shock protecting, round-shaped, 3-dial, (start, stop & fly back to zero).*	72A 13''	~	30mm x 6,95mm	17J	18,000	1939
13''' 72VZHC (13''')	*Manual wind, Chronograph w/ hr. recorder, shock protecting, round-shaped, 3-dial, (start, stop & fly back to zero).*	72A 13''	~	30mm x 6,95mm	17J	18,000	1939
REF. 90 (4-6''')	*Manual wind, no seconds, rectangle-shaped.*	Basic Caliber	~	10,3mm x 14,1mm	17J	~	1950

ROLEX MOVEMENTS (continued)

Caliber (Size) [Old Ref]	Movement Description	Base Caliber	Engraved Info	Ø Size	# Jewel	Beats per hr	Intro Year
REF. 100 (4'''U) [Size U.]	*Manual wind, no seconds, rectangle-shaped.*	Basic Caliber	~	11,3mm x 14,7mm	17J	~	1942
REF. 150 (7'''U) [Size U-7]	*Manual wind, no seconds, round-shaped.*	100	~	16mm	17J	~	1942
REF. 160 (4'''113) [Size 113]	*Manual wind, no seconds, rectangle-shaped.*	100	~	11,3mm x 14,7mm	17J	17,886	1945
REF. 161 (4'''113)	*Manual wind, no seconds, rectangle-shaped.*	100	*"161" on plate, lateral edge.*	11,3mm x 14,7mm	17J	18,000	1947
REF. 170 (4¼''') M. Baguette [Size M.]	*Manual wind, no seconds, long rect-shaped.*	Basic Caliber	~	10mm x 24mm	17J	~	1938
REF. 180 (5'''F) [Size F.]	*Manual wind, no seconds, long rect-shaped.*	Basic Caliber	~	11,8mm x 20,9mm	17J	~	1943
REF. 190 (4''')	*Manual wind, no seconds, rectangle-shaped.*	160	*"190" on hub sinking of balance wheel.*	11,3mm x 14,7mm	17J	18,000	1950
REF. 191 (4''')	*Manual wind, no seconds, shock protecting, rectangle-shaped.*	160	*"191" on hub sinking of balance wheel.*	11,3mm x 14,7mm	17J	18,000	1952
REF. 192 (4''')	*Manual wind, no seconds, shock protecting, rectangle-shaped.*	160	*"192" on hub sinking of balance wheel.*	11,3mm x 14,7mm	17J	21,600	1952
REF. 193 (4''')	*Manual wind, no seconds, shock protecting, rectangle-shaped.*	160	*"193" on hub sinking of balance wheel.*	11,3mm x 14,7mm	17J	21,600	1956
REF. 200 (6¾''') [Size T: oval R: rect.]	*Manual wind, no seconds, oval (or) rectangle-shaped (cut-corners).*	Basic Caliber	~	15,2mm x 24,6mm	17J	~	1937
REF. 210 (6¾''') [Size T: oval R: rect.]	*Manual wind, sweep-seconds, oval (or) rectangle-shaped (cut-corners).*	200	~	15,2mm x 24,6mm	17J	~	1938

ROLEX MOVEMENTS (continued)

Caliber (Size) [Old Ref]	Movement Description	Base Caliber	Engraved Info	Ø Size	# Jewel	Beats per hr	Intro Year
REF. 250 (5¾''') [Size O.]	*Manual wind, no seconds, oval-shaped.*	Basic Caliber	~	13,5mm x 22,5mm	15J	~	1938
REF. 270 (6''')	*Manual wind, no seconds, round-shaped.*	Basic Caliber	~	13,5mm	17J	18,000	1940
REF. 280 (6''')	*Manual wind, no seconds, round-shaped.*	270	*"280" on hub sinking of balance wheel.*	13,5mm	17J	21,600	1950
REF. 281 (6''')	*Manual wind, no seconds, round-shaped.*	270	*"281" on hub sinking of balance wheel.*	13,5mm	17J	21,600	1955
REF. 282 (6''')	*Manual wind, no seconds, shock protecting, round-shaped.*	270	*"282" on hub sinking of balance wheel.*	13,5mm	17J	21,600	1958
REF. 300 [Size T.S.]	*Manual wind, Chronometer, small seconds, rectangle-shaped.*	Basic Caliber	~	16,9mm x 32,7mm	18J	~	1932
REF. 310 [Size T.S.]	*Manual wind, Chronometer, sweep-seconds, rectangle-shaped.*	300	~	16,9mm x 32,7mm	18J	~	1932
REF. 350 [Size T.S.]	*Manual wind, Chronometer, small seconds, jump hour dial, rectangle-shaped.*	300	~	16,9mm x 32,7mm	18J	~	1932
REF. 360 [Size H.W.]	*Manual wind, Chronometer, small seconds, rectangle-shaped.*	Basic Caliber	~	18mm x 27mm	18J	~	1937
REF. 400 (7¾''') [Size 7¾"-H.]	*Manual wind, small seconds, round-shaped.*	Basic Caliber	~	17,2mm	17J	~	1941
REF. 420 (7¾''') [Size P.A.]	*Self wind, small seconds, round-shaped.*	400 (replaced by 1120)	~	19,4mm	18J	~	1941
REF. 500 (8¾''') [Size 8¾"-H.]	*Manual wind, small seconds, precision, round-shaped.*	Basic Caliber	~	19,4mm	17J	~	1935

ROLEX MOVEMENTS (continued)

Caliber (Size) [Old Ref]	Movement Description	Base Caliber	Engraved Info	Ø Size	# Jewel	Beats per hr	Intro Year
REF. 510 (8¾''') [Size 8¾"–H.]	*Manual wind, sweep-seconds, precision, round-shaped.*	500	~	19,4mm	17J	~	1935
REF. 520 (8¾''') [Size A.R.]	*Self wind, small seconds, round-shaped.*	500	~	24mm	18J	~	1936
REF. 530 (8¾''') [Size A.R.]	*Self wind, sweep-second, round-shaped,*	500	~	24mm	17J	~	1936
REF. 600 (9¾''') [Size 9¾" Hunter Patent]	*Manual wind, small seconds, round-shaped.*	Basic Caliber	~	21,7mm	17J	~	1933
REF. 620 (9¾''') [Size N.A.]	*Self wind, Chronometer, small seconds, round-shaped.*	600	~	26,4mm	18J	~	1936
REF. 630 (9¾''') [Size N.A.]	*Self wind, sweep-seconds, round-shaped.*	600	~	26,4mm	18J	~	1937
REF. 635 (9¾''') [Size A.260]	*Self wind, small seconds, shock protecting, round-shaped.*	600	~	26,4mm	18J	~	1950
REF. 640 (9¾''') [Size A.260]	*Self wind, sweep-seconds, moonphase, calendar, round-shaped.*	635	~	26,4mm	18J	~	1950
REF. 645 (9¾''') [Size A.260]	*Self wind, sweep-seconds, shock protecting, round-shaped.*	635	~	26,4mm	18J	~	1950
REF. 650	*Manual wind, ultra-slim, no seconds, round-shaped.*	Basic Caliber	"650" on train wheel bridge.	20,8mm x 1,80mm	17J	18,000	1958
REF. 651	*Manual wind, ultra-slim, no seconds, round-shaped.*	650	"651" on train wheel bridge.	20,8mm x 1,80mm	18J	21,600	1978
REF. 700 (10½''') [Size 10½"-H]	*Manual wind, Chronometer, small seconds, round-shaped.*	Basic Caliber	~	23,4mm	18J	~	1938

ROLEX MOVEMENTS (continued)

Caliber (Size) [Old Ref]	Movement Description	Base Caliber	Engraved Info	Ø Size	# Jewel	Beats per hr	Intro Year
REF. 710 (10½''') [Size 10½"-H]	*Manual wind, sweep-seconds, precision, round-shaped.*	700	~	23,4mm	17J	~	1938
REF. 720 (10½''') [Size A.295]	*Self wind, Chronometer, small seconds, shock protecting, round-shaped.*	Basic Caliber	~	29,5mm	18J	~	1945
REF. 722 (10½''') Same as 72B	*Manual wind, Chronograph w/ hr. recorder, shock protecting, round-shaped, 3-dial, (hairspring protection added to 72A).*	72A 13"	"722" on hub sinking of balance wheel.	30mm x 6,95mm	17J	18,000	1962
REF. 722-1 (10½''')	*Manual wind, Chronograph w/ hr. recorder, shock protecting, round shaped, 3-dial, (conveyor spring added to 72B/722).*	72A 13"	"722-1" on hub sinking of balance wheel.	30mm x 6,95mm	17J	18,000	1969
REF. 727 (10½''')	*Manual wind, Chronograph w/ hr. recorder, shock protecting, round shaped, 3-dial, (conveyor spring added to 72BC/72cB).*	72A 13"	"727" on hub sinking of balance wheel.	30mm x 6,95mm	17J	21,600	1970
REF. 730 (10½''') [Size A.295]	*Self wind, Chronometer, sweep-seconds, shock protecting, round-shaped.*	720	~	29,5mm	18J	~	1945
REF. 740 (10½''') [Size A.295]	*Self wind, Chronometer, sweep-seconds, calendar, round-shaped.*	720-730	~	29,5mm	18J	~	1950

ROLEX MOVEMENTS (continued)

Caliber (Size) [Old Ref]	Movement Description	Base Caliber	Engraved Info	Ø Size	# Jewel	Beats per hr	Intro Year
REF. 745 (10½''') [Size A.295]	*Self wind, sweep-seconds, calendar, round-shaped.*	720-740	~	29,5mm	18J	~	1950
REF. 750 (10½''')	*Manual wind, pocket watch, round-shaped.*	Basic Caliber	~	35,64mm x 1,90mm	20J	21,000	~
REF. 760 (10½''')	*Manual wind, sweep-seconds, calendar, round-shaped.*	710	~	29,5mm	18J	~	1950
REF. 765 (10½''') [Size A.296]	*Self wind, sweep-seconds, calendar, round-shaped.*	720	~	29,5mm	18J	~	1950
REF. 775 (10½''') [Size A.296]	*Self wind, sweep-seconds, shock protecting, round-shaped.*	720	~	29,5mm	18J	~	1950
REF. 780 (10½''')	*Self wind, sweep-seconds, moonphase, calendar, round-shaped.*	720	~	29,5mm	18J	~	1950
REF. 800 (10½''') [Size D.D.]	*Manual wind, Chronometer, small seconds, shock protecting, pocket watch, round-shaped.*	Basic Caliber	~	29,5mm	17J	~	1934
REF. 850 (10½''') [Size D.D.]	*Manual wind, Chronometer, small seconds, shock protecting, pocket watch, round-shaped.*	800	~	29,5mm	17J	~	1934
1000	*Manual wind, small seconds, shock protecting, round-shaped.*	1030	*"1000" on hub sinking of balance wheel.*	28,5mm x 3,45mm	18J	18,000	1955
1030	*Self winding, sweep-seconds, shock protecting, round-shaped.*	Basic Caliber	*"1030" on bridge for self-winding mechanism.*	28,5mm x 5,85mm	17J/ 25J	18,000	1950

ROLEX MOVEMENTS (continued)

Caliber (Size) [Old Ref]	Movement Description	Base Caliber	Engraved Info	Ø Size	# Jewel	Beats per hr	Intro Year
1035	*Self winding, sweep-seconds, shock protecting, progressive calendar, round-shaped.*	1030	*"1030" on bridge for self-winding mechanism.*	28,5mm x 6,66mm	25J	18,000	1957
1036	*Self wind, sweep-seconds, shock protecting, instant-calendar, round-shaped.*	1030	*"1030" on bridge for self-winding mechanism.*	28,5mm x 6,26mm	25J	18,000	1957
1036 GMT	*Self wind, sweep-seconds, shock protecting, instant-calendar, round-shaped.*	1030	*"1030" on bridge for self-winding mechanism.*	28,5mm x 6,44mm	25J	18,000	1957
1040	*Self wind, jumping sweep-seconds, shock protecting, round-shaped.*	1030	*"1040" on bridge for self-winding mechanism.*	28,5mm x 6,47mm	25J	18,000	1954
1055	*Self wind, sweep-seconds, shock protecting, day-date (Pres.), round-shaped.*	1030	*"1055" on bridge for self-winding mechanism.*	28,5mm x 7,00mm	25J	18,000	1954
1055B	*Self wind, sweep-seconds, shock protecting, day-date (Pres.), round-shaped (dial plate diff-from 1055).*	1030	*"1055B" on bridge for self-winding mechanism.*	28,5mm x 7,10mm	25J	18,000	1954
1065	*Self wind, sweep-seconds, instant-calendar, shock protecting, round-shaped.*	1030	*"1065" on bridge for self-winding mechanism.*	28,5mm x 6,25mm	25J	18,000	1955
1065 GMT	*Self wind, sweep-seconds, calendar, 12/24 hr hand, shock protecting, round-shaped.*	1030	*"1065" on bridge for self-winding mechanism.*	28,5mm x 6,44mm	25J	18,000	1957

ROLEX MOVEMENTS (continued)

Caliber (Size) [Old Ref]	Movement Description	Base Caliber	Engraved Info	Ø Size	# Jewel	Beats per hr	Intro Year
1065M Same as 1080	*Self wind, sweep-seconds, shock protecting, anti-magnetic, round-shaped.*	1030	*"1065 M" on bridge for self-winding mechanism.*	28,5mm x 5,85mm	25J	18,000	1955
1066	*Self wind, sweep-seconds, shock protecting, instant-calendar, round-shaped.*	1030	*"1066 M" on bridge for self-winding mechanism*	28,5mm x 6,25mm	25J	18,000	1957
1066 GMT	*Self wind, sweep-seconds, calendar, 12/24 hr hand, shock protecting, round-shaped.*	1030	*"1066" on bridge for self-winding mechanism.*	28,5mm x 6,44mm	25J	18,000	1957
1066M	*Self wind, sweep-seconds, shock protecting, anti-magnetic, round-shaped.*	1030	*"1066 M" on bridge for self-winding mechanism.*	28,5mm x 5,85mm	25J	18,000	1955
1080 Same as 1065M	*Self wind, sweep-seconds, shock protecting, anti-magnetic, round-shaped.*	1030	*"1080" on bridge for self-winding mechanism.*	28,5mm x 5,85mm	25J	18,000	1955
1100 7½'''	*Manual wind, small seconds, shock protecting, round-shaped.*	Basic Caliber	*"1100" on hub sinking of balance wheel.*	17,7mm x 3,05mm	18J	19,800	1954
1120	*Self wind, small seconds, shock protecting, round-shaped.*	Basic Caliber	*"1120" on bridge for self-winding mechanism.*	20,0mm x 5,25mm	17/ 27J	19,800	1953
1130	*Self wind, sweep-seconds, shock protecting, round-shaped.*	1120	*"1130" on bridge for self-winding mechanism.*	20,0mm x 5,40mm	26J	19,800	1955
1135	*Self wind, sweep-seconds, progress-calendar, round-shaped.*	1120	*"1130" on bridge for self-winding mechanism.*	20,0mm x 5,90mm	26J	19,800	1955

ROLEX MOVEMENTS (continued)

Caliber (Size) [Old Ref]	Movement Description	Base Caliber	Engraved Info	Ø Size	# Jewel	Beats per hr	Intro Year
1160	*Self wind, sweep-seconds, shock protecting, round-shaped.*	1120	*"1160" on bridge for self-winding mechanism.*	20,0mm x 5,40mm	26J	19,800	1964
1161	*Self wind, sweep-seconds, shock protecting, round-shaped.*	1120	*"1161" on bridge for self-winding mechanism.*	20,0mm x 5,40mm	26J	19,800	1964
1165	*Self wind, sweep-seconds, progress-calendar, shock protecting, round-shaped.*	1120	*"1160" on bridge for self-winding mechanism.*	20,0mm x 5,90mm	26J	19,800	1965
1166	*Self wind, sweep-seconds, progress-calendar, shock protecting, round-shaped.*	1120	*"1161" on bridge for self-winding mechanism.*	20,0mm x 5,90mm	26J	19,800	1967
1200	*Manual wind, small seconds, shock protecting, round-shaped.*	1210	*"1200" on hub sinking of balance wheel.*	23,8mm x 3,65mm	17J	18,000	1961
1210	*Manual wind, sweep-seconds, shock protecting, round-shaped.*	Basic Caliber	*"1210" on hub sinking of balance wheel.*	23,8mm x 4,27mm	18J	18,000	1954
1215	*Manual wind, sweep-seconds, Oysterdate-cal, shock protecting, round-shaped.*	1210	*"1210" on hub sinking of balance wheel.*	23,8mm x 5,07mm	18J	18,000	1954
1216	*Manual wind, sweep-seconds, Oysterdate-cal, shock protecting, round-shaped.*	1210	*"1216" on hub sinking of balance wheel.*	23,8mm x 5,07mm	17J	18,000	1954
1220	*Manual wind, sweep-seconds, shock protecting, round-shaped.*	1210	*"1225" on hub sinking of balance wheel.*	23,8mm x 4,27mm	17/ 18J	21,600	1957
1225	*Manual wind, sweep-seconds, Oysterdate-cal, shock protecting, round-shaped.*	1210	*"1225" on hub sinking of balance wheel.*	23,8mm x 5,07mm	17/ 18J	21,600	1967

ROLEX MOVEMENTS (continued)

Caliber (Size) [Old Ref]	Movement Description	Base Caliber	Engraved Info	Ø Size	# Jewel	Beats per hr	Intro Year
1300	*Manual wind, no seconds, shock protecting, diamond-shaped.*	Basic Caliber	*"1300" on hub sinking of balance wheel.*	17,8mm x 15,3mm x 3,48mm	17J	18,000	1956
1310	*Manual wind, sweep-seconds, shock protecting, diamond-shaped.*	1300	*"1310" on hub sinking of balance wheel.*	17,8mm x 15,3mm x 3,95mm	18J	18,000	1956
1315	*Manual wind, sweep-seconds, calendar, shock protecting, diamond-shaped.*	1300	*"1315" on hub sinking of balance wheel.*	17,8mm x 13,5mm x 4,35mm	17J	18,000	1956
1400	*Manual wind, no seconds, shock protecting, round-shaped.*	Basic Caliber	*"1400" on hub sinking of balance wheel.*	13,75mm x 3,23mm	15J	21,600	1960
1401	*Manual wind, no seconds, shock protecting, round-shaped.*	1400	*"1401" on hub sinking of balance wheel.*	13,75 x 3,23mm	15J	21,600	1960
1520	*Self wind, sweep-seconds, (hack after '72), shock protecting, round-shaped.*	1530	*"1520" on hub sinking of balance wheel.*	28,5mm x 5,75mm	26J	19,800	1963
1525	*Self wind, sweep-seconds, (hack after '72), progress-calendar, shock protecting, round-shaped.*	1530	*"1520" on hub sinking of balance wheel.*	28,5mm x 6,30mm	26J	19,800	1965
1530	*Self wind, sweep-seconds, shock protecting, round-shaped.*	Basic Caliber	*"1530" on bridge of self-winding mechanism.*	28,5mm x 6,30mm	17/ 26J	18,000	1957
1535	*Self wind, sweep-seconds, progress-calendar, shock protecting, round-shaped.*	1530	*"1530" on bridge of self-winding mechanism.*	28,5mm x 6,30mm	26J	18,000	1957

ROLEX MOVEMENTS (continued)

Caliber (Size) [Old Ref]	Movement Description	Base Caliber	Engraved Info	Ø Size	# Jewel	Beats per hr	Intro Year
1536	*Self wind, sweep-seconds, progress-calendar, shock protecting, round-shaped.*	1530	*"1530" on bridge of self-winding mechanism.*	28,5mm x 6,30mm	26J	18,000	1964
1555	*Self wind, sweep-seconds, day-date (Pres.), shock protecting, round-shaped.*	Basic Caliber	*"1555" on bridge of self-winding mechanism.*	28,5mm x 7,03mm	26J	18,000	1959
1556	*Self wind, sweep-seconds, (hack after '72), day-date (Pres.), shock protecting, round-shaped.*	1530	*"1556" on bridge of self-winding mechanism.*	28,5mm x 7,03mm	26J	19,800	1965
1560	*Self wind, sweep-seconds, shock protecting, round-shaped.*	1530	*"1560" on bridge of self-winding mechanism.*	28,5mm x 5,75mm	26J	18,000	1965
1565	*Self wind, sweep-seconds, instant-calendar, shock protecting, round-shaped.*	1530	*"1560" on bridge of self-winding mechanism.*	28,5mm x 6,30mm	26J	18,000	1959
1565 GMT	*Self wind, sweep-seconds, instant-calendar, shock protecting, round-shaped.*	1530	*"1560" on bridge of self-winding mechanism.*	28,5mm x 6,30mm	26J	18,000	1962
1570	*Self wind, sweep-seconds, (hack after '72), shock protecting, round-shaped.*	1530	*"1570" on bridge of self-winding mechanism.*	28,5mm x 5,75mm	26J	19,800	1965
1575	*Self wind, sweep-seconds, (hack after '72), instant-calendar, shock protecting, round-shaped.*	1530	*"1570" on bridge of self-winding mechanism.*	28,5mm x 6,30mm	26J	19,800	1965

ROLEX MOVEMENTS (continued)

Caliber (Size) [Old Ref]	Movement Description	Base Caliber	Engraved Info	Ø Size	# Jewel	Beats per hr	Intro Year
1575 GMT	*Self wind, sweep-seconds, (hack after '72), instant-calendar, shock protecting, round-shaped.*	1530	*"1570" on bridge of self-winding mechanism.*	28,5mm x 6,47mm	26J	19,800	1965
1580	*Self wind, sweep-seconds, (hack after '72), shock protecting, anti-magnetic, round-shaped.*	1530	*"1580" on bridge of self-winding mechanism.*	28,5mm x 5,75mm	26J	19,800	1963
1600	*Manual wind, no seconds, shock protecting, round-shaped.*	Basic Caliber	*"1600" on hub sinking of balance wheel (and) on train wheel bridge.*	20,8mm x 2,32mm	19J	19,800	1964
1601	*Manual wind, no seconds, shock protecting, round-shaped.*	1600	*"1601" on hub sinking of balance wheel (and) on train wheel bridge.*	20,8mm x 2,32mm	19/ 20J	19,800	1977
1602	*Manual wind, No seconds, Shock protecting, Round-shaped.*	1600	*"1602" on hub sinking of balance wheel (and) on train wheel bridge.*	20,8mm x 2,32mm	20J	21,600	1993
1800	*Manual wind, no seconds, shock protecting, short-oval-shaped.*	Basic Caliber	*"1800" on hub sinking of balance wheel.*	11,7mm x 14,3mm	17J	21,600	1964
2030	*Self wind, sweep-seconds, shock protecting, round-shaped.*	Basic Caliber	*"2030" on bridge for self-winding mechanism.*	20,0mm x 5,40mm	28J	28,800	1970
2035	*Self wind, sweep-seconds, progress-calendar, shock protecting, round-shaped.*	2030	*"2030" on bridge for self-winding mechanism.*	20,0mm x 5,83mm	28J	28,800	1970

ROLEX MOVEMENTS (continued)

Caliber (Size) [Old Ref]	Movement Description	Base Caliber	Engraved Info	Ø Size	# Jewel	Beats per hr	Intro Year
2130	*Self wind, sweep-seconds, (hack stop), shock protecting, round-shaped.*	Basic Caliber	*"2130" on bridge for self-winding mechanism.*	20,0mm x 5,40mm	29J	28,800	1983
2135	*Self wind, sweep-seconds, (hack stop), quick set day-date, shock protecting, round-shaped.*	2130	*"2035" on bridge for self-winding mechanism.*	20,0mm x 5,90mm	29J	28,800	1983
3035	*Self wind, sweep-seconds, (hack stop), quick set calendar, shock protecting, round-shaped.*	Basic Caliber	*"3035" on automatic device bridge.*	28,5mm x 6,35mm	27J	28,800	1977
3055	*Self wind, sweep-seconds, (hack stop), quick set day-date, shock protecting, round-shaped.*	3035	*"3055" on automatic device bridge.*	28,5mm x 7,11mm	27J	28,800	1977
3075	*Self wind, sweep-seconds, (hack stop), quick set calendar, 12/24 hr hand, shock protecting, round-shaped.*	3035	*"3075" on automatic device bridge.*	28,5mm x 6,35mm	27J	28,800	1981
3085	*Self wind, sweep-seconds, (hack stop), quick set calendar, 12/24 hr hand, shock protecting, round-shaped.*	3035	*"3085" on automatic device bridge.*	28,5mm x 7,20mm	27J	28,800	1982
3135	*Self wind, sweep-seconds, (hack stop) quick set calendar, shock protecting, round-shaped.*	Basic Caliber	*"3135" on bridge for self-winding mechanism.*	28,5mm x 6,35mm	31J	28,800	1988

ROLEX MOVEMENTS (continued)

Caliber (Size) [Old Ref]	Movement Description	Base Caliber	Engraved Info	Ø Size	# Jewel	Beats per hr	Intro Year
3155	*Self wind, sweep-seconds, (hack stop) quick set day-date, shock protecting, round-shaped.*	3135	*"3155" on bridge for self-winding mechanism.*	28,5mm x 6,35mm	31J	28,800	1988
3175	*Self wind, sweep-seconds, (hack stop) quick set calendar, 12/24 hr hand, shock protecting, round-shaped.*	3135	*"3175" on bridge for self-winding mechanism.*	28,5mm x 6,35mm	31J	28,800	1988
3185	*Self wind, sweep-seconds, (hack stop) quick set calendar, 12/24 hr hand, shock protecting, round-shaped.*	3135	*"3185" on bridge for self-winding mechanism.*	28,5mm x 6,35mm	31J	28,800	1988
4030	*Self wind, Chronograph, (hack stop) shock protecting, round-shaped, 3-dial, (start, stop & fly back to zero).*	Basic Caliber (Zenith 400)	*"4030" on upper module bridge.*	30mm x 6,55mm	31J	28,800	1989
4130	*Self wind, Chronograph, (hack stop) shock protecting, round-shaped, 3-dial, (start, stop & fly back to zero).*	Basic Caliber	*"4130" on upper module bridge.*	30mm x 6,50mm	44J	28,800	2000
5035	*Electronic Quartz, sweep-seconds, (hack stop), quick set calendar, round-shaped.*	Basic Caliber	*"5035" on upper module bridge.*	29,75mm x 6,35mm	11J	32,768 Hz Quartz	1977
5055	*Electronic Quartz, sweep-seconds, (hack stop), quick set day-date, round-shaped.*	5035	*"5055" on upper module bridge.*	29,75mm x 7,11mm	11J	32,768 Hz Quartz	1977

**Two things about the way we make our watches
that haven't changed since we started.**

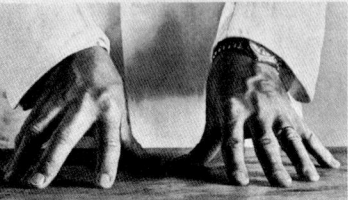

We've introduced a lot of technical innovations into the watchmaking world.

The world's first successful self-winding watch, for instance.

And the world's first officially certified wrist chronometer.

And the world's first watch that truly locked out water, even at great depths. (The famous Rolex Oyster.)

But it's what we *haven't* changed that makes a Rolex a Rolex: The two awesomely skilled hands of proud Swiss watchmakers are still our most valuable asset.

The fact is, we still make each Rolex the Old World way. Slowly. One at a time. By dedicated men who demand perfection.

The Oyster case is a good example of the care that's lavished on each Rolex.

Step 1 sees it hewn from one solid block of stainless steel, or gold, lest it contain any seams that might yield under pressure.

Not until after Step 162 (hand polishing) is it ready to receive the movement.

Now consider the winding crown. It's our own Rolex-patented Twinlock design. The name comes from the way it screws down into the Oyster case (similar to a submarine hatch) to provide a second barrier against dirt and water.

Even the Rolex crystal is exceptional.

Each is meticulously diamond-cut for a micro-perfect match with its case. And ingeniously designed so that it actually seals tighter under pressure. (Deep underwater, for instance.)

What about the movement that receives all this protection?

We call it the Perpetual, which says it all. It's the apex of the watchmaker's art. It's hand-tuned to extraordinary accuracy. And a gravity-powered rotor (invented by Rolex) makes it self-winding.

Then each one is submitted to one of the Swiss Institutes for Official Chronometer Tests for 15 days and nights of demanding trials. Only when it passes is it certified as a chronometer.

Still not satisfied, Rolex' own inspectors spare no mercy in a final barrage of tests.

Not until now is it ready to leave our hands.

The sum of all this pride and patience and craftsmanship is what makes a Rolex unique in all the world.

Which is why a man like Sir Francis Chichester was able to rely on one during his solo voyage around the world.

And why Grand Prix driver Jackie Stewart wouldn't race without one.

And why Rolex is the official timepiece of Pan American World Airways.

Truly, Rolex has earned the recognition it enjoys. And you'll start to share it as soon as you wear one.

**Owning one
is almost as satisfying
as making one.**

♛ **ROLEX**

The Rolex Oyster Day-Date:
a 30-jewel, self-winding chronometer
(with day available in 18 languages) in 18 kt. gold, $1,250.
Also in 18 kt. white gold or platinum.

American Rolex Watch Corporation, 580 Fifth Avenue, New York, N.Y. 10036. Write for free color brochure.

Rhythm, tempo, harmony, measuring and movement.
—Rolex's company motto

ABOVE: Magazine advertisement celebrating the fact that Rolex watches are in fact 'made by hand'. Circa 1971

PART IV

From the Factory to your Wrist...

The Rolex Facilities

In 1905, *Wilsdorf & Davis Ltd.* opened their first offices at 83, Hatton Gardens (London), but shortly thereafter moved to 44, Holborn Viaduct (near Clerkenwell). At this time, *Rebberg* movements were supplied by Jean Aegler's firm in Bienne, Switzerland, and in 1915, Wilsdorf made an agreement with Hermann Aegler to move Rolex's center of operations to his factory.

Early advertisement for Jean Aegler's *Rebberg* movement factory
Fabrication D' Horlogerie, founded in 1878, in Bienne, Switzerland.

In 1919, Wilsdorf moved to Geneva and founded the new headquarters: *Montres Rolex SA*, located at 88, rue de Marche. That same year, Rolex entered into a 3-way partnership with Aegler & Gruen, whereby Rolex would exclusively buy movements from Aegler's firm, now called: *Aegler Incorporated, Manufacturer of Rolex & Gruen Guild A Watches.* Thus the movements were manufactured in Bienne, then sent to Geneva where they were finished before being shipped to the retailer.

The *Aegler SA Rolex Watch Company* factories in Bienne, Switzerland.

Rolex took full advantage of the consistency in quality that a single source (Aegler) afforded them and made incredible advancements over the following years, with respect to wristwatch accuracy. However, the only way this could be maintained was *quality control*, thus, to this day Rolex rarely sources out any of their manufacturing. Instead, Rolex has maintained a strong level of control by staying very "hands on" with the entire manufacturing process.

A rare exception was that of the *Valjoux* movements used in Rolex Chronographs since 1937. In 1988, Rolex replaced the manual wind *Valjoux* with a heavily modified *Zenith* 'El Primero' for the first *Oyster Perpetual Cosmograph Daytona*. Then in 2000, Rolex released their first completely in-house chronograph movement (cal. 4130)—It could now be said that *all* Rolex models featured Rolex-made movements, exclusively.

Around 1930, Gruen sold off their final shares of the 3-way partnership, thus strengthening the remaining partnership between Rolex and Aegler—A partnership which would eventually see Rolex as the primary stock holder. However, while it is now owned by Rolex, the facility is still run by the Aegler-Borer family to this day, but only provides movements to Rolex.

In the 1950s, Rolex began expanding the size of their facilities in Geneva and by the end of the decade, the headquarters was comprised of five buildings and employed 750 workers—while the factories in Bienne employed another 450.

In 1965, the new facility: *Rolex I* was completed. This new modern structure was designed by the architects Julliard & Addor. In 1981, *Rolex III* was completed, with notable technical improvements to some environmental problems, and in 1984, a panoramic lift was added to the main building. In 1995, *Rolex VII* was finally completed which is now home to some 1200 employees.

In what has been called an "internal reorganization", *Montres Rolex SA* was recently renamed as *Rolex SA*, combining both *Montres Rolex SA* and *Rolex Industrie SA*. This industrial consolidation has also led to Rolex's recent acquisition of *Boninchi SA* (in Geneva) which has been Rolex's primary supplier of crowns since 1919. According to Rolex, the company will remain independent (with some 184 employees) and will not become part of the Rolex entity.

Birth of a Rolex

The construction of a Rolex timepiece is a very complex procedure, its case housing over 220 pieces working together, within tolerances measured in microns (thousandths of a millimeter). While the process is aided by means of sophisticated "computers, robots, microscopes and lasers"[43], the actual assembly is meticulously done by hand, then checked and rechecked.[44] Here is a basic explanation of that process:

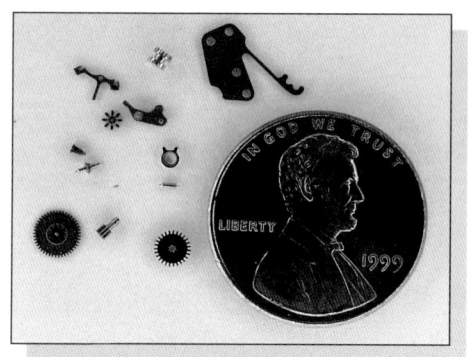

This is an example of the tiny parts used in a wristwatch, some not much wider than a human hair.

The birth of a Rolex watch starts with the **Movement**, which takes over a year to produce. The parts are calibrated and matched by computer and the marriage of some parts is done by laser. "At least 400 operations are performed on the mainplate alone."[43]

The assembly is then tested for accuracy, photo-mechanically (in four positions) for 24-hours and compared with an atomic *überclock*. If the movement deviates by no more than −1 or +5 seconds per day, it is then sent to the COSC for independent chronometer testing. If the movement fails, it is dismantled and rebuilt from scratch. It is important to note that the movement is sent to the COSC, without its *case*, *date* or *automatic winding* mechanisms.

The **Oyster Case** is a work of art in itself. Hewn from a solid ingot of stainless steel, 18kt gold, or platinum, it takes 163 detailed steps to complete the year-long process. Before the movement is even installed, the case (temporarily) receives its crystal, crown and case back (creating a hermetic seal), so it can be pressure-proof tested. A special tank, called a *Mariotte* meter, uses high-tech electronics and vacuum air-pressure to test the watch at its guaranteed depth—if any imperfections are identified, the case is rejected.

Once the movement successfully completes its chronometer testing at the COSC, it is returned to Rolex for final assembly. The **Date** mechanism is installed (if so equipped), then the movement is placed on a base and fitted with its **Dial**, by hand. Next the **Hands** are carefully installed: hour, minute and second, respectively.

Date Wheel

After the Oyster Case passes the pressure-proof test, it is disassembled and the process of housing the movement begins. First, the movement assembly is placed inside the case and it is fitted with the screw down **Winding Crown**. This is a vital link in the Oyster chain, as it helps to maintain the hermetic seal against moisture, dust, etc... The crown is "machined in 35 minutely precise operations."[45]

Winding Crown

With the movement assembly in place, the case receives its **Crystal**. Cut from a laboratory grown, synthetic sapphire, it is then sliced, shaped and polished to perfection. A special **Cyclops Lens** is added (on date models), to magnify the date aperture two and a half times. The crystal is attached to the Oyster assembly with a *zytel* washer and then the bezel is fitted to complete the hermetic seal. It is worth noting that the bezel is merely considered a cosmetic feature and is not necessary to maintain the pressure-proof seal—"the precisely cut threading of the case bottom is enough to guarantee watertightness."[46] Furthermore, the seal of the crystal is so designed that the excessive pressure that builds up when submerged at depth, actually *increases* the effectiveness of the seal.

Finally, the auto-winding **Rotor** mechanism is installed and tested for effectiveness, by a special machine which simulates wrist motion. Next, the assembly is again photo-mechanically tested for accuracy and compared with an atomic *überclock*. If the watch passes this test, then the **Case Back** is screwed shut with a special *blocking tool* creating a pressure-proof seal. The watch is now assembled, but the process is far from complete, as the new assembly is put through another series of 'torture tests'.

Auto-Winding Rotor

Final Pressure-Proof Testing: The completed watch assembly is again tested in the *Mariotte* meter, to guarantee its hermetic seal against moisture, dust, etc… This is the same test that the Oyster case assembly was put through before the movement was installed.

Final Timing Reliability Testing: The watch is yet again photo-mechanically tested for its accuracy and compared with an atomic *überclock*. Upon completion, the watch receives its bracelet and is issued a serial number before being shipped out.

Random Durability Testing: In addition to the tests listed above, watches are chosen at random for testing in a special 'tropical chamber'. "Here they are exposed to a highly corrosive climate of recycled vapor which in four weeks simulates approximately five years of use in an extremely smoggy humidity."[43]

Magazine advertisement celebrating one of the 'torture tests' that Rolex watches have been exposed to.

Superlative Chronometer Officially Certified

Chronometer Certificate Testing Standards

Chronometer 'hang tag'
included with every
Rolex currently sold.

A Chronometer is a highly accurate timepiece, whose precision has been tested and certified by the official Swiss testing stations – the *Contrôle Officiel Suisse des Chronomètres* (C.O.S.C.).

If successful, the institute bestows a rating certificate of chronometer status, thus the inscription 'Superlative Chronometer Officially Certified' means the that watch earned the accolade "especially good results".

On November 15, 1951, the Swiss Horological Federation set forth a mandate, whereas any watch bearing the name *"Chronometer"* on the dial must be accompanied by its *"Bulletin"* (or Certificate).

The rigorous testing lasts 15 days and nights, during which time, the movement (not the entire watch) is testing in five positions and at various temperatures.

Testing Positions		Testing Temperatures	
Days 1 & 2:	Crown left.	**Days 1 thru 10:**	18° Celsius (64° Fahrenheit).
Days 3 & 4:	Crown up.	**Day 11:**	8° Celsius (46° Fahrenheit).
Days 5 & 6:	Crown down.	**Day 12:**	18° Celsius (64° Fahrenheit).
Days 7 & 8:	Face down.	**Day 13:**	38° Celsius (100° Fahrenheit).
Days 9 thru 13:	Face up.	**Days 14 & 15:**	18° Celsius (64° Fahrenheit).
Days 14 & 15:	Crown left.		

Using the positions and temperatures listed above, the following seven tests are performed.
Please Note: If the movement fails to pass any of these tests it is rejected.

Test 1 "Mean Daily Rate": The MDR is described as the difference between the time indicated on the movement (after 24 hours) and the correct time, thus the 'daily error' of the timepiece. This test is performed for 10 days and the movement must fall within the range of –4 to +6 seconds per day.

Test 2 "Mean Variation in Rates": This is described as the difference (or variation) between 2 daily rates in each position. The movement's rate is recorded in five different positions (two horizontal, three vertical) each day for 10 days, thus a total of 50 rates are recorded. This variation in rates can be no more than 2 seconds

Test 3 "Maximum Variation in Rates": This is the maximum variation in daily rates in any one of the 5 positions. The variation can be no more than 5 seconds per day.

Test 4 "Horizontal and Vertical Difference": This is the difference in the average of the rates in the vertical position (measured on the 1st and 2nd days) from the average of the rates in the horizontal position (measured on the 9th and 10th days). The difference must be no more than –6 to +8 seconds.

Test 5 "Greatest Variation in Rates": This is the difference between the greatest individual daily rate and the Mean Daily Rate. The difference must be no more than 10 seconds per day.

Test 6 "Rate Variation Due to Temperature": The movement's rate is recorded at 8 degrees Celsius and again at 38 degrees Celsius. The difference between these rates is then divided by 30. The resulting variation must be no more than 0.6 seconds per day.

Test 7 "Resumption of the Rate": This is calculated by subtracting the MDR of the first two days from the MDR of the last day. The difference must be no more than 5 seconds.

In 2000, the C.O.S.C tested 1,066,938 movements from over 60 watch companies. However, only 1,032,258 received a chronometer certificate. Of those certificates issued, Rolex received a staggering 635,209—comprising 61% of all those issued. Others worth mentioning were: Breitling (148,380), Omega (146,144), Bulgari (21,345), Panerai (19,231) and TAG Heuer (13,270).[47]

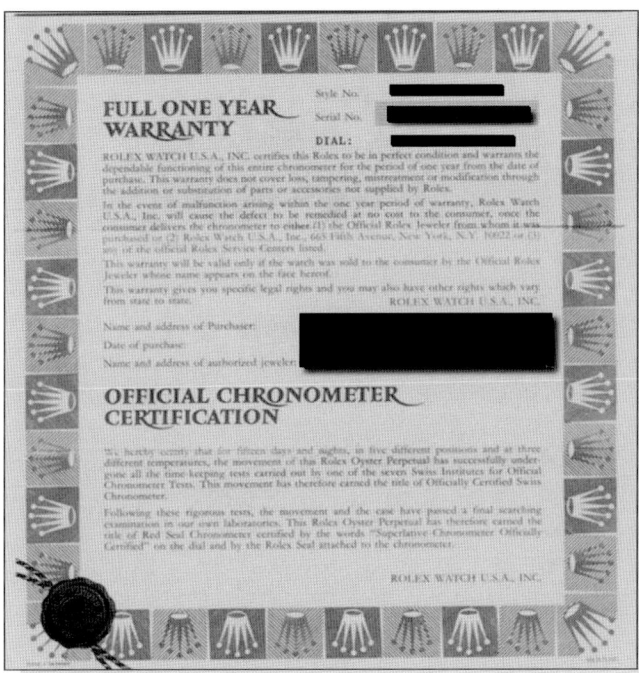

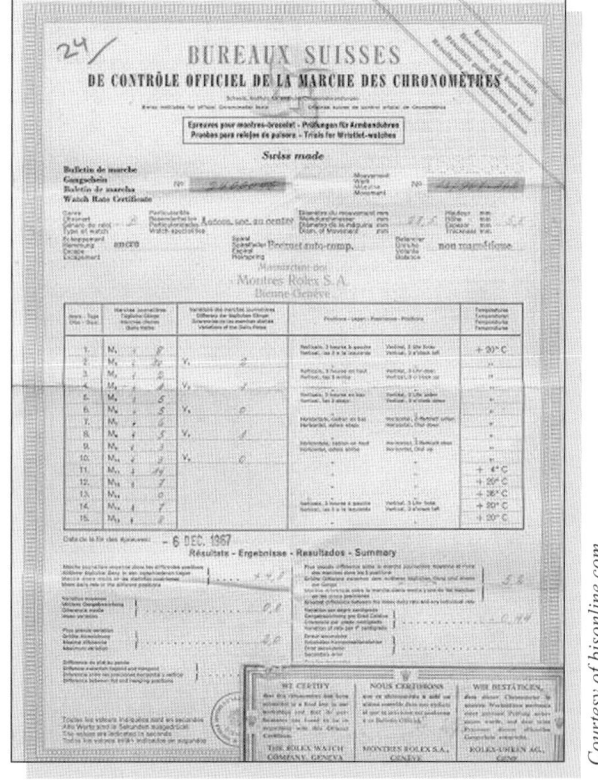

ABOVE: Certificate issued by Rolex explaining the *One Year Warranty*, as well as the *Official Chronometer Certification*.

RIGHT: *Official Chronometer Certificate* issued by the C.O.S.C.

In 1935, the chronometer designation printed on the dial was originally *"Chronomètre"* (French), but was replaced with the English version *"Chronometer"* in 1947. In 1948, this changed to *"Certified Chronometer"* and then in 1949, changed again to *"Officially Certified Chronometer"*. The Current designation *"Superlative Chronometer Officially Certified"* did not appear until 1957.

It is also worth mentioning that Rolex watches in the past that did not receive a chronometer certificate were labeled as *"Precision"* in lieu of *"Chronometer"*.

Basic Operation of the *Winding Crown.*
(for most models)

Crown Position: 1

The crown is screwed down fully. In this position, the watch is completely sealed and is ready to be worn.

Crown Position: 2

Unscrew the crown by turning it in the counterclockwise direction until it just becomes free of the screw threads. In this position (in mechanical models), the watch can be hand wound, by turning the crown in the clockwise direction—In quartz models, this is considered the neutral position.

Crown Position: 3

Pull the crown out to the first notch. In this position, the watch will continue to run normally and the day/date can be set. (on quick set models) Turning the crown counterclockwise will rapidly set the numbered date. (on double-quick set models) Turning the crown clockwise will set the numbered date, and turning the crown counterclockwise will rapidly set the day of the week.

Crown Position: 4

Pull the crown out (fully) to the last notch. In this position, the watch will stop. From here the time (hours and minutes) can be set. Notice the seconds will stop (or hack) allowing the time to be synchronized with another source. By pushing the crown back in (to position 3) will restart the watch.

Basic Operation of the *Elapse Time Bezel*
(Submariner and Sea-Dweller)

Rolex diving watches (i.e. Submariner & Sea-Dweller) feature a *uni-directional* elapse time bezel. The operation of this bezel is as follows:

When starting your dive, set the bezel so that the triangle points at the (current) minute hand position. From this position, the bezel will measure elapsed bottom time (i.e. informing the wearer how long he has been diving). This is done by counting the number of minutes elapsed from the triangle's position.

You will notice that the triangle has a luminous circle to coordinate with the luminous hands and hour markers on the dial. Thus making it easier to read in the darkness of the water's depths.

When beginning your final ascent, again set the bezel so that the triangle points at the (current) minute hand position. This will allow the diver to time their ascent at a slow, safe pace in accordance with standard diving safety procedures.

Submariner bezel positioned with triangle pointing at the minute hand position. This would be the initial position when starting a dive or ascent.

Furthermore, the diver can time safety decompression stops. (e.g. one minute at twenty feet and three minutes at ten feet.) Thus, the bezel is calibrated to individual markers for the first fifteen minutes.

Please note: Since the 1980s, Rolex diving watches have been equipped with a uni-directional (one way), counterclockwise rotating bezel. Thus, protecting the diver from an erroneous (and potentially dangerous) reading when measuring decompression times, since any accidental movement (of the bezel) could only err on the side of safety. This means that an incorrect reading could only indicate to the diver that he has spent 'more' bottom time than he actually has. If the bezel was allowed to move in the opposite direction (clockwise), it would indicate to the diver that he has spent *less* bottom time and thus give the indication of *more* air in reserve than is actually available.

WARNING: All adjustments done while underwater are to the bezel and NOT to the crown. The crown should NEVER be unscrewed when submerged, as this will FLOOD the case.

Basic Operation of the *24-hour Hand & Bezel*
(GMT-Master, GMT-Master II and Explorer II)

GMT-Master II displaying the time 'ten past ten' (AM) Notice the position of the 24-hour hand.

The Rolex GMT models utilize a special 24-hour hand and bezel, allowing the wearer to tell the time in two different time zones. The operation of this feature is as follows:

The *24-hour bezel* is divided into two equal parts which are color coordinated (on some bezels). The time 06:00 to 18:00 (6AM to 6PM) is colored red to represent 'day'. Whereas, 18:00 to 06:00 (6PM to 6AM) is colored blue (or black on some bezels) to represent 'night'.

The *24-hour hand* points to the appropriate 24-hour time represented on the bezel. For example, ten past ten, with the 24-hour hand pointing to the "10" on the red portion of the dial, tells us that it is 10:10 AM. Whereas, if the 24-hour hand was pointing to the "22" in the blue (or black) portion of the dial would indicate 10:10 PM. Thus, the bezel expresses the time in 24 hour "military time".

(GMT-Master): With the bezel in the 'zero' or 'neutral' position, the triangle on the bezel is aligned with the triangle on the dial (i.e. 12 o'clock position). From here, the time reads ten past ten in the morning (as indicated by the 24-hour hand).

Lets say you are in New York (Eastern time zone), and you want to set the 24-hour hand to indicate the time in California (Pacific time zone). Since Pacific time is 3-hours behind Eastern time, it would make it ten past seven in the morning in California. Simply turn the bezel until the number '7' faces the 24-hour hand. Now the hour/minute hands indicate New York time, while the 24-hour hand indicates California time.

(GMT-Master II): In addition to the function listed above, the GMT-Master II has an additional convenience feature. This model allows the regular hour hand to be set to a different time zone without adjusting the 24-hour hand and bezel, or affecting the watch's accuracy. This is done by unscrewing the winding crown to the first notch (position 3). In this position, the watch operates normally and the time does not stop. Now, by *slowly* turning the crown clockwise or counterclockwise will 'jump' the hour hand one hour at a time without affecting the operation of the minute or second hand. Therefore, using the example above, the wearer could simply turn the hour hand back three hours (to ten past seven AM) and thus the watch would indicate the time in California (Eastern time).

Explorer II with 24-hour hand and bezel.

(Explorer II): While the Explorer II does not have the *rotating* bezel like the GMT models, it does have the same 24-hour hand and 'jump' hour feature as the GMT-Master II. Therefore, the operation would be identical to that listed above.

Basic Operation of the *Tachymeter Bezel Scale*
(Cosmograph "Daytona")

The Rolex Cosmograph "Daytona" is basically a chronograph (stop watch) with the aid of a Tachymeter (logarithmic) scale printed around the bezel. The screw down push-buttons (located on either side of the winding crown) are used to start, stop and reset the timer. The Tachymeter scale allows the wearer to calculate two basic timed functions when used in conjunction with the stop watch. These functions are to *Measuring Elapsed Time* & *Calculating Average Speed*, and their explanation is as follows:

Measuring Elapsed Time:

To perform this function you will need to unscrew the push-buttons, so they are in the operational position. By pressing the upper button, the large sweep second hand starts the timing sequence (to within $1/5$ of a second), while two mini-registers on the dial record the elapsed hours and minutes respectively. (Please Note: The third mini-register constantly measures seconds and is not part of the stop watch function.) Press the upper button again and the timing sequence is stopped. Pressing the lower button will reset the large sweep second hand and both mini-registers to zero.

Calculating Average Speed:

This function is performed similarly to *Measuring Elapsed Time*, but you are measuring the time it takes to travel a predetermined distance (such as a mile or kilometer). The only requirement is that the total measured time must fall between 9 seconds to 60 seconds, which is calibrated within the scale 60 to 400 units per hour. Please Note: Earlier chronographs featured 1000, 200 and 300 unit per hour scales, respectively.

Cosmograph 'Daytona'
with Tachymeter scale bezel.

If you were timing a car as it travels around a one mile track, then you would press the upper button to start the timing sequence, then press the upper button again when the car has completed the distance—in this case one lap around the track. Once a time has been established, then you would simply read the Tachymeter scale as it corresponds to the time. For instance, if it took 30 seconds for the car to travel one mile, then the corresponding number on the Tachymeter scale would be 120. Therefore, the car maintained an *Average Speed* of 120 mph.

If you are unable to keep the timed sequence between 9 seconds to 60 seconds, then you can use a different distance and perform a simple calculation. If it took 40 seconds for a bicycle to travel ½ kilometer, then the corresponding number on the Tachymeter scale would be 90. However, since it only traveled ½ kilometer, then the *Average Speed* would be ½ as well which is 45 km/hour.

Now lets say you are measuring the speed of an airplane which traveled 10 miles in 45 seconds. The corresponding number on the Tachymeter scale would be 80. Since the airplane traveled 10 miles, then the *Average Speed* would be 80 mph x10 which is 800 mph.

How to Photograph your Rolex

When photographing your watches (or any close-up photography for that matter), it is important to maintain a good level of lighting—natural light is best, but artificial light can be used if done correctly.

The biggest cause of poor quality photos is low light or shadows, thus preventing a clear focus. (i.e. When you zoom into the subject the camera blocks out your light source.) A simple way to overcome this is to use a *light magnifier*—a good inexpensive example is a frosted (or milk glass) light fixture. You don't want it to be totally clear, nor do you want it painted, or any patterns on the glass. However, scalloped sides (as seen in the example on the right) seem to work fine. These can be purchased from a home improvement store for around $5-$10.

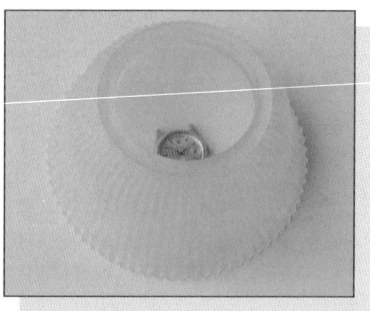

Glass *light fixture* used as a light magnifier.

The theory behind this is as follows: A light fixture normally takes the light from *inside* the fixture (i.e. the light bulb) and magnifies it *outward*. However, by placing the light source *outside* the fixture, it will magnify the light *into* the fixture, thus illuminating your subject.

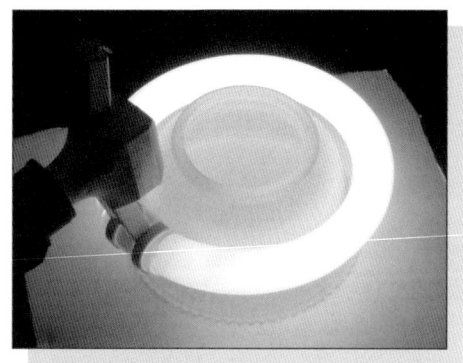

Circular *fluorescent tube* used as an external light source when doing close-up photography.

These fixtures can be used outdoors (thus utilizing the natural ambient light), however, you want to take your pictures around "noon time" so the sun is directly overhead and thereby reduces shadows cast from angled light. If you use the fixture indoors you will need to have multiple light sources *around* the fixture. A great way to improvise is with a circular fluorescent tube*. These can also be purchased for around $5-$10, and will fit a standard light bulb socket—making it convenient to attach to a portable work light.

If you have a glass top table, you can use an additional light source *under* the fixture, just make sure to place a *semi-opaque* panel between the bottom light source and the subject—a few sheets of paper will suffice.

Place your subject *inside* the fixture, and then place the circular light source *around* the fixture. Now insert your camera's lens into the top opening. From here you will be able to focus onto the subject (i.e. the watch dial) very closely. The digital camera on the right is a *Sony Mavica MVC-FD95* (priced around $800) which has been outfitted with a macro (close-up) lens attachment (priced around $50) allowing you to focus at around one inch from the subject.

It is worth mentioning that (for advertising purposes) Rolex watches are photographed in the following position: **Time** set at "10:10:31", with the **Day** at "Monday", and the **Date** at "28". Adjustable **Bezels** are set at the "12 o'clock" (or neutral) position, with **24-Hour hands** set at "10AM", and on Daytonas, the **Tachymeter hand** is set at "54" seconds.

Sony Mavica MVC-FD95 digital camera fitted with a special macro (close-up) lens.

* If using a 'fluorescent light', it may be necessary to use a *filter* on traditional cameras, or adjust the *white balance* on digital cameras.

Basic Care and Cleaning for your Rolex

"Winding Your Watch"

Occasionally, if not worn for a few days, you may find that your watch needs winding. This of course is due to the fact that a perpetual (or self-winding) watch will only hold about 48 hours of reserve power (on average) before it runs dead. In this event, you should not 'shake' the watch to get it going again. Simply unscrew the crown (to position 2) and wind it about 30 to 40 times, then screw the crown back down. (*Please Note: You should never try to wind a watch while it is on your wrist.*)

Don't worry about 'over-winding' the watch. Rolex movements have a protection built-in that will not allow them to be over-wound. Again, if the watch does not start running immediately after you wind it—do not shake it. Sometimes, the movement just needs a little coaxing to get started. While holding the watch in your hand, gently rotate your wrist, allowing the watch to rotate as well. This will cause the rotor inside to make a revolution and should 'kick start' the watch. In the event that the watch still won't run, you should let the watch set for a few minutes, as it will often start running on its own.

"Cleaning Your Clock"

From time to time your watch may require a cleaning, due to dirt, grime and body oils accumulating in the cracks and crevices. It is also recommended to rinse the watch with fresh water (shortly) after taking a salt water swim.

A good cleaning is a simple procedure, but there are a few precautions that should be followed.

1: Check to make sure the winding crown is securely screwed onto the case, to ensure a tight seal.
2: Wash your hands to remove any grime or body oils.
3: Rinse off the watch with lukewarm water (not too hot).
4: Fill a bowl with lukewarm water and a mild soap—avoid using anything containing ammonia.
5: Using your fingers, apply the soapy water all over the watch.
6: Now, using a soft bristled brush (an old toothbrush works well) gently scrub clean the watch.

Give special attention to the areas around the cyclops (on the crystal) and between the links (on the bracelet), as they tend to collect an excessive amount of dirt and grime.

7: Periodically submerge the brush and/or watch in the bowl of soapy water.
8: After sufficient cleaning, rinse the watch with lukewarm water.
9: Using a clean, soft cotton towel, blot the watch dry.
10: Blow through the sides of the bracelet to remove excess water between the links.
11: Finally, using the towel, dry remaining water from the watch.

Servicing for your Rolex

Every Rolex is manufactured and tested to the most stringent of levels. However, like a finely tuned automobile, it may require periodic servicing or "scheduled maintenance" over the life of the watch. Unfortunately, most people don't have their watches serviced until they experience a problem—thus, "if it ain't broke don't fix it." This can be an expensive philosophy, as the watch only bears a one-year warranty. Therefore, the chances of the watch breaking down during the warranty period is very unlikely.

Probably the biggest cause of watch malfunctions results from neglect. This often comes from the lubricants coagulating (or hardening) and thus causing friction within the movement's gears—just imagine running your car on the same oil for 5 years! Over time, this friction can cause excessive wear to the parts and will eventually result in damage to the movement. Remember, these parts are so tiny they function within tolerances measured in microns (thousandths of a millimeter).

Therefore, the best recommendation for keeping your watch in proper running order is to wear the watch regularly. By wearing the watch it will keep a constant flow of the lubricants, thereby reducing the possibility of coagulation.

Of course conditions may arise which make it impossible to wear the watch everyday—especially if you are lucky enough to own more than one! In this case, I recommend winding the watch at least once per week. The reserve power should keep the watch running for approximately 40 hours, so the more often you wind it the better. To aid in this process, some companies manufacture special "winding boxes" which will actually keep your watches constantly wound. The designs vary, but the one common factor they share is the price, starting around $200-$500 on average.

With this being said, Rolex recommends the watch to be cleaned and oiled every five years (depending on the wearer's habits) by an Official Rolex Jeweler. In some cases, a complete overhaul (or refurbishment) is needed. The following is a brief explanation of that process, as performed by one of the Rolex Service Centers:

Visual Identification Inspection: First the watch's reference and serial numbers are recorded and checked against a database of reported stolen Rolex watches. Furthermore, the watch is visually inspected for potential counterfeit parts. If the watch is found to be stolen, then it is returned to the proper owner. In the event that the watch (or parts of the watch) are found to be counterfeit, then the watch (or counterfeit parts) are confiscated and are not returned to the owner.

Please Note: If aftermarket parts are detected, you may be required to replace the parts with genuine-Rolex parts before having the watch serviced. This is due to the inferior quality of non-genuine Rolex parts, which may not perform properly.

Visual Diagnosis Inspection: The technician then inspects the appearance and operation of the watch, noting any errors or problems to be corrected during servicing.

Timekeeping Diagnosis: The watch is tested for accuracy, photo-mechanically (in four positions) for 24-hours and compared with an atomic *überclock*. The results are then recorded, to be corrected during servicing.

Servicing: With the diagnosis complete, the watch is ready to be serviced. The movement is completely disassembled, with every part being inspected and cleaned thoroughly. A special solution is used that not only dissolves dirt, but also emulsifies congealed lubricants. All worn or damaged parts and seals are replaced. The winding crown and case tube are given special attention and replaced if necessary.

Clean and Polish: The Oyster case and bracelet are (ultrasonically) cleaned and hand-polished. At this time, the bracelet receives repairs as needed.

Pressure-Proof Test: Before the movement is reinstalled, the Oyster case is pressure-proof tested in a special tank called a *Mariotte* meter, which uses high-tech electronics and vacuum air-pressure to test the watch at its guaranteed depth.

Timekeeping Test: The watch is now reassembled, re-oiled (with five different types of lubricants) and then re-tested for timekeeping accuracy, photo-mechanically (in four positions) for 24-hours and compared with an atomic *überclock* (much the same as when it was originally manufactured). If necessary, micro-adjustments are then made to the balance wheel with a special *Microstella* tool.

Final Pressure-Proof Test: With the watch reassembled, it is again pressure-proof tested in the special *Mariotte* meter vacuum tank.

Final Quality Control: Once the watch has been repaired and tested, it is again inspected by a technician (by hand) for any possible errors or problems before it is returned to the customer.

One Year Warranty: After receiving a complete overhaul (by an Official Rolex Jeweler), the watch is reissued a full one-year warranty, as it was when it was originally manufactured! This warranty is honored at any of the worldwide Rolex service locations. A list of these locations is printed on the following pages).

In addition to the servicing listed above, Rolex recommends testing the watch every eighteen months to ensure its pressure-proof integrity—especially if the watch is used for diving.

Estimated Service Prices from 'Independent' (non-Rolex) Service Centers:

Complete Overhaul

Rolex Automatic:	$125-$250
Rolex Automatic (Date):	$150-$350
Rolex Automatic (Day-Date):	$175-$400

Partial Service

Dial Refinishing:	$30-$50 (and up)
Crown Replacement:	$15-$30 (and up)
Stem Replacement:	$15-$30 (and up)
Crystal Replacement (Plastic):	$20-$30 (and up)
Crystal Replacement (Mineral):	$25-$35 (and up)

Please Note: Prices listed are for *labor only* and do not include parts—Vintage models may be higher.

Rolex International Service Centers

Bangkok: The Rolex Centre, S.A.B. (Thailand) Ltd.,
89/9, Wireless Road, Lumpini, Patumwan, Bangkok 10330, Thailand.
Tel. + 66 2 650 91 18 **Fax**: + 66 2 651 49 79

Beverly Hills: Rolex Watch Service Center (California) Inc.,
9420 Wilshire Blvd., Beverly Hills, California 90212, United States.
Tel. + 1 310 271 6200 **Fax**: + 1 310 271 6250

Brussels: Montres Rolex Bénélux S.A., 250,
Avenue Louise 250, Bt 101, 1050 Bruxelles 1, Belgium.
Tel. + 32 2 648 58 90 **Fax**: + 32 2 640 17 19

Buenos Aires: Relojes Rolex Argentina S.A.I.,
Suipacha 1111, piso 24, C1008AAW Buenos Aires, Argentina.
Tel. + 54 11 4 312 90 56 **Fax**: + 54 11 4 312 90 59

Caracas: Rolex de Venezuela, C.A., Apartado Postal 6617, Torre Las Mercedes, Piso 5,
Ciudad Comercial Tamanaco, Chuao, Caracas 1010-A, Venezuela.
Tel. + 58 212 991 0666 **Fax**: + 58 212 992 7289

Cologne: Rolex-Deutchland GMBH, Dompropst-Ketzer-Str. 1-9,
50667 Köln, Deutchland, Germany
Tel. + 49 221 16 500 **Fax**: + 49 221 1650 580

Dallas: Rolex Watch Service Corp.,
Rolex Building, 2651 North Harwood, Dallas, Texas 75201, United States.
Tel. + 1 214 871 0500 **Fax**: + 1 214 871 2767

Geneva: The Rolex Watch Co. Ltd.,
3-7 rue François-Dussaud, CH-1211 Genève 24, Switzerland.
Tel. + 41-22 308 22 00 **Fax**: 41-22 300 22 55`

Hong Kong: Rolex (Hong Kong) Ltd.,
G.P.O. Box 4123, 14/F, Jardine House, Hong Kong, Hong Kong.
Tel. + 852 2 525 61 56 **Fax**: + 852 2 810 69 64

Johannesburg: Rolex Watch Company, (S.A.) (Pty) Ltd.,
PO Box 786635, Sandton 2196, Rep. of South Africa.
Tel. + 27 11 784 92 30 **Fax**: + 27 11 784 07 18

Kuala Lumpur: The Rolex Centre, Ground Floor, Bangunan Arab-
Malaysian, 55 Jalan Raja Chulan, 50200 Kuala Lumpur, Malaysia.
Tel. +60 32 072 27 09 **Fax**. + 60 32 072 31 12

London: The Rolex Watch Company Ltd.,
19 St. James's Square, London SW1Y 4JE, United Kingdom.
Tel. + 44 207 024 7300 **Fax**: + 44 207 024 7317

Madrid: Relojes Rolex de España S.A.,
Serrano 45, 5ª Planta, 28001 Madrid, Spain.
Tel. + 34 91 426 49 00 **Fax**: + 34 91 435 41 99

Manila: Rolex Centre Phil. Limited, Corinthian Plaza, G/F,
121 Paseo de Roxas, Makati City, Metro Manila 3117, The Philippines.
Tel. + 632 811 3029 **Fax**: + 632 811 3030

Melbourne: Rolex Watch Australia Pty Ltd.,
70 Collins Street, Melbourne Vic. 3000, Australia.
Tel. + 61 3 9654 39 88 **Fax**: + 61 3 9650 44 99

Mexico City: Relojes Rolex de México S.A., Paseo de la Reforma 300,
15.° Piso, Col. Juarez, Del. Cuauhtemoc, 06600 Mexico, D.F., Mexico.
Tel. + 52 5 533 57 50 **Fax**: + 52 5 208 08 89

Milan: Rolex Italia S.p.A.,
Via Romagnosi, 1, 20121 Milano, Italy.
Tel. + 39 02 88 00 00 1 **Fax**: + 39 02 72 00 21 41

Mumbai: Rolex Watch Co. Pvt Ltd., N.M. Wadia Building, 1st Floor,
123, Mahatma Gandhi Road, 400 023 Mumbai/India.
Tel. + 91 22 261 78 46 **Fax**: + 91 22 363 03 25

New York (US Headquarters): Rolex Watch U.S.A. Inc.,
Rolex Building, 665 Fifth Avenue, N.Y. 10022, United States.
Tel. + 1 212 758 77 00 **Fax**: + 1 212 371 03 71

Paris: Rolex France,
3, Avenue Ruysdaël, 75008, Paris, Francis.
Tel. + 33 1 44 29 01 50 **Fax**: + 33 1 44 29 01 55

Sao Paulo: Relógios Rolex Ltda.,
Avenue Paulista, 2006, Andar 14, 01310-200 São Paulo, Brazil.
Tel. + 55 11 287 45 33 **Fax**: + 55 11 285 23 71

Singapore: Rolex Singapore Private Limited,
The Rolex Centre, 302 Orchard Road, 01-01 Tong Building, Singapore 238 862.
Tel. + 65 6 737 90 33 **Fax**: + 65 6 235 01 83

Taipei: Rolex Centre Ltd., Taiwan Branch,
105, Tun Hwa South Road, Section 2 Taipei - Taiwan.
Tel. + 886 2 2709 88 99 **Fax**: + 886 2 2709 88 00

Tokyo: Rolex (Japan) Limited, Yusen Building,
2-3-2 Marunouchi, C.P.O. 721, Chiyoda-ku, Tokyo 100-8345, Japan.
Tel. + 81 3 32 16 56 71 **Fax**: + 81 3 32 13 83 28

Toronto: Rolex Canada Limited, Rolex Building,
50, St. Clair Avenue West, Toronto, Ontario M4V 3B7, Canada.
Tel. + 1 416 968 11 00 **Fax**: + 1 416 968 23 15

---

[43] Quoted from *Talking Points*, by The Rolex Watch Company.
[44] The year-long process of creating a single Rolex wristwatch, requires the services of over 200 craftsmen and technicians.
[45] Quoted from *Oyster Service Booklet*, by The Rolex Watch Company.
[46] Quoted from *Time in Gold, Wristwatches*, by Viola & Brunner.
[47] Source: *Federation of the Swiss Watch Industry*. http://www.fhs.ch

There is no such thing as absolute value in this world.
You can only estimate what a thing is worth to you.
—Charles Dudley Warner

PRICE LIST

Wholesale & Suggested Retail

August 15, 2001

How To Use The ROLEX Price List Appendix:

The watches are listed in numeric order by their *Case Reference Number*. The prices listed include: *Suggested Retail* (what a NEW Rolex should list for from an Authorized Rolex Dealer), and *Wholesale* (what an Authorized Rolex Dealer would pay for the NEW watch from Rolex.) You will notice from these prices that Rolex watches have a mark-up of around 40-42%

PLEASE NOTE: Rolex does not sell watches directly to the general public. The only way to purchase at wholesale is to be an Authorized Rolex Dealer. Buying a Rolex is not like buying a car (although it can be just as expensive), that is to say Rolex dealers do not sell at or near "invoice." In fact, it is quite common for high demand Rolex models to sell ABOVE retail during busy seasons (i.e. Christmas, Fathers Day, etc...)

Also, as stated on Rolex's website: **"Genuine Rolex products are sold through Official Rolex Jewelers, and are not available on the Internet."**

Yes, you read that right—Rolex does not allow their dealers to sell NEW Rolex watches over the Internet. This means if you're purchasing a new Rolex from a dealer via the Internet, then they're not an Authorized Rolex Dealer, and the watch you're buying is probably what is called *gray market* goods - Please Note: This does NOT mean the watch is fake, stolen or refurbished.

"Gray market" simply means the dealer did not get it directly from Rolex. It was probably purchased through an authorized Rolex dealer who was either going out of business, or simply ordered a large quantity of watches with the intention of selling them to a non-dealer for this very reason. It is important to note that if you purchase gray market, Rolex may not cover the watch under its factory warranty. This is due to the fact that warranty papers must be completed by the dealer at the time of retail purchase. In this event, you want to make sure the seller is willing to warranty the watch themselves.

The *Wholesale Price* section is included for INFORMATION PURPOSES ONLY, and to give someone a "general" idea as to the value a Rolex *may* keep in the secondary market after being just a few years old. (e.g. A Rolex in good condition can maintain a value greater than the "wholesale" price listed even after it is 3-4 years old.) **This is not written in stone**, however, it will give you a good starting range when determining the value of late model Rolex watches—this is due to the fact that Rolex has one of the highest resale values of any watch line.

ROLEX OYSTER WATCHES

Style	Description	Suggested Retail Price	Wholesale
14000	**Air King Oyster Perpetual**, ∅ 34mm, stainless steel, polished bezel, 27 jewel movement, synthetic sapphire crystal, with Oyster bracelet 78350......	2,775.00	1,631.00
14010	**Air King Oyster Perpetual**, ∅ 34mm, stainless steel, finely engine-turned bezel, 27 jewel movement, synthetic sapphire crystal, with Oyster bracelet 78350......	2,825.00	1,661.00
14060	**Submariner Oyster Perpetual**, ∅ 40mm, stainless steel, pressure-proof to 1,000 feet, Special time-lapse bezel, 27 jewel movement, synthetic sapphire crystal, with special fliplock clasp and extension link Oyster bracelet 93150......	3,250.00	1,911.00
14203	**Oyster Perpetual**, ∅ 34mm, stainless steel case, 18kt. yellow gold, polished bezel, 27 jewel chronometer movement, synthetic sapphire crystal, with Oyster bracelet 78353......	4,200.00	2,471.00
14208	**Oyster Perpetual**, ∅ 34mm, 18kt. yellow gold, polished bezel, 27 jewel chronometer movement, synthetic sapphire crystal, with Oyster bracelet 7205/8......	12,300.00	7,311.00
14233	**Oyster Perpetual**, ∅ 34mm, stainless steel case, 18kt. yellow gold, fluted bezel, 27 jewel chronometer movement, synthetic sapphire crystal, with Oyster bracelet 78353......	4,250.00	2,501.00
14238	**Oyster Perpetual**, ∅ 34mm, 18kt. yellow gold, fluted bezel, 27 jewel chronometer movement, synthetic sapphire crystal, with Jubilee bracelet 6311/8......	13,950.00	8,291.00
	with Oyster bracelet 7205/8......	12,350.00	7,341.00
14270	**Explorer Oyster Perpetual**, ∅ 36mm, stainless steel, polished bezel, 27 jewel chronometer movement, synthetic sapphire crystal, with special Oysterlock bracelet 78790......	3,200.00	1,881.00
15200	**Oyster Perpetual Date**, ∅ 34mm, stainless steel, polished bezel, 31 jewel chronometer movement, synthetic sapphire crystal, with Oyster bracelet 78350......	3,100.00	1,821.00
15203	**Oyster Perpetual Date**, ∅ 34mm, stainless steel case, 18kt. yellow gold, polished bezel, 31 jewel chronometer movement, synthetic sapphire crystal, with Oyster bracelet 78353......	4,650.00	2,741.00
	with 10 brilliants set on Roman dial and Oyster bracelet 78353......	6,100.00	3,591.00
15210	**Oyster Perpetual Date**, ∅ 34mm, stainless steel, finely engine-turned bezel, 31 jewel chronometer movement, synthetic sapphire crystal, with Oyster bracelet 78350......	3,150.00	1,851.00
15223	**Oyster Perpetual Date**, ∅ 34mm, stainless case, 18kt. yellow gold engine-turned bezel, 31 jewel chronometer movement, synthetic sapphire crystal, with Oyster bracelet 78353......	4,700.00	2,761.00
	with 10 brilliants set on Roman dial and Oyster bracelet 78353......	6,150.00	3,611.00
15238	**Oyster Perpetual Date**, ∅ 34mm, 18kt. yellow gold, fluted bezel, 31 jewel chronometer movement, synthetic sapphire crystal, with Oyster bracelet 7205/8......	12,850.00	7,641.00
	with Jubilee bracelet 6311/8......	14,450.00	8,591.00
	with 10 brilliants set on Roman dial and Oyster bracelet 7205/8......	14,300.00	8,491.00
16200	**Oyster Perpetual Datejust**, ∅ 36mm, stainless steel, polished bezel, 31 jewel chronometer movement, synthetic sapphire crystal, with Oyster bracelet 78360......	3,200.00	1,881.00
	with Jubilee bracelet 62510......	3,300.00	1,941.00

ROLEX OYSTER WATCHES

Style	Description	Suggested Retail Price	Wholesale
16248	**Oyster Perpetual Datejust**, ∅ 36mm, 18kt. yellow gold, bark finish bezel, 31 jewel chronometer movement, synthetic sapphire crystal,		
	with bark finish Jubilee bracelet 8210/8..	14,850.00	8,821.00
	with 10 brilliants set on dial and bark finish Jubilee bracelet 8210/8............................	16,300.00	9,681.00
	Refer to model 16238 for a complete listing of available additional cost bezels.		
16263	**Oyster Perpetual Datejust**, ∅ 36mm, stainless steel case, special 18kt. yellow gold "turn-o-graph" bezel, 31 jewel chronometer movement, synthetic sapphire crystal,		
	with Jubilee bracelet 62523...	5,900.00	3,471.00
	with Oyster bracelet 78363...	5,600.00	3,291.00
	With 10 brilliants set on dial and Jubilee bracelet 62523....................................	7,350.00	4,321.00
16264	**Oyster Perpetual Datejust**, ∅ 36mm, stainless steel case, special 18kt. white gold "turn-o-graph" bezel, 31 jewel chronometer movement, synthetic sapphire crystal,		
	with Oyster bracelet 78360...	4,200.00	2,471.00
	with Jubilee bracelet 62510...	4,300.00	2,521.00
	With 10 brilliants set on dial and Jubilee bracelet 62510....................................	5,650.00	3,321.00
16518	**Daytona Oyster Perpetual Cosmograph**, ∅ 40mm, 18kt. yellow gold, tachometer engraving on bezel, special screw-down push buttons, 31 jewel chronometer movement, synthetic sapphire crystal,		
	with 18kt. yellow gold deployable fliplock clasp on brown strap............................	14,550.00	8,641.00
	with 8 brilliants set on dial and 18kt. yellow gold deployable fliplock clasp on strap.........	15,800.00	9,391.00
	with mother-of-pearl Arabic dial and 18kt. yellow gold deployable fliplock clasp on strap..	16,250.00	9,651.00
	with mother-of-pearl Serti dial and 18kt. yellow gold deployable fliplock clasp on strap....	17,550.00	10,421.00
16519	**Daytona Oyster Perpetual Cosmograph**, ∅ 40mm, 18kt. white gold, tachometer engraving on bezel, special screw-down push buttons, 31 jewel chronometer movement, synthetic sapphire crystal,		
	with 18kt. white gold deployable fliplock clasp on brown strap............................	14,550.00	8,641.00
	with 8 brilliants set on dial and 18kt. white gold deployable fliplock clasp on strap..........	15,800.00	9,391.00
	with mother-of-pearl Arabic dial and 18kt. white gold deployable fliplock clasp on strap...	16,250.00	9,651.00
	with mother-of-pearl Serti dial and 18kt. white gold deployable fliplock clasp on strap......	17,550.00	10,421.00
	with 8 brilliants set on semi-precious stone dial (sodalite) and 18kt. white gold, deployable fliplock clasp on blue strap...	18,800.00	11,171.00
16520	**Daytona Oyster Perpetual Cosmograph**, ∅ 40mm, stainless steel, tachometer engraving on bezel, special screw-down push buttons, 31 jewel chronometer movement, synthetic sapphire crystal,		
	with special Oysterlock bracelet 78390..	5,500.00	3,231.00
16523	**Daytona Oyster Perpetual Cosmograph**, ∅ 40mm, stainless steel case, tachometer engraving on 18kt. yellow gold bezel, special screw-down push buttons, 31 jewel chronometer movement, synthetic sapphire crystal,		
	with special Oysterlock bracelet 78393..	9,650.00	5,681.00
	with 8 brilliants set on dial and special Oysterlock bracelet 78393.........................	9,950.00	5,861.00
16528	**Daytona Oyster Perpetual Cosmograph**, ∅ 40mm, 18kt. yellow gold, tachometer engraving on bezel, special screw-down push buttons, 31 jewel chronometer movement, synthetic sapphire crystal,		
	with special Oysterlock bracelet 78398..	20,450.00	12,151.00
	with 8 brilliants set on dial and special Oysterlock bracelet 78398.........................	21,700.00	12,891.00
	with mother-of-pearl Arabic dial and special Oysterlock bracelet 78398....................	22,150.00	13,161.00
	with mother-of-pearl Serti dial and special Oysterlock bracelet 78398.....................	23,450.00	13,931.00

ROLEX OYSTER WATCHES

Style	Description	Suggested Retail Price	Wholesale
16568	**Daytona Oyster Perpetual Cosmograph**, ∅ 40mm, 18kt. yellow gold, bezel set with 24 baguette diamonds, 8 brilliants set on dial, screw-down push buttons, 31 jewel chronometer movement, synthetic sapphire crystal, with special Oysterlock bracelet 78398..	67,500.00	40,101.00
	with mother-of-pearl Arabic dial and special Oysterlock bracelet 78398....................	67,950.00	40,371.00
16570	**Explorer II Oyster Perpetual Date**, ∅ 40mm, stainless steel, 24-hour bezel and hand, independently adjustable 12-hour hand, 31 jewel chronometer movement, synthetic sapphire crystal, with special Oysterlock bracelet 78790..	3,800.00	2,231.00
16588P	**Daytona Oyster Perpetual Cosmograph**, ∅ 40mm, 18kt. yellow gold, bezel set with 24 baguette pink sapphires, "Pave Extra Large" diamond dial set with 8 rubies, screw-down push buttons, 31 jewel chronometer movement, synthetic sapphire crystal, with 18kt. yellow gold deployable fliplock clasp on pink strap................................	73,750.00	43,821.00
16589	**Daytona Oyster Perpetual Cosmograph**, ∅ 40mm, 18kt. white gold, bezel set with 24 baguette diamonds, 8 brilliants set on dial, special screw-down push buttons, 31 jewel chronometer movement, synthetic sapphire crystal, with 18kt. white gold deployable fliplock clasp on strap....................................	61,250.00	36,401.00
16589R	**Daytona Oyster Perpetual Cosmograph**, ∅ 40mm, 18kt. white gold, bezel set with 24 baguette rubies, "Pave Extra Large" diamond dial set with 8 rubies, screw-down push buttons, 31 jewel chronometer movement, synthetic sapphire crystal, with 18kt. white gold deployable fliplock clasp on red strap..................................	76,000.00	45,161.00
	with 8 brilliants set on semi-precious stone dial (grossular) and 18kt. white gold deployable fliplock clasp on red strap..	67,250.00	39,961.00
16589S	**Daytona Oyster Perpetual Cosmograph**, ∅ 40mm, 18kt. white gold, bezel set with 24 baguette sky-blue sapphires, "Pave Extra Large" diamond dial set with 8 sapphires, screw-down push buttons, 31 jewel chronometer movement, synthetic sapphire crystal, with 18kt. white gold deployable fliplock clasp on blue strap..................................	67,750.00	40,261.00
	with 8 brilliants set on semi-precious stone dial (sodalite) and 18kt. white gold deployable fliplock clasp on blue strap..	59,000.00	35,061.00
16598E	**Daytona Oyster Perpetual Cosmograph**, ∅ 40mm, 18kt. yellow gold, bezel set with 36 baguette emeralds, flash-fit set with 48 brilliants, "Pave Extra Large" diamond dial set with 8 emeralds, special screw-down push buttons, 31 jewel chronometer movement, synthetic sapphire crystal, with 18kt. yellow gold deployable fliplock clasp on green strap..............................	102,000.00	60,611.00
16599S	**Daytona Oyster Perpetual Cosmograph**, ∅ 40mm, 18kt. white gold, bezel set with 36 baguette sapphires, flash-fit set with 48 brilliants, "Pave Extra Large" diamond dial set with 8 sapphires, special screw-down push buttons, 31 jewel chronometer movement, synthetic sapphire crystal, with 18kt. white gold deployable fliplock clasp on blue strap..................................	85,000.00	50,501.00
	with 8 brilliants set on semi-precious stone dial (sodalite) and 18kt. white gold deployable fliplock clasp on blue strap..	76,250.00	45,301.00
16600	**Sea-Dweller 4000 Oyster Perpetual Date**, ∅ 40mm, stainless steel, pressure-proof to 4,000 ft, helium escape valve, special time-lapse bezel, 31 jewel chronometer movement, synthetic sapphire crystal, with tool kit and special fliplock clasp and interchangeable extension links Oyster bracelet 93160....................................	4,000.00	2,351.00
16610	**Submariner Oyster Perpetual Date**, ∅ 40mm, stainless steel, pressure-proof to 1,000 ft, special time-lapse bezel, 31 jewel chronometer movement, synthetic sapphire crystal, with special fliplock clasp and extension link Oyster bracelet 93250..........................	3,875.00	2,271.00

ROLEX OYSTER WATCHES

Style	Description	Suggested Retail Price	Wholesale
16613	**Submariner Oyster Perpetual Date**, ∅ 40mm, stainless steel, pressure-proof to 1,000 ft, special 18kt. yellow gold time-lapse bezel, 31 jewel chronometer movement, synthetic sapphire crystal,		
	with special fliplock clasp and extension link Oyster bracelet 93253............................	6,000.00	3,521.00
	with champagne or steel dial set with 8 brilliants, 1 triangular and 2 baguette sapphires and special fliplock clasp and extension link Oyster bracelet 93253............................	8,050.00	4,751.00
16618	**Submariner Oyster Perpetual Date**, ∅ 40mm, 18kt. yellow gold, pressure-proof 1,000ft, special time-lapse bezel, 31 jewel chronometer movement, synthetic sapphire crystal,		
	with special fliplock clasp and extension link Oyster bracelet 92908............................	19,250.00	11,441.00
	with champagne dial set with 8 brilliants, 1 triangular and 2 baguette sapphires and special fliplock clasp and extension link Oyster bracelet 92908............................	21,400.00	12,721.00
16622	**Yacht-Master Oyster Perpetual Date**, ∅ 40mm, stainless steel case, special platinum time-lapse bezel, platinum dial, 31 jewel chronometer movement, synthetic sapphire crystal,		
	with special Oysterlock bracelet 78760............................	6,800.00	4,001.00
16628	**Yacht-Master Oyster Perpetual Date**, ∅ 40mm, 18kt. yellow gold, time-lapse bezel, 31 jewel chronometer movement, synthetic sapphire crystal,		
	with special Oysterlock bracelet 78768............................	19,750.00	11,731.00
	with mother-of-pearl dial set with 8 brilliants, 1 triangular and 2 baguette sapphires and special Oysterlock bracelet 78768............................	24,950.00	14,821.00
	with mother-of-pearl dial set with 8 round, 1 triangular and 2 baguette rubies and special Oysterlock bracelet 78768............................	25,650.00	15,241.00
16700	**GMT-Master Oyster Perpetual Date**, ∅ 40mm, stainless steel, 24-hour bezel and hand, 31 jewel chronometer movement, synthetic sapphire crystal,		
	with special Oysterlock bracelet 78790............................	3,375.00	1,981.00
16710	**GMT-MasterII Oyster Perpetual Date**, ∅ 40mm, stainless steel, special 24-hour bezel and hand, independently adjustable 12-hour hand, 31 jewel chronometer movement, synthetic sapphire crystal,		
	with special Oysterlock bracelet 78790............................	3,875.00	2,271.00
16713	**GMT-MasterII Oyster Perpetual Date**, ∅ 40mm, stainless steel, special 24-hour bezel and hand, 18kt. yellow gold bezel, independently adjustable 12-hour hand, 31 jewel chronometer movement, synthetic sapphire crystal,		
	with special Oysterlock bracelet 78793............................	6,000.00	3,521.00
	with Jubilee bracelet 62523............................	5,925.00	3,481.00
	with champagne or steel dial set with 8 brilliants, 1 triangular and 2 baguette rubies and Jubilee bracelet 62523............................	9,575.00	5,661.00
16718	**GMT-MasterII Oyster Perpetual Date**, ∅ 40mm, 18kt. yellow gold, special 24-hour bezel and hand, independently adjustable 12-hour hand, 31 jewel chronometer movement, synthetic sapphire crystal,		
	with special Oysterlock bracelet 78798............................	17,550.00	10,431.00
	with Super Jubilee bracelet 8386/8............................	16,950.00	10,071.00
	with Jubilee bracelet 6311/8............................	16,550.00	9,831.00
	with Oyster bracelet 7206/8............................	14,950.00	8,881.00
	with champagne dial set with 8 brilliants, 1 triangular and 2 baguette rubies and Super Jubilee bracelet 8386/8............................	20,700.00	12,301.00
168622	**Yacht-Master Oyster Perpetual Date**, ∅ 35mm, stainless steel case, special platinum time-lapse bezel, platinum dial, 31 jewel chronometer movement, synthetic sapphire crystal,		
	with special men's Oysterlock bracelet 78750............................	5,975.00	3,511.00
	with special ladies' Oysterlock bracelet 78740............................	5,950.00	3,491.00

ROLEX OYSTER WATCHES

Style	Description	Suggested Retail Price	Wholesale
168623	**Yacht-Master Oyster Perpetual Date**, ⌀ 35mm, stainless steel case, special 18kt. yellow gold time-lapse bezel, 31 jewel chronometer movement, synthetic sapphire crystal,		
	with special men's Oysterlock bracelet 78753..	6,500.00	3,821.00
	with special ladies' Oysterlock bracelet 78743...	6,400.00	3,761.00
168628	**Yacht-Master Oyster Perpetual Date**, ⌀ 35mm, 18kt. yellow gold, special time-lapse bezel, 31 jewel chronometer movement, synthetic sapphire crystal,		
	with special men's Oysterlock bracelet 78758..	16,250.00	9,661.00
	with special ladies' Oysterlock bracelet 78748..	15,850.00	9,421.00
	with mother-of-pearl dial set with 8 brilliants, 1 triangular and 2 baguette sapphires and special men's Oysterlock bracelet 78758............................	21,250.00	12,631.00
	with mother-of-pearl dial set with 8 round, 1 triangular and 2 baguette rubies and special men's Oysterlock bracelet 78758............................	21,950.00	13,051.00
169622	**Lady Yacht-Master Oyster Perpetual Date**, ⌀ 29mm, 18kt. stainless steel case, special platinum time-lapse bezel, platinum dial, 31 jewel chronometer movement, synthetic sapphire crystal,		
	with special Oysterlock bracelet 78730...	5,225.00	3,071.00
169623	**Lady Yacht-Master Oyster Perpetual Date**, ⌀ 29mm, 18kt. stainless steel case, special 18kt. yellow gold time-lapse bezel, 31 jewel chronometer movement, synthetic sapphire crystal,		
	with special Oysterlock bracelet 78733...	5,700.00	3,351.00
169628	**Lady Yacht-Master Oyster Perpetual Date**, ⌀ 29mm, 18kt. 18kt. yellow gold, special time-lapse bezel, 31 jewel chronometer movement, synthetic sapphire crystal,		
	with special Oysterlock bracelet 78738...	13,950.00	8,291.00
	with mother-of-pearl dial set with 8 brilliants, 1 triangular and 2 baguette sapphires and special men's Oysterlock bracelet 78738............................	18,700.00	11,111.00
	with mother-of-pearl dial set with 8 round, 1 triangular and 2 baguette rubies and special men's Oysterlock bracelet 78738............................	19,400.00	11,531.00
17000	**Oysterquartz Datejust**, ⌀ 36mm, stainless steel case, polished bezel, 11 jewel chronometer movement, synthetic sapphire crystal, integral bracelet.................	3,025.00	1,781.00
17013	**Oysterquartz Datejust**, ⌀ 36mm, stainless steel case, 18kt. yellow gold fluted bezel, 11 jewel chronometer movement, synthetic sapphire crystal,		
	stainless steel and 18kt. yellow gold integral bracelet.............................	5,050.00	2,971.00
	with 10 brilliants set on dial...	6,500.00	3,831.00
	with 10 brilliants set on Jubilee dial...	6,550.00	3,861.00
17014	**Oysterquartz Datejust**, ⌀ 36mm, stainless steel case, 18kt. white gold fluted bezel, 11 jewel chronometer movement, synthetic sapphire crystal, integral bracelet..............	3,575.00	2,101.00
	with 10 brilliants set on dial...	5,025.00	2,961.00
18206	**Oyster Perpetual Day-Date**, ⌀ 36mm, platinum, polished bezel, 8 brilliants and 2 baguette diamonds set on dial, 31 jewel chronometer movement, synthetic sapphire crystal,		
	with Super President bracelet 8385/6..	36,500.00	21,691.00
	with 18kt. gold Mother-of-Pearl Myriad Serti diamond dial and Super President bracelet 8385/6..	41,100.00	24,421.00

Refer to model 18239 for a complete listing of available additional cost dials.

ROLEX OYSTER WATCHES

Style	Description	Suggested Retail Price	Wholesale
18208	**Oyster Perpetual Day-Date**, ⌀ 36mm, 18kt. yellow gold, polished bezel, 31 jewel chronometer movement, synthetic sapphire crystal, with Super President bracelet 8385/8..	**15,850.00**	9,421.00
	with 8 brilliants and 2 baguette diamonds set on dial and Super President bracelet 8385/8...	**17,850.00**	10,601.00
	Refer to model 18239 for a complete listing of available additional cost dials.		
18238	**Oyster Perpetual Day-Date**, ⌀ 36mm, 18kt. yellow gold, fluted bezel, 31 jewel chronometer movement, synthetic sapphire crystal, with Super President bracelet 8385/8..	**15,900.00**	9,451.00
	with 8 brilliants and 2 baguette diamonds set on dial and Super President bracelet 8385/8...	**17,900.00**	10,631.00
	with 10 brilliants set on dial and Super President bracelet 8385/8..............................	17,900.00	10,631.00
	with 10 brilliants set on Jubilee dial and Super President bracelet 8385/8.......................	17,900.00	10,631.00
	with 10 baguette diamonds set on dial and Super President bracelet 8385/8....................	20,400.00	12,101.00
	with 2 rubies set on dial and Super President bracelet 8385/8....................................	18,700.00	11,111.00
	with mother-of-pearl Arabic, Roman or decorated Roman dial and Super President bracelet 8385/8...	17,250.00	10,251.00
	with 2 brilliants set on mother-of-pearl Arabic dial and Super President bracelet 8385/8...	19,350.00	11,501.00
	with mother-of-pearl Serti dial and Super President bracelet 8385/8.........................	19,550.00	11,621.00
	with 10 baguette diamonds set on mother-of-pearl dial and Super President bracelet 8385/8	21,950.00	13,041.00
	with 10 sapphires set on mother-of-pearl dial and Super President bracelet 8385/8...........	19,300.00	11,471.00
	with 10 rubies set on mother-of-pearl dial and Super President bracelet 8385/8...............	19,300.00	11,471.00
	with 10 emeralds set on mother-of-pearl dial and Super President bracelet 8385/8...........	21,550.00	12,811.00
	with onyx dial and Super President bracelet 8385/8..	17,000.00	10,101.00
	with 2 brilliants set on onyx Arabic dial and Super President bracelet 8385/8.................	17,500.00	10,401.00
	with onyx Serti dial and Super President bracelet 8385/8..	19,000.00	11,291.00
	with malachite dial and Super President bracelet 8385/8..	17,500.00	10,401.00
	with 2 brilliants set on lapis lazuli Arabic dial and Super President bracelet 8385/8..........	20,250.00	12,031.00
	with lapis lazuli Serti dial and Super President bracelet 8385/8...............................	22,150.00	13,161.00
	with semi-precious stone dial with applied gold Roman numerals (aventurine, ferrite, obsidienne) and Super President bracelet 8385/8..	17,250.00	10,251.00
	with 2 brilliants set on semi-precious stone dial with Arabic numerals (cacholong) and Super President bracelet 8385/8...	17,500.00	10,401.00
	with 10 brilliants set on semi-precious stone dial (ammonite, aventurine, cacholong, ferrite, grossular, jasper) and Super President bracelet 8385/8..................................	19,250.00	11,441.00
	with 8 brilliants and 2 baguette diamonds set on semi-precious stone dial (meteorite) and Super President bracelet 8385/8..	21,600.00	12,831.00
	with diamond string and 10 brilliants set on 18kt. gold dial and Super President bracelet 8385/8...	21,850.00	12,981.00
	with diamond string and 10 sapphires set on 18kt. gold dial and Super President bracelet 8385/8...	22,000.00	13,071.00
	with diamond string and 10 rubies set on 18kt. gold dial and Super President bracelet 8385/8...	22,750.00	13,521.00
	with diamond string and 10 emeralds set on 18kt. gold dial and Super President bracelet 8385/8...	27,750.00	16,491.00
	with 18kt. gold "Pleide" diamond dial and Super President bracelet 8385/8....................	24,650.00	14,651.00
	with 18kt. gold "Myriad" diamond dial and Super President bracelet 8385/8..................	25,250.00	15,001.00
	with 18kt. gold "Myriad Arabic" diamond dial and Super President bracelet 8385/8........	21,500.00	12,781.00
	with 18kt. gold "Myriad Roman" diamond dial and Super President bracelet 8385/8........	20,250.00	12,031.00
	with 18kt. gold "Myriad Serti" diamond dial and Super President bracelet 8385/8...........	22,500.00	13,371.00
	with 18kt. gold "Mother-of-Pearl Myriad" diamond dial set with 10 sapphires and Super President bracelet 8385/8...	24,000.00	14,261.00

Continued

ROLEX OYSTER WATCHES

Style	Description	Suggested Retail Price	Wholesale
	with 18kt. gold "Mother-of-Pearl Myriad" diamond dial set with 10 rubies and Super President bracelet 8385/8..	24,000.00	14,261.00
	with 18kt. gold "Mother-of-Pearl Myriad" diamond dial set with 10 emeralds and Super President bracelet 8385/8..	26,250.00	15,601.00
	with 18kt. gold "Mother-of-Pearl Pave Roman" diamond dial and Super President bracelet 8385/8..	31,250.00	18,571.00
	with 18kt. gold "Pave" diamond dial with 2 rows of rubies, ruby markers and Super President bracelet 8385/8..	40,900.00	24,301.00
	with 18kt. gold "Pave Sapphires and Brilliants" dial and Super President bracelet 8385/8..	40,900.00	24,301.00
	with 18kt. gold "Pave Rubies and Brilliants" dial and Super President bracelet 8385/8..	43,400.00	25,791.00
	with 18kt. gold "Pave Extra Large" diamond dial and Super President bracelet 8385/8..	45,250.00	26,891.00
	with 18kt. gold "Pave Losange" diamond, ruby and sapphire dial and Super President bracelet 8385/8..	45,400.00	26,981.00
18239 Bic	**Tridor Oyster Perpetual Day-Date**, ∅ 36mm, 18kt. white gold case, 18kt. yellow gold fluted bezel, 31 jewel chronometer movement, synthetic sapphire crystal, with "Tridor" Super President bracelet 8285/9.................................	20,450.00	12,151.00
	with 8 brilliants and 2 baguette diamonds set on dial and "Tridor" Super President bracelet 8285/9.................................	22,450.00	13,331.00
	Refer to model 18238 for a complete listing of available additional cost dials.		
18239	**Oyster Perpetual Day-Date**, ∅ 36mm, 18kt. white gold, fluted bezel, 31 jewel chronometer movement, synthetic sapphire crystal, with Super President bracelet 8385/9.................................	17,350.00	10,311.00
	with 8 brilliants and 2 baguette diamonds set on dial and Super President bracelet 8285/9.................................	19,350.00	11,491.00
	with 10 brilliants set on dial and Super President bracelet 8385/9.................................	19,350.00	11,491.00
	with 10 brilliants set on Jubilee dial and Super President bracelet 8385/9.................................	19,350.00	11,491.00
	with 10 baguette diamonds set on dial and Super President bracelet 8385/9.................................	21,850.00	12,961.00
	with 2 sapphires set on dial and Super President bracelet 8385/9.................................	19,250.00	11,441.00
	with mother-of-pearl decorated Roman dial and Super President bracelet 8385/9.................................	18,700.00	11,111.00
	with mother-of-pearl Serti dial and Super President bracelet 8385/9.................................	21,000.00	12,481.00
	with 10 baguette diamonds set on mother-of-pearl dial and Super President bracelet 8385/9	23,400.00	13,901.00
	with 2 brilliants set on lapis lazuli Arabic dial and Super President bracelet 8385/9.........	21,700.00	12,891.00
	with lapis lazuli Serti dial and Super President bracelet 8385/9.................................	23,600.00	14,021.00
	with 2 brilliants set on semi-precious stone dial with Arabic numerals (meteorite) and Super President bracelet 8385/9.................................	21,600.00	12,831.00
	with 18kt. gold "Pleide" diamond dial and Super President bracelet 8385/9....................	26,100.00	15,511.00
	with 18kt. gold "Myriad Arabic" diamond dial and Super President bracelet 8385/9.........	22,950.00	13,641.00
	with 18kt. gold "Myriad Serti" diamond dial and Super President bracelet 8385/9............	23,950.00	14,231.00
	with 18kt. gold "Mother-of-Pearl Myriad Serti" diamond dial and Super President bracelet 8385/9.................................	25,450.00	15,121.00
	with 18kt. gold "Pave" diamond dial with onyx markers and Super President bracelet 8385/9.................................	40,700.00	24,181.00
	with 18kt. gold "Pave" diamond dial with sapphire markers and Super President bracelet 8385/9.................................	40,700.00	24,181.00
	with 18kt. gold "Pave Extra Large" diamond dial and Super President bracelet 8385/9.................................	46,700.00	27,751.00

ROLEX OYSTER WATCHES

Style	Description	Suggested Retail Price	Wholesale
18248	**Oyster Perpetual Day-Date**, ∅ 36mm, 18kt. yellow gold, bark finish bezel, 31 jewel chronometer movement, synthetic sapphire crystal, with bark finish Super President bracelet 8723/8..............	16,500.00	9,801.00
	with 8 brilliants and 2 baguette diamonds set on dial and bark finish Super President bracelet 8723/8..............	18,500.00	10,981.00
	Refer to model 18238 for a complete listing of available additional cost dials.		
18249	**Oyster Perpetual Day-Date**, ∅ 36mm, 18kt. white gold, bark finish bezel, 31 jewel chronometer movement, synthetic sapphire crystal, with bark finish Super President bracelet 8723/9..............	17,700.00	10,511.00
	with 8 brilliants and 2 baguette diamonds set on dial and bark finish Super President bracelet 8723/9..............	19,700.00	11,691.00
	Refer to model 18239 for a complete listing of additional cost dials.		
18296	**Oyster Perpetual Day-Date**, ∅ 36mm, platinum, polished bezel, case lugs set with 28 brilliants, 8 brilliants and 2 baguette diamonds on dial, 31 jewel chronometer movement, synthetic sapphire crystal, with Super President bracelet 8385/6..............	39,350.00	23,381.00
	Refer to model 18239 for a complete listing of additional cost dials.		
18308	**Oyster Perpetual Day-Date**, ∅ 36mm, 18kt. yellow gold, bark finish bezel set with 12 brilliants, 31 jewel chronometer movement, synthetic sapphire crystal, with bark finish Super President bracelet 8723/8..............	19,500.00	11,591.00
	with 8 brilliants and 2 baguette diamonds set on dial and bark finish Super President bracelet 8723/9..............	21,500.00	12,771.00
	Refer to model 18238 for a complete listing of additional cost dials.		
18338	**Oyster Perpetual Day-Date**, ∅ 36mm, 18kt. yellow gold, fluted bezel, lugs set with 28 brilliants, 31 jewel chronometer movement, synthetic sapphire crystal, with Super President bracelet 8385/8..............	18,750.00	11,141.00
	with 8 brilliants and 2 baguette diamonds set on dial and Super President bracelet 8385/8..............	20,750.00	12,321.00
	Refer to model 18238 for a complete listing of additional cost dials.		
18346	**Oyster Perpetual Day-Date**, ∅ 36mm, platinum, bezel set with 44 brilliants, 8 brilliants and 2 baguette diamonds set on dial, 31 jewel chronometer movement, synthetic sapphire crystal, with Super President bracelet 8385/6..............	43,900.00	26,091.00
	with "Super President Karat" bracelet 8485/6..............	75,000.00	44,571.00
	with 18kt. gold "Pave" diamond dial and sapphire markers and "Super President Karat" bracelet 8485/6..............	94,850.00	56,361.00
	Refer to model 18239 for a complete listing of additional cost dials.		
18348	**Oyster Perpetual Day-Date**, ∅ 36mm, 18kt. yellow gold, bezel set with 44 brilliants, 8 brilliants and 2 baguette diamonds set on dial, 31 jewel chronometer movement, synthetic sapphire crystal, with Super President bracelet 8385/8..............	24,950.00	14,821.00
	with bark finish Super President bracelet 8723/8..............	25,550.00	15,181.00
	with "Super Jubilee Karat" bracelet 8486/8..............	52,000.00	30,891.00
	with "Super President Karat" bracelet 8485/8..............	56,550.00	33,601.00
	with "Super President Baguette" bracelet 8385/8B..............	102,000.00	60,601.00
	with 18kt. gold "Pave Extra Large" diamond dial and "Super Jubilee Karat" bracelet 8486/8..............	79,350.00	47,151.00
	Refer to model 18238 for a complete listing of additional cost dials.		

ROLEX OYSTER WATCHES

Style	Description	Suggested Retail Price	Wholesale
18349 Bic	**Tridor Oyster Perpetual Day-Date**, ⌀ 36mm, 18kt. white gold case, 18kt. yellow gold bezel set with 44 brilliants, 8 brilliants and 2 baguette diamonds set on dial, 31 jewel chronometer movement, synthetic sapphire crystal,		
	with "Tridor" Super President bracelet 8285/9..	29,500.00	17,521.00
	with "Bicolor Super Jubilee Karat" bracelet 8486/9.................................	53,500.00	31,781.00
	with 10 brilliants set on "Jubilee" dial and "Bicolor Super Jubilee Karat" bracelet 8486/9.................................	53,500.00	31,781.00
	Refer to model 18238 for a complete listing of additional cost dials.		
18366	**Oyster Perpetual Day-Date**, ⌀ 36mm, platinum, bezel set with 24 baguette diamonds, 31 jewel chronometer movement, synthetic sapphire crystal,		
	with Super President bracelet 8385/6..	73,750.00	43,821.00
	with 8 brilliants and 2 baguette diamonds set on dial and Super President bracelet 8385/6..	77,250.00	45,901.00
	Refer to model 18239 for a complete listing of additional cost dials.		
18368	**Oyster Perpetual Day-Date**, ⌀ 36mm, 18kt. yellow gold, bezel set with 24 baguette diamonds, 31 jewel chronometer movement, synthetic sapphire crystal,		
	with Super President bracelet 8385/8..	56,650.00	33,661.00
	with 8 brilliants and 2 baguette diamonds set on dial and Super President bracelet 8385/8..	58,650.00	34,841.00
	Refer to model 18238 for a complete listing of additional cost dials.		
18378	**Oyster Perpetual Day-Date**, ⌀ 36mm, 18kt. yellow gold, bezel set with 44 brilliants and 4 baguette rubies, 8 brilliants and 2 baguette diamonds set on dial, 31 jewel chronometer movement, synthetic sapphire crystal,		
	with Super President bracelet 8385/8..	26,250.00	15,601.00
	with 10 brilliants set on Jubilee dial and Super President bracelet 8385/8.................	26,250.00	15,601.00
	with diamond string and 10 rubies set on 18kt. gold dial and "Super President Karat" bracelet 8485/8..	62,700.00	37,271.00
	Refer to model 18238 for a complete listing of additional cost dials.		
18388	**Oyster Perpetual Day-Date**, ⌀ 36mm, 18kt. yellow gold, bezel set with 44 brilliants, case lugs set with 28 brilliants, 8 brilliants and 2 baguette diamonds set on dial, 31 jewel chronometer movement, synthetic sapphire crystal,		
	with Super President bracelet 8385/8..	27,800.00	16,511.00
	Refer to model 18238 for a complete listing of additional cost dials.		
18389	**Oyster Perpetual Day-Date**, ⌀ 36mm, 18kt. white gold, bezel set with 44 brilliants, case lugs set with 28 brilliants, 8 brilliants and 2 baguette diamonds set on dial, 31 jewel chronometer movement, synthetic sapphire crystal,		
	with Super President bracelet 8385/9..	29,250.00	17,371.00
	with 10 brilliants set on Jubilee dial and "Super Jubilee Karat" bracelet 8486/9..	56,350.00	33,471.00
	Refer to model 18239 for a complete listing of additional cost dials.		
18946	**Oyster Perpetual Master Day-Date**, ⌀ 39mm, platinum, bezel set with 40 brilliants, 8 brilliants and 2 baguette diamonds set on dial, 31 jewel chronometer movement, synthetic sapphire crystal,		
	with Super President bracelet 72746..	61,500.00	36,541.00
	with mother-of-pearl "Serti" dial and Super President bracelet 72746..................	61,650.00	36,631.00
	Refer to model 18239 for a complete listing of additional cost dials.		

ROLEX OYSTER WATCHES

Style	Description	Suggested Retail Price	Wholesale

18948 Bic Tridor Oyster Perpetual Master Day-Date, ∅ 39mm, 18kt. yellow gold, bezel set with 40 brilliants, 8 brilliants and 2 baguette diamonds set on dial, 31 jewel chronometer movement, synthetic sapphire crystal,
with "Tridor" Super President bracelet 72748...32,750.00 19,461.00
with 8 brilliants and 2 baguette diamonds set on semi-precious stone dial (meteorite) and "Tridor" Super President bracelet 72748.......................36,450.00 21,661.00
Refer to model 18238 for a complete listing of additional cost dials.

18956 Oyster Perpetual Master Day-Date, ∅ 39mm, platinum, bezel set with 42 baguette diamonds, 8 brilliants and 2 bag. diamonds set on dial, 31 jewel chronometer movement, synthetic sapphire crystal,
with Super President bracelet 72746.. 105,000.00 62,391.00
Refer to model 18239 for a complete listing of additional cost dials.

19018 Oysterquartz Day-Date, ∅ 36mm, 18kt. yellow gold, fluted bezel, 11 jewel chronometer movement, synthetic sapphire crystal,
integral bracelet, concealed clasp... 16,500.00   9,801.00
with 8 brilliants and 2 baguette diamonds set on dial............................18,500.00 10,981.00
with 10 bezel set brilliants set on dial..18,500.00 10,981.00
with 10 brilliants set on Jubilee dial...18,500.00 10,981.00
with 10 baguette diamonds set on dial.. 21,000.00 12,451.00
with African mahogany or walnut dial..16,900.00 10,041.00
with diamond string and 10 brilliants set on 18kt. gold dial.....................22,450.00 13,341.00
with diamond string and 10 sapphires set on 18kt. gold dial.....................22,600.00 13,431.00
with diamond string and 10 emeralds set on 18kt. gold dial......................28,350.00 16,841.00
with 18kt. gold "Pleiade" diamond dial.......................................25,250.00 15,001.00
with 18kt. gold "Myriad" diamond dial.......................................25,850.00 15,361.00
with 18kt. gold "Myriad Arabic" diamond dial.................................22,100.00 13,131.00
with 18kt. gold "Mother-of-Pearl Pave Roman" diamond dial...................31,850.00 18,921.00
with 18kt. gold "Pave" diamond dial with 2 rows of rubies and ruby markers..................41,500.00 24,661.00
with 18kt. gold "Pave Sapphires and Brilliants" dial.............................41,500.00 24,661.00
with 18kt. gold "Pave Rubies and Brilliants" dial................................44,000.00 26,141.00
with 18kt. gold "Pave Extra Large" diamond dial.................................45,850.00 27,241.00
with 18kt. gold "Pave Losange" diamond, ruby and sapphire dial.................46,000.00 27,331.00

19019 Oysterquartz Day-Date, ∅ 36mm, 18kt. white gold, fluted bezel, 11 jewel chronometer movement, synthetic sapphire crystal,
integral bracelet, concealed clasp... 18,200.00 10,811.00
with 8 brilliants and 2 baguette diamonds set on dial............................20,200.00 11,991.00
with 10 brilliants set on Jubilee dial...20,200.00 11,991.00
with 18kt. gold "Pleiade" diamond dial.......................................26,950.00 16,011.00
with 18kt. gold "Pave" diamond dial with sapphire markers.....................41,550.00 24,691.00
with 18kt. gold "Pave Extra Large" diamond dial.................................47,550.00 28,251.00

19028 Oysterquartz Day-Date, ∅ 36mm, 18kt. yellow gold, "Pyramid" bezel, 11 jewel chronometer movement, synthetic sapphire crystal,
"Pyramid" integral bracelet, concealed clasp....................................18,500.00 10,991.00
with 8 brilliants and 2 baguette diamonds set on dial............................20,500.00 12,171.00
Refer to model 19018 for a complete listing of available cost dials.

19038 Oysterquartz Day-Date, ∅ 36mm, 18kt. yellow gold, "Pyramid" bezel with 12 brilliants, 11 jewel chronometer movement, synthetic sapphire crystal,
"Pyramid" integral bracelet, concealed clasp....................................21,250.00 12,631.00
with 8 brilliants and 2 baguette diamonds set on dial............................23,250.00 13,811.00
Refer to model 19018 for a complete listing of available cost dials.

ROLEX OYSTER WATCHES

Style	Description	Suggested Retail Price	Wholesale
19048	**Oysterquartz Day-Date**, ⌀ 36mm, 18kt. yellow gold, bezel set with 44 brilliants, 8 brilliants and 2 baguette diamonds set on dial, 11 jewel chronometer movement, synthetic sapphire crystal, integral bracelet, concealed clasp.................................... *Refer to model 19018 for a complete listing of available cost dials.*	25,550.00	15,171.00
19049	**Oysterquartz Day-Date**, ⌀ 36mm, 18kt. white gold, bezel set with 44 brilliants, 8 brilliants and 2 baguette diamonds set on dial, 11 jewel chronometer movement, synthetic sapphire crystal, integral bracelet, concealed clasp...................................	27,250.00	16,181.00
	with 18kt. gold "Pleide" diamond dial.. *Refer to model 19019 for a complete listing of available cost dials.*	34,000.00	20,201.00
19068	**Oysterquartz Day-Date**, ⌀ 36mm, 18kt. yellow gold, bezel set with 44 brilliants, 8 brilliants and 2 baguette diamonds set on dial, 11 jewel chronometer movement, synthetic sapphire crystal, "Pyramid" integral bracelet, concealed clasp...................... *Refer to model 19018 for a complete listing of available cost dials.*	27,500.00	16,341.00
19148	**Oysterquartz Day-Date**, ⌀ 36mm, 18kt. yellow gold, bezel set with 44 brilliants, case set with 8 brilliants, 8 brilliants and 2 baguette diamonds set on dial, 11 jewel chronometer movement, synthetic sapphire crystal, "Karat" integral bracelet set with 308 brilliants, concealed clasp.............................	60,000.00	35,651.00
	with 10 brilliants set on Jubilee dial.. *Refer to model 19018 for a complete listing of available cost dials.*	60,000.00	35,651.00
69028R	**Oyster Perpetual Lady-Datejust**, ⌀ 26mm, 18kt. yellow gold, bezel set with 40 square cut rubies, case lugs set with 24 brilliants, 10 brilliants set on dial, 29 jewel chronometer movement, synthetic sapphire crystal, with Super President bracelet 8570/8.. *Refer to model 79178 for a complete listing of available cost dials.*	28,250.00	16,781.00
69038S	**Oyster Perpetual Lady-Datejust**, ⌀ 26mm, 18kt. yellow gold, bezel set with 16 brilliants and 24 sapphires, case lugs set with 24 brilliants, 10 brilliants set on dial, 29 jewel chronometer movement, synthetic sapphire crystal, with Super President bracelet 8570/8.. *Refer to model 79178 for a complete listing of available cost dials.*	20,750.00	12,331.00
69108	**Oyster Perpetual Lady-Datejust**, ⌀ 26mm, 18kt. yellow gold, bezel set with 40 square cut emeralds, 10 brilliants set on dial, 29 jewel chronometer movement, synthetic sapphire crystal, with Super President bracelet 8570/8.. *Refer to model 79178 for a complete listing of available cost dials.*	48,500.00	28,821.00
6919BE	**Oyster Perpetual Lady-Datejust**, ⌀ 26mm, 18kt. yellow gold, bezel with 16 brilliants and 16 oval cut emeralds, case lugs set with 24 brilliants, 10 brilliants set on dial, 29 jewel chronometer movement, synthetic sapphire crystal, with Super President bracelet 8570/8.. *Refer to model 79178 for a complete listing of available cost dials.*	30,500.00	18,121.00
76030	**Lady Oyster Perpetual**, ⌀ 24mm, stainless steel, finely engine-turned bezel, 31 jewel chronometer movement, synthetic sapphire crystal,		
	with Oyster bracelet 78240..	2,675.00	1,571.00
	with Jubilee bracelet 62510..	2,775.00	1,631.00
76080	**Lady Oyster Perpetual**, ⌀ 24mm, stainless steel, polished bezel, 31 jewel chronometer movement, synthetic sapphire crystal,		
	with Oyster bracelet 78240..	2,625.00	1,541.00
	with Jubilee bracelet 62510..	2,725.00	1,601.00

ROLEX OYSTER WATCHES

Style	Description	Suggested Retail Price	Wholesale
76094	**Lady Oyster Perpetual**, ⌀ 24mm, stainless steel case, 18kt. white gold fluted bezel, 31 jewel chronometer movement, synthetic sapphire crystal,		
	with Oyster bracelet 78240..	**3,175.00**	**1,861.00**
	with Jubilee bracelet 62510..	**3,275.00**	**1,921.00**
76183	**Lady Oyster Perpetual**, ⌀ 24mm, stainless steel case, 18kt. yellow gold polished bezel, 31 jewel chronometer movement, synthetic sapphire crystal,		
	with Oyster bracelet 78243..	**3,650.00**	**2,141.00**
	with Jubilee bracelet 62523..	**3,925.00**	**2,301.00**
	with 11 brilliants set on dial and Oyster bracelet 78243........................	**4,950.00**	**2,911.00**
76188	**Lady Oyster Perpetual**, ⌀ 24mm, 18kt. yellow gold, polished bezel, 31 jewel chronometer movement, synthetic sapphire crystal,		
	with Oyster bracelet 7204/8..	**9,200.00**	**5,471.00**
	with Jubilee bracelet 6251/8..	**9,500.00**	**5,651.00**
	with Super Jubilee bracelet 8571/8..	**11,050.00**	**6,571.00**
	with 11 brilliants set on dial and Oyster bracelet 7204/8......................	**10,500.00**	**6,231.00**
76193	**Lady Oyster Perpetual**, ⌀ 24mm, stainless steel case, 18kt. yellow gold fluted bezel, 31 jewel chronometer movement, synthetic sapphire crystal,		
	with Oyster bracelet 78243..	**3,700.00**	**2,171.00**
	with Jubilee bracelet 62523..	**3,975.00**	**2,341.00**
	with 11 brilliants set on dial and Jubilee bracelet 62523.......................	**5,275.00**	**3,101.00**
76198	**Lady Oyster Perpetual**, ⌀ 24mm, 18kt. yellow gold, fluted bezel, 31 jewel chronometer movement, synthetic sapphire crystal,		
	with Super Jubilee bracelet 8571/8..	**11,100.00**	**6,601.00**
	with Jubilee bracelet 6251/8..	**9,550.00**	**5,681.00**
	with Oyster bracelet 7204/8..	**9,250.00**	**5,501.00**
	with 11 brilliants set on dial and Super Jubilee bracelet 8571/8............	**12,400.00**	**7,361.00**
76233	**Lady Oyster Perpetual**, ⌀ 24mm, stainless steel, 18kt. yellow gold finely engine-turned bezel, 31 jewel chronometer movement, synthetic sapphire crystal,		
	with Oyster bracelet 78243..	**3,700.00**	**2,171.00**
	with Jubilee bracelet 62523..	**3,975.00**	**2,341.00**
	with 11 brilliants set on dial and Oyster bracelet 78243........................	**5,000.00**	**2,941.00**
76243	**Lady Oyster Perpetual**, ⌀ 24mm, stainless steel, 18kt. yellow gold "Zephyr" engraved bezel, 31 jewel chronometer movement, synthetic sapphire crystal,		
	with Oyster bracelet 78243..	**3,700.00**	**2,171.00**
	with Jubilee bracelet 62523..	**3,975.00**	**2,341.00**
	with 11 brilliants set on dial and Oyster bracelet 78243........................	**5,000.00**	**2,941.00**
77014	**Oyster Perpetual**, ⌀ 31mm, stainless steel case, 18kt. white gold fluted bezel, 31 jewel chronometer movement, synthetic sapphire crystal,		
	with men's Jubilee bracelet 63110...	**3,400.00**	**1,991.00**
	with ladies' Jubilee bracelet 62510..	**3,375.00**	**1,981.00**
	with men's Oyster bracelet 78350..	**3,275.00**	**1,921.00**
	with ladies' Oyster bracelet 78050...	**3,250.00**	**1,911.00**
77080	**Oyster Perpetual**, ⌀ 31mm, stainless steel case, polished bezel, 31 jewel chronometer movement, synthetic sapphire crystal,		
	with men's Jubilee bracelet 63110...	**2,870.00**	**1,681.00**
	with ladies' Jubilee bracelet 62510..	**2,825.00**	**1,661.00**
	with men's Oyster bracelet 78350..	**2,725.00**	**1,601.00**
	with ladies' Oyster bracelet 78050...	**2,700.00**	**1,581.00**

ROLEX OYSTER WATCHES

Style	Description	Suggested Retail Price	Wholesale
77483	**Oyster Perpetual**, ⌀ 31mm, stainless steel case, 18kt. yellow gold polished bezel, 31 jewel chronometer movement, synthetic sapphire crystal,		
	with men's Oyster bracelet 78353...	4,350.00	2,561.00
	with ladies' Oyster bracelet 78053...	4,150.00	2,441.00
	with men's Jubilee bracelet 63113..	4,650.00	2,731.00
	with ladies' Jubilee bracelet 62513..	4,450.00	2,621.00
77488	**Oyster Perpetual**, ⌀ 31mm, 18kt. yellow gold, polished bezel, 31 jewel chronometer movement, synthetic sapphire crystal,		
	with Oyster bracelet 7205/8...	11,250.00	6,681.00
	with Jubilee bracelet 6311/8..	12,850.00	7,631.00
77513	**Oyster Perpetual**, ⌀ 31mm, stainless steel case, 18kt. yellow gold fluted bezel, 31 jewel chronometer movement, synthetic sapphire crystal,		
	with men's Jubilee bracelet 63113..	4,700.00	2,761.00
	with ladies' Jubilee bracelet 62523..	4,500.00	2,651.00
	with men's Oyster bracelet 78353...	4,400.00	2,591.00
	with ladies' Oyster bracelet 78053...	4,200.00	2,471.00
77518	**Oyster Perpetual**, ⌀ 31mm, 18kt. yellow gold, fluted bezel, 31 jewel chronometer movement, synthetic sapphire crystal,		
	with Jubilee bracelet 6311/8..	12,900.00	7,661.00
	with Oyster bracelet 7205/8...	11,300.00	6,711.00
78158	**Oyster Perpetual Datejust**, ⌀ 31mm, 18kt. yellow gold, bezel set with 44 brilliants, case lugs set with 24 brilliants, 10 brilliants set on dial, 31 jewel chronometer movement, synthetic sapphire crystal,		
	with men's Super President bracelet 8389/8...................................	23,750.00	14,111.00
	with ladies' Super President bracelet 8390/8.................................	23,200.00	13,781.00
	with Super Jubilee bracelet 8391/8...	23,000.00	13,661.00
	with 10 brilliants set on Jubilee dial and men's Super President bracelet 8389/8..............	23,800.00	14,141.00
	Refer to model 78278 for a complete listing of available additional cost dials.		
78159	**Oyster Perpetual Datejust**, ⌀ 31mm, 18kt. white gold, bezel set with 44 brilliants, case lugs set with 24 brilliants, 10 brilliants set on dial, 31 jewel chronometer movement, synthetic sapphire crystal,		
	with men's Super President bracelet 8389/9...................................	24,750.00	14,701.00
	with ladies' Super President bracelet 8390/9.................................	24,200.00	14,381.00
	Refer to model 78279 for a complete listing of available additional cost dials.		
78238	**Oyster Perpetual Datejust**, ⌀ 31mm, 18kt. yellow gold, fluted bezel, case lugs set with 24 brilliants, 31 jewel chronometer movement, synthetic sapphire crystal,		
	with men's Super President bracelet 8389/8...................................	16,800.00	9,991.00
	with ladies' Super President bracelet 8390/8.................................	16,250.00	9,661.00
	with Super Jubilee bracelet 8391/8...	16,050.00	9,541.00
	with 10 brilliants set on Jubilee dial and men's Super President bracelet 8389/8..............	18,150.00	10,781.00
	Refer to model 78278 for a complete listing of available additional cost dials.		
78240	**Oyster Perpetual**, ⌀ 31mm, stainless steel case, polished bezel, 31 jewel chronometer movement, synthetic sapphire crystal,		
	with men's Jubilee bracelet 63110..	3,280.00	1,921.00
	with ladies' Jubilee bracelet 62510..	3,250.00	1,911.00
	with men's Oyster bracelet 78350...	3,150.00	1,851.00
	with ladies' Oyster bracelet 78050...	3,125.00	1,831.00

ROLEX OYSTER WATCHES

Style	Description	Suggested Retail Price	Wholesale
78243	**Oyster Perpetual**, ⌀ 31mm, stainless steel case, 18kt. yellow gold polished bezel, 31 jewel chronometer movement, synthetic sapphire crystal,		
	with men's Jubilee bracelet 63113..	5,050.00	2,971.00
	with ladies' Jubilee bracelet 62523..	4,850.00	2,851.00
	with men's Oyster bracelet 78353...	4,750.00	2,791.00
	with ladies' Oyster bracelet 78053...	4,550.00	2,681.00
	with 10 brilliants set on dial and men's Jubilee bracelet 63113................................	6,400.00	3,761.00
	with 10 brilliants set on Jubilee dial and men's Jubilee bracelet 63113......................	6,450.00	3,791.00
78246	**Oyster Perpetual**, ⌀ 31mm, platinum, polished bezel, 10 brilliants set on dial, 31 jewel chronometer movement, synthetic sapphire crystal,		
	with men's Super Presidents bracelet 8389/6..	23,750.00	14,111.00
	with ladies' Super Presidents bracelet 8390/6..	22,400.00	13,311.00
	Refer to model 78279 for a complete listing of available additional cost dials.		
78248	**Oyster Perpetual Datejust**, ⌀ 31mm, 18kt. yellow gold, polished bezel, 31 jewel chronometer movement, synthetic sapphire crystal,		
	with Oyster bracelet 7205/8...	11,650.00	6,921.00
	with Jubilee bracelet 6311/8..	13,250.00	7,871.00
	with Super Jubilee bracelet 8391/8...	13,700.00	8,141.00
	with men's Super President bracelet 8389/8..	14,450.00	8,591.00
	with ladies' Super President bracelet 8390/8...	13,900.00	8,261.00
	with 10 brilliants set on dial and men's Super President bracelet 8389/8....................	15,800.00	9,381.00
	Refer to model 78278 for a complete listing of available additional cost dials.		
78258	**Oyster Perpetual Datejust**, ⌀ 31mm, 18kt. yellow gold, "Pyramid" bezel set with 24 brilliants, 31 jewel chronometer movement, synthetic sapphire crystal,		
	with men's Super President bracelet 8389/8..	17,750.00	10,551.00
	with ladies' Super President bracelet 8390/8...	17,200.00	10,221.00
	with Super Jubilee bracelet 8391/8...	17,000.00	10,101.00
	with Jubilee bracelet 6311/8..	16,550.00	9,831.00
	with 10 brilliants set on dial and men's "Super Jubilee Karat" bracelet 6411/8...............	45,000.00	26,731.00
	Refer to model 78278 for a complete listing of available additional cost dials.		
78266	**Oyster Perpetual Datejust**, ⌀ 31mm, platinum, bezel set with 24 baguette diamonds, 31 jewel chronometer movement, synthetic sapphire crystal,		
	with men's Super President bracelet 8389/8..	47,650.00	28,321.00
	with ladies' Super President bracelet 8390/6...	46,300.00	27,511.00
	with 10 brilliants set on dial and men's Super President bracelet 8389/6....................	49,000.00	29,111.00
	Refer to model 78279 for a complete listing of available additional cost dials.		
78268	**Oyster Perpetual Datejust**, ⌀ 31mm, 18kt. yellow gold, bezel set with 24 baguette diamonds, 31 jewel chronometer movement, synthetic sapphire crystal,		
	with men's Super President bracelet 8389/8..	39,750.00	23,621.00
	with ladies' Super President bracelet 8390/8...	39,200.00	23,291.00
	with 10 brilliants set on dial and men's Super President bracelet 8389/6....................	41,100.00	24,411.00
	Refer to model 78278 for a complete listing of available additional cost dials.		

ROLEX OYSTER WATCHES

Style	Description	Suggested Retail Price	Wholesale
78273	**Oyster Perpetual Datejust**, ⌀ 31mm, stainless steel case, 18kt. yellow gold fluted bezel, 31 jewel chronometer movement, synthetic sapphire crystal,		
	with men's Jubilee bracelet 63113..	5,100.00	3,001.00
	with ladies' Jubilee bracelet 62523...	4,900.00	2,881.00
	with men's Oyster bracelet 78353...	4,800.00	2,821.00
	with ladies' Oyster bracelet 78053...	4,600.00	2,711.00
	with 10 brilliants set on dial and men's Jubilee bracelet 63113................................	6,450.00	3,791.00
	with 10 brilliants set on Jubilee dial and men's Oyster bracelet 78353........................	6,200.00	3,651.00
	with mother-of-pearl Roman or decorated Roman dial and men's Jubilee bracelet 63113....	6,300.00	3,711.00
	With mother-of-pearl "Serti" dial and men's Jubilee bracelet 63113............................	8,350.00	4,931.00
78274	**Oyster Perpetual Datejust**, ⌀ 31mm, stainless steel case, 18kt. white gold fluted bezel, 31 jewel chronometer movement, synthetic sapphire crystal,		
	with men's Jubilee bracelet 63110...	3,650.00	2,141.00
	with ladies' Jubilee bracelet 62510...	3,625.00	2,131.00
	with men's Oyster bracelet 78350...	3,525.00	2,071.00
	with ladies' Oyster bracelet 78050...	3,500.00	2,051.00
	with 10 brilliants set on dial and men's Jubilee bracelet 63110................................	4,900.00	2,881.00
	with mother-of-pearl Arabic or decorated Roman dial and men's Jubilee bracelet 63110....	4,750.00	2,801.00
	with mother-of-pearl "Serti" dial and men's Jubilee bracelet 63110............................	6,800.00	4,021.00
	with 10 brilliants on semi-precious stone dial (sodalite) and men's Jubilee bracelet 63110...	6,400.00	3,781.00
78278	**Oyster Perpetual Datejust**, ⌀ 31mm, 18kt. yellow gold, fluted bezel, 31 jewel chronometer movement, synthetic sapphire crystal,		
	with men's Super President bracelet 8389/8..	14,500.00	8,621.00
	with ladies' Super President bracelet 8390/8...	13,950.00	8,291.00
	with Super Jubilee bracelet 8391/8...	13,750.00	8,171.00
	with Jubilee bracelet 6311/8..	13,300.00	7,901.00
	with Oyster bracelet 7205/8...	11,700.00	6,951.00
	with 10 brilliants set on dial and men's Super President bracelet 8389/8......................	15,850.00	9,411.00
	with 10 brilliants set on dial and Oyster bracelet 7205/8......................................	13,050.00	7,751.00
	with 10 bezel set brilliants on dial and men's Super President bracelet 8389/8................	16,000.00	9,511.00
	with 10 brilliants set on Jubilee dial and men's Super President bracelet 8389/8..............	15,900.00	9,441.00
	with 2 rubies set on dial and men's Super President bracelet 8389/8...........................	17,150.00	10,191.00
	with mother-of-pearl Roman or decorated Roman dial and men's Super President bracelet 8389/8...	15,700.00	9,331.00
	with 2 brilliants set on mother-of-pearl dial and men's Super President bracelet 8389/8.....	17,600.00	10,461.00
	with mother-of-pearl "Serti" dial and men's Super President bracelet 8389/8...................	17,750.00	10,551.00
	with 8 brilliants and 2 baguette diamonds set on mother-of-pearl Jubilee dial and men's Super President bracelet 8389/8...	18,100.00	10,761.00
	with 10 sapphires set on mother-of-pearl dial and men's Super President bracelet 8389/8...	17,350.00	10,311.00
	with 10 rubies set on mother-of-pearl dial and men's Super President bracelet 8389/8...	17,350.00	10,311.00
	with 10 emeralds set on mother-of-pearl dial and men's Super President bracelet 8389/8...	19,500.00	11,591.00
	with onyx dial and men's Super President bracelet 8389/8......................................	15,450.00	9,181.00
	with 2 brilliants set on onyx Arabic dial and men's Super President bracelet 8389/8.........	15,750.00	9,361.00
	with onyx Serti dial and men's Super President bracelet 8389/8................................	17,000.00	10,101.00
	with 2 brilliants set on lapis lazuli Arabic dial and men's Super President bracelet 8389/8.	18,300.00	10,881.00
	with semi-precious stone dial with applied gold Roman numerals (howlite) and men's Super President bracelet 8389/8...	15,700.00	9,331.00

Continued

ROLEX OYSTER WATCHES

Style	Description	Suggested Retail Price	Wholesale
	with onyx Serti dial and men's Super President bracelet 8389/8..............................	17,000.00	10,101.00
	with 2 brilliants set on lapis lazuli Arabic dial and men's Super President bracelet 8389/8...	18,300.00	10,881.00
	with semi-precious stone dial with applied gold Roman numerals (howlite) and men's Super President bracelet 8389/8...	15,700.00	9,331.00
	with 18kt. gold "Myriad Arabic" diamond dial and men's Super President bracelet 8389/8.	19,800.00	11,771.00
	with 18kt. gold "Myriad Roman" diamond dial and men's Super President bracelet 8389/8.	18,250.00	10,851.00
	with 18kt. gold "Myriad Serti" diamond dial and men's Super President bracelet 8389/8...	20,550.00	12,211.00
	with 18kt. gold "Mother-of-Pearl Myriad" diamond dial set with 11 sapphires and men's Super President bracelet 8389/8..	21,350.00	12,691.00
	with 18kt. gold "Mother-of-Pearl Myriad" diamond dial set with 11 rubies and men's Super President bracelet 8389/8..	21,350.00	12,691.00
	with 18kt. gold "Mother-of-Pearl Myriad" diamond dial set with 11 emeralds and men's Super President bracelet 8389/8..	23,650.00	14,061.00
	with 18kt. gold "Pave" diamond dial set with 11 rubies and men's Super President bracelet 8389/8..	31,100.00	17,891.00
	with 18kt. gold "Pave" diamond dial set with 11 sapphires and men's Super President bracelet 8389/8..	30,100.00	17,891.00
	with 18kt. gold "Pave Extra Large" diam. dial and men's Super President bracelet 8389/8..	33,500.00	19,911.00
78279 Bic	**Tridor Oyster Perpetual Datejust**, ∅ 31mm, 18kt. white gold case, 18kt. yellow gold fluted bezel, 31 jewel chronometer movement, synthetic sapphire crystal,		
	with "Tridor" Super President bracelet 8289/9...	18,750.00	11,141.00
	with 10 brilliants set on dial and "Tridor" Super President bracelet 8289/9.................	21,100.00	11,931.00
	with 10 brilliants set on dial and men's "Bicolor Super Jubilee Karat" bracelet 6411/9...	42,800.00	25,421.00
	Refer to model 78278 for a complete listing of available additional cost dials.		
78279	**Oyster Perpetual Datejust**, ∅ 31mm, 18kt. white gold, fluted bezel, 31 jewel chronometer movement, synthetic sapphire crystal,		
	with men's Super President bracelet 8389/9..	15,500.00	9,211.00
	with ladies' Super President bracelet 8390/9...	14,950.00	8,881.00
	with 10 brilliants set on dial and men's Super President bracelet 8389/9..................	16,850.00	10,001.00
	with 10 brilliants set on Jubilee dial and men's Super President bracelet 8389/9..........	16,900.00	10,031.00
	with 2 sapphires set on dial and men's Super President bracelet 8389/9...................	17,300.00	10,281.00
	with mother-of-pearl Arabic or decorated Roman dial and men's Super President bracelet 8389/9..	16,700.00	9,921.00
	with mother-of-pearl "Serti" dial and men's Super President bracelet 8389/9.............	18,750.00	11,141.00
	with 10 brilliants set on semi-precious stone dial (sodalite) and men's Super President bracelet 8389/9..	18,350.00	10,901.00
	with 18kt. gold "Myriad Serti" diamond dial and men's Super President bracelet 8389/9...	21,550.00	12,801.00
	with 18kt. gold "Pave" diamond dial set with 11 sapphires and men's Super President bracelet 8389/9..	31,100.00	18,481.00
	with 18kt. gold "Pave Extra Large" diam. dial and men's Super President bracelet 8389/9..	34,500.00	20,501.00
78286	**Oyster Perpetual Datejust**, ∅ 31mm, platinum, bezel set with 44 brilliants, 10 brilliants set on dial, 31 jewel chronometer movement, synthetic sapphire crystal,		
	with men's Super President bracelet 8389/6..	29,350.00	17,441.00
	with ladies' Super President bracelet 8390/6...	28,000.00	16,641.00
	with 10 brilliants set on Jubilee dial and men's "Super President Karat" bracelet 8489/6...	57,150.00	33,961.00
	Refer to model 78279 for a complete listing of available additional cost dials.		

ROLEX OYSTER WATCHES

Style	Description	Suggested Retail Price	Wholesale
78288	**Oyster Perpetual Datejust**, ∅ 31mm, 18kt. yellow gold, bezel set with 44 brilliants, 10 brilliants set on dial, 31 jewel chronometer movement, synthetic sapphire crystal,		
	with men's Super President bracelet 8389/8..............................	21,450.00	12,741.00
	with ladies' Super President bracelet 8390/8..............................	20,900.00	12,411.00
	with Super Jubilee bracelet 8391/8..............................	20,700.00	12,291.00
	with men's "Super Jubilee Karat" bracelet 6411/8..............................	47,350.00	28,131.00
	with men's "Super President Karat" bracelet 8489/8..............................	49,250.00	29,261.00
	with 18kt. gold "Pave" diamond dial set with 11 rubies and men's "Super President Karat" bracelet 8489/8..............................	63,500.00	37,731.00
	Refer to model 78278 for a complete listing of available additional cost dials.		
78289	**Bic Tridor Oyster Perpetual Datejust**, ∅ 31mm, 18kt. white gold case, 18kt. yellow gold bezel set with 44 brilliants, 10 brilliants set on dial, 31 jewel chronometer movement, synthetic sapphire crystal,		
	with "Tridor" Super President bracelet 8289/9..............................	25,700.00	15,261.00
	with men's "Bicolor Super Jubilee Karat" bracelet 6411/9..............................	48,400.00	28,751.00
	Refer to model 78278 for a complete listing of available additional cost dials.		
79068	**Oyster Perpetual Lady-Datejust**, ∅ 26mm, 18kt. yellow gold, bezel set with 32 brilliants and 4 baguette rubies, 10 brilliants set on dial, 31 jewel chronometer movement, synthetic sapphire crystal,		
	with Super President bracelet 8570/8..............................	18,250.00	10,841.00
	Refer to model 79178 for a complete listing of available cost dials.		
79069	**Oyster Perpetual Lady-Datejust**, ∅ 26mm, 18kt. white gold, bezel set with 32 brilliants and 4 baguette rubies, 10 brilliants set on dial, 31 jewel chronometer movement, synthetic sapphire crystal,		
	with Super President bracelet 8570/9..............................	18,850.00	11,201.00
	Refer to model 79179 for a complete listing of available cost dials.		
79078	**Oyster Perpetual Lady-Datejust**, ∅ 26mm, 18kt. yellow gold, bezel set with 32 brilliants and 4 baguette emeralds, 10 brilliants set on dial, 31 jewel chronometer movement, synthetic sapphire crystal,		
	with Super President bracelet 8570/8..............................	19,350.00	11,501.00
	with 10 brilliants set on Jubilee dial and Super President bracelet 8570/8..............................	19,400.00	11,531.00
	Refer to model 79178 for a complete listing of available cost dials.		
79079	**Oyster Perpetual Lady-Datejust**, ∅ 26mm, 18kt. white gold, bezel set with 32 brilliants and 4 baguette emeralds, 10 brilliants set on dial, 31 jewel chronometer movement, synthetic sapphire crystal,		
	with Super President bracelet 8570/9..............................	19,950.00	11,851.00
	with 10 brilliants set on Jubilee dial and "Super President Karat" bracelet 8570/8..............................	41,250.00	24,511.00
	Refer to model 79179 for a complete listing of available cost dials.		
79088	**Oyster Perpetual Lady-Datejust**, ∅ 26mm, 18kt. yellow gold, bezel set with 32 brilliants and 4 baguette sapphires, 10 brilliants set on dial, 31 jewel chronometer movement, synthetic sapphire crystal,		
	with Super President bracelet 8570/8..............................	18,200.00	10,811.00
	with "Super Karat" bracelet 6454/8..............................	33,450.00	19,871.00
	with 18kt. gold "Pave" diamond dial set with 11 sapphires and "Super President Karat" bracelet 8470/8..............................	52,150.00	31,001.00
	Refer to model 79178 for a complete listing of available cost dials.		

ROLEX OYSTER WATCHES

Style	Description	Suggested Retail Price	Wholesale
79089	**Oyster Perpetual Lady-Datejust**, ⌀ 26mm, 18kt. white gold, bezel set with 32 brilliants and 4 baguette sapphires, 10 brilliants set on dial, 31 jewel chronometer movement, synthetic sapphire crystal,		
	with Super President bracelet 8570/9.........................	18,800.00	11,171.00
	with "Super Karat" bracelet 6454/9..........................	34,050.00	20,231.00
	with 18kt. gold "Pave Extra Large" diamond dial and "Super President Karat" bracelet 6451/9........................	49,200.00	29,241.00
	Refer to model 79179 for a complete listing of available cost dials.		
79126	**Oyster Perpetual Lady-Datejust**, ⌀ 26mm, platinum, bezel set with 40 square cut diamonds, 10 brilliants set on dial, 31 jewel chronometer movement, synthetic sapphire crystal,		
	with Super President bracelet 8570/6.........................	38,950.00	23,151.00
	Refer to model 79179 for a complete listing of available cost dials.		
79128	**Oyster Perpetual Lady-Datejust**, ⌀ 26mm, 18kt. yellow gold, bezel set with 40 square cut diamonds, 10 brilliants set on dial, 31 jewel chronometer movement, synthetic sapphire crystal,		
	with Super President bracelet 8570/8.........................	31,500.00	18,721.00
	Refer to model 79178 for a complete listing of available cost dials.		
79136	**Oyster Perpetual Lady-Datejust**, ⌀ 26mm, platinum, bezel set with 40 brilliants, 10 brilliants set on dial, 31 jewel chronometer movement, synthetic sapphire crystal,		
	with Super President bracelet 8570/6.........................	25,750.00	15,301.00
	with "Super President Karat" bracelet 8470/6.................	47,700.00	28,341.00
	Refer to model 79179 for a complete listing of available cost dials.		
79138	**Oyster Perpetual Lady-Datejust**, ⌀ 26mm, 18kt. yellow gold, bezel set with 40 brilliants, 10 brilliants on dial, 31 jewel chronometer movement, synthetic sapphire crystal,		
	with Super President bracelet 8570/8.........................	18,000.00	10,691.00
	with bark finish Super President bracelet 9235/8.............	18,200.00	10,811.00
	with Super Jubilee bracelet 8571/8...........................	17,600.00	10,461.00
	with "Super Jubilee Karat" bracelet 6451/8..................	36,250.00	21,541.00
	with "Super Jubilee Karat" bracelet 6453/8..................	41,250.00	24,511.00
	with "Super Karat" bracelet 6454/8..........................	33,200.00	19,721.00
	with "Super President Karat" bracelet 8470/8................	39,200.00	23,291.00
	with "Super President Karat" bracelet 8472/8................	39,250.00	23,321.00
	with "Super President Karat" bracelet 8473/8................	50,700.00	30,121.00
	with "Super President Baguette" bracelet 8570/8B............	56,300.00	33,451.00
	with 10 brilliants set on Jubilee dial and Super President bracelet 8570/8......................	18,000.00	10,701.00
	with diamond string and 10 brilliants set on 18kt. gold dial and "Super President Karat" bracelet 8470/8........................	42,150.00	25,051.00
	Refer to model 79178 for a complete listing of available additional cost dials.		
79139 Bic	**Tridor Oyster Perpetual Lady-Datejust**, ⌀ 26mm, 18kt. white gold case, 18kt. yellow gold bezel set with 40 brilliants, 10 brilliants set on dial, 31 jewel chronometer movement, synthetic sapphire crystal,		
	with "Tridor" Super President bracelet 8270/9...............	21,600.00	12,831.00
	with "Bicolor Super Jubilee Karat" bracelet 6451/9..........	36,750.00	21,831.00
	with 10 brilliants set on Jubilee dial and "Tridor" Super President bracelet 8270/9............	21,650.00	12,861.00
	Refer to model 79178 for a complete listing of available additional cost dials.		

ROLEX OYSTER WATCHES

Style	Description	Suggested Retail Price	Wholesale
79158	**Oyster Perpetual Lady-Datejust**, ∅ 26mm, 18kt. yellow gold, bezel set with 40 brilliants, case lugs set with 24 brilliants, 10 brilliants set on dial, 31 jewel chronometer movement, synthetic sapphire crystal,		
	with Super President bracelet 8570/8..	19,950.00	11,851.00
	with "Super Karat" bracelet 6454/8..	35,200.00	20,911.00
	Refer to model 79178 for a complete listing of available additional cost dials.		
79159	**Oyster Perpetual Lady-Datejust**, ∅ 26mm, 18kt. white gold, bezel set with 40 brilliants, case lugs set with 24 brilliants, 10 brilliants set on dial, 31 jewel chronometer movement, synthetic sapphire crystal,		
	with Super President bracelet 8570/9..	20,550.00	12,201.00
	with "Super Karat" bracelet 6454/9..	35,800.00	21,261.00
	with 10 brilliants set on Jubilee dial and Super President bracelet 8570/9.....................	20,600.00	12,241.00
	Refer to model 79179 for a complete listing of available additional cost dials.		
79160	**Oyster Perpetual Lady-Date**, ∅ 26mm, stainless steel, polished bezel, 31 jewel chronometer movement, synthetic sapphire crystal,		
	with Jubilee bracelet 62510..	3,050.00	1,791.00
	with Oyster bracelet 78240..	2,950.00	1,731.00
79163	**Oyster Perpetual Lady-Datejust**, ∅ 26mm, stainless steel, 18kt. yellow gold polished bezel, 31 jewel chronometer movement, synthetic sapphire crystal,		
	with Oyster bracelet 78243..	3,975.00	2,331.00
	with Jubilee bracelet 62523..	4,250.00	2,501.00
	with 10 brilliants set on dial and Oyster bracelet 78243..............................	5,275.00	3,101.00
	with mother-of-pearl Roman or decorated Roman dial and Oyster bracelet 78243..........	5,075.00	2,991.00
	with mother-of-pearl "Serti" dial and Oyster bracelet 78243...........................	7,075.00	4,171.00
	with 2 brilliants set on onyx Arabic dial and Oyster bracelet 78243.....................	5,175.00	3,051.00
79166	**Oyster Perpetual Lady-Datejust**, ∅ 26mm, platinum, polished bezel, 10 brilliants set on dial, 31 jewel chronometer movement, synthetic sapphire crystal,		
	with Super President bracelet 8570/6..	20,500.00	12,181.00
	Refer to model 79179 for a complete listing of available additional cost dials.		
79168	**Oyster Perpetual Lady-Datejust**, ∅ 26mm, 18kt. yellow gold, polished bezel, 31 jewel chronometer movement, synthetic sapphire crystal,		
	with Jubilee bracelet 6251/8..	9,800.00	5,831.00
	with Oyster bracelet 7204/8...	9,500.00	5,651.00
	with Super Jubilee bracelet 8571/8..	11,350.00	6,751.00
	with Super President bracelet 8570/8..	11,700.00	6,951.00
	with 10 brilliants set on dial and Super President bracelet 8570/8.....................	13,000.00	7,721.00
	Refer to model 79178 for a complete listing of available additional cost dials.		
79173	**Oyster Perpetual Lady-Datejust**, ∅ 26mm, stainless steel, 18kt. yellow gold fluted bezel, 31 jewel chronometer movement, synthetic sapphire crystal,		
	with Jubilee bracelet 62523...	4,300.00	2,531.00
	with Oyster bracelet 78243...	4,025.00	2,361.00
	with 10 brilliants set on dial and Jubilee bracelet 62523.............................	5,600.00	3,291.00
	with 10 brilliants set on Jubilee dial and Oyster bracelet 78243......................	5,375.00	3,161.00
	with mother-of-pearl Roman or decorated Roman dial and Jubilee bracelet 62523..........	5,400.00	3,181.00
	with mother-of-pearl "Serti" dial and Jubilee bracelet 62523.........................	7,400.00	4,371.00
	with 2 brilliants set on mother-of-pearl dial and Jubilee bracelet 62523...............	7,250.00	4,281.00
	with 2 brilliants set on onyx Arabic dial and Jubilee bracelet 62523..................	5,500.00	3,241.00
	with semi-precious stone dial with applied gold Roman numerals (obsidienne) and Jubilee bracelet 62523...	5,400.00	3,181.00

ROLEX OYSTER WATCHES

Style	Description	Suggested Retail Price	Wholesale
79174	**Oyster Perpetual Lady-Datejust**, ∅ 26mm, stainless steel, 18kt. white gold fluted bezel, 31 jewel chronometer movement, synthetic sapphire crystal,		
	with Jubilee bracelet 62510..	3,600.00	2,111.00
	with Oyster bracelet 78240..	3,500.00	2,051.00
	with 10 brilliants set on dial and Jubilee bracelet 62510................	4,725.00	2,781.00
	with 10 brilliants set on Jubilee dial and Jubilee bracelet 62510........	4,775.00	2,811.00
	with mother-of-pearl Arabic, Roman or decorated Roman dial and Jubilee bracelet 62510..	4,525.00	2,671.00
	with mother-of-pearl "Serti" dial and Jubilee bracelet 62510............	6,525.00	3,851.00
	with 2 sapphires set on dial and Jubilee bracelet 62510.................	5,175.00	3,051.00
	with 10 brilliants set on semi-precious stone dial (sodalite) and Jubilee bracelet 62510......	6,175.00	3,651.00
79178	**Oyster Perpetual Lady-Datejust**, ∅ 26mm, 18kt. yellow gold, fluted bezel, 31 jewel chronometer movement, synthetic sapphire crystal,		
	with Super President bracelet 8570/8......................................	11,750.00	6,981.00
	with Super Jubilee bracelet 8571/8..	11,400.00	6,781.00
	with Jubilee bracelet 6251/8..	9,850.00	5,861.00
	with Oyster bracelet 7204/8...	9,550.00	5,681.00
	with 2 brilliants set on Arabic dial and Super President bracelet 8570/8....	12,200.00	7,251.00
	with 10 brilliants set on dial and Super President bracelet 8570/8.........	13,050.00	7,751.00
	with 10 brilliants set on dial and Oyster bracelet 7204/8.................	10,850.00	6,441.00
	with 10 brilliants set on Jubilee dial and Super President bracelet 8570/8..	13,100.00	7,781.00
	with 2 rubies set on dial and Super President bracelet 8570/8.............	14,350.00	8,531.00
	with mother-of-pearl Roman or decorated Roman dial and Super President bracelet 8570/8	12,850.00	7,641.00
	with 2 brilliants set on mother-of-pearl dial and Super President bracelet 8570/8..............	14,700.00	8,741.00
	with mother-of-pearl "Serti" dial and Super President bracelet 8570/8.........	14,850.00	8,821.00
	with 8 brilliants and 2 baguette diamonds set on mother-of-pearl Jubilee dial and Super President bracelet 8570/8......	15,250.00	9,061.00
	with 10 sapphires set on mother-of-pearl dial and Super President bracelet 8570/8...........	14,500.00	8,621.00
	with 10 rubies set on mother-of-pearl dial and Super President bracelet 8570/8..............	14,500.00	8,621.00
	with 10 emeralds set on mother-of-pearl dial and Super President bracelet 8570/8...........	16,600.00	9,861.00
	with onyx dial and Super President bracelet 8570/8........................	12,400.00	7,371.00
	with onyx Serti dial and Super President bracelet 8570/8..................	14,000.00	8,321.00
	with lapis lazuli dial and Super President bracelet 8570/8................	13,150.00	7,821.00
	with 2 brilliants set on lapis lazuli Arabic dial and Super President bracelet 8570/8..........	13,700.00	8,141.00
	with lapis lazuli "Serti" dial and Super President bracelet 8570/8............	14,750.00	8,771.00
	with lapis lazuli "Pyramid Serti" dial and Super President bracelet 8570/8....................	18,050.00	10,731.00
	with semi-precious stone dial with applied gold Roman numerals (obsidienne) and Super President bracelet 8570/8......	12,850.00	7,641.00
	with 10 brilliants set on semi-precious stone dial (ammonite, aventurine, azurite, cacholong, cornelian, ferrite, jade, jasper, opal, pyrite, turquoise) and Super President bracelet 8570/8..........	14,500.00	8,621.00
	with rubellite "Serti" dial and Super President bracelet 8570/8..............	14,750.00	8,771.00
	with diamond string and 10 brilliants set on 18kt. gold dial and Super President bracelet 8570/8......	16,000.00	9,511.00
	with diamond string and 10 sapphires set on 18kt. gold dial and Super President bracelet 8570/8......	16,100.00	9,571.00
	with diamond string and 10 rubies set on 18kt. gold dial and Super President bracelet 8570/8......	16,500.00	9,811.00
	with diamond string and 10 emeralds set on 18kt. gold dial and Super President bracelet 8570/8......	21,200.00	12,601.00

Continued.

ROLEX OYSTER WATCHES

Style	Description	Suggested Retail Price	Wholesale
	with 18kt. gold "Pleiade" diamond dial and Super President bracelet 8570/8.................	18,500.00	10,991.00
	with 18kt. gold "Myriad" diamond dial and Super President bracelet 8570/8..................	17,200.00	10,221.00
	with 10 brilliants set on semi-precious stone dial (ammonite, aventurine, azurite, cacholong, cornelian, ferrite, jade, jasper, opal, pyrite, turquoise) and Super President bracelet 8570/8..	14,500.00	8,621.00
	with rubellite "Serti" dial and Super President bracelet 8570/8................................	14,750.00	8,771.00
	with diamond string and 10 brilliants set on 18kt. gold dial and Super President bracelet 8570/8..	16,000.00	9,511.00
	with diamond string and 10 sapphires set on 18kt. gold dial and Super President bracelet 8570/8..	16,100.00	9,571.00
	with diamond string and 10 rubies set on 18kt. gold dial and Super President bracelet 8570/8..	16,500.00	9,811.00
	with diamond string and 10 emeralds set on 18kt. gold dial and Super President bracelet 8570/8..	21,200.00	12,601.00
	with 18kt. gold "Pleiade" diamond dial and Super President bracelet 8570/8.................	18,500.00	10,991.00
	with 18kt. gold "Myriad" diamond dial and Super President bracelet 8570/8.................	17,200.00	10,221.00
	with 18kt. gold "Myriad Arabic" diamond dial and Super President bracelet 8570/8.........	16,750.00	9,951.00
	with 18kt. gold "Myriad Roman" diamond dial and Super President bracelet 8570/8.........	14,850.00	8,821.00
	with 18kt. gold "Myriad Serti" diamond dial and Super President bracelet 8570/8............	17,450.00	10,371.00
	with 18kt. gold "Mother-of-Pearl Myriad" diamond dial set with 11 sapphires and Super President bracelet 8570/8..	17,450.00	10,371.00
	with 18kt. gold "Mother-of-Pearl Myriad" diamond dial set with 11 rubies and Super President bracelet 8570/8..	17,450.00	10,371.00
	with 18kt. gold "Mother-of-Pearl Myriad" diamond dial set with 11 emeralds and Super President bracelet 8570/8..	19,850.00	11,801.00
	with 18kt. gold "Mother-of-Pearl Pave Roman" diamond dial and Super President bracelet 8570/8..	20,500.00	12,181.00
	with 18kt. gold "Pave" diamond dial set with 11 sapphires and Super President bracelet 8570/8..	25,750.00	15,301.00
	with 18kt. gold "Pave" diamond dial set with 11 rubies and Super President bracelet 8570/8..	26,100.00	15,511.00
	with 18kt. gold "Pave" diamond dial set with 11 emeralds and Super President bracelet 8570/8..	31,750.00	18,871.00
	with 18kt. gold "Pave Extra Large" diamond dial and Super President bracelet 8570/8......	25,250.00	15,011.00
	with 18kt. gold "Pave Extra Large" diamond dial set with 11 sapphires and Super President bracelet 8570/8..	25,750.00	15,301.00
	with 18kt. gold "Pave Extra Large" diamond dial set with 11 rubies and Super President bracelet 8570/8..	26,100.00	15,511.00
	with 18kt. gold "Pave Extra Large" diamond dial set with 11 emeralds and Super President bracelet 8570/8..	31,750.00	18,871.00
79179 Bic	**Tridor Oyster Perpetual Lady-Datejust**, ⌀ 26mm, 18kt. white gold case, 18kt. yellow gold fluted bezel, 31 jewel chronometer movement, synthetic sapphire crystal,		
	with "Tridor" Super President bracelet 8270/9..	15,400.00	9,151.00
	with 10 brilliants set on dial and "Tridor" Super President bracelet 8270/9...................	16,700.00	9,911.00
	Refer to model 79178 for a complete listing of available additional cost dials.		

ROLEX OYSTER WATCHES

Style	Description	Suggested Retail Price	Wholesale
79179	**Oyster Perpetual Lady-Datejust**, ⌀ 26mm, 18kt. white gold, fluted bezel, 31 jewel chronometer movement, synthetic sapphire crystal,		
	with Super President bracelet 8570/9.....................	12,350.00	7,341.00
	with 10 brilliants set on dial and Super President bracelet 8570/9..............................	13,650.00	8,101.00
	with 10 brilliants set on Jubilee dial and Super President bracelet 8570/9......................	13,700.00	8,141.00
	with 2 sapphires set on dial and Super President bracelet 8570/9..............................	14,100.00	8,381.00
	with mother-of-pearl Arabic, Roman or decorated Roman dial and Super President bracelet 8570/9...........................	13,450.00	7,991.00
	with mother-of-pearl "Serti" dial and Super President bracelet 8570/9........................	15,450.00	9,181.00
	with 10 rubies set on mother-of-pearl dial and Super President bracelet 8570/9...............	15,100.00	8,971.00
	with 10 sapphires set on mother-of-pearl dial and Super President bracelet 8570/9...........	15,100.00	8,971.00
	with lapis lazuli "Serti" dial and Super President bracelet 8570/9............................	15,350.00	9,121.00
	with semi-precious stone dial with applied gold Roman numerals (obsidienne) and Super President bracelet 8570/9............................	13,450.00	7,991.00
	with 10 brilliants set on semi-precious stone dial (sodalite, turquoise) and Super President bracelet 8570/9............................	15,100.00	8,971.00
	with 18kt. gold "Pleiade" diamond dial and Super President bracelet 8570/9..................	19,100.00	11,351.00
	with 18kt. gold "Myriad Arabic" diamond dial and Super President bracelet 8570/9.........	17,350.00	10,311.00
	with 18kt. gold "Myriad Serti" diamond dial and Super President bracelet 8570/9...........	18,050.00	10,721.00
	with 18kt. gold "Pave" diamond dial set with 11 sapphires and Super President bracelet 8570/9............................	26,350.00	15,661.00
	with 18kt. gold "Pave Extra Large" diamond dial and Super President bracelet 8570/9......	25,850.00	15,361.00
	with 18kt. gold "Pave Extra Large" diamond dial set with 11 sapphires and Super President bracelet 8570/8............................	26,350.00	15,661.00
79188	**Oyster Perpetual Lady-Datejust**, ⌀ 26mm, 18kt. yellow gold, "Pyramid" bezel, case lugs set with 24 brilliants, 31 jewel chronometer movement, synthetic sapphire crystal,		
	with Super President bracelet 8570/8....................	13,800.00	8,201.00
	with Super Jubilee bracelet 8571/8.....................	13,450.00	7,991.00
	with 10 brilliants set on dial and Super President bracelet 8570/8............................	15,100.00	8,961.00
	with 10 brilliants set on Jubilee dial and "Super President Karat" bracelet 8472/8............	36,450.00	21,661.00
	Refer to model 79178 for a complete listing of available additional cost dials.		
79190	**Oyster Perpetual Lady-Datejust**, ⌀ 26mm, stainless steel, finely engine-turned bezel, 31 jewel chronometer movement, synthetic sapphire crystal,		
	with Jubilee bracelet 62510............................	3,100.00	1,821.00
	with Oyster bracelet 78240............................	3,000.00	1,761.00
79198R	**Oyster Perpetual Lady-Datejust**, ⌀ 26mm, 18kt. yellow gold, bezel set with 16 brilliants and 16 oval cut rubies, 10 brilliants set on dial, 31 jewel chronometer movement, synthetic sapphire crystal,		
	with Super President bracelet 8570/8....................	19,950.00	11,851.00
	with diamond string and 10 rubies set on 18kt. gold dial and "Super President Karat" bracelet 8473/8........................	56,150.00	33,371.00
	Refer to model 79178 for a complete listing of available additional cost dials.		
79198S	**Oyster Perpetual Lady-Datejust**, ⌀ 26mm, 18kt. yellow gold, bezel set with 16 brilliants and 16 oval cut sapphires, 10 brilliants set on dial, 31 jewel chronometer movement, synthetic sapphire crystal,		
	with Super President bracelet 8570/8....................	18,250.00	10,841.00
	Refer to model 79178 for a complete listing of available additional cost dials.		

ROLEX OYSTER WATCHES

Style	Description	Suggested Retail Price	Wholesale
79238	**Oyster Perpetual Lady-Datejust**, ⌀ 26mm, 18kt. yellow gold, fluted bezel, case lugs set with 24 brilliants, 31 jewel chronometer movement, synthetic sapphire crystal,		
	with Super President bracelet 8570/8……..............................	13,750.00	8,171.00
	with 10 brilliants set on dial and Super President bracelet 8570/8…........................	15,050.00	8,931.00
	Refer to model 79178 for a complete listing of available additional cost dials.		
79240	**Oyster Perpetual Lady-Datejust**, ⌀ 26mm, stainless steel, engine-turned bezel, 31 jewel chronometer movement, synthetic sapphire crystal,		
	with Jubilee bracelet 62510……….....…......................................	3,100.00	1,821.00
	with Oyster bracelet 78240……….....…...................................…...	3,000.00	1,761.00
79258	**Oyster Perpetual Lady-Datejust**, ⌀ 26mm, 18kt. yellow gold, "Pyramid" bezel set with 24 brilliants, 31 jewel chronometer movement, synthetic sapphire crystal,		
	with Super President bracelet 8570/8……..............................	14,850.00	8,821.00
	with Super Jubilee bracelet 8571/8……..................................	14,500.00	8,621.00
	with 10 brilliants set on dial and Super President bracelet 8570/8…........................	16,150.00	9,591.00
	with 10 brilliants set on Jubilee dial and "Super Jubilee Karat" bracelet 6451/8…........	34,450.00	20,461.00
	Refer to model 79178 for a complete listing of available additional cost dials.		
79268	**Oyster Perpetual Lady-Datejust**, ⌀ 26mm, 18kt. yellow gold, "Pyramid" bezel set with 24 brilliants, 31 jewel chronometer movement, synthetic sapphire crystal,		
	with Super President bracelet 8570/8……..............................	15,250.00	9,061.00
	with 10 brilliants set on dial and Super President bracelet 8570/8…........................	16,550.00	9,831.00
	with 10 brilliants set on Jubilee dial and "Super Jubilee Karat" bracelet 6453/8…..........	39,850.00	23,671.00
	Refer to model 79178 for a complete listing of available additional cost dials.		
79278	**Oyster Perpetual Lady-Datejust**, ⌀ 26mm, 18kt. yellow gold, bark finish bezel, 31 jewel chronometer movement, synthetic sapphire crystal,		
	with bark finish Super President bracelet 9235/8….................................	12,000.00	7,131.00
	with bark finish Jubilee bracelet 8211/8…................................….....	10,250.00	6,091.00
	with 10 brilliants set on dial and bark finish Super President bracelet 8570/8…................	13,300.00	7,901.00
	with diamond string and 10 brilliants set on 18kt. gold dial and bark finish Super President bracelet 9235/8…................................	16,250.00	9,661.00
	Refer to model 79178 for a complete listing of available additional cost dials.		
79279	**Oyster Perpetual Lady-Datejust**, ⌀ 26mm, 18kt. white gold, bark finish bezel, 31 jewel chronometer movement, synthetic sapphire crystal,		
	with bark finish Super President bracelet 9235/9….................................	12,950.00	7,691.00
	with bark finish Jubilee bracelet 8211/9…................................…....	11,200.00	6,651.00
	with 10 brilliants set on dial and bark finish Super President bracelet 8570/8…................	14,250.00	8,461.00
	Refer to model 79179 for a complete listing of available additional cost dials.		
79288	**Oyster Perpetual Lady-Datejust**, ⌀ 26mm, 18kt. yellow gold, bark finish bezel set with 12 brilliants, 31 jewel chronometer movement, synthetic sapphire crystal,		
	with bark finish Super President bracelet 9235/8….................................	14,750.00	8,761.00
	with 10 brilliants set on dial and bark finish Jubilee bracelet 8570/8…......................	14,300.00	8,491.00
	Refer to model 79178 for a complete listing of available additional cost dials.		

ROLEX OYSTER WATCHES

Style	Description	Suggested Retail Price	Wholesale
80298	**Oyster Perpetual Lady-Datejust**, ∅ 29mm, 18kt. yellow gold, bezel set with 32 brilliants, 10 brilliants on dial, 31 jewel chronometer movement, synthetic sapphire crystal,		
	with Oyster 14mm bracelet 72948...	25,750.00	15,301.00
	with "Oyster Karat" 14mm bracelet 74948..	43,250.00	25,701.00
	with "Super Oyster Karat" 14mm bracelet 74908..	68,500.00	40,701.00
	with "Super Oyster Karat" 14mm bracelet 74978..	47,450.00	28,181.00
	with "Super Oyster Karat" 14mm bracelet 74988..	45,950.00	27,301.00
	with "Super Karat" 14mm bracelet 64908...	63,550.00	37,771.00
	with mother-of-pearl "Serti" dial and "Oyster Karat" 14mm bracelet 74948............	45,050.00	26,771.00
	with 18kt. gold "Pave Extra Large" diamond dial and "Super Karat" 14mm bracelet 64908	75,750.00	45,011.00
	with Roman numerals on dial and "Super Oyster Karat" 14mm bracelet 74978..........	46,150.00	27,421.00
	Refer to model 79178 for a complete listing of available additional cost dials.		
80298 Bic	**Tridor Oyster Perpetual Lady-Datejust**, ∅ 29mm, 18kt. yellow gold, bezel set with 32 brilliants, 10 brilliants set on dial, 31 jewel chronometer movement, synthetic sapphire crystal,		
	with "Tridor" Oyster 14mm bracelet 72948...	26,450.00	15,711.00
	with "Tridor" Oyster Karat 14mm bracelet 74948..	46,500.00	27,631.00
	Refer to model 79178 for a complete listing of available additional cost dials.		
80299	**Oyster Perpetual Lady-Datejust**, ∅ 29mm, 18kt. white gold, bezel set with 32 brilliants, 10 brilliants set on dial, 31 jewel chronometer movement, synthetic sapphire crystal,		
	with Oyster 14mm bracelet 72949...	26,500.00	15,741.00
	with "Oyster Karat" 14mm bracelet 74949..	44,250.00	26,291.00
	with "Super Oyster Karat" 14mm bracelet 74909..	69,500.00	41,291.00
	with "Super Oyster Karat" 14mm bracelet 74979..	48,450.00	28,791.00
	with "Super Oyster Karat" 14mm bracelet 74989..	46,750.00	27,781.00
	with "Super Karat" 14mm bracelet 64909...	64,550.00	38,351.00
	with 18kt. gold "Pave Extra Large" diamond dial set with 11 sapphires and "Oyster Karat" 14mm bracelet 74949..	56,950.00	33,841.00
	with mother-of-pearl Arabic dial and "Super Oyster Karat" 14mm bracelet 74979.....	48,250.00	28,681.00
	Refer to model 79179 for a complete listing of available additional cost dials.		
80299 Bic	**Tridor Oyster Perpetual Lady-Datejust**, ∅ 29mm, 18kt. yellow gold, bezel set with 32 brilliants, 10 brilliants set on dial, 31 jewel chronometer movement, synthetic sapphire crystal,		
	with "Tridor" Oyster 14mm bracelet 72948...	26,500.00	15,741.00
	Refer to model 79178 for a complete listing of available additional cost dials.		
80308	**Oyster Perpetual Lady-Datejust**, ∅ 29mm, 18kt. yellow gold, bezel set with 40 baguette diamonds, 10 brilliants set on dial, 31 jewel chronometer movement, synthetic sapphire crystal,		
	with Oyster 14mm bracelet 72948...	36,000.00	21,391.00
	with "Oyster Karat" 14mm bracelet 74948..	53,500.00	37,791.00
	with "Super Oyster Karat" 14mm bracelet 74908..	78,750.00	46,791.00
	Refer to model 79178 for a complete listing of available additional cost dials.		
80308P	**Oyster Perpetual Lady-Datejust**, ∅ 29mm, 18kt. yellow gold, bezel set with 40 baguette pink sapphires, 10 brilliants on dial, 31 jewel chron. movement, synthetic sapphire crystal,		
	with Oyster 14mm bracelet 72948...	30,500.00	18,121.00
	with "Oyster Karat" 14mm bracelet 74948..	48,000.00	28,521.00
	with "Super Oyster Karat" 14mm bracelet 74908..	73,250.00	43,521.00
	with "Super Oyster Karat" 14mm bracelet 74908P..	57,000.00	33,871.00
	with "Super Karat" 14mm bracelet 64908P...	65,300.00	38,801.00
	Refer to model 79178 for a complete listing of available additional cost dials.		

ROLEX OYSTER WATCHES

Style	Description	Suggested Retail Price	Wholesale
80308R	**Oyster Perpetual Lady-Datejust**, ⌀ 29mm, 18kt. yellow gold, bezel set with 40 baguette rubies, 10 brilliants set on dial, 31 jewel chronometer movement, synthetic sapphire crystal,		
	with Oyster 14mm bracelet 72948	45,000.00	26,741.00
	with "Oyster Karat" 14mm bracelet 74948	62,500.00	37,141.00
	with "Super Oyster Karat" 14mm bracelet 74908	87,750.00	52,141.00
	with "Super Oyster Karat" 14mm bracelet 74908R	89,700.00	53,301.00
	with 10 rubies on mother-of-pearl dial and "Super Oyster Karat" 14mm bracelet 74908R	91,150.00	54,171.00
	Refer to model 79178 for a complete listing of available additional cost dials.		
80308S	**Oyster Perpetual Lady-Datejust**, ⌀ 29mm, 18kt. yellow gold, bezel set with 40 baguette sapphires, 10 brilliants set on dial, 31 jewel chronometer movement, synthetic sapphire crystal,		
	with Oyster 14mm bracelet 72948	30,500.00	18,121.00
	with "Oyster Karat" 14mm bracelet 74948	48,000.00	28,521.00
	with "Super Oyster Karat" 14mm bracelet 74908	73,250.00	43,521.00
	with "Super Oyster Karat" 14mm bracelet 74908S	57,000.00	33,871.00
	with 10 sapphires set on mother-of-pearl dial and "Super Oyster Karat" 14mm bracelet 74988	52,150.00	30,991.00
	Refer to model 79178 for a complete listing of available additional cost dials.		
80309	**Oyster Perpetual Lady-Datejust**, ⌀ 29mm, 18kt. white gold, bezel set with 40 baguette diamonds, 10 brilliants set on dial, 31 jewel chronometer movement, synthetic sapphire crystal,		
	with Oyster 14mm bracelet 72949	39,750.00	23,621.00
	with "Oyster Karat" 14mm bracelet 74949	57,500.00	34,161.00
	with "Super Oyster Karat" 14mm bracelet 74909	82,750.00	49,171.00
	Refer to model 79179 for a complete listing of available additional cost dials.		
80309P	**Oyster Perpetual Lady-Datejust**, ⌀ 29mm, 18kt. white gold, bezel set with 40 baguette pink sapphires, 10 brilliants set on dial, 31 jewel chronometer movement, synthetic sapphire crystal,		
	with Oyster 14mm bracelet 72949	34,500.00	20,501.00
	with "Oyster Karat" 14mm bracelet 74949	52,250.00	31,041.00
	with "Super Oyster Karat" 14mm bracelet 74909	77,500.00	46,051.00
	Refer to model 79179 for a complete listing of available additional cost dials.		
80309S	**Oyster Perpetual Lady-Datejust**, ⌀ 29mm, 18kt. white gold, bezel set with 40 baguette sky-blue sapphires, 10 brilliants set on dial, 31 jewel chronometer movement, synthetic sapphire crystal,		
	with Oyster 14mm bracelet 72949	34,500.00	20,501.00
	with "Oyster Karat" 14mm bracelet 74949	52,250.00	31,041.00
	with "Super Oyster Karat" 14mm bracelet 74909	77,500.00	46,051.00
	with "Super Oyster Karat" 14mm bracelet 74909S	61,300.00	36,421.00
	with "Super Karat" 14mm bracelet 64909S	75,000.00	44,561.00
	with mother-of-pearl "Serti" dial and "Super Oyster Karat" 14mm bracelet 74989	56,550.00	33,611.00
	Refer to model 79179 for a complete listing of available additional cost dials.		
80318	**Oyster Perpetual Lady-Datejust**, ⌀ 29mm, 18kt. yellow gold, bezel set with 12 brilliants, 31 jewel chronometer movement, synthetic sapphire crystal,		
	with Oyster 14mm bracelet 72948	15,450.00	9,181.00
	with 10 brilliants set on dial and Oyster 14mm bracelet 72948	16,750.00	9,941.00
	Refer to model 79178 for a complete listing of available additional cost dials.		

ROLEX OYSTER WATCHES

Style	Description	Suggested Retail Price	Wholesale
80318 Bic	**Tridor Oyster Perpetual Lady-Datejust**, ∅ 29mm, 18kt. yellow gold, bezel set with 12 brilliants, 31 jewel chronometer movement, synthetic sapphire crystal,		
	with "Tridor" Oyster 14mm bracelet 72948..	**16,150.00**	**9,591.00**
	with 10 brilliants set on dial and "Tridor" Oyster 14mm bracelet 72948.........................17,450.00		**10,361.00**
	Refer to model 79178 for a complete listing of available additional cost dials.		
80319	**Oyster Perpetual Lady-Datejust**, ∅ 29mm, 18kt. white gold, bezel set with 12 brilliants, 31 jewel chronometer movement, synthetic sapphire crystal,		
	with Oyster 14mm bracelet 72949..	**17,250.00**	**10,251.00**
	with 10 brilliants set on dial and Oyster 14mm bracelet 72949...................................	**18,550.00**	**11,011.00**
	Refer to model 79179 for a complete listing of available additional cost dials.		
80319 Bic	**Tridor Oyster Perpetual Lady-Datejust**, ∅ 29mm, 18kt. white gold, bezel set with 12 brilliants, 31 jewel chronometer movement, synthetic sapphire crystal,		
	with "Tridor" Oyster 14mm bracelet 72949...17,250.00		**10,251.00**
	with 10 brilliants set on dial and "Tridor" Oyster 14mm bracelet 72949.........................18,550.00		**11,011.00**
	Refer to model 79179 for a complete listing of available additional cost dials.		
80328	**Oyster Perpetual Lady-Datejust**, ∅ 29mm, 18kt. yellow gold, bezel set with 1 diamond, 31 jewel chronometer movement, synthetic sapphire crystal,		
	with Oyster 14mm bracelet 72948...	**15,450.00**	**9,181.00**
	with 10 brilliants set on dial and Oyster 14mm bracelet 72948..................................	**16,750.00**	**9,941.00**
	with 10 brilliants set on dial and "Oyster Karat" 14mm bracelet 72948.........................34,250.00		**20,341.00**
	Refer to model 79178 for a complete listing of available additional cost dials.		
80328 Bic	**Tridor Oyster Perpetual Lady-Datejust**, ∅ 29mm, 18kt. yellow gold, bezel set with 1 diamond, 31 jewel chronometer movement, synthetic sapphire crystal,		
	with "Bicolor" Oyster 14mm bracelet 72958...	**17,950.00**	**10,661.00**
	with 10 brilliants set on dial and "Bicolor" Oyster 14mm bracelet 72958.........................19,250.00		**11,431.00**
	with 10 brilliants set on dial and "Tridor Oyster Karat" 14mm bracelet 74958................37,500.00		**22,271.00**
	Refer to model 79178 for a complete listing of available additional cost dials.		
80329	**Oyster Perpetual Lady-Datejust**, ∅ 29mm, 18kt. white gold, bezel set with 1 diamond, 31 jewel chronometer movement, synthetic sapphire crystal,		
	with Oyster 14mm bracelet 72949..	**16,150.00**	**9,591.00**
	with 10 brilliants set on dial and Oyster 14mm bracelet 72949..................................	**17,450.00**	**10,361.00**
	Refer to model 79178 for a complete listing of available additional cost dials.		
80329 Bic	**Tridor Oyster Perpetual Lady-Datejust**, ∅ 29mm, 18kt. white gold, bezel set with 1 diamond, 31 jewel chronometer movement, synthetic sapphire crystal,		
	with "Bicolor" Oyster 14mm bracelet 72959...	**17,950.00**	**10,661.00**
	with 10 brilliants set on dial and "Bicolor" Oyster 14mm bracelet 72959.........................19,250.00		**11,431.00**
	Refer to model 79178 for a complete listing of available additional cost dials.		
80359	**Oyster Perpetual Lady-Datejust**, ∅ 29mm, 18kt. white gold, bezel set with 116 brilliants, case lugs set with 24 brilliants, 10 brilliants set on dial, 31 jewel chronometer movement, synthetic sapphire crystal,		
	with Oyster 14mm bracelet 72949..	**26,950.00**	**16,011.00**
	with "Oyster Karat" 14mm bracelet 74949...	**44,700.00**	**26,561.00**
	with "Super Oyster Karat" 14mm bracelet 74909..69,950.00		**41,561.00**
	Refer to model 79179 for a complete listing of available additional cost dials.		

ROLEX CELLINI WATCHES

Style	Description	Suggested Retail Price	Wholesale
2011/8	**Cellini Karat**, Ladies' 18kt. yellow gold case set with 2 full-cut brilliants, with 18kt. yellow gold bracelet,		
	with 3 brilliants set on dial..	12,850.00	7,561.00
	with mother-of-pearl dial..	12,850.00	7,561.00
	with 11 brilliants set on dial..	13,350.00	7,851.00
	with "Pave" diamond dial..	15,550.00	9,151.00
2035/8	**Cellini Karat**, Ladies' 18kt. yellow gold case and bracelet,		
	with mother-of-pearl dial..	10,650.00	6,261.00
	with 11 brilliants set on dial..	11,150.00	6,561.00
	with "Pave" diamond dial..	13,350.00	7,851.00
2037/8	**Cellini Karat**, Ladies' 18kt. yellow gold case and bracelet, bracelet set with 193 full-cut brilliants,		
	with 3 brilliants set on dial..	19,750.00	11,611.00
	with mother-of-pearl dial..	19,750.00	11,611.00
	with "Pave" diamond dial..	22,450.00	13,201.00
2253/8	**Cellini Parentheses**, Ladies' 18kt. yellow gold case set with 28 full-cut brilliants, with 18kt. yellow gold bracelet,		
	with 3 brilliants set on dial..	18,350.00	10,791.00
	with ferrite or mother-of-pearl Roman dial..	18,350.00	10,791.00
2255/8	**Cellini Karat**, Ladies' 18kt. yellow gold case set with 28 full-cut brilliants, with 18kt. yellow gold bracelet,		
	with 3 brilliants set on dial..	18,500.00	10,881.00
	with ferrite or mother-of-pearl Roman dial..	18,500.00	10,881.00
2294/8	**Cellini Gourmette**, Ladies' 18kt. yellow gold case and bracelet,		
	with 3 brilliants set on dial..	13,250.00	7,791.00
	with 11 brilliants set on dial..	13,750.00	8,091.00
	with "Pleiade" diamond dial..	15,850.00	9,321.00
	with "Pave" diamond dial..	18,750.00	11,031.00
2294/8 Bic	**Cellini Bicolor Gourmette**, Ladies' 18kt. yellow gold case with 18kt. yellow and white gold combination bracelet,		
	with 3 brilliants set on dial..	13,600.00	8,001.00
	with 11 brilliants set on dial..	14,100.00	8,291.00
	with "Pleiade" diamond dial..	16,200.00	9,531.00
	with "Pave" diamond dial..	19,100.00	11,231.00
2295/8	**Cellini Gourmette**, Ladies' 18kt. yellow gold case and bracelet set with 118 full-cut brilliants, with 3 brilliants set on dial........................	25,400.00	14,941.00
	with mother-of-pearl Roman dial..	25,400.00	14,941.00
	with 11 brilliants set on dial..	25,900.00	15,241.00
	with "Pleiade" diamond dial..	28,000.00	16,471.00
	with "Pave" diamond dial..	30,900.00	18,181.00
2295/8 Bic	**Cellini Bicolor Gourmette**, Ladies' 18kt. yellow gold case with 18kt. yellow and white gold combination bracelet, case and bracelet set with 118 full-cut brilliants,		
	with 3 brilliants set on dial..	25,850.00	15,201.00
	with 11 brilliants set on dial..	26,350.00	15,501.00
	With "Pleiade" diamond dial..	28,450.00	16,731.00
	With "Pave" diamond dial..	31,350.00	18,441.00

ROLEX CELLINI WATCHES

Style	Description	Suggested Retail Price	Wholesale
2296/8	**Cellini Gourmette**, Ladies' 18kt. yellow gold case and bracelet set with 92 full-cut brilliants, with 3 brilliants set on dial	22,600.00	13,291.00
	with 11 brilliants set on dial	23,100.00	13,591.00
	with "Pleiade" diamond dial	25,200.00	14,821.00
	with "Pave" diamond dial	28,100.00	16,531.00
2296/8 Bic	**Cellini Bicolor Gourmette**, Ladies' 18kt. yellow gold case with 18kt. yellow and white gold combination bracelet, case and bracelet set with 92 full-cut brilliants, with 3 brilliants set on dial	23,000.00	13,531.00
	with 11 brilliants set on dial	23,500.00	13,821.00
	With "Pleiade" diamond dial	25,600.00	15,061.00
	With "Pave" diamond dial	28,500.00	16,761.00
2435/8	**Cellini Gourmette**, Ladies' 18kt. yellow gold case and bracelet set with 62 full-cut brilliants, with 3 brilliants set on dial	17,300.00	10,181.00
	with 11 brilliants set on dial	17,800.00	10,471.00
2466/8C	**Cellini Karat**, Ladies' 18kt. yellow gold case set with 36 full-cut brilliants, with 18kt. yellow gold bracelet, with 2 citrine cabochons and tigrite dial	15,750.00	9,261.00
2504/8	**Cellini Karat**, Ladies' 18kt. yellow gold case set with 18 full-cut brilliants, with 18kt. yellow gold bracelet, with 3 brilliants set on dial	11,300.00	6,651.00
	with mother-of-pearl dial	11,300.00	6,651.00
	with 11 brilliants set on dial	11,800.00	6,941.00
	with "Pleiade" diamond dial	13,900.00	8,181.00
	with "Pave" diamond dial	16,800.00	9,881.00
2708/8	**Cellini Almond**, Ladies' 18kt. yellow gold case set with 50 full-cut brilliants, with 18kt. yellow gold plaited bracelet, with champagne Roman dial	23,550.00	13,881.00
	with mother-of-pearl Roman dial	24,150.00	14,201.00
	with "Pave" diamond dial	30,000.00	17,651.00
3612/8	**Cellini Classic**, 22kt. yellow gold U.S. twenty dollar coin watch	9,450.00	5,561.00
3717/8	**Cellini Classic**, 18kt. yellow gold pocket watch	3,250.00	1,911.00
	Also available in white gold, model 3717/9	3,700.00	2,181.00
3729/8	**Cellini Classic**, 18kt. yellow gold pocket watch	3,700.00	2,181.00
	Also available in white gold, model 3729/9	3,900.00	2,291.00
3759/8	**Cellini Classic**, 18kt. yellow gold pocket watch	14,550.00	8,561.00
	with chain 787/8	19,200.00	11,291.00
3761/8	**Cellini Classic**, 18kt. yellow gold pocket watch	6,900.00	4,061.00
	with chain 787/8	11,550.00	6,791.00
3767/8	**Cellini First**, 18kt. yellow gold pocket watch	6,150.00	3,621.00
	with mother-of-pearl Arabic dial	7,000.00	4,121.00
	with chain 787/8	10,800.00	6,351.00
3771/8	**Cellini First**, 18kt. yellow gold pocket watch	6,150.00	3,621.00
	with chain 787/8	10,800.00	6,351.00
3783/8	**Cellini Midas-First Smooth**, 18kt. yellow gold pocket watch	6,150.00	3,621.00
	with chain 787/8	10,800.00	6,351.00
3787/8	**Cellini Midas-First Smooth**, 18kt. yellow gold pocket watch	6,150.00	3,621.00
	with chain 787/8	10,800.00	6,351.00

ROLEX CELLINI WATCHES

Style	Description	Suggested Retail Price	Wholesale
4047/8	**Cellini Zephyr**, Ladies' 18kt. yellow gold strap watch..	3,300.00	1,941.00
	with 3 brilliants set on dial...	3,900.00	2,301.00
	Also available in white gold, model 4047/9...	3,450.00	2,031.00
	with 3 brilliants set on dial...	4,050.00	2,381.00
4056/8	**Cellini Zephyr**, Men's 18kt. yellow gold strap watch..	3,700.00	2,181.00
	Also available in white gold, model 4056/9...	3,850.00	2,261.00
	with 3 brilliants set on dial...	4,450.00	2,621.00
4080/8	**Cellini Zephyr**, Ladies' 18kt. yellow gold strap watch..	3,300.00	1,941.00
	with 3 brilliants set on dial...	3,900.00	2,301.00
	Also available in white gold, model 4080/9...	3,450.00	2,031.00
	with 3 brilliants set on dial...	4,050.00	2,381.00
4081/8	**Cellini Zephyr**, Ladies' 18kt. yellow gold strap watch..	3,000.00	1,761.00
	with 3 brilliants set on dial...	3,600.00	2,151.00
	Also available in white gold, model 4081/9...	3,150.00	1,881.00
	with 3 brilliants set on dial...	3,750.00	2,241.00
4082/8	**Cellini Zephyr**, Ladies' 18kt. yellow gold strap watch..	3,050.00	1,791.00
	with 3 brilliants set on dial...	3,650.00	2,151.00
	Also available in white gold, model 4082/9...	3,200.00	1,881.00
	with 3 brilliants set on dial...	3,800.00	2,241.00
4083/8	**Cellini Zephyr**, Men's 18kt. yellow gold strap watch..	3,400.00	2,001.00
	with 3 brilliants set on dial...	4,000.00	2,351.00
	Also available in white gold, model 4083/9...	3,550.00	2,091.00
	with 3 brilliants set on dial...	4,150.00	2,441.00
4084/8	**Cellini Zephyr**, Men's 18kt. yellow gold strap watch..	3,450.00	2,031.00
	with 3 brilliants set on dial...	4,050.00	2,381.00
	Also available in white gold, model 4084/9...	3,600.00	2,121.00
	with 3 brilliants set on dial...	4,200.00	2,471.00
4087/8	**Cellini Zephyr**, Men's 18kt. yellow gold strap watch..	3,700.00	2,181.00
	with 3 brilliants sct on dial...	4,300.00	2,531.00
	Also available in white gold, model 4087/9...	3,850.00	2,261.00
	with 3 brilliants set on dial...	4,450.00	2,621.00
4109/8	**Cellini Biseau**, Ladies' 18kt. yellow gold strap watch..	2,900.00	1,711.00
	Also available in white gold, model 4109/9...	3,050.00	1,791.00
4110/8	**Cellini Biseau**, Ladies' 18kt. yellow gold strap watch..	2,500.00	1,471.00
	Also available in white gold, model 4110/9...	2,650.00	1,561.00
4111/8	**Cellini Biseau**, Ladies' 18kt. yellow gold strap watch..	3,050.00	1,791.00
	Also available in white gold, model 4111/9...	3,200.00	1,881.00
4112/8	**Cellini Biseau**, Men's 18kt. yellow gold strap watch..	3,200.00	1,881.00
	with mother-of-pearl Arabic dial...	4,050.00	2,381.00
	Also available in white gold, model 4112/9...	3,350.00	1,971.00
4113/8	**Cellini Biseau**, Men's 18kt. yellow gold strap watch..	3,450.00	2,031.00
	Also available in white gold, model 4113/9...	3,600.00	2,121.00
4114/8	**Cellini Biseau**, Men's 18kt. yellow gold strap watch..	3,450.00	2,031.00
	Also available in white gold, model 4114/9...	3,600.00	2,121.00
4126/8	**Cellini Midas-First Clous de Paris**, Men's 18kt. yellow gold strap watch...................	4,000.00	2,351.00
	with African mahogany dial..	4,300.00	2,531.00
	Also available in white gold, model 4126/9...	4,150.00	2,441.00
4127/8	**Cellini Midas-First Clous de Paris**, Men's 18kt. yellow gold strap watch...................	4,000.00	2,351.00
	with African mahogany dial..	4,300.00	2,531.00
	Also available in white gold, model 4127/9...	4,150.00	2,441.00

ROLEX CELLINI WATCHES

Style	Description	Suggested Retail Price	Wholesale
4129/8	**Cellini Ligne Douce**, Ladies' 18kt. yellow gold strap watch..................................	3,000.00	1,761.00
	Also available in white gold, model 4129/9...	3,150.00	1,851.00
4131/8	**Cellini Ligne Douce**, Ladies' 18kt. yellow gold strap watch..................................	2,900.00	1,701.00
	Also available in white gold, model 4131/9...	3,050.00	1,791.00
4133/8	**Cellini Ligne Douce**, Men's 18kt. yellow gold strap watch..................................	3,300.00	1,941.00
	Also available in white gold, model 4133/9...	3,450.00	2,031.00
4135/8	**Cellini Ligne Douce**, Men's 18kt. yellow gold strap watch..................................	3,300.00	1,941.00
	Also available in white gold, model 4135/9...	3,450.00	2,031.00
4136/8	**Cellini Ligne Douce**, Men's 18kt. yellow gold strap watch..................................	3,500.00	2,061.00
	Also available in white gold, model 4136/9...	3,700.00	2,181.00
4139/8 Bic	**Cellini Bicolor**, Ladies' 18kt. yellow and white gold combination strap watch............	3,350.00	1,971.00
4140/8 Bic	**Cellini Bicolor**, Men's 18kt. yellow and white gold combination strap watch..............	4,150.00	2,441.00
4143/8 Bic	**Cellini Midas-First Smooth Bicolor**, Men's 18kt. yellow and white gold combination strap watch, case set with 12 full-cut brilliants, with 3 brilliants set on dial....................	5,350.00	3,151.00
4150/8 Bic	**Cellini First Bicolor**, Men's 18kt. yellow and white gold combination strap watch........	4,550.00	2,681.00
4160/8	**Cellini First**, Ladies' 18kt. yellow gold strap watch...................................	3,450.00	2,031.00
	with 11 brilliants set on dial...	4,750.00	2,791.00
	Also available in white gold, model 4160/9...	3,600.00	2,121.00
4170/8	**Cellini First**, Men's 18kt. yellow gold strap watch.....................................	4,150.00	2,441.00
	Also available in white gold, model 4170/9...	4,300.00	2,531.00
4311/8	**Cellini Biseau**, Men's 18kt. yellow gold case and bracelet...............................	10,100.00	5,941.00
4312/8	**Cellini Clous de Paris**, Men's 18kt. yellow gold case and bracelet.............................	13,900.00	8,181.00
4317/8	**Cellini Zephyr**, Ladies' 18kt. yellow gold case and bracelet..................................	9,100.00	5,351.00
	with 3 brilliants set on dial..	9,700.00	5,711.00
4318/8	**Cellini Zephyr**, Ladies' 18kt. yellow gold case and bracelet..................................	9,100.00	5,351.00
	with 3 brilliants set on dial..	9,700.00	5,711.00
4319/8	**Cellini Zephyr**, Men's 18kt. yellow gold case and bracelet...................................	10,750.00	6,321.00
4320/8	**Cellini Zephyr**, Men's 18kt. yellow gold case and bracelet...................................	10,750.00	6,321.00
	with 3 brilliants set on dial..	11,350.00	6,681.00
4339/8 Bic	**Cellini Bicolor**, Ladies' 18kt. yellow and white gold combination case and bracelet......	9,450.00	5,561.00
4340/8 Bic	**Cellini Bicolor**, Men's 18kt. yellow and white gold combination case and bracelet........	11,400.00	6,701.00
4345/8 Bic	**Cellini Midas Bicolor**, Ladies' 18kt. yellow and white gold combination case with 18kt. yellow gold bracelet...	9,950.00	5,851.00
4346/8 Bic	**Cellini Alpha Bicolor**, Men's 18kt. yellow and white gold combination case with 18kt. yellow gold bracelet...	13,150.00	7,731.00
4347/8 Bic	**Cellini Alpha Bicolor**, Ladies' 18kt. yellow gold case with 18kt. yellow and white gold combination bracelet...	9,100.00	5,351.00
4349/8 Bic	**Cellini Alpha Bicolor**, Men's 18kt. yellow gold case with 18kt. yellow and white gold combination bracelet...	10,350.00	6,091.00
4350/8	**Cellini First**, Men's 18kt. yellow gold case and bracelet.....................................	15,400.00	9,061.00
	with African mahogany dial...	15,700.00	9,241.00
	Also available in white gold, model 4350/9...	17,150.00	10,091.00
4355/8	**Cellini Midas-First Clous de Paris**, Men's 18kt. yellow gold case and bracelet..............	15,400.00	9,061.00
	with African mahogany dial...	15,700.00	9,241.00
	with "Pleiade" diamond dial..	20,250.00	11,911.00

ROLEX CELLINI WATCHES

Style	Description	Suggested Retail Price	Wholesale
4378/8 Bic	**Cellini Bicolor**, Ladies' 18kt. yellow gold combination case with 18kt. yellow and white gold combination bracelet..	**8,400.00**	**4,941.00**
	with 12 brilliants set on dial...	**9,700.00**	**5,711.00**
4623/8	**Cellini Biseau**, Ladies' 18kt. yellow gold case set with 20 full-cut brilliants		
	with 18kt. yellow gold bracelet...	**9,400.00**	**5,531.00**
4628/8	**Cellini Ligne Douce**, Ladies' 18kt. yellow gold case set with 10 full-cut brilliants		
	with 18kt. yellow gold bracelet, lapis lazuli dial...................................	**10,750.00**	**6,321.00**
4650/8	**Cellini First**, Men's 18kt. yellow gold case set with 50 full-cut brilliants		
	with 18kt. yellow gold bracelet...	**20,250.00**	**11,911.00**
	with African Mahogany dial..	**20,550.00**	**12,091.00**
4933/8	**Cellini Jubilee**, Ladies' 18kt. yellow gold case		
	with 18kt. yellow gold "Jubilee" finish bracelet...................................	**7,800.00**	**4,591.00**
4934/8	**Cellini Jubilee**, Men's 18kt. yellow gold case		
	with 18kt. yellow gold "Jubilee" finish bracelet...................................	**9,350.00**	**5,501.00**
4951/8	**Cellini First**, Men's 18kt. yellow gold case set with 32 full-cut brilliants		
	with 18kt. yellow gold bracelet...	**24,900.00**	**14,651.00**
5041/8	**Cellini Classic**, Ladies' 18kt. yellow gold case and bracelet.................	**8,050.00**	**4,731.00**
	with 11 brilliants set on mother-of-pearl Roman dial.............................	**9,350.00**	**5,501.00**
5042/8	**Cellini Classic**, Men's 18kt. yellow gold case and bracelet..................	**9,950.00**	**5,851.00**
	with 11 brilliants set on mother-of-pearl Roman dial.............................	**11,250.00**	**6,621.00**
5071/8	**Cellini Midas-First Smooth**, Men's 18kt. yellow gold strap watch..........	**3,600.00**	**2,121.00**
	with African mahogany dial..	**3,900.00**	**2,301.00**
5072/8	**Cellini Midas-First Smooth**, Men's 18kt. yellow gold strap watch..........	**3,850.00**	**2,261.00**
5078/8	**Cellini Clous de Paris**, Men's 18kt. yellow gold strap watch.................	**6,300.00**	**3,701.00**
5109/8	**Cellini Classic**, Ladies' 18kt. yellow gold strap watch........................	**2,900.00**	**1,711.00**
	with mother-of-pearl Arabic dial...	**3,700.00**	**2,181.00**
	with 11 brilliants set on dial...	**3,900.00**	**2,291.00**
	with 11 brilliants set on mother-of-pearl Roman dial.............................	**4,200.00**	**2,471.00**
5112/8	**Cellini Classic**, Men's 18kt. yellow gold strap watch...........................	**3,100.00**	**1,821.00**
	with mother-of-pearl Arabic dial...	**3,900.00**	**2,291.00**
	with 11 brilliants set on dial...	**4,100.00**	**2,411.00**
	with 11 brilliants set on mother-of-pearl Roman dial.............................	**4,400.00**	**2,591.00**
5113/8	**Cellini Classic**, Ladies' 18kt. yellow gold strap watch, case set with 58 full-cut brilliants...	**7,750.00**	**4,561.00**
	with mother-of-pearl Arabic dial...	**8,550.00**	**5,031.00**
5114/8	**Cellini Classic**, Men's 18kt. yellow gold strap watch, case set with 68 full-cut brilliants.....	**8,100.00**	**4,761.00**
	with mother-of-pearl Arabic dial...	**8,900.00**	**5,231.00**
	with 11 brilliants set on dial...	**9,100.00**	**5,351.00**
	with 11 brilliants set on mother-of-pearl Roman dial.............................	**9,400.00**	**5,531.00**
5133/8	**Cellini Jubilee**, Ladies' 18kt. yellow gold case set with 58 full-cut brilliants		
	with 18kt. yellow gold "Jubilee" finish bracelet...................................	**10,450.00**	**6,151.00**
	with mother-of-pearl Arabic dial...	**11,250.00**	**6,621.00**
5134/8	**Cellini Jubilee**, Men's 18kt. yellow gold case set with 58 full-cut brilliants		
	with 18kt. yellow gold "Jubilee" finish bracelet...................................	**12,750.00**	**7,501.00**
	with mother-of-pearl Arabic dial...	**13,550.00**	**7,971.00**
	With 11 brilliants set on mother-of-pearl Roman dial.............................	**14,050.00**	**8,261.00**
5150/8	**Cellini Pyramid**, Men's 18kt. yellow gold case and "Pyramid" bracelet......................	**15,400.00**	**9,061.00**
5156/8 Bic	**Cellini Midas-First Smooth Bicolor**, Men's 18kt. yellow and white gold combination strap watch..	**4,550.00**	**2,681.00**

ROLEX CELLINI WATCHES

Style	Description	Suggested Retail Price	Wholesale
5161/8	**Cellini Classic**, Ladies' 18kt. yellow gold case and bracelet	10,950.00	6,441.00
	with mother-of-pearl Arabic dial	11,750.00	6,911.00
	with 11 brilliants set on mother-of-pearl Roman dial	12,250.00	7,211.00
5162/8	**Cellini Classic**, Men's 18kt. yellow gold case and bracelet	13,100.00	7,701.00
	with mother-of-pearl Arabic dial	13,900.00	8,171.00
	with 11 brilliants set on mother-of-pearl Roman dial	14,400.00	8,471.00
5173/8	**Cellini Parentheses**, Ladies' 18kt. yellow gold case set with 48 full-cut brilliants with 18kt. yellow gold bracelet	15,100.00	8,881.00
5174/8	**Cellini Parentheses**, Ladies' 18kt. yellow gold case set with 48 full-cut brilliants with 18kt. yellow gold bracelet, with ferrite Roman dial	15,700.00	9,231.00
5183/8	**Cellini Parentheses**, Ladies' 18kt. yellow gold case set with 42 full-cut brilliants		
	with 18kt. yellow gold bracelet	13,950.00	8,201.00
	with 11 brilliants set on dial	15,250.00	8,971.00
	with "Pave Extra Large" diamond dial	19,650.00	11,561.00
5184/8	**Cellini Parentheses**, Ladies' 18kt. yellow gold case with 42 full-cut brilliants and 2 rubies		
	with 18kt. yellow gold bracelet	16,150.00	9,501.00
	with rubellite dial	16,950.00	9,971.00
	with 11 brilliants set on dial	17,450.00	10,261.00
	with "Pleiade" diamond dial	18,750.00	11,031.00
5185/8	**Cellini Parentheses**, Ladies' 18kt. yellow gold case set with 28 full-cut brilliants		
	with 18kt. yellow gold bracelet	13,900.00	8,181.00
	with 11 brilliants set on dial	15,200.00	8,941.00
5186/8	**Cellini Parentheses**, Ladies' 18kt. yellow gold case set with 28 full-cut brilliants		
	with 18kt. yellow gold bracelet	14,000.00	8,231.00
	with 11 brilliants set on dial	15,300.00	9,001.00
	with "Pleiade" diamond dial	16,600.00	9,761.00
	with "Pave" diamond dial	19,700.00	11,591.00
5204/8	**Cellini Parentheses**, Ladies' 18kt. yellow gold case set with 20 full-cut brilliants		
	with chestnut ostrich strap	6,450.00	3,791.00
	with 11 brilliants set on dial	7,750.00	4,561.00
	with "Pleiade" diamond dial	9,050.00	5,321.00
	with "Pave" diamond dial	12,150.00	7,151.00
5205/8	**Cellini Parentheses**, Ladies' 18kt. yellow gold case set with 44 full-cut brilliants		
	with chestnut ostrich strap	13,750.00	8,091.00
	with 11 brilliants set on dial	15,050.00	8,851.00
	with "Pleiade" diamond dial	16,350.00	9,621.00
	with "Pave" diamond dial	19,450.00	11,441.00
5206/8	**Cellini Parentheses**, Ladies' 18kt. yellow gold case set with 28 full-cut brilliants		
	with chestnut ostrich strap	10,400.00	6,121.00
	with 11 brilliants set on dial	11,700.00	6,881.00
5214/8	**Cellini Parentheses**, Ladies' 18kt. yellow gold case set with 20 full-cut brilliants		
	with chestnut ostrich strap	6,600.00	3,881.00
	with 11 brilliants set on dial	7,900.00	4,651.00
5218/8	**Cellini Parentheses**, Ladies' 18kt. yellow gold case set with 64 full-cut brilliants		
	with 18kt. yellow gold bracelet	19,250.00	11,321.00
	with 11 brilliants set on dial	20,550.00	12,091.00
5219/8	**Cellini Parentheses**, Ladies' 18kt. yellow gold case set with 54 full-cut brilliants		
	with 18kt. yellow gold bracelet	18,150.00	10,681.00
	with 11 brilliants set on dial	20,750.00	12,201.00

ROLEX CELLINI WATCHES

Style	Description	Suggested Retail Price	Wholesale
5220/8	**Cellini Parentheses**, Ladies' 18kt. yellow gold case set with 52 full-cut brilliants		
	with 18kt. yellow gold bracelet...	18,350.00	10,791.00
	with 11 brilliants set on dial..	19,650.00	11,561.00
	with "Pleiade" diamond dial..	20,950.00	12,321.00
5310/5	**Cellini Or Rose**, Ladies' 18kt. pink gold strap watch..	4,350.00	2,561.00
5320/5	**Cellini Or Rose**, mid-size 18kt. pink gold strap watch..	4,850.00	2,851.00
5330/5	**Cellini Or Rose**, Men's 18kt. pink gold strap watch..	5,350.00	3,151.00
6621/8	**Cellini Quartz**, Ladies', 18kt. yellow gold, 8 jewel movement, synthetic sapphire crystal,		
	with 18kt. yellow gold deployable clasp on black, blue or chestnut ostrich strap..............	5,200.00	3,061.00
	with 11 brilliants set on dial and ostrich strap..	6,450.00	3,791.00
	with 18kt. yellow gold "Damier" bracelet 211/8..	8,850.00	5,201.00
	with 11 brilliants set on dial and "Damier" bracelet 211/8.......................................	10,100.00	5,941.00
	with 18kt. yellow gold "Milanese" bracelet 213/8..	9,400.00	5,531.00
	with 11 brilliants set on dial and "Milanese" bracelet 213/8.....................................	10,650.00	6,261.00
	with 18kt. yellow gold "Milanese" bracelet 313/8..	9,400.00	5,531.00
	with 11 brilliants set on dial and "Milanese" bracelet 313/8.....................................	10,650.00	6,261.00
6621/9	**Cellini Quartz**, Ladies', 18kt. white gold, 8 jewel movement, synthetic sapphire crystal,		
	with 18kt. white gold deployable clasp on blue, brown or red leather strap....................	5,200.00	3,061.00
	with 11 brilliants set on dial and leather strap...	6,450.00	3,791.00
	with 11 brilliants set on "Jubilee" dial and leather strap...	6,450.00	3,791.00
6622/8	**Cellini Quartz**, mid-size, 18kt. yellow gold, 8 jewel movement, synthetic sapphire crystal,		
	with 18kt. yellow gold deployable clasp on black, blue or chestnut ostrich strap..............	6,250.00	3,681.00
	with 11 brilliants set on dial and ostrich strap..	7,500.00	4,411.00
	with 18kt. yellow gold Ladies' "Damier" bracelet 221/8..	10,500.00	6,181.00
	with 11 brilliants set on dial and Ladies' "Damier" bracelet 221/8...........................	11,750.00	6,911.00
	with 18kt. yellow gold Men's "Damier" bracelet 222/8...............................	10,750.00	6,321.00
	with 11 brilliants set on dial and Men's "Damier" bracelet 222/8...............................	12,000.00	7,061.00
	with 18kt. yellow gold Ladies' "Milanese" bracelet 223/8......................................	11,000.00	6,471.00
	with 11 brilliants set on dial and Ladies' "Milanese" bracelet 223/8...........................	12,250.00	7,211.00
	with 18kt. yellow gold Ladies' "Milanese" bracelet 323/8......................................	11,000.00	6,471.00
	with 11 brilliants set on dial and Ladies' "Milanese" bracelet 323/8...........................	12,250.00	7,211.00
	with 18kt. yellow gold Men's "Milanese" bracelet 224/8..	11,300.00	6,651.00
	with 11 brilliants set on dial and Men's "Milanese" bracelet 224/8.............................	12,550.00	7,381.00
	with 18kt. yellow gold Men's "Milanese" bracelet 324/8..	11,300.00	6,651.00
	with 11 brilliants set on dial and Men's "Milanese" bracelet 324/8.............................	12,550.00	7,381.00
6622/9	**Cellini Quartz**, mid-size, 18kt. white gold, 8 jewel movement, synthetic sapphire crystal,		
	with 18kt. white gold deployable clasp on blue, brown or red leather strap....................	6,250.00	3,681.00
	with 11 brilliants set on dial and leather strap...	7,500.00	4,411.00
	with 11 brilliants set on "Jubilee" dial and leather strap...	7,500.00	4,411.00
6623/8	**Cellini Quartz**, Men's, 18kt. yellow gold, 8 jewel movement, synthetic sapphire crystal,		
	with 18kt. yellow gold deployable clasp on black, blue or chestnut ostrich strap..............	7,100.00	4,181.00
	with 11 brilliants set on dial and ostrich strap..	8,600.00	5,061.00
	with 18kt. yellow gold "Damier" bracelet 231/8..	12,000.00	7,061.00
	with 11 brilliants set on dial and "Damier" bracelet 231/8.......................................	13,500.00	7,951.00
	with 18kt. yellow gold "Milanese" bracelet 233/8..	12,500.00	7,351.00
	with 11 brilliants set on dial and "Milanese" bracelet 233/8.....................................	14,000.00	8,241.00
	with 18kt. yellow gold "Milanese" bracelet 333/8..	12,500.00	7,351.00
	with 11 brilliants set on dial and "Milanese" bracelet 333/8.....................................	14,000.00	8,241.00

ROLEX CELLINI WATCHES

Style	Description	Suggested Retail Price	Wholesale
6623/9	**Cellini Quartz**, Men's, 18kt. white gold, 8 jewel movement, synthetic sapphire crystal,		
	with 18kt. white gold deployable clasp on blue, brown or red leather strap................	7,100.00	4,181.00
	with 11 brilliants set on dial and leather strap...................................	8,600.00	5,061.00
	with 11 brilliants set on "Jubilee" dial and leather strap............................	8,600.00	5,061.00
6631/8	**Cellini Quartz**, Ladies', 18kt. yellow gold, 8 jewel movement, synthetic sapphire crystal,		
	with 18kt. yellow gold deployable clasp on black, blue or chestnut ostrich strap............	5,450.00	3,211.00
	with 18kt. yellow gold "Damier" bracelet 212/8..................................	9,100.00	5,351.00
6631/9	**Cellini Quartz**, Ladies', 18kt. white gold, 8 jewel movement, synthetic sapphire crystal,		
	with 18kt. white gold deployable clasp on blue, brown or red leather strap................	5,450.00	3,211.00
6633/8	**Cellini Quartz**, Men's, 18kt. yellow gold, 8 jewel movement, synthetic sapphire crystal,		
	with 18kt. yellow gold deployable clasp on black, blue or chestnut ostrich strap............	7,100.00	4,181.00
	with 18kt. yellow gold "Damier" bracelet 231/8..................................	12,000.00	7,061.00
6633/9	**Cellini Quartz**, Men's, 18kt. white gold, 8 jewel movement, synthetic sapphire crystal,		
	with 18kt. white gold deployable clasp on blue, brown or red leather strap................	7,100.00	4,181.00
6651/8	**Cellini Quartz**, Ladies', 18kt. yellow gold, 8 jewel movement, synthetic sapphire crystal,		
	with 18kt. yellow gold bracelet 264/8..	13,900.00	8,181.00
	with mother-of-pearl Roman dial..	14,500.00	8,531.00
	with 11 brilliants set on dial...	15,150.00	8,911.00
	with 11 brilliants set on mother-of-pearl dial....................................	15,900.00	9,351.00
6651/8 Bic	**Cellini Quartz**, Ladies', 18kt. yellow gold, 8 jewel mvmnt., synthetic sapphire crystal,		
	with 18kt. yellow and white gold combination bracelet 264/8 Bic.......................	13,900.00	8,181.00
	with mother-of-pearl Roman dial..	14,500.00	8,531.00
	with 11 brilliants set on dial...	15,150.00	8,911.00
	with 11 brilliants set on mother-of-pearl dial....................................	15,900.00	9,351.00
6661/8	**Cellini Quartz**, Ladies', 18kt. yellow gold case set with 36 full-cut brilliants, 8 jewel movement, synthetic sapphire crystal,		
	with 18kt. yellow gold bracelet...	17,750.00	10,441.00
	with mother-of-pearl Roman dial..	18,600.00	10,941.00
	with 11 brilliants set on dial...	19,000.00	11,181.00
	with 11 brilliants set on mother-of-pearl dial....................................	19,750.00	11,621.00
6661/9	**Cellini Quartz**, Ladies', 18kt. white gold case set with 36 full-cut brilliants, 8 jewel movement, synthetic sapphire crystal,		
	with 18kt. white gold bracelet..	17,750.00	10,441.00
	with mother-of-pearl Roman dial..	18,600.00	10,941.00
	with 11 brilliants set on dial...	19,000.00	11,181.00
	with 11 brilliants set on mother-of-pearl dial....................................	19,750.00	11,621.00
6663/8	**Cellini Quartz**, Men's, 18kt. yellow gold case set with 40 full-cut brilliants, 11 brilliants set on dial, 8 jewel movement, synthetic sapphire crystal,		
	with 18kt. yellow gold bracelet...	23,450.00	13,791.00
6663/9	**Cellini Quartz**, Men's, 18kt. white gold case set with 40 full-cut brilliants, 8 jewel movement, synthetic sapphire crystal,		
	with 18kt. white gold bracelet..	21,950.00	12,911.00
	with mother-of-pearl Roman dial..	22,800.00	13,411.00
	with 11 brilliants set on mother-of-pearl dial....................................	24,250.00	14,261.00
6664/8	**Cellini Quartz**, Ladies', 18kt. yellow gold case set with 36 full-cut brilliants, 8 jewel movement, synthetic sapphire crystal,		
	with 18kt. yellow gold bracelet...	17,750.00	10,441.00
	with mother-of-pearl Roman dial..	18,600.00	10,941.00
	with 11 brilliants set on dial...	19,000.00	11,181.00
	with 11 brilliants set on mother-of-pearl, pink opal or pyrite dial......................	19,750.00	11,621.00

ROLEX DIAMOND DIALS & BEZELS

Style	Description	Suggested Retail Price	Wholesale

DIAMOND DIALS:

FOR STEEL/GOLD, 18KT. GOLD OR PLATINUM MODELS ONLY

Ladies'

Style	Description	Suggested Retail Price	Wholesale
LDG/U10	Ten brilliants set on dial for "Oyster Perpetual Lady-Datejust" models	1,300.00	761.00
LDR10	Ten brilliants set on Roman dial for "Oyster Perpetual Lady-Datejust" models	1,300.00	761.00
LDC11	Eleven brilliants set on dial for "Lady Oyster Perpetual" models	1,300.00	761.00

31mm (Mid-size)

Style	Description	Suggested Retail Price	Wholesale
MSG/U10	Ten brilliants set on dial for "Oyster Perpetual Datejust" models	1,350.00	791.00
MSR10	Ten brilliants set on Roman dial for "Oyster Perpetual Datejust" models	1,350.00	791.00

Men's

Style	Description	Suggested Retail Price	Wholesale
MDA10	Eight brilliants and two baguette diamonds set on dial for "Oyster Perpetual Day-Date" models	2,000.00	1,181.00
MDB10	Ten baguette diamonds set on dial for "Oyster Perpetual Day-Date" models	4,500.00	2,651.00
MDG/U10	Ten brilliants set on dial for "Oyster Perpetual Datejust" models	1,450.00	851.00
MDR10	Ten brilliants set on Roman dial for "Oyster Perpetual Date" models	1,450.00	851.00
MQA10	Eight brilliants and two baguette diamonds set on dial for "Oysterquartz Day-Date" models	2,000.00	1,181.00
MQG10	Ten brilliants set on dial for "Oysterquartz Datejust" models	1,450.00	851.00

DIAMOND BEZELS:

FOR 18KT. GOLD OR PLATINUM MODELS ONLY

Ladies'

Style	Description	Suggested Retail Price	Wholesale
LBZ4066	Platinum bezel set with 40 full-cut brilliants for "Oyster Perpetual Lady-Datejust" models with synthetic sapphire crystal	5,250.00	3,121.00
LBZ4088	18kt. yellow gold bezel set with 40 full-cut brilliants for "Oyster Perpetual Lady-Datejust" models with synthetic sapphire crystal	4,900.00	2,911.00
LBZ4099	18kt. white gold bezel set with 40 full-cut brilliants for "Oyster Perpetual Lady-Datejust" models with synthetic sapphire crystal	4,900.00	2,911.00

31mm (Mid-size)

Style	Description	Suggested Retail Price	Wholesale
MSB4488	18kt. yellow gold bezel set with 44 full-cut brilliants for "Oyster Perpetual Datejust" models with synthetic sapphire crystal	5,600.00	3,331.00
MSB4499	18kt. white gold bezel set with 44 full-cut brilliants for "Oyster Perpetual Datejust" models with synthetic sapphire crystal	5,600.00	3,331.00

Men's

Style	Description	Suggested Retail Price	Wholesale
MBZ4466	Platinum bezel set with 44 full-cut brilliants for "Oyster Perpetual and Oysterquartz Day-Date" with synthetic sapphire crystal	7,400.00	4,401.00
MBZ4488	18kt. yellow gold bezel set with 44 full-cut brilliants for "Oyster Perpetual and Oysterquartz Day-Date" with synthetic sapphire crystal	7,050.00	4,191.00

Please Note:

The above prices reflect the trade-in of the customer's existing dial and/or 18kt. gold or platinum bezel. The following additional charges apply when the existing items are not traded-in.

Diamond Dials	Suggested Retail	Wholesale	Diamond Bezels	Suggested Retail	Wholesale
Ladies'	150.00	100.00	Ladies'	410.00	275.00
31mm (Mid-size)	150.00	100.00	31mm (Mid-size)	560.00	375.00
Men's	180.00	120.00	Men's	710.00	475.00
Day-Date	225.00	150.00			

ROLEX BRACELETS

Style	Description	Suggested Retail Price	Wholesale
63113	17mm (11/16") with endpiece #487B for models 77483, 77513, 78243 and 78273.............	2,100.00	1,231.00
	additional link...	165.00	110.00

Jubilee 18kt. Yellow Gold and 18kt. White Gold

Style	Description	Suggested Retail Price	Wholesale
6251/8	13mm Regular clasp for models 76188, 76198, 79138, 79168 and 79178....................	4,100.00	2,441.00
	additional link...	170.00	115.00
6311/8	17mm Regular clasp for models 77518, 78248, 78278 and 78288............................	6,300.00	3,741.00
	additional link...	305.00	205.00
6311/8	19mm Regular clasp for models 14208, 14238 and 15238....................................	6,800.00	4,041.00
	additional link...	370.00	250.00
6311/8	20mm Regular clasp for models 16238, 16718, 16018, 16258 and 16758....................	6,800.00	4,041.00
	additional link...	370.00	250.00
6411/8	17mm Concealed clasp "Super Jubilee Karat" set with 263 brilliants for model 78288..	33,400.00	19,841.00
	additional link...	815.00	545.00
6411/9 Bic	17mm White gold, concealed clasp "Bicolor Super Jubilee Karat" set with 263 brilliants for models 78279 Bic and 78289 Bic..	33,950.00	20,171.00
	additional link...	815.00	545.00
6411/9	17mm White gold, concealed clasp "Super Jubilee Karat" set with 263 brilliants for model 78159..	33,950.00	20,171.00
	additional link...	815.00	545.00
6451/8	13mm Concealed clasp "Super Jubilee Karat" set with 344 brilliants for model 79138..	24,300.00	14,401.00
	additional link...	620.00	415.00
6451/9 Bic	13mm White gold, concealed clasp "Bicolor Super Jubilee Karat" set with 344 brilliants for model 79139 Bic...	24,600.00	14,621.00
	additional link...	620.00	415.00
6451/9	13mm White gold, concealed clasp "Super Jubilee Karat" set with 344 brilliants for model 79159..	24,600.00	14,621.00
	additional link...	620.00	415.00
6453/8	13mm Concealed clasp "Super Jubilee Karat" set with 360 brilliants for model 79159..	29,300.00	17,411.00
	additional link...	700.00	470.00
6454/8	13mm Concealed clasp "Super Karat" set with 89 large brilliants for model 79138..	29,650.00	17,621.00
	additional link...	700.00	470.00
6454/9	13mm White gold, concealed clasp "Super Karat" set with 89 large brilliants for model 79159..	21,250.00	12,621.00
	additional link...	650.00	435.00
8210/8	20mm Bark finish, regular clasp for models 16248 and 16078...............	7,100.00	4,221.00
	additional link...	370.00	250.00
8211/8	13mm Bark finish, regular clasp for models 79138 and 79278...............	4,500.00	2,671.00
	additional link...	225.00	150.00
8211/9	13mm White gold, bark finish, regular clasp for models 79279...............	5,250.00	3,121.00
	additional link...	225.00	150.00
8386/8	20mm Concealed clasp Super Jubilee for models 16238, 16718, 16018, 16258 and 16758..	7,200.00	4,281.00
	additional link...	370.00	250.00

ROLEX BRACELETS

Style	Description	Suggested Retail Price	Wholesale
Jubilee Stainless Steel			
62510	13mm (1/2") with endpiece #591B for models 76030, 76080 and 76094......................	525.00	311.00
	additional link...	35.00	25.00
62510	13mm (1/2") with endpiece #568B for models 79160, 79174, 79190 and 79240..............	525.00	311.00
	additional link...	35.00	25.00
62510	17mm (11/16") with endpiece #587B for models 77014, 77080, 78240 and 78274...........	525.00	311.00
	additional link...	35.00	25.00
62510	19mm (3/4") with endpiece #574B for models 14000, 14010, 15200 and 15210.............. (available for replacement only)	525.00	311.00
	additional link...	35.00	25.00
62510	19mm (3/4") with endpiece #574 for models 1002/0, 15000, 15010, 5500/0, 6426/0 and 6694/0...	525.00	311.00
	additional link...	35.00	25.00
62510	20mm (13/16") with endpiece #555B for models 16200, 16220, 16234 and 16264...........	525.00	311.00
	additional link...	35.00	25.00
62510	20mm (13/16") with endpiece #555 for models 16000, 16014 and 16030....................	525.00	311.00
	additional link...	35.00	25.00
62510	20mm (13/16") with endpiece #550 for models 1019/0 and 16750.............................	525.00	311.00
	additional link...	35.00	25.00
62510	20mm (13/16") with endpiece #502B for models 16700 and 16710........................... (available for replacement only)	525.00	311.00
	additional link...	35.00	25.00
62510	20mm (13/16") with endpiece #502 for model 16760...	525.00	311.00
	additional link...	35.00	25.00
63110	17mm (11/16") with endpiece #587B for models 77014, 77080, 78240 and 78274...........	550.00	321.00
	additional link...	35.00	25.00
Jubilee Stainless Steel With 18kt. Yellow Gold Middle Links			
62523	13mm (1/2") with endpiece #491B for models 76183, 76193, 76233 and 76243..............	1,500.00	881.00
	additional link...	115.00	80.00
62523	13mm (1/2") with endpiece #468B for models 79163 and 79173...............................	1,500.00	881.00
	additional link...	115.00	80.00
62523	17mm (11/16") with endpiece #487B for models 77483, 77513, 78243 and 78273...........	1,900.00	1,121.00
	additional link...	165.00	110.00
62523	19mm (3/4") with endpiece #474B for models 14230, 14233, 15203 and 15223.............. (available for replacement only)	2,225.00	1,311.00
	additional link...	185.00	125.00
62523	19mm (3/4") with endpiece #474 for models 1002/3, 1005/3, 15003, 15053 and 5501/3.....	2,225.00	1,310.00
	additional link...	185.00	125.00
62523	20mm (13/16") with endpiece #455B for models 16203, 16233 and 16263....................	2,225.00	1,311.00
	additional link...	185.00	125.00
62523	20mm (13/16") with endpiece #455 for models 16003, 16013 and 16253....................	2,225.00	1,311.00
	additional link...	185.00	125.00
62523	20mm (13/16") with endpiece #450 for model 16753...	2,225.00	1,311.00
	additional link...	185.00	125.00
62523	20mm (13/16") with endpiece #402B for model 16713..	2,225.00	1,311.00
	additional link...	185.00	125.00
78730	14mm (1/2") with endpiece #806 special Oysterlock for model 169622......................	625.00	371.00
	additional link...	50.00	35.00
78740	17mm (11/16") with endpiece #807 special Oysterlock for model 168622....................	625.00	371.00
	additional link...	50.00	35.00

ROLEX BRACELETS

Style	Description	Suggested Retail Price	Wholesale
78750	17mm (11/16") with endpiece #807 special Oysterlock for model 168622....................	650.00	371.00
	additional link...	50.00	35.00
78760	20mm (13/16") with endpiece #808 special Oysterlock for model 16622..................….....	650.00	371.00
	additional link...	50.00	35.00
78790	20mm (13/16") with endpiece #558B special Oysterlock for model 14270....................	525.00	311.00
	additional link...	35.00	25.00
78790	20mm (13/16") with endpiece #501B special Oysterlock for models 16570, 16700 and 16710.........	525.00	311.00
	additional link...	35.00	25.00
93150	20mm (13/16") with endpiece #558B special fliplock clasp with extension link for model 14270.........	525.00	311.00
	(available for replacement only)		
	additional link...	35.00	25.00
93150	20mm (13/16") with endpiece #580 special fliplock clasp with extension link for models 1016/0, 1019/0, 16750 and 5513/0............	525.00	311.00
	additional link...	35.00	25.00
93150	20mm (13/16") with endpiece #501B special fliplock clasp with extension link for model 14060.........	525.00	311.00
	additional link...	35.00	25.00
93150	20mm (13/16") with endpiece #593 special fliplock clasp with extension link for models 16550, 16760 and 16800.........	525.00	311.00
	additional link...	35.00	25.00
93160	20mm (13/16") with endpiece #892 special fliplock clasp with interchangeable extension links and tool kit for models 16600 and 16660.........	625.00	371.00
	additional link...	50.00	35.00
93250	20mm (13/16") with endpiece #801 special fliplock clasp with extension link for model 16610.........	625.00	371.00
	additional link...	50.00	35.00

Oyster Stainless Steel With 18kt. Yellow Gold Middle Links

Style	Description	Suggested Retail Price	Wholesale
78053	17mm (11/16") with endpiece #451B for models 77483, 77513, 78243 and 78273..........	1,600.00	941.00
	additional link...	200.00	135.00
78243	13mm (1/2") with endpiece #466B for models 76183, 76193, 76233 and 76243.............	1,225.00	721.00
	additional link...	155.00	105.00
78243	13mm (1/2") with endpiece #490B for models 79163 and 79173.............................	1,225.00	721.00
	additional link...	155.00	105.00
78353	17mm (11/16") with endpiece #451B for models 77483, 77513, 78243 and 78273..........	1,800.00	1,061.00
	additional link...	200.00	135.00
78353	19mm (3/4") with endpiece #457B for models 14203, 14233, 15203 and 15233.............	1,925.00	1,131.00
	additional link...	265.00	180.00
78353	19mm (3/4") with endpiece #457 for models 1002/3, 1038/3, 1005/3, 15003, 15053 and 5501/3.........	1,925.00	1,131.00
	additional link...	265.00	180.00
78363	20mm (13/16") with endpiece #458B for models 16203, 16233 and 16263....................	1,925.00	1,131.00
	additional link...	265.00	180.00
78363	20mm (13/16") with endpiece #458 for models 16003, 16013 and 16253....................	1,925.00	1,131.00
	additional link...	265.00	180.00
8391/8	17mm Concealed clasp Super Jubilee for models 78158, 78238, 78248 and 78278..........	6,750.00	4,011.00
	additional link...	305.00	205.00
9486/8	20mm Concealed clasp "Super Jubilee Karat" set with 218 brilliants for model 18348.........	34,750.00	20,651.00
	additional link...	1,540.00	1,030.00

ROLEX BRACELETS

Style	Description	Suggested Retail Price	Wholesale
8486/9 Bic	20mm White gold, concealed clasp "Bicolor Super Jubilee Karat" set with 218 brilliants for model 18349 Bic...	**35,450.00**	**21,061.00**
	additional link...	**1,540.00**	**1,030.00**
8486/9	20mm White gold, concealed clasp "Super Jubilee Karat" set with 218 brilliants for model 18389..	**35,450.00**	**21,061.00**
	additional link...	**1,540.00**	**1,030.00**
8571/8	13mm Concealed clasp Super Jubilee for models 76188, 76198, 79138, 79168 and 79178..	**5,650.00**	**3,361.00**
	additional link...	**220.00**	**145.00**

Oyster Stainless Steel

Style	Description	Suggested Retail Price	Wholesale
78050	17mm (11/16") with endpiece #551B for models 77014, 77080, 78240 and 78274............	**400.00**	**231.00**
	additional link...	**35.00**	**25.00**
78240	13mm (1/2") with endpiece #566B for models 76030, 76080 and 76094........................	**425.00**	**251.00**
	additional link...	**35.00**	**25.00**
78240	13mm (1/2") with endpiece #590B for models 79160, 79174, 79190 and 79240..............	**425.00**	**251.00**
	additional link...	**35.00**	**25.00**
78350	17mm (11/16") with endpiece #562 for model 6466/0...	**425.00**	**251.00**
	additional link...	**35.00**	**25.00**
78350	17mm (11/16") with endpiece #551B for models 77014, 77080, 78240 and 78274............	**425.00**	**251.00**
	additional link...	**35.00**	**25.00**
78350	19mm (3/4") with endpiece #557B for models 14000, 14010, 15200 and 15210..............	**425.00**	**251.00**
	additional link...	**35.00**	**25.00**
78350	19mm (3/4") with endpiece #557 for models 1002/0, 15000, 15010, 5500/0, 6426/0 and 6694/0..	**425.00**	**251.00**
	additional link...	**35.00**	**25.00**
78350	19mm (3/4") with endpiece #571 for model 6263/0...	**425.00**	**251.00**
	additional link...	**35.00**	**25.00**
78360	20mm (13/16") with endpiece #558B for models 16200, 16220, 16234 and 16264............	**425.00**	**251.00**
	additional link...	**35.00**	**25.00**
78360	20mm (13/16") with endpiece #558 for models 16000, 16014 and 16030.......................	**425.00**	**251.00**
	additional link...	**35.00**	**25.00**
78360	20mm (13/16") with endpiece #580 for models 1016/0, 1019/0 and 16750....................	**425.00**	**251.00**
	additional link...	**35.00**	**25.00**
78360	20mm (13/16") with endpiece #501B for models 16570, 16700 and 16710..................... (available for replacement only)	**425.00**	**251.00**
	additional link...	**35.00**	**25.00**
78360	20mm (13/16") with endpiece #501 for models 16550 and 16760...............................	**425.00**	**251.00**
	additional link...	**35.00**	**25.00**
78390	20mm (13/16") with endpiece #803 special Oysterlock for model 16520.....................	**625.00**	**371.00**
	additional link...	**50.00**	**35.00**

President 18kt. Yellow Gold, 18kt. White Gold, 18kt. Tridor and Platinum

Style	Description	Suggested Retail Price	Wholesale
72746	20mm Platinum, concealed clasp Super President for models 18946 and 18956...............	**29,500.00**	**17,531.00**
	additional full link..	**1,900.00**	**1,270.00**
	additional half link..	**1,500.00**	**1,000.00**
72748	20mm "Tridor" yellow gold, center links pink and white gold, concealed clasp Super President for model 18948 Bic..	**12,500.00**	**7,431.00**
7286/8	20mm Yellow gold, regular clasp for models 18208, 18238, 18348, 18028, 18038 and 18048..	**7,250.00**	**4,311.00**
	additional link...	**370.00**	**250.00**

ROLEX BRACELETS

Style	Description	Suggested Retail Price	Wholesale
7286/9	20mm White gold, regular clasp for models 18239, 18039 and 18049	7,900.00	4,691.00
	additional link	370.00	250.00
8153/8	13mm Yellow gold, regular clasp for models 79138, 79168 and 79178	5,750.00	3,421.00
	additional link	225.00	150.00
8153/9	13mm White gold, regular clasp for model 79179	6,150.00	3,651.00
	additional link	225.00	150.00
8209/8	20mm Yellow gold, bark finish, regular clasp for models 18248, 18308, 18348, 18048, 18078 and 18108	7,600.00	4,511.00
	additional link	370.00	250.00
8209/9	20mm White gold, bark finish, regular clasp for models 18249, 18049 and 18079	8,250.00	4,901.00
	additional link	370.00	250.00
8228/8	13mm Yellow gold, bark finish, regular clasp for models 79138 and 79278	6,000.00	3,561.00
	additional link	230.00	155.00
8228/9	13mm White gold, bark finish, regular clasp for model 79279	6,400.00	3,801.00
	additional link	230.00	155.00
8270/9	13mm "Tridor" white gold, center links pink, yellow and white gold, concealed clasp Super President for models 79139 Bic and 79179 Bic	9,450.00	5,611.00
	additional link	395.00	265.00
8285/9	20mm "Tridor" white gold, center links pink, yellow and white gold, concealed clasp Super President for models 18239 Bic, 18349 Bic, 18039 Bic and 18129 Bic	11,450.00	6,801.00
	additional link	545.00	365.00
8289/9	17mm "Tridor" white gold, center links pink, yellow and white gold, concealed clasp Super President for models 78279 Bic and 78289 Bic	11,250.00	6,681.00
	additional link	420.00	280.00
8385/6	20mm Platinum, concealed clasp Super President for models 18206, 18296, 18346, 18366, 18026 and 18046	22,400.00	13,311.00
	additional link	925.00	620.00
8385/8	20mm Yellow gold, concealed clasp Super President for models 18208, 18238, 18348, 18028, 18038 and 18048	7,700.00	4,571.00
	additional link	370.00	250.00
8385/8B	20mm Yellow gold, concealed clasp "Super President Baguette" set with 50 brilliants and 23 baguette diamonds for model 18348	84,750.00	50,361.00
	additional link	3,750.00	2,500.00
8385/9	20mm White gold, concealed clasp Super President for models 18239, 18389, 18039 and 18049	8,350.00	4,961.00
	additional link	370.00	250.00
8385/9B	20mm White gold, concealed clasp "Super President Baguette" set with 50 brilliants and 23 baguette diamonds for model 18389	84,950.00	50,471.00
	additional link	3,750.00	2,500.00
78363	20mm (13/16") with endpiece #480 for model 16753	1,925.00	1,131.00
	additional link	265.00	180.00
78363	20mm (13/16") with endpiece #401B for model 16713 (available for replacement only)	1,925.00	1,131.00
	additional link	265.00	180.00
78393	20mm (13/16") with endpiece #703 special Oysterlock for model 16523	2,350.00	1,381.00
	additional link	265.00	180.00
78733	14mm (1/2") with endpiece #706 special Oysterlock for model 169623	1,950.00	1,151.00
	additional link	250.00	170.00
78743	17mm (11/16") with endpiece #707 special Oysterlock for model 168623	2,000.00	1,171.00
	additional link	265.00	180.00

ROLEX BRACELETS

Style	Description	Suggested Retail Price	Wholesale
78753	17mm (11/16") with endpiece #707 special Oysterlock for model 168623.....................	2,100.00	1,231.00
	additional link...	265.00	180.00
78793	20mm (13/16") with endpiece #401B special Oysterlock for model 16713.....................	2,300.00	1,351.00
	additional link...	265.00	180.00
93153	20mm (13/16") with endpiece #493 special fliplock clasp with extension link for model 16803...	2,050.00	1,201.00
	additional link...	265.00	180.00
93253	20mm (13/16") with endpiece #701 special fliplock clasp with extension link for model 16613...	2,150.00	1,261.00
	additional link...	265.00	180.00

Oyster 18kt. Yellow Gold and 18kt. White Gold

Style	Description	Suggested Retail Price	Wholesale
7204/8	13mm Regular clasp for models 76188, 76198, 79138, 79168 and 79178.....................	3,800.00	2,261.00
	additional link...	265.00	180.00
7205/8	17mm Regular clasp for models 77488, 77518, 78248, 78278 and 78288.....................	4,700.00	2,791.00
	additional link...	380.00	255.00
7205/8	19mm Regular clasp for models 14208, 14238 and 15238.........................	5,200.00	3,091.00
	additional link...	405.00	270.00
7206/8	20mm Regular clasp for models 16238 and 16718.........................	5,200.00	3,091.00
	additional link...	405.00	270.00
78398	20mm Special Oysterlock for models 16528 and 16568.........................	8,000.00	4,751.00
	additional link...	715.00	480.00
78738	14mm Special Oysterlock for model 169628.........................	6,050.00	3,591.00
	additional link...	525.00	350.00
78748	17mm Ladies' Special Oysterlock for model 168628.........................	7,200.00	4,281.00
	additional link...	570.00	380.00
78758	17mm Men's Special Oysterlock for model 168628.........................	7,600.00	4,521.00
	additional link...	570.00	380.00
78768	20mm Special Oysterlock for model 16628.........................	7,800.00	4,631.00
	additional link...	715.00	480.00
78798	20mm Special Oysterlock for model 16718.........................	7,800.00	4,631.00
	additional link...	715.00	480.00
92908	20mm Special fliplock clasp with extension link for models 16618, 16718, 16758 and 16808.........................	8,000.00	4,751.00
	additional link...	725.00	485.00
8570/6	13mm Platinum, concealed clasp Super President for models 79126, 79136 and 79166......	8,850.00	5,261.00
	additional link...	370.00	250.00
8570/8	13mm Yellow gold, concealed clasp Super President for models 79138, 79168 and 79178.........................	6,000.00	3,561.00
	additional link...	225.00	150.00
8570/8B	13mm Yellow gold, concealed clasp "Super President Baguette" set with 74 brilliants and 35 baguette diamonds for model 79138.........................	44,350.00	25,351.00
	additional link...	1,234.00	825.00
8570/9	13mm White gold, concealed clasp Super President for model 79179.........................	6,400.00	3,801.00
	additional link...	225.00	150.00
8570/9B	13mm White gold, concealed clasp "Super President Baguette" set with 74 brilliants and 35 baguette diamonds for model 79159.........................	44,750.00	26,591.00
	additional link...	1,235.00	825.00
8723/8	20mm Yellow gold, bark finish, concealed clasp Super President for models 18248, 18308 18348, 18048, 18078 and 18108.........................	8,300.00	4,931.00
	additional link...	370.00	250.00

ROLEX BRACELETS

Style	Description	Suggested Retail Price	Wholesale
8723/9	20mm White gold, bark finish, concealed clasp Super President for models 18249, 18049 and 18079	8,700.00	5,171.00
	additional link	370.00	250.00
9235/8	13mm Yellow gold, bark finish, concealed clasp Super President for models 79138, 79278 and 79288	6,250.00	3,711.00
	additional link	230.00	155.00
9235/9	13mm White gold, bark finish, concealed clasp Super President for models 79279	7,000.00	4,161.00
	additional link	230.00	155.00

Oyster 14mm 18kt. Yellow Gold, 18kt. White Gold and 18kt. Tridor

Style	Description	Suggested Retail Price	Wholesale
64908	Yellow gold, concealed clasp "Super Karat" set with 100 large brilliants for model 80298	44,950.00	26,701.00
	additional full link	1,425.00	950.00
64908P	Yellow gold, concealed clasp "Super Karat" set with 100 pink sapphires for model 80308P	41,950.00	24,921.00
	additional full link	1,325.00	885.00
64909	White gold, concealed clasp "Super Karat" set with 100 large brilliants for model 80299	45,900.00	27,271.00
	additional full link	1,425.00	950.00
64909S	White gold, concealed clasp "Super Karat" set with 100 sky-blue sapphires for model 80309S	48,350.00	28,721.00
	additional full link	1,525.00	1,020.00
72948	Yellow gold, concealed clasp for models 80298, 80308, 80318 and 80328	7,150.00	4,251.00
	additional full link	450.00	300.00
	additional half link	365.00	245.00
72948	"Tridor" yellow gold, center links pink and white gold, concealed clasp for models 80298 Bic, 80299 Bic, 80318 Bic and 80319 Bic	7,850.00	4,661.00
	additional full link	750.00	500.00
	additional half link	625.00	420.00
72949	White gold, concealed clasp for models 80299, 80319, 80329 and 80359	7,850.00	4,661.00
	additional full link	505.00	340.00
	additional half link	420.00	280.00
72958 Bic	"Bicolor" yellow gold, center links white gold, concealed clasp for model 80328 Bic	9,650.00	5,731.00
	additional full link	650.00	435.00
8389/6	17mm Men's platinum, concealed clasp Super President for models 78246, 78266 and 78286	13,450.00	8,791.00
	additional link	620.00	415.00
8389/8	17mm Men's yellow gold, concealed clasp Super President for models 78248, 78278 and 78288	7,500.00	4,461.00
	additional link	370.00	250.00
8389/9	17mm Men's white gold, concealed clasp Super President for model 78279	8,000.00	4,751.00
	additional link	370.00	250.00
8390/6	17mm Ladies' platinum, concealed clasp Super President for models 78246, 78266 and 78286	12,100.00	7,191.00
	additional link	620.00	415.00
8390/8	17mm Ladies' yellow gold, concealed clasp Super President for models 78248, 78278 and 78288	6,950.00	4,131.00
	additional link	370.00	250.00
8390/9	17mm Ladies' white gold, concealed clasp Super President for model 78279	7,450.00	4,431.00
	additional link	370.00	250.00

ROLEX BRACELETS

Style	Description	Suggested Retail Price	Wholesale
8470/6	13mm Platinum, concealed clasp "Super President Karat" set with 460 brilliants for model 79136..	30,800.00	18,301.00
	additional link...	870.00	580.00
8470/8	13mm Yellow gold, concealed clasp "Super President Karat" set with 460 brilliants for model 79138..	27,250.00	16,191.00
	additional link...	760.00	510.00
8470/9	13mm White gold, concealed clasp "Super President Karat" set with 460 brilliants for model 79159..	27,650.00	16,431.00
	additional link...	760.00	510.00
8472/8	13mm Yellow gold, concealed clasp "Super President Karat" set with 204 brilliants for model 79138..	27,300.00	16,231.00
	additional link...	760.00	510.00
8473/8	13mm Yellow gold, concealed clasp "Super President Karat" set with 446 brilliants for model 79138..	38,750.00	23,021.00
	additional link...	1,120.00	750.00
8485/6	20mm Platinum, concealed clasp "Super President Karat" set with 288 brilliants for model 18346..	53,500.00	31,791.00
	additional link...	1,960.00	1,310.00
8485/8	20mm Yellow gold, concealed clasp "Super President Karat" set with 288 brilliants for model 18348..	39,300.00	23,351.00
	additional link...	1,795.00	1,200.00
8485/9	20mm White gold, concealed clasp "Super President Karat" set with 288 brilliants for model 18389..	39,900.00	23,711.00
	additional link...	1,795.00	1,200.00
8489/6	17mm Men's platinum, concealed clasp "Super President Karat" set with 340 brilliants for model 78286..	41,200.00	24,481.00
	additional link...	1,680.00	1,120.00
8489/8	17mm Men's yellow gold, concealed clasp "Super President Karat" set with 340 brilliants for model 78288..	35,300.00	20,971.00
	additional link...	1,515.00	1,010.00
8489/9	17mm Men's white gold, concealed clasp "Super President Karat" set with 340 brilliants for model 78159..	35,850.00	21,301.00
	additional link...	1,515.00	1,010.00

Oysterquartz Integral

Style	Description	Suggested Retail Price	Wholesale
17000	Oyster-Type stainless steel for model 17000..	425.00	251.00
	additional link...	51.00	34.00
17010	Jubilee-Type stainless steel for model 17014..	600.00	351.00
	additional link...	60.00	40.00
17013	Jubilee-Type stainless steel and 18kt. yellow gold for model 17013....................	1,900.00	1,121.00
	additional link...	240.00	160.00
19018	President-Type 18kt. yellow gold, concealed clasp for models 19018 and 19048..........	9,400.00	5,591.00
	additional link...	370.00	250.00
19019	President-Type 18kt. white gold, concealed clasp for models 19019 and 19049...........	10,250.00	6,091.00
	additional link...	370.00	250.00
19028	"Pyramid" 18kt. yellow gold, concealed clasp for models 19028, 19038 and 19068 (available for replacement only).......................................	11,350.00	6,751.00
	additional link...	370.00	250.00
19148	"Karat" 18kt. yellow gold, concealed clasp for model 19148 (available for replacement only).......................................	43,000.00	25,551.00
	additional link...	1,750.00	1,170.00

ROLEX BRACELETS

Style	Description	Suggested Retail Price	Wholesale

Damier 18kt. Yellow Gold

Style	Description	Suggested Retail Price	Wholesale
211/8	Damier for model 6621/8	4,700.00	2,761.00
	additional link	225.00	150.00
212/8	Damier for model 6631/8	4,700.00	2,761.00
	additional link	225.00	150.00
221/8	Ladies' Damier for model 6622/8	5,375.00	3,161.00
	additional link	325.00	215.00
222/8	Men's Damier for model 6622/8	5,625.00	3,311.00
	additional link	325.00	215.00
231/8	Damier for models 6623/8 and 6633/8	6,250.00	3,681.00
	additional link	350.00	235.00

Milanese 18kt. Yellow Gold

Style	Description	Suggested Retail Price	Wholesale
213/8	Milanese for model 6621/8	5,250.00	3,091.00
	extension bar	375.00	250.00
223/8	Ladies' Milanese for model 6622/8	5,875.00	3,461.00
	extension bar	400.00	265.00
224/8	Men's Milanese for model 6622/8	6,175.00	3,631.00
	extension bar	400.00	265.00
233/8	Milanese for model 6623/8	6,750.00	3,971.00
	extension bar	425.00	285.00
313/8	Milanese for model 6621/8	5,250.00	3,091.00
	extension bar	375.00	250.00
323/8	Ladies' Milanese for model 6622/8	5,875.00	3,091.00
	extension bar	400.00	250.00
324/8	Men's Milanese for model 6622/8	6,175.00	3,631.00
	extension bar	400.00	265.00
333/8	Milanese for model 6623/8	6,750.00	3,971.00
	extension bar	425.00	285.00
72959 Bic	"Bicolor" white gold, center links yellow gold, concealed clasp for model 80329 Bic	9,650.00	5,731.00
	additional full link	650.00	435.00
74908	Yellow gold, concealed clasp "Super Oyster Karat" set with 174 brilliants and 14 large brilliants for models 80298 and 80308	49,900.00	29,651.00
	additional full link	3,475.00	2,320.00
74908E	Yellow gold, concealed clasp "Super Oyster Karat" set with 174 brilliants and 14 large emeralds for model 80298	81,400.00	48,361.00
	additional full link	5,700.00	3,800.00
74908P	Yellow gold, concealed clasp "Super Oyster Karat" set with 174 brilliants and 14 large pink sapphires for model 80308P	33,650.00	19.991.00
	additional full link	2,350.00	1,570.00
74908R	Yellow gold, concealed clasp "Super Oyster Karat" set with 174 brilliants and 14 large rubies for model 80308R	51,850.00	30,811.00
	additional full link	3,600.00	2,400.00
74908S	Yellow gold, concealed clasp "Super Oyster Karat" set with 174 brilliants and 14 large sapphires for model 80308S	33,650.00	19,991.00
	additional full link	2,350.00	1,570.00
74909	White gold, concealed clasp "Super Oyster Karat" set with 174 brilliants and 14 large brilliants for models 80299 and 80359	50,850.00	30,211.00
	additional full link	3,475.00	2,320.00

ROLEX BRACELETS

Style	Description	Suggested Retail Price	Wholesale
74909S	White gold, concealed clasp "Super Oyster Karat" set with 174 brilliants and 14 large sapphires for model 80309S	34,650.00	20,581.00
	additional full link	2,350.00	1,570.00
74948	Yellow gold, concealed clasp "Oyster Karat" set with 174 brilliants for models 80298 and 80308	24,650.00	14,651.00
	additional full link	1,570.00	1,050.00
	additional half link	1,260.00	840.00
74949	White gold, concealed clasp "Oyster Karat" set with 174 brilliants for models 80299 and 80359	25,600.00	15,211.00
	additional full link	1,570.00	1,050.00
	additional half link	1,260.00	840.00
74958	"Tridor" yellow gold, center links pink and white gold, concealed clasp "Oyster Karat" set with 15 large brilliants for models 80298 Bic, 80318 Bic and 80328 Bic	27,900.00	16,581.00
	additional full link	1,900.00	1,270.00
74978	Yellow gold, concealed clasp "Super Oyster Karat" set with 270 brilliants for models 80298 and 80308	28,850.00	17,131.00
	additional full link	1,900.00	1,270.00
74979	White gold, concealed clasp "Super Oyster Karat" set with 270 brilliants for models 80299 and 80359	29,800.00	17,711.00
	additional full link	1,900.00	1,270.00
74988	Yellow gold, concealed clasp "Super Oyster Karat" set with 286 brilliants for models 80298 and 80308	27,350.00	16,251.00
	additional full link	1,800.00	1,200.00
74989	White gold, concealed clasp "Super Oyster Karat" set with 286 brilliants for models 80299 and 80359	28,100.00	16,701.00
	additional full link	1,800.00	1,200.00

Chevrons 18kt. Yellow Gold and 18kt. White Gold

Style	Description	Suggested Retail Price	Wholesale
264/8	Chevron for models 6651/8 and 6664/8	7,500.00	4,411.00
	additional link	800.00	535.00
264/8 Bic	Chevron for models 6651/8 Bic and 6664/8 Bic	7,500.00	4,411.00
	additional link	800.00	535.00

ROLEX
CASE REFERENCE NUMBERS

How To Use The ROLEX Case Reference Numbers Appendix:

The following pages provide a detailed resource for identifying Rolex watches. Models are listed in numeric order by the *Case Reference Number*.

Case#: This column identifies the *Case Reference Number*, which is often known as the watch's 'model number'.

Movements: This identifies known movements which have been present in the given watch. In many cases there will be more than one movement listed and they are listed either by *Caliber/ Reference, Linges*, or *Old Reference Number*. Many of these movements are identified in the *Movements* section of *Part III: Rolex Parts Identification* in this book. (*Please Note: This is not a complete list.*)

Style: This indicates the watch style (or model) that is associated with the particular *Case Reference Number*. In many cases there will be more than one style listed, as well as additional notes. (*Please Note: This is not a complete list.*)

Unfortunately, due to the limited information available from Rolex, resources are not publicly available to identify every Rolex *Case Reference Number* by *Movement* and *Style*. Therefore, if you have verifiable information not listed in the following appendix, please notify the author so it may be added for the next edition.

Case#:	Movements:	Style:
Deep Sea Special	1000/419343	Experimental Diving Watch
60		Chronograph
333		MW
514		
537		
578	Rebberg	MW (Tonneau case)
678		MW 'Aviator'
713	8 ¾"	
714	8 ¾"	
756		
758		
781		MW (Tonneau case)
813		
814		MW (Tonneau case)
829		
861		MW (Hexagon case)
868		
870		
871		Chronograph 'Moon Phase'
895	8 ¾", 131	
912		
913	10 ½", 65	
913	8 ¾"	
920	8 ¾", 131	
930		
931		
951	8 ¾", 11 ¼", 1250	
971 A/U		Prince
978	10 ½", 65	
1002	1560, 1570	OP, Air-King
1003	1560, 1570	OP
1004	1560	OP 'Zephyr'
1005	1560, 1570	OP
1006	1560	OP
1007	1560, 1570	OP
1008	1560, 1570	OP
1009	1560, 1570	OP
1010	1560, 1570	OP
1011	1560, 1570	OP
1012	1560, 1570	OP
1013	1560, 1570	OP
1014	1560	OP
1016	1560, 1570	Explorer
1018	1560, 1570	OP
1019	1560	Milgauss
1020	1560	Tru-Beat
1022	1560, 1570	OP
1023	1560, 1570	OP
1024	1560, 1570	OP

Case#:	Movements:	Style:
1025	1560, 1570	OP
1026	1560	OP
1027	1560, 1570	OP
1028	1560	OP
1029	1560, 1570	OP
1030	1560, 1570	OP
1031	1570	OP
1035	1570	OP
1036	1570	OP
1038	1570	OP
1039	1570	OP
1069		MW
1070		MW
1072		Speed-King
1074		Chronograph
1102	TS300	OP Date
1147		MW
1223		Chronograph
1237		MW
1343		Prince
1381		
1387		MW (Rect. Case)
1400		Air-King
1401		Air-King
1406	3000	Submariner
1420		OP
1423		OP
1427	3000	Explorer
1490		Prince '¼ Century'
1491		Prince
1500	1565, 1575	OP Date
1501	1565, 1575	OP Date
1502	1565, 1575	OP Date
1503	1575	OP Date
1503g	1565, 1575	OP Date
1504	1565, 1575	OP Date
1505	1565, 1575	OP Date
1506	1565, 1575	OP Date
1507	1565, 1575	OP Date
1508	1565, 1575	OP Date
1509	1565, 1575	OP Date
1510	1565, 1575	OP Date
1511	1575	OP Date
1512	1575	OP Date
1513	1575	OP Date
1514	1575	OP Date
1520		OP Date
1521		OP Date
1522		OP Date
1523		OP Date
1527	300	Prince 'JH, Railway'
1530	1575	OP Date

Case#:	Movements:	Style:
1541		Prince
1550	1575	OP Date
1560		
1564		'Sporting' Prince
1573	9 ¾"	MW 'Imperial'
1587		
1599		'Sporting' Prince
1600	1565, 1575	Datejust
1601	1565, 1575	Datejust
1602	1565, 1575	Datejust
1603	1565, 1575	Datejust, OP
1604	1565, 1575	Datejust
1605	1565	Datejust
1607	1565, 1575	Datejust
1610	1565, 1575	Datejust
1611	1565, 1575	Datejust
1620		Datejust
1622		Datejust
1623		Datejust
1624		Datejust
1625	1565, 1575	Datejust 'T-Bird'
1626		Datejust
1630	1575	Datejust
1650		Cosmograph
1651	4030	Cosmograph
1652	13L, 4030	Cosmograph
1655	1575	Explorer II
1656	4030	Cosmograph
1657	3185	Explorer II
1658	4030	Cosmograph
1659		Cosmograph
1660	3135	Sea-Dweller
1661	3135	Submariner Date
1662	3135	Yacht-Master
1665	1575	Sea-Dweller
1666	3000, 3035	Sea-Dweller
1670		GMT Master
1671	3085	GMT Master II
1675	1565, 1575	GMT Master
1676	3085	GMT Master II
1680	1575	Submariner Date
1768		Prince
1770		Prince 'JH'
1774		
1779	8 ¾"	
1800		Day Date
1802	1555, 1556	Day Date
1803	1555, 1556	Day Date
1804	1555, 1556	Day Date
1805	1555	Day Date
1806	1555, 1556	Day Date
1807	1555, 1556	Day Date

Case#:	Movements:	Style:
1808	1555	Day Date
1809	1555, 1556	Day Date
1810	1555, 1556	Day Date
1811	1555, 1556	Day Date
1812	1555	Day Date
1813	1556	Day Date
1814	1556	Day Date
1815	1556	Day Date
1816		Day Date
1817		Day Date
1820		Day Date
1823		Day Date
1824		Day Date
1829		Day Date
1830		Day Date
1831	1556	Day Date
1833		Day Date
1834		Day Date
1836		Day Date
1837		Day Date
1838		Day Date
1839		Day Date
1852		Bubbleback
1855		Prince
1858	8 ¾"	Bubbleback
1862		Prince 'Railway'
1871		'Sporting' Prince
1873	10 ½"	Bubbleback
1879		
1880		MW (Rect. Case)
1894		Master Day Date
1895		Master Day Date
1921		MW
1925		MW (Cushion case)
1936		MW 'Egyptian'
2005		MW (Rect. Case)
2021		Chronograph
2022		Chronograph
2023		Chronograph
2057		Chronograph
2081	10 ¾"	MW 'Scientific'
2121	9 ¾", 10 ½"	
2136	10 ½"	MW
2190	10 ½"	
2226		Chronograph
2227	9 ¾"	
2233	10 ½"	
2240		Bubbleback
2253	10 ½"	
2280	10 ½", 65	MW 'Observatory, Royal'
2295	8 ¾"	

Case#:	Movements:	Style:		Case#:	Movements:	Style:
2296	8 ¾"			2588	8 ¾"	
2297	8 ¾"			2589	8 ¾"	
2301				2590	8 ¾"	
2303		Chronograph		2591	8 ¾"	
2317				2592	8 ¾"	
2318		MW		2593	9 ¾"	MW
2319	10 ½"	MW 'Royal'		2595	10 ½"	MW 'Royal, Speed-King, Imperial'
2320	10 ½"					
2322	10 ½"			2596	9 ¾"	
2323	9 ¾"			2612	8 ¾"	
2324	9 ¾"			2613	8 ¾"	
2325	9 ¾"			2618	8 ¾"	
2329	8 ¾"			2632	8 ¾"	
2330	8 ¾"			2633	8 ¾"	
2331	8 ¾"	MW		2636	8 ¾"	
2332	9 ¾"			2638	8 ¾"	
2333	9 ¾"			2701	8 ¾"	MW
2349	10 ½"			2705	13L	Chronograph
2387				2716	8 ¾"	
2407	8 ¾"			2717	8 ¾"	
2408	8 ¾"			2730	"HW"	Prince
2416	10 ½"	MW		2737		Chronograph
2420	10 ½"	MW 'Precision'		2764	9 ¾"	Bubbleback
2422				2765	10 ½"	Bubbleback
2446	8 ¾"			2771		Prince
2467				2784	10 ½", 65	Bubbleback
2490		Bubbleback		2811	13" 23	Chronograph
2496		MW (Cushion case)		2819	8 ¾"	
2499				2820	8 ¾"	
2507		Chronograph		2821	8 ¾"	
2508		Chronograph		2848	10 ½"	
2514	8 ¾"			2849	8 ¾"	MW
2515	8 ¾"			2855	8 ¾"	
2516	8 ¾"			2861	8 ¾"	
2517	8 ¾"			2891		MW
2518	9 ¾"	MW 'Egyptian'		2917		Chronograph
2524	8 ¾"			2918		Chronograph
2525	8 ¾"			2920		Chronograph
2528				2940	9 ¾"	Bubbleback
2529				2941	10 ½"	
2530				2942		MW 'Scientific'
2532				2945		Bubbleback
2533				2949	10 ½"	MW 'Life-Saver'
2536				2984		MW (Flexible lugs)
2537				2996		Prince
2540				3003		
2541				3004		
2574	10 ½"	MW 'Chronometer'		3009	10 ½"	Bubbleback
2576				3019	8 ¾"	Bubbleback
2585	8 ¾"			3028		
2586	8 ¾"			3029		
2587	8 ¾"			3036		Chronograph

Case#:	Movements:	Style:
3038		
3039	10 ½"	
3055		Chronograph
3059		MW (Rect. Case)
3064	9 ¾"	OP
3065	9 ¾"N.A.	Bubbleback
3078		MW 'Chronometer'
3082		Chronograph
3085	13L	Chronograph
3096	10 ½"	MW
3116	10 ½"	MW 'Speed-King, Royal'
3121	9 ¾", 10 ½"	MW 'Speed-King, Royal'
3130	9 ¾"	Bubbleback
3131	9 ¾"N.A.	Bubbleback
3132	9 ¾"	Bubbleback
3133	9 ¾"	Bubbleback
3134	9 ¾"	Bubbleback
3135	9 ¾"	Bubbleback
3136	10 ½", 65	MW
3139	10 ½"	MW 'Army' (Cushion case)
3140		MW (Rect. Case)
3143	10 ½"	
3144	10 ½"	
3159	9 ¾"	
3172	9 ¾"	OP
3181	13L	Chronograph
3189	10 ½"	
3190	10 ½"	
3201	9 ¾"	
3202	9 ¾"	OP
3203	10 ½"	
3204	10 ½"	
3205	10 ½"	
3206	10 ½"	
3233		Chronograph
3241	10 ½"	
3242	10 ½"	
3243	10 ½"	
3244	10 ½"	
3255		
3260		
3263	10 ½"	
3265		
3270	10 ½"	MW
3272		OP
3284		
3311	10 ½"	
3312	10 ½"	
3314	10 ½"	

Case#:	Movements:	Style:
3320		
3323	8 ¾"	OP
3326	10 ½"	
3330		Chronograph
3333		Chronograph
3335		Chronograph
3346	10 ½"	Chronograph
3347		Bubbleback
3348		Bubbleback
3351	10 ½"	MW (Cushion case)
3352		OP
3353	8 ¾", 10 ½"	Bubbleback
3355		
3358		Bubbleback
3359	10 ½"	MW 'Viceroy, Sky Rocket'
3361		Prince (Center sec.)
3362		Prince
3367		
3370	8 ¾"	OP
3371		
3372	9 ¾"	Bubbleback
3373	10 ½", 65	
3374	9 ¾"	
3386	10 ½"	Royal
3405	10 ½"	
3406	10 ½"	
3421	7"	
3456		
3458	9 ¾"N.A.	Bubbleback
3462	10 ½"	Chronograph
3474	10 ½"	Centregraph
3478	10 ½", 65M.T.	Centregraph
3479	10 ½"	
3481	10 ½"	Chronograph
3483	8 ¾"	OP
3484		Chronograph
3486	7"	
3487	7"	
3488	7"	
3489	7"	
3490	8 ¾"	OP
3492	8 ¾"	MW
3495	8 ¾"	OP
3496	8 ¾"	OP
3497	8 ¾"	OP
3501	8 ¾"	
3502	8 ¾"	
3503	8 ¾"	
3505	8 ¾"	OP
3506		
3511		MW (Square case)

Case#:	Movements:	Style:
3514		
3525	13" 72	Chronograph
3529		Chronograph
3535		
3536	9 ¾"	OP
3537	8 ¾"s/c	
3538	9 ¾"	OP
3540		MW 'Precision'
3548	9 ¾"	Bubbleback 'Athlete'
3549		Bubbleback
3562		
3570		
3578		
3573		
3580		
3591	8 ¾"	OP 'Felsa'
3593	9 ¾"	OP
3594	9 ¾"	OP
3595	9 ¾"	Bubbleback
3596	9 ¾"	OP
3597	9 ¾"	OP
3598	9 ¾"	Bubbleback
3599	9 ¾"	Bubbleback
3604	10 ½"	
3606	7"	
3616	10 ½"	
3624		
3626	7"	
3627	9 ¾"	OP
3635		Chronograph
3639	9 ¾"	OP
3640	7 ¾", 80	MW
3642		Chronograph
3645	8 ¾"	OP
3646	16"	MW 'Divers'
3665		
3668	13"	Chronograph
3672		
3684		
3685		OP
3686		OP
3689		
3693	9 ¾"	Speed-King
3694		
3695		Chronograph
3696	9 ¾"N.A.	Bubbleback
3704		
3705		
3706		
3707		
3708	8 ¾"	OP
3715		

Case#:	Movements:	Style:
3716	9 ¾"	OP 'Athlete'
3724		OP
3725	9 ¾"N.A.	Bubbleback
3732	8 ¾"	
3735		Chronograph
3737		
3745		
3746		
3754		
3765		MW 'Royal'
3766	10 ½"	
3767	8 ¾"	Bubbleback
3771		
3772	8 ¾"s/c	OP
3778	8 ¾"	OP
3782		
3785	8 ¾"	OP
3786	10 ½"	
3794	8 ¾"	OP 'Lifesaver'
3795	8 ¾"	Bubbleback
3796	8 ¾"	Bubbleback
3801	8 ¾"	Bubbleback
3802		
3827		Chronograph
3830		
3834		Chronograph
3835		Chronograph
3852		
3858		
3868		MW 'Precision'
3869		OP
3873	10 ½"	
3874	10 ½"	
3875	10 ½"	
3876		
3877	9 ¾"	OP 'Empire'
3882		MW 'Precision'
3884	8 ¾"	
3885	8 ¾"	OP
3886	8 ¾"	OP
3887	8 ¾"	OP
3888	8 ¾"	OP
3890	10 ½"	
3893		
3894		
3923		
3924	10 ½"	
3926		OP
3936		
3937		Prince '¼ Century'
3938	8 ¾"	
3940		Bubbleback

Case#:	Movements:	Style:
3942	10 ½"	
3946	10 ½"	
3949	10 ½"	
3951	8 ¾"	Bubbleback
3967		OP
3977		
3978		MW 'Pioneer'
3980	10 ½"	
3997		Chronograph
4013	8 ¾"	OP
4021		OP
4024	8 ¾"	OP
4025	8 ¾"	OP
4027		OP
4029		
4048	13"	Chronograph
4052		MW
4055	8 ¾"	OP
4059		
4060		
4061		
4062		Chronograph
4064	10 ½"	
4065	10 ½"	
4068		MW
4070	10 ½"	MW 'Falcon'
4099		Chronograph
4100		Chronograph
4111		
4113		Chronograph
4114		
4116		
4119		MW (ultra thin)
4125	10 ½"	MW 'King-of-Wings'
4127	10 ½"	MW 'Athlete'
4130	9 ¾"	OP
4134		OP
4136	9 ¾"	
4156		
4157		
4163	7 ¾"	OP
4164	7 ¾"	OP
4165	7 ¾"	OP
4166	7 ¾"	OP
4167	7 ¾"	OP
4168	7 ¾"	OP
4171	7 ¾"	OP
4172	7 ¾"	OP
4181		MW 'Precision'
4185	7 ¾"	OP
4186	7 ¾"	OP
4187	7 ¾"	OP

Case#:	Movements:	Style:
4190	7 ¾"	OP
4203	7 ¾"	OP
4205		
4211		
4214	7 ¾"	OP
4219		MW 'Precision'
4220	10 ½"	MW 'Speed-King, Royal, Observatory'
4222		MW 'Precision'
4225	7"	
4242	9 ¾"	OP
4255	9 ¾"	OP
4262		
4270	10 ½"	'Elegante'
4271	8 ¾"	MW
4281		
4291		
4294		
4296	10 ½"	
4297	10 ½"	
4302	10 ½"	OP
4306	9 ¾"	OP
4311		Chronograph
4313		Chronograph
4323		
4325		
4327		
4330		MW (Square case)
4332	9 ¾", 10 ½"	OP, Chronograph
4337	7 ¾"	OP
4341	10 ½"	
4350	7 ¾"	OP
4352	14L	Chronograph
4357		
4360	7 ¾"	
4361	10 ½"	MW 'Speed-King'
4362	9 ¾"	OP
4363		
4364		
4365	10 ½"	MW 'Precision'
4366		
4374		
4376		Prince 'JH, Railway'
4377	10 ½"	
4378	10 ½"	
4381		
4389		
4391		
4392	9 ¾"	Bubbleback
4394		
4401		
4402		Prince

Case#:	Movements:	Style:
4405		
4407		
4408	10 ½"	OP
4411		
4417		
4430		
4436		OP
4437	7 ¾"	MW
4444	10 ½"	MW 'Air-Giant, Royal'
4446		
4448		MW
4449	9 ¾", 65	OP
4453	10 ½"	
4454	10 ½", 65	
4455	10 ½", 65	
4457		
4461	10 ½"	MW
4463	10 ½", 65	
4467	10 ½", 740, A.295	DateJust 'Big Bubbleback'
4470		
4471		
4473		
4474		
4476		MW (Square case)
4480	7 ¾"	OP
4483		MW (Square case)
4484		
4486	7 ¾"	OP
4487		OP
4491		
4492		
4493		
4494		
4495		
4496		
4499	10 ½"	MW
4500	13"	Chronograph
4501	10 ½"	
4513		
4528	9 ¾"	OP
4534	9 ¾"	OP
4535	10 ½"	
4537	13"	Chronograph
4540	10 ½", 65	
4547	10 ½", 65	MW Date
4556		MW 'Precision'
4626		MW (Cushion case)
4643		
4645		
4647	10 ½"	MW 'Observatory'

Case#:	Movements:	Style:
4672	9 ¾"	OP
4686	7 ¾"	OP
4767	13", 76C	Chronograph
4768	72C	Chronograph
4771		
4777	9 ¾"	Bubbleback
4804	7 ¾"	OP
4816		
4817	10 ½"	
4845		
4846	8 ¾"	OP
4853		
4857	8 ¾"	OP
4892	7 ¾"	
4900	10 ½"	
4919	9 ¾"	Bubbleback
4925	10 ½"	
4934	10 ½"	
4935	10 ½"	
4937	9 ¾"	OP
4939		Bubbleback
4943	10 ½"	
4961	9 ¾"	Bubbleback
4984	9 ¾"	OP 'Precision'
5000	7 ¾"	MW
5001	7 ¾"	Bubbleback
5002	7 ¾"P.A.	Bubbleback
5003	7 ¾"P.A.	Bubbleback
5004	8 ¾"	MW 'Precision'
5005	8 ¾"	
5006	8 ¾"N.A.	Bubbleback
5007	8 ¾"N.A.	Bubbleback
5009	9 ¾"N.A.	Bubbleback
5010	9 ¾"N.A.	Bubbleback
5011	9 ¾"N.A.	Bubbleback
5013	9 ¾"N.A.	Bubbleback
5015	9 ¾"N.A.	Bubbleback
5016	8 ¾"N.A.	Bubbleback -Bombe'
5018	9 ¾"N.A.	OP - Bombe'
5020	10 ½"	MW
5021	10 ½"	
5022	10 ½"	
5023	10 ½"	OP
5024	10 ½"	
5025	10 ½"	MW 'Precision'
5026	10 ½", A.295	Bubbleback
5027	10 ½", A.295	
5028	10 ½", A.295	Bubbleback
5029	10 ½", A.295	
5030	10 ½", A.295	Datejust
5031	10 ½", A.295, 730	Datejust
5034	13"	Chronograph

Case#:	Movements:	Style:
5036		Chronograph
5045	9 ¾"N.A.	Bubbleback
5048	9 ¾"N.A.	Bubbleback
5050	9 ¾"N.A.	Bubbleback
5051		Bubbleback
5052	9 ¾"N.A.	Bubbleback
5053	10 ½"	
5055	8 ¾"A.R.	Bubbleback
5056	10 ½"	MW 'Speed-King, Kew A'
5058	10 ½"	
5059	10 ½"	
5065		OP
5068		Prince 'JH'
5070	10 ½"	
5076	10 ½"	
5077	10 ½"	
5080	10 ½"	OP
5087	9 ¾"N.A.	Bubbleback
5100		Quartz Date
5105		Bubbleback
5173		Bubbleback
5488		Bubbleback
5500	1520, 1530	Explorer, Air-King
5501	1520, 1530	Explorer, Air-King
5502	1530	Air-King
5503		
5504	1520, 1530	Explorer, Air-King
5505	1530	OP Everest
5506	1530	OP Explorer
5508	1530	Submariner
5510	1530	Submariner
5512	1530, 1570	Submariner
5513	1520, 1530	Submariner
5514	1570	Submariner
5516	1530	
5518	1530	
5520	1520	Air-King
5552	1520, 1530	OP
5590	1520, 1530	
5700	1525, 1535	Air-King, Date
5701	1525, 1535	Explorer, Air-King
6006	8 ¾"A.R.	Bubbleback
6007	8 ¾"A.R.	Bubbleback
6011	9 ¾"N.A.	Bubbleback
6015	9 ¾"N.A.	Bubbleback
6016	9 ¾"N.A.	Bubbleback
6018	9 ¾"N.A.	OP
6020	10 ½"	MW 'Precision'
6021	10 ½"	MW 'Speed-King'
6022	10 ½"	MW 'Air-Giant'
6023	10 ½"	OP

Case#:	Movements:	Style:
6024	10 ½"	
6025	10 ½"	
6026	10 ½", A.295	
6028	10 ½", A.295	
6029	10 ½", A.295	
6030	10 ½", A.295	
6031	10 ½", A.295	Big Bubbleback
6032	13"	Chronograph
6034	13"	Chronograph
6036	13"	Chronograph
6044	10 ½"	MW 'Royal'
6048		Bubbleback
6050	9 ¾" N.A.	OP
6052	9 ¾"N.A.	Bubbleback
6053	10 ½"	
6054		
6056	10 ½"	
6057	10 ½"	
6062	9 ¾"C.P.L.	P-Chronograph 'Moon Phase'
6064	9 ¾"N.A.	Bubbleback
6065	9 ¾"N.A.	Bubbleback
6066	10 ½"	MW Date
6074	10 ½", A.295	Big Bubbleback
6075	10 ½", A.295	Big Bubbleback
6076	9 ¾"N.A.	Bubbleback
6082	10 ½"	OP
6083	10 ½"	
6084	645, 9¾", A.260	OP
6085	9 ¾", A.260	OP (Charles Poluzzi enamel dial)
6085/9	9 ¾", A.260	OP
6087	9 ¾"N.A.	Bubbleback
6088	9 ¾", A.260	OP
6090	9 ¾", A.260	OP (Bombe' lugs)
6092	9 ¾", A.260	OP
6094	10 ½"	
6097	10 ½"	
6098	10 ½", A.296	OP, Explorer
6099	10 ½", A.296	OP
6100	9 ¾", A.260	OP
6101	9 ¾", A.260	OP
6102	9 ¾", A.260	OP
6103	9 ¾", A.260	OP
6104	10 ½", A.296	Datejust
6105	10 ½", A.296	Datejust, OP Date
6106	9 ¾", A.260	Bubbleback
6107	9 ¾", A.260	OP
6108	9 ¾", A.260	
6109	9 ¾", A.260	
6110	9 ¾", A.260	
6111	9 ¾", A.260	

Case#:	Movements:	Style:
6112	10 ½", A.296	
6113	9 ¾", A.260	
6114	9 ¾", A.260	
6115	9 ¾", A.260	
6117	9 ¾", A.260	
6118	9 ¾", A.260	
6119	9 ¾", A.260	OP
6121	9 ¾", A.260	
6122	10 ½"	
6122/5	10 ½"	
6124	10 ½"	
6126	10 ½"	
6127	10 ½"	
6127/5	10 ½"	
6143	9 ¾", A.260	
6144	10 ½"	MW 'Royal'
6145	10 ½"	
6150	10 ½", A.296	Explorer
6152	16"	
6152/1	16"	
6154	16"	
6155	10 ½", A.296	Datejust
6200	10 ½", A.296	Submariner
6202	A.296, A.260	Turn-O-Graph
6204	9 ¾", A.260	Submariner
6205	9 ¾", A.260	Submariner
6206	9 ¾", A.260	
6210	10 ½"	OP 'Observatory, Kew A'
6220	10 ½"	
6221	10 ½"	
6222	10 ½"	
6223	10 ½"	
6224	10 ½"	
6225	10 ½"	
6227	9 ¾", A.260	
6228	9 ¾", A.260	
6232	13"	Chronograph
6234	13"	Chronograph
6236	13"	Chronograph
6238	13"722	Chronograph
6239	13"722	Cosmograph
6240	13"722	Cosmograph
6241	13"722	Cosmograph
6244	10 ½"	MW 'Royal'
6245	10 ½"	
6246	10 ½"	MW
6251		Datejust
6262	13"727	Cosmograph
6263	13"727	Cosmograph
6264	13"727	Cosmograph
6265	13"727	Cosmograph

Case#:	Movements:	Style:
6266	10 ½"	MW Date
6270	13"	Chronograph
6282	10 ½"	
6283	10 ½"	
6284	9 ¾", A.260	OP
6285	9 ¾", A.260	OP
6286	9 ¾", A.260	OP
6285/1	9 ¾", A.260	
6286	9 ¾", A.260	
6290	9 ¾", A.260	OP
6292	9 ¾", A.260	
6294	10 ½"	Date
6298	10 ½", A.296	
6299	10 ½", A.296	Explorer
6300	9 ¾", A.260	
6301	9 ¾", A.260	OP
6303	9 ¾", A.260	OP
6304	10 ½", A.296	Datejust
6305	760, 10 ½", A.296	Datejust
6305/1	1065, 10 ½", A.296	
6305/2	10 ½", A.296	Datejust 'Chronometer'
6307	10 ½", A.296	
6309	760, 10 ½", 1065, A.296	Datejust 'Thunder-Bird'
6332	9 ¾", A.260	OP
6334	9 ¾", A.260	OP
6342		OP 'Speed-King'
6350	10 ½", A.296	Explorer
6352	10 ½", A.296	
6353	10 ½", A.296	
6363		MW
6406	1315	
6410	1310	
6411	1310	
6418	1210	MW, Date 'Speed-King'
6420	1210	MW 'Precision'
6421	1210	MW 'Speed-King'
6422	1210	MW 'Precision'
6423	1210	MW 'Precision'
6424	1210	MW
6425	1210	MW
6426	1210	MW 'Royal'
6427	1210, 1220	MW 'Precision'
6428	10 ½", A.295	Bubbleback
6429	1220	MW
6430	1210, 1220	MW 'Speed-King'
6431	1210, 1220	MW
6432	1210	MW
6434	10 ½"	
6444	1210	MW

Case#:	Movements:	Style:
6466	1215, 1225	MW Date 'Precision'
6480	1210	MW 'Precision'
6482	1210	
6484	10 ½"	
6494	1215	MW Date
6495		
6498	1215	
6500	1030	
6502	1030	OP
6503	1120	OP
6504	1120	OP
6505	1120	
6506	1120	
6507	1120	OP
6508	1130	OP
6509	1120	OP
6510	1055	Day Date
6511	1055	Day Date
6512	1000	OP 'Veriflat'
6513	1135, 1165	
6515	1035, 1120, 1135, 1166	
6516	1135, 1166	Datejust, OP Date
6517	1135, 1166	Datejust, OP Date
6518	1035	OP Date
6519	1135, 1166	OP Date
6520	1135, 1166	
6521	1135, 1166	
6522	1100	
6523	1100	
6524	1166	
6525	1100	
6526	1120	
6527	1135, 1166	
6528	1130	
6529	1135, 1166	
6530	1035	OP Date
6531	1135, 1166	
6532	1030	OP
6533	1135, 1166	
6534	1036	OP Date
6535	1036	OP Date
6536	1030	Submariner
6536-1	1030	Submariner 'Chronometer'
6537	1036	OP Date
6538	1030	Submariner
6538A	1030	Submariner 'Chronometer'
6539		OP
6540	1030	OP
6541	1065M, 1030, 1080	Milgauss

Case#:	Movements:	Style:
6542	1036	GMT Master
6543	1080	OP
6544	1161	OP
6545	1161	OP
6546	1120	OP
6547	1130, 1160	OP Date
6548	1130, 1161	OP
6549	1130, 1161	OP
6551	1130, 1161	OP
6552	1030	OP
6553	1130, 1161	OP
6554	1130, 1161	OP
6555	1130, 1160	
6556	1040	Tru-Beat
6557	1130, 1160	
6558	1040	OP
6559	1130, 1160	OP
6560	1030	OP
6564	1030	OP
6565	1030	OP
6566	1030	OP
6567	1030	OP
6569	1030	OP
6571	1060, 1161	
6580	1030	OP
6581	1030	OP (Octagonal)
6582	1030	OP (Zephyr)
6583	1030	OP
6584	1030	OP
6585	1030	OP
6586	1030	OP
6587	1030	OP
6590	1030	OP
6591		
6592	1030	OP
6593	1030	OP (Bombe lugs)
6594	1030	OP
6598	1030	OP
6599	1030	OP
6602	1065	Datejust
6604	1065	Datejust
6605	1065	Datejust
6609	1065	Datejust 'Thunder-Bird'
6610	1030	Explorer
6611	1055	OP, Day Date
6612	1055	Day Date
6613	1055	Day Date
6614	1030	OP
6615	1130, 1161	
6616	1130, 1160	
6617	1130, 1161	

Case#:	Movements:	Style:
6618	1130, 1161	OP
6619	1130, 1161	OP
6620	1130, 1161	
6621	1130, 1161	OP
6622	1130, 1160	
6623	1130, 1161	OP
6624	1135, 1166	Datejust, OP Date
6625	1135, 1166	OP Date
6626	1135	
6627	1135, 1166	Datejust, OP Date
6628	1135	
6629	1135, 1166	
6630	1135, 1166	
6631	1134, 1166	
6632	1165, 1166	
6633	1135, 1166	
6634	1030	OP
6635	1135, 1166	
6636	1135	
6638	1135, 1165	
6639	1135, 1166	
6646	1036	
6664	1030	MW Date
6694	1215, 1225	MW Date 'Precision'
6700	1135, 1165	
6701	1135, 1166	
6702	1135, 1166	
6703	1165, 1166	
6704	1135, 1166	
6705	1135, 1166	
6706	2030	OP
6707	2030	OP
6710	2030	OP
6711	2030	OP
6712	2030	OP
6713	2030	OP
6715	2030	OP
6717	2030	OP
6718	2030	OP
6719	2030	OP
6720	2030	OP
6721	2030	OP
6723	2030	OP
6724	2030	OP
6740		OP Date
6744	2030	OP
6745	2030	OP
6747	2030	OP
6748	2030	OP
6749	2030	OP
6751	2030	OP
6753	2030	OP

Case#:	Movements:	Style:
6754	2030	OP
6757	2030	OP
6771	2030	OP
6800	1130, 1160	Datejust
6801	1130, 1160	
6802	1130, 1161	
6803	1161	
6804	1161	
6806	1161	
6807	1161	
6815		Datejust
6823		Datejust
6824	2035	Datejust
6824ac	2035	
6825	1035	Datejust
6826		Datejust
6827	2035	Datejust, OP Date
6828	2035	Datejust
6829	2035	Datejust
6830	2035	Datejust
6831	2035	Datejust
6832	2035	Datejust
6833	2035	Datejust
6835	2035	Datejust
6839	2035	Datejust
6862		Yacht-Master
6900	2035	Datejust
6901	2035, 2135	Datejust
6902	2035	Datejust
6903	2035	Datejust
6904	2035	
6905	2035	Datejust
6906	2035	Datejust
6907	2035	Datejust
6908	2135	Datejust
6909		Datejust
6910		Datejust
6911	2135	Datejust
6912	2135	Datejust
6913	2035, 2135	Datejust
6914	2035	Datejust
6915		Datejust
6916	2035	Datejust
6917	2035	Datejust
6918		Datejust
6919	2035	Datejust
6920	2035	
6921	2035	
6923		Datejust
6924	2035	OP Date
6925		Datejust
6926		Datejust

Case#:	Movements:	Style:
6927	2035	Datejust
6928		Datejust
6929	2035	Yacht-Master
6930		Yacht-Master
6931		Yacht-Master
6933	2035	
6935		Yacht-Master
6944		OP Date
6962		Yacht-Master
6994		Date
7016	2461, 2483	
7017	1895	
7019	1895	
7020	1895	
7021	2484	
7024A	2772	
7025	2772	
7025A	2772	
7031	7734	
7032	7734	
7106	2772	
7107	2772	
7109	2784	
7116	2784	
7117	2772	
7126	2784	
7127	2772	
7131		Chronograph
7132		Chronograph
7137	2784	
7149	234	
7157	2784	
7159	234	Chronograph
7169	234	Chronograph
7205/0 Piccard		Experimental Diving Watch
7206	2784	
7535A	2546, 2784	MW
7575A	2554	OP
7576A	2555	OP Date
7580A	2554	
7581A	2555	
7582A	2555	
7583A	2554	
7586A	2554	
7588A	2554	
7590A	2554	
7592A	2555	
7594A	2555	
7596A	2555	
7597	2554	
7599A	2554	

Case#:	Movements:	Style:
7600A	2555	OP Date
7601A	2555	
7602A	2555	
7603		OP
7604	2650	
7605	2650	OP
7606	2651	OP Date
7607	2651	
7608		OP
7609		OP
7614	2650	OP
7615	2650	
7616	2651	
7617	2651	
7618		OP
7619		OP
7623		OP
7624		OP
7626	2651	
7637	2651	
7701		OP
7708		OP
7748		OP
7751		OP
7802	10 ½", 1156, 1182	
7803	10 ½", 1156, 1182	
7804	10 ½", 1156, 1182	
7805	7 ¾", 1173	
7806	9", 9 ¼", 1410	OP
7807	9", 9 ¼", 1412	OP
7808	12 ½", 390	
7809	12 ½", 390	
7810	10 ½", 1412	
7811	10 ½"	OP
7812	12 ½", 390	
7813	10 ½", 1260, 1272	
7815		Datejust
7816	10 ½", 1156, 1182	
7823		Datejust
7824		Datejust
7825		Datejust
7826		Datejust
7827		Datejust
7828		Datejust
7900		
7902	10 ½", 1182, 1156	
7903	10 ½", 1182, 1156	
7904	10 ½", 1156, 1182	
7905	7 ¾", 1173	
7906	9 ¼", 1410	Datejust
7907	9 ¼", 1412	Datejust
7908		Datejust

Case#:	Movements:	Style:
7909	12 ½", 390	
7910	10 ½", 1411, 1412	
7911	10 ½", 1413	
7912		Datejust
7913	10 ½", 1272, 1262, 1260	Datejust
7914	12 ½", 395	
7915		Datejust
7916		Datejust, OP Date
7917	9 ¼"A.S, 1410	Datejust
7918		Datejust
7919	12 ½", 425	Datejust, OP Date
7922	12 ½", 390	
7923	10 ½", 1156, 1182	Datejust
7924	12 ½", 390	Datejust, OP Date
7925		Datejust
7926	12 ½", 1475, 3475	Datejust
7927	10 ½", 1260, 1272	Datejust
7928	12 ½", 390	Datejust
7929	12 ½", 425	
7931	10 ½", 1413	
7935	7 ¾", 1173	
7936	9 ¼", 1410	
7937	9 ¼", 1412	
7939	12 ½", 425	
7944	12 ½", 395	
7949	12 ½", 390	
7950	12 ½", 390	
7951	12 ½", 395	
7952	9 ¼", 1412	
7953	7", 1566	
7954	7", 1566	
7955	10 ½", 1411	
7956	10 ½", 1413	
7957	10 ½", 1156	
7958	10 ½", 1260, 1272	
7959	10 ½", 1156	
7972	290	OP Date
7973	10 ½", 290	
7974	11 ½", 380/2	
7975	7 ¾", 2446	
7976	2447	
7977	1130, 1161	
7980	2446	
7981	2447	
7982	2447	
8011		MW 'Air-Giant'
8012		MW 'Air-Giant'
8015		MW 'Drake'
8023		MW 'Canadian'
8027		MW 'Viceroy'
8029		Datejust

Case#:	Movements:	Style:
8030		Datejust
8031		Datejust
8032		Datejust
8035		Datejust
8044		Explorer
8045		Explorer
8050		Bubbleback
8052		Bubbleback
8053		OP 'Canadian'
8055		OP 'Canadian'
8056		Bubbleback
8058		OP 'Canadian'
8060		OP
8065		Datejust
8066		Datejust
8067		Datejust
8074		OP 'Canadian'
8075		OP 'Canadian'
8076		OP 'Canadian'
8077		OP 'Canadian'
8078		OP 'Canadian'
8079		OP 'Canadian'
8080		OP 'Canadian'
8094		
8113		
8124		
8148		
8171		P-Chronograph 'Moon Phase'
8180		Chronograph
8206		Chronograph
8237		Chronograph 'Moon Phase'
8317		
8389		MW (Rect. Case)
8405		
8437		
8443		
8570		
8717		
8896		
8940		
8950		
8952		
9000	2750	
9010	2763	
9020	2766	
9021	2766	
9031	2766	
9041	2766	
9081	1000	
9090	2784	

Case#:	Movements:	Style:
9091	2671	
9101	2784	
9111	2784	
9121	940.111	
9130	940.111	
9140	940.111	
9150	940.111	
9151	940.111	
9156	2772	
9161	940.111	
9162		Chronograph
9210	2670	OP
9211	2670	OP
9220	2670	OP
9221	2670	OP
9230	2671	
9231	2671	
9240	2671	
9241	2671	
9301	2671	
9303	2671	
9311	2671	
9313	2671	
9321	2651	
9323	2671	
9333	951.111	
9343	951.111	
9346		
9350	951.111	
9351	951.111	
9401	2776	
9411	2784	
9420	7750	
9421	7750	
9430	7750	
9440	2671	
9450	2834	
9451	2834	
9461	2834	
9630		
9659		MW Date
9829		
9919		
9937		
9972		
10000	10 ½", 65	
10008	10 ½", 1182	
10009	10 ½", 1182	
10010	10 ½", 1280	
10050	3475	
14000		Air-King
14010		Air-King

Case#:	Movements:	Style:
14060		Submariner
14203		OP
14208		OP
14233		OP
14238		OP
14270		Explorer
15000	3035	OP Date
15003	3035	OP Date
15007	3035	OP Date
15008	3035	OP Date
15010	3035	OP Date
15017	3035	OP Date
15018	3035	OP Date
15037	3035	OP Date
15038	3035	OP Date
15053	3035	OP Date
15148	3035	OP Date
15200		OP Date
15203		OP Date
15210		OP Date
15223		OP Date
15238		OP Date
15505	3035	OP Date
16000	3035	Datejust
16003	3035	Datejust
16008	3035	Datejust
16009	3035	Datejust
16013	3035	Datejust
16014	3035	Datejust
16018	3035	Datejust
16019	3035	Datejust
16030	3035	Datejust
16058		Datejust
16078	3035	Datejust
16200		Datejust
16203		Datejust
16220		Datejust
16233		Datejust
16234		Datejust
16238		Datejust
16248		Datejust
16250	3035	Datejust
16253	3035	Datejust (T-Bird)
16258	3035	Datejust
16263		Datejust
16264		Datejust
16520		Cosmograph
16523		Cosmograph
16528		Cosmograph
16550	3085	Explorer II
16570		Explorer II
16600		Sea-Dweller

Case#:	Movements:	Style:	Case#:	Movements:	Style:
16610		Submariner Date	19058	5055	OysterQuartz DD
16613		Submariner Date	19068	5055	OysterQuartz DD
16618		Submariner Date	19078	5055	OysterQuartz DD
16650		Sea-Dweller	19148	5055	OysterQuartz DD
16660	3035	Sea-Dweller	19168	5055	OysterQuartz DD
16700		GMT Master	66466	1210	
16710		GMT Master II	67180	2130	OP
16713		GMT Master II	67183	2130	OP
16718		GMT Master II	67187	2130	OP
16750	3075	GMT Master	67188	2130	OP
16753	3075	GMT Master	67193	2130	OP
16758	3075	GMT Master	67194	2130	OP
16760	3085	GMT Master II	67197	2130	OP
16800	3035	Submariner Date	67198	2130	OP
16803	3035	Submariner Date	67230	2130	OP
16808	3035	Submariner Date	67243	2130	OP
17000	5035	OysterQuartz DJ	67480	2130	OP
17013	5035	OysterQuartz DJ	67483	2130	OP
17014	5035	OysterQuartz DJ	67488	2130	OP
18000	3055	Day Date	67513	2130	OP
18026	3055	Day Date	67514	2130	OP
18028	3055	Day Date	67518	2130	OP
18029	3055	Day Date	68158		Datejust
18038	3055	Day Date	68159		Datejust
18039	3055	Day Date	68240	2135	Datejust
18046	3055	Day Date	68243	2135	Datejust
18048	3055	Day Date	68248	2135	Datejust
18049	3055	Day Date	68258		Datejust
18078	3055	Day Date	68273	2135	Datejust
18079	3055	Day Date	68274	2135	Datejust
18178		Day Date	68278	2135	Datejust
18206		Day Date	68279	2135	Datejust
18206B		Day Date	68288	2135	Datejust
18208		Day Date	68289	2135	Datejust
18238		Day Date	69008	2135	Datejust
18239		Day Date	69008A	2135	Datejust
18248		Day Date	69018	2135	Datejust
18249		Day Date	69018A	2135	Datejust
18308		Day Date	69038R	2135	Datejust
18346		Day Date	69038S	2135	Datejust
18348		Day Date	69068	2135	Datejust
18349		Day Date	69068A	2135	Datejust
18368		Day Date	69069	2135	Datejust
18369		Day Date	69069A	2135	Datejust
18388		Day Date	69078	2135	Datejust
18389		Day Date	69078A	2135	Datejust
19018	5055	OysterQuartz DD	69079	2135	Datejust
19019	5055	OysterQuartz DD	69079A	2135	Datejust
19028	5055	OysterQuartz DD	69088	2135	Datejust
19038	5055	OysterQuartz DD	69088A	2135	Datejust
19048	5055	OysterQuartz DD	69089	2135	Datejust
19049	5055	OysterQuartz DD	69089A	2135	Datejust

Case#:	Movements:	Style:
69098	2135	Datejust
69108	2135	Datejust
69108A	2135	Datejust
69118A	2135	Datejust
69128	2135	Datejust
69128A	2135	Datejust
69136	2135	Datejust
69138	2135	Datejust
69138A	2135	Datejust
69139	2135	Datejust
69139A	2135	Datejust
69148	2135	Datejust
69148A	2135	Datejust
69158	2135	Datejust
69159	2135	Datejust
69160A	2135	OP Date
69163	2135	Datejust
69163A	2135	Datejust
69166		Datejust
69168	2135	Datejust
69168A	2135	Datejust
69169	2135	Datejust
69169A	2135	Datejust
69173	2135	Datejust
69173A	2135	Datejust
69174A		Datejust
69174	2135	Datejust
69178	2135	Datejust
69178A	2135	Datejust
69179	2135	Datejust
69179A	2135	Datejust
69188		Datejust
69190A	2135	OP Date
69198E		Datejust
69198R		Datejust
69198S		Datejust
69240	2135	OP Date
69258		Datejust
69268		Datejust
69278	2135	Datejust
69279	2135	Datejust
69279A	2135	Datejust
69288		Datejust
72000		
72033		
73090		
74000	2841-1	
74001	2841-1	
74003	2841-1	
74008	2841-1	
74100	2841-1	
74300	2841-1	

Case#:	Movements:	Style:
75000	2841-1	
75090		
75100	2841-1	
75201	2841-1	
75203	2841-1	
75204	2841-1	
75205	2841-1	
75208	2841-1	
75301	2841-1	
75303	2841-1	
75304	2841-1	
75403	2841-1	
76100	2841-1	
79090		
79160		
79170		
79180		
84000		
84033		
84040		
85000		
85033		
85040		
90020	2750	
90021	2750	
90120	2763	
90121	2763	
92200	2670	
96080		

FREQUENTLY ASKED QUESTIONS

Why do some Roman numeral dials represent the 4th hour as IIII instead of IV?

There are a number of theories on this matter, but for simplicities' sake, I will only discuss the three most common opinions.

One explanation is that a famous clockmaker was commissioned to build a clock for a powerful king in Europe. The clockmaker printed the dial with the 4th hour represented as *IV*, as is the correct manner. The king informed the clockmaker that it was wrong and should be represented as *IIII*. The clockmaker assured the king that *IV* was correct. However, the king persisted and the clockmaker wanting to keep his head attached to his body, changed the dial to feature the *IIII* configuration— thus, the tradition was born. This of course is very unlikely, but it does sound colorful.

The next explanation dates back to Roman mythology, when apparently *IV* was too similar to the name for the Roman god 'Jupiter', whose name in Latin begins *IV*. *I* representing the *J* and *V* being used instead of *U* in ancient times, thus *IV* (in Latin) represented the abbreviation *JU* for 'Jupiter'. They felt it was disrespectful to display the name of a god on the face of a clock. Again, this seems a bit far fetched, but you never know—it's just crazy enough to be true.

Roman numeral watch dial featuring the 4th hour as *IIII*.

The final explanation (and likely the correct one), is also the simplest. It's just a matter of symmetry on the dial. With the 4th hour represented as *IIII,* then you would have the first 4 hours displaying the *I* numeral, the second 4 hours displaying the *V* numeral and the last 4 hours displaying the *X* numeral. Furthermore, the hour positioned opposite the *IIII* is the *VIII*. These numerals are more similar if physical appearance (and size) than *IV & VIII* would be, thus the *IIII* configuration makes for a more balanced appearance on the dial. As usual, the simplest explanation is often the correct one.[48]

What can I do if my watch is stolen?

In addition to notifying the local authorities, you should contact Rolex who will place the *Case Reference Number & Serial Number* in their database. Thus if the watch is ever returned for service you will be notified. Also, the N.A.W.C.C. (National Association of Watch & Clock Collectors) has a resource on their website, whereby you can post (free of charge) information on any stolen Horological items. Their website is located at http://www.nawcc.org

270

How was the standard direction of clockwise (left to right) determined?

Although this is difficult to conclusively determine, there is a general consensus regarding why the hands of a clock move from left to right, thus clockwise.

The explanation dates back thousands of years to the earliest civilizations: the Sumerians and Babylonians, who tracked the movement of the stars in the heavens from left to right. This was due to the fact that they were located in the *Northern Hemisphere,* and since the Sun was located to the South, you would have to face South to the track the Sun's path across the sky. They even wrote of religious ceremonies and events that required left to right motions. This could also have been the inspiration for modern writing flowing from left to right, as well as a number of other habits and rituals which utilize a left to right motion.

Centuries later, the Egyptians created giant obelisk-shaped sundials called *Cleopatra Needles,* which cast shadows onto the ground to track the 12 parts of the day. Due to the size of these sundials (or sun-clocks, as they are often called), one had to stand back, facing the North, if they wanted to easily view the shadows—thus, the shadows would travel across the ground from left to right. Otherwise, if you faced the South, you would constantly be looking over your shoulder to view the shadows. Again, this was due to the fact that they were located in the Northern Hemisphere, and the Sun, being to the South, would cast the shadows to the North.

With this being said, the evolution of clocks took a natural progression toward a left to right movement. This of course poses the question: If modern civilization had developed from Africa or Australia, being in the Southern Hemisphere, would clockwise be right to left, thus counter-clockwise?[48]

Where did the term 'Horology' originate?

While the exact origin is unknown, an early use of the term is as follows. The ancient Roman water clock was known as a *Horologium,* and after the fall of the Roman Empire, many Latin-speaking cultures adopted variations of the name to describe subsequent timekeepers. Some of those variations were: *horloge, orloge, orologio, orloige* and *oreloige.*

Centuries later, in 1656, Christian Huygens invented the first Pendulum clock, based on Galileo's design. Seventeen years later, in 1673, Huygens chronicled the invention (among others) in a book entitled: *Horologium Oscillatorium.* Then around 1751, Abbé Nicolas Louis de Lacaille borrowed the term to name an obscure constellation in the southern hemisphere ("the pendulum"), thus honoring Huygens' invention. The name was later shortened to *Horologium,* and thus the term 'Horology' has been used to describe "the science of measuring time".

What is the most money ever paid for a Rolex?

Rolex wristwatches are known for being of the utmost quality and therefore are also known for being quite expensive. However, Rolex does not hold the 'World Record' for the most money ever paid for a wristwatch. That record goes to *Patek Philippe,* when one of their watches recently sold for SFr. 6'603'500 ($4,026,524; £2,774,579) at the Antiquorum's auction in Geneva, on April 14, 2002. The watch, Lot 608, was a 1939, (probably unique) Platinum *World-Timer* (Ref. 1415HU "Heures Universelles"; No. 929693; Case No. 656462), featuring 41 names of cities & locations engraved around the milled dial.

At the same auction, Rolex set a world record of their own when a 1952 Oyster Chronograph sold for SFr. 322'500 ($196,646; £135,504)—the most money ever paid at auction for a Rolex wristwatch. This watch, Lot 125, was the famed *Jean-Claude Killy* (Ref. 6036), 50m=165ft Anti-Magnetic.[49]

Why does a quartz movement 'tick' instead of 'sweeping' like a mechanical watch?

Before answering this we must first give a very basic explanation of how a mechanical watch operates. There are three basic parts to a watch's movement:

1: A power source (or mainspring).
2: An oscillating mass (or balance wheel) which provides the timed rate.
3: A series of gears which regulate the beat of the balance wheel and transfers this rate to the hands.

What results is the step (or action) of the second hand. This action is so fast (upwards of 8 times per second) that the second hand gives the *illusion* of sweeping (or floating) around the dial.

Quartz watches use a tiny energy cell (or battery) to replace the mainspring as the power source. The oscillating mass is replaced by a tiny piece of shaped quartz crystal, which is tuned to a frequency of 32,768 Hz (cycles per second)—this is often called the piezoelectric effect and is similar to that of a tuning fork. A system of integrated circuits then divides the frequency into one-second pulses to drive a tiny motor, which in turn drives the hands.

The purpose of these pulses being timed to one-second is simply a matter of power. To achieve a faster pulse, it would require a higher frequency which would require a much larger power source. Therefore, a one-second pulse is used, resulting in the second hand 'ticking' in one-second intervals.

It is worth noting that the accuracy of a particular timepiece is directly-proportional to the beats or cycles per second. Whereas, a timepiece with a higher 'per second' rate has the capability of being more accurate. This rate for current Rolex models is 8 beats per second, where a quartz clock is 32,768 cycles per second and an atomic clock is 9,192,631,770 cycles per second.

Therefore, the accuracy error for a mechanical chronometer is rated at no more than a few seconds per day, while a quartz is a fraction of a second per day, but an atomic clock is accurate to less than one second in over 1,000 years!

LEFT: Generic mechanical watch movement shown without the automatic winding rotor.
CENTER: Generic mechanical watch movement shown with its automatic winding rotor.
RIGHT: Generic quartz watch movement.

Is it illegal to sell 'Replica' Rolex watches?

In a word—Yes! Replica watches are in fact counterfeit and therefore are illegal. On January 17, 2001, the U.S. District Court in Columbia, S.C. charged two individuals with selling allegedly counterfeit versions of Rolex watches. Their website fakegifts.com claimed the watches to be "replicas". Mark Dipadova was later sentenced to 24 months in prison and was ordered to pay $138,264 in restitution for "trafficking counterfeited trademarks", while Rufus Todd Jones was sentenced to 36 months in prison, and was ordered to pay $116,779 in restitution on a similar charge.

What does the "T" designation at the bottom of the dial mean?

This refers to the chemical used on the hands and hour markers, which causes them to illuminate. Around 1950, watch makers started using Tritium as their luminous material, and began indicating the amount of that radioactive material with a designation at the bottom of the dial (i.e. T SWISS T or SWISS T < 25). Around 1998, watchmakers changed the designation to read: SWISS MADE, when they replaced the Tritium with LumiNova (an organic, non-radioactive chemical), as their source of luminescence.

T SWISS MADE T indicates that the radioactive material Tritium is present on the wristwatch. The amount of radioactive material emitted is limited to a maximum of 25 milliCurie.

SWISS T < 25 more specifically indicates that the wristwatch emits an amount of Tritium that is *less* than the 25 milliCurie limit.

SWISS T 25 indicates that the wristwatch emits the *maximum* allowable amount of Tritium (i.e. a full 25 milliCurie).

SWISS MADE on wristwatches produced after (around) 1998, this indicates the presence of Lumi-Nova as the luminous material. (*Please Note: "SWISS MADE" was also the indication on wrist-watches produced prior to the 1950s, when Radium was used as the luminous material. However, at that time "SWISS MADE" simply indicated that the watch was in fact made in Switzerland.*)

The following is a brief history of these luminous materials:

Around 1913, watchmakers began using a radioactive alpha emitter called *Radium* which, over a period of time, disintegrates into Radon (also known as Radon gas), a radioactive beta emitter which is considerably more hazardous—especially when inhaled.

Radium didn't pose a direct hazard to the wearer (since there is no physical contact), but did to those working in the factories producing the luminous paints. It was later determined that workers who applied the Radium paint to watch dials were experiencing health problems as well. This was due to the fact that they would often *lick* the tips of their paint brushes, thus creating a finer point and making it easier to apply. This prolonged contact eventually resulted in many cancerous conditions.

Radium was widely used into the 1940s, but was subsequently replaced by *Tritium* around 1950. Since Radium has a substantial half life (meaning how long the material lasts before losing its radioactive properties), it was feared that old watches containing the Radium paint could pose a health hazard to the public if the crystals were broken, thus an increased possibility for physical contact.

Tritium is a low-level radioactive beta emitting version of hydrogen, thus was considered less of a health risk. That's not to say that Tritium is a completely safe chemical. Since it does have a radioactive content, prolonged physical contact could be harmful as well. However, the radiation exposure to the wearer (under normal conditions) is nominal. Furthermore, due to the reduced half life (being only around 10-15 years), Tritium will lose its illumination and begin to fade after only a few years.

With that being said, watch manufacturers did the 'politically correct' thing and began phasing out Tritium in favor of the newer (and safer) chemical *LumiNova* around 1998. This new material is not only safe, but also maintains its illumination substantially longer. It is worth noting that the chemical LumiNova actually glows 'green', and is considered by some to be less cosmetically appealing than the clean 'white' appearance of Tritium.

What is the difference between a 'Chronometer' and a 'Chronograph'?

This is a very common question since people often confuse the two. While their names may sound similar, these terms have very little in common.

Chronometer is a term used to describe a highly-precise timepiece which, after rigorous testing, has received an official timing certificate from the official Swiss timing bureau *Contrôle Officiel Suisse des Chronometres* (COSC). Thus, it is a rating or accolade given for the watch's accuracy.

A **chronograph** on the other hand is a timepiece that, in addition to the normal time telling functions, also performs a separate time *measuring* function such as a stop watch—with a separate seconds hand which can be started, stopped and reset to zero, via push-buttons on the side of the case. Please do not confuse 'chronographs' with 'complications' (which are described below). While *all* chronographs can be considered complications, not all complications are in fact chronographs.

What do "complications" mean when referring to a wristwatch?

A **complication** is described as *any* additional function the wristwatch performs beyond *basic time telling* (i.e. hour, minute and second). A common example of wristwatch complications are calendar models which display the day/date. Additional complications include chronograph models, whereas the watch performs like a basic 'stop watch' (as described above). Other complications worth mentioning are: second time zone, moonphase and alarms.

What does it mean by a 'jeweled movement'?

A **jeweled movement** refers to precious stones (typically synthetic sapphires, or rubies), which are used on the movement in key pivot points to reduce friction, thus reducing wear. This is due to the hardness of the jewel which will not wear out when under constant friction from the metal parts.

The idea was introduced over three hundred years ago, and today is used in most mechanical watch movements. The more common configuration is a 17 jewel movement, however, more complicated watches are often found with 29 jewels (or more). In fact, a rare example exists with a highly complicated movement featuring 76 jewels (i.e. IWC II Destriero Scafusia). It is worth noting that movements were created in the 1980s featuring upwards of 100 jewels, but upon closer examination, it was easily determined that most of the jewels were merely cosmetic.

When jeweled movements were first introduced they frequently used real (or natural) garnets or even diamonds. However, modern watch movements typically feature synthetic jewels, which are laboratory grown and are quite inexpensive to produce.

How many watches does Rolex manufacture each year?

Rolex doesn't release exact numbers, however, according to industry estimates and considering the number of Chronometer certificates issued to Rolex over the past few years, it's safe to assume that Rolex produces somewhere between 650,000 to 700,000 watches annually. On the other hand, it is believed that counterfeiters produce ten times that number!

---

[48] Source: *British Horological Institute* website. http://www.bhi.co.uk
[49] Source: *Antiquorum* website. http://www.antiquorum.com

GLOSSARY OF TERMINOLOGY

ACRYLIC CRYSTAL: First introduced in the 1920s, these are also called plastic crystals.

AFTERMARKET ROLEX PARTS: Any non-genuine, or non-Rolex made parts that DO NOT bear counterfeit Rolex trademarks, logos or hallmarks.

APERTURE: Small openings on the dials of some watches. It is inside these apertures where indications are given (e.g. numbered date, hour or day of the week).

ARABIC NUMERALS: Figures on a dial representing the hours (i.e. 1, 2, 3, 4) , as opposed to Roman Numerals (i.e. I, II, III, IV).

ARBOR: The shaft or axle that a gear rides on. At each end is a narrower segment called the "pivot"

ATMOSPHERE: Used as a measure of the watertightness of a watch case. One atmosphere equals average air pressure at sea level, approximately 14.7 pounds per square inch. Since one atmosphere equals 33.90 feet of water, a 3 ATM water resistant watch is considered water resistant to approximately 100 feet.

AUTOMATIC WINDING (also Self Winding): An automatic watch is wound by the movement of the wearer's wrist. This movement causes a weight inside the watch to rotate backwards and forwards. The weight is connected by a gear train to the barrel arbor, which is hooked to the mainspring, thus winding it and keeping it in constant tension.

AUTO ROTOR: Rolex patented perpetual movement invented by Emil Borer in 1931.

BAGUETTE: A ladies style watch (or movement) featuring a thin rectangular or oval shape.

BAKELITE: The transparent acrylic material used on the bezel of early model GMT-Masters in 1954.

BALANCE: The governor or controller of a watch; it consists of a metal wheel, now commonly made of Invar, a special steel resistant to changes in dimension due to fluctuations of heat or humidity and usually is mounted with a hairspring also of Invar or a similar alloy.

BALANCE SPRING: Also referred to as the "hair spring", this spring controls the swing of the balance.

BALANCE WHEEL: A portion of the escapement, which divides time into equal sections.

BARK FINISH: The finish on some bracelet links that resembles the bark of a tree.

BARREL: Often called the "mainspring barrel" this is a circular box, often connected to a gear, which holds the mainspring, which drives the watch.

BEAT: Measured in either Beats Per Hour (BPH) or Beats Per Second (BPS), this is the number of times per hour or second that the balance wheel goes through a full arc of motion in either direction. The usual number of Beats Per Hour is 18,000, however current Rolex watches are 28,800 BPH.

BEZEL: The ring around the crystal on the top portion of a watch. Often, the bezel is made from varying materials (i.e. stainless steel or gold) within a watch line—See also **rotating bezel**, **bi-directional rotating bezel** and **uni-directional rotating bezel**.

BI-DIRECTIONAL ROTATING BEZEL: A bezel which can be rotated either clockwise or counterclockwise, and is used for making calculations.

BOY'S SIZE WATCH: 2mm smaller than that of a standard men's size watch.

BRANCARD: Rolex Prince model with flared ends. From the French word meaning 'stretcher'.

BREATHE: This is a term for the expansion and contraction of the hairspring. When breathing correctly, the spring is working at it's optimum efficiency.

BREVET: From the French work *Brevette* meaning patented.

BRIDGE: Any movement plate secured by a minimum of two screws.

BUBBLEBACK: Term used to describe the early Rolex Perpetual models, due to the thickness of the case used to house the oversized Auto-Rotor movement.

CALENDAR WATCH: A watch with a mechanism that shows the date, or on more complex watches, the month, day, moonphase and even the year. Most calendar watches have to be adjusted manually at the end of the month, but the mechanism of a perpetual calendar watch adjusts itself automatically.

CALIBER (or Calibre U.K.): Refers to the size, style or shape of a watch movement.

CALIFORNIA DIAL (also Roman-Arabic): Dial featuring a combination of Roman & Arabic numerals. Roman on the top half, with Arabic on bottom. The term "California Dial" refers to a California-based company who became known for *reproducing* the dial over the years.

CENTER SECONDS (or Centre Seconds U.K.): Also called sweep seconds. Mounted on the center post of the watch for greater visibility and ease in reading

CHRONOGRAPH: A timepiece that, in addition to the normal time telling functions, also performs a separate time *measuring* function such as a stop watch—with a separate seconds hand which can be started, stopped and reset to zero, via push-buttons on the side of the case

CHRONOMETER (or Chronometre U.K.): A highly-precise timepiece which, after rigorous testing, has received a timing certificate from the official Swiss timing bureau *Contrôle Officiel Suisse des Chronometres* (COSC). (Greek for Chronos = time / Meter = measure.)

COCK: Any retaining device secured by one screw.

COMEX: A French commercial diving company (**CO**mpagnie **M**aritime d'**EX**pertise), which in the 1960s, aided in the development of the one-way gas escape valve in the Rolex Sea-Dweller.

COMPLICATIONS: Any additional function the wristwatch performs beyond *basic time telling* (i.e. hour, minute and second), such as date, day of the week, moonphase, perpetual calendars or even sop/start chronograph functions.

CONCEALED CLASP: Clasp used, whereby the buckle is concealed under the bracelet's links, giving the appearance of a continuous flowing bracelet. This clasp is found on modern Rolex *President* models.

COSC (*Contrôle Officiel Suisse des Chronomètres*): Official Swiss testing station, whereby watches are tested for the chronometer rating.

COSMOGRAPH: A Rolex trademarked term, which is similar to the chronograph, the cosmetic difference being that the tachymeter scale is printed (or engraved) on the bezel rather than on the outer rim of the dial.

COUNTERFEIT ROLEX PARTS: Any aftermarket parts that bear illegal, fake or otherwise non-authentic Rolex trademarks, logos or hallmarks. These parts are used with the sole intention of deceiving someone, by misrepresenting the watch/parts as authentic Rolex made.

CROWN: The button used to wind and set the time of a watch.

CROWN GUARDS (also Shoulders): Protective rails protruding from the watch's case on either side of the crown for the purpose of protecting it from damage.

CUSHION CASE: Squared shape with rounder edges, used on older model watch cases.

CYCLOPS: Glass bubble positioned over the date aperture for the purpose of magnifying the date to be more easily read. First patented on May 1, 1952, and publicly released on the *Datejust* at the Basel fair in 1954.

DCI (Decompression Illness): A condition, especially in divers, caused by the release of nitrogen bubbles in the tissue and blood upon too rapid a return from high pressure to atmospheric pressure—characterized by pains in the joints, cramps, paralysis and possibly death. This condition is often referred to as "the bends"

DIAL: This is the face of the watch, on which the hour markers (or indices) and hands are attached. On date and day-date models, an aperture is cut in the dial to allow the number wheels to be read.

DIVERS' EXTENSION: Used on divers' watches, a "hinged" extension within the watch's bracelet, which allows the bracelet to be lengthened so as to fit over a wet suit.

DOUBLE QUICK SET: Introduced in late 1990, this feature allows both the day and the date to be rapidly set via the winding crown—See also **quick set**.

DOUBLE NAMED WATCHES (also Co-Branded): Refers to watches that bear more than one company name on the dial (i.e. the manufacturer and retailer).

EBAUCHE: A movement blank. Typically, an ebauche does not include a mainspring or balance. These items are added as a movement is completed.

ELAPSED TIME ROTATING BEZEL: A graduated rotating bezel often found on divers' models, used to keep track of elapsed time while diving.

END PIECE: The small (usually hollow) piece of metal, crafted to look like a bracelet link, which allows the bracelet to be attached to the case via tiny spring bars.

ESCAPEMENT: Allows the power stored in the mainspring to be released through the gears in a regular and controlled manner—See also **lever escapement**.

ESCAPE WHEEL: In a lever escapement, this is the last gear in the train, but does not turn other gears. Instead it has specially shaped teeth that are alternately locked and unlocked by the motion of the balance and lever to regulate the motion of the watch in a controlled manner.

FLIP LOCK CLASP: Clasp used on special Oyster bracelets, whereas the buckle utilizes a 'flip-lock' safety clasp to help prevent accidental loss. These are often found on divers' models (i.e. Submariner, Sea-Dweller).

GAS ESCAPE VALVE: A one-way valve used in the Sea-Dweller, by which the helium particles are allowed to escape from the watch's case during decompression. Sometimes called a *helium escape valve*.

GAUSS: The centimeter-gram-second electromagnetic unit of magnetic flux density, equal to one maxwell per square centimeter. [After Karl F. Gauss (1777-1855).] - *The American Heritage Dictionary*, Second College Edition. Copyright © 1985 by Houghton Mifflin Company. All rights reserved. Please Note: The Rolex Milgauss gets part of its name from this term (i.e. Mill-Gauss).

GILT (or Gild): Gold plated, or having a gold color or hue.

G.M.T: Abbreviation for Greenwich mean time. Time is calculated from the naval observatory at Greenwich, England, which is located at zero degrees longitude.

GUILLOCHÉ: French term meaning "engine-turned". This term is also used to describe the 'honeycomb' textured dial found on some Rolex models.

HACKING: Introduced around 1972, this feature causes the second hand to 'stop dead' when the winding crown is pulled out fully to set the time, thus allowing for more easily synchronizing of one or more watches.

HALLMARK: A mark or stamp indicating the purity of a metal, or the date, and/or country of import.

HAIRSPRING: See **Balance Spring**.

HERMETIC: Completely sealed, especially against the escape or entry of air and/or dust.

HONEYCOMB DIAL: A Rolex dial model featuring a honeycomb-like texture—See also **guilloché**.

HOROLOGY: 1—The science of measuring time. 2—The art of making timepieces.

HUNTER CASE: A case used on pocket watches and even some early wrist watches, whereas the front and back are protected by hinged covers, which are usually spring loaded.

INCABLOC: The best known of the various competing shock absorbers for watches, it is manufactured by Potescap SA and considered an industry standard.

INDICES: Another term for the hour markers on a watch's dial.

JEWEL: A precious stone (usually a synthetic sapphire or ruby) that is used as a bearing for watch gears to reduce friction. The top of the jewel has a depression to hold oil. Jewels are set in the metal plates that support the gears. The pivot (the tip of the gear arbor) goes though a hole in the jewel.

JUMP HOUR: From *Heures Sautantes*, a watch were the hour hand is replaced with a tiny aperture at the 12 o'clock position. Through this window one could view a miniature wheel displaying the numbers 1 thru 12. When the minute hand passed the 60-minute mark, the wheel would turn, thus the hour marker 'jumping' into place at the start of each hour.

LADY PRESIDENT: This nickname is often used to refer to the ladies' Rolex Datejust fitted with a President bracelet.

LEVER ESCAPEMENT: Invented by Thomas Mudge in 1759, it subsequently replaced all other types of watch escapements, and is currently the only type of escapement manufactured for watches. Consisting of an escape wheel, "lever" and a balance wheel, the lever, when initiated by the balance wheel, locks and unlocks the escape wheel, thus transferring power through the gear train in an even and controlled motion.

LIGNE: A pre-metric system of measurement still used in Switzerland to measure watch movements. One ligne (''') is approximately 2.256 mm.

LOUPE: Often called a jewelers' or magnifier loupe. It is used to inspect fine detailed markings, and very small parts.

LUGS: The two pointed edges on either end of the case, by which the bracelet is attached to the case through the end pieces. These are often called the 'horns'.

LUMINOVA: Organic, non-radioactive, luminous material now used on the hands and hour markers of a watch. It replaced the older (and more dangerous) radioactive material *Tritium* around 1998.

MAINSPRING: The principal spring of a watch that supplies the force of motion to the gear trains.

MECHANICAL: Movement used on traditional timepieces, whereas the watch uses a main spring for its power source and must be hand wound.

MERCEDES HANDS: Nickname used to describe a style of hands used on some sports model watches. The name comes from the hour hand which features a round emblem which resembles the logo of the German automobile manufacturer *Mercedes Benz*. Rolex refers to these hands as *skelette* or skeleton hands.

MICRO-STELLA: Tiny screws used for adjustment of the balance.

MID-SIZED WATCHES: Refers to Rolex models that are 80% of the size of a standard men's watch.

MILLED EDGE: Having a grooved or coined edge. First used on watch cases by the Dennison Watch Case Company in the early 1900s, and is still featured on the back of all Rolex Oyster cases.

MOON PHASE: A type of dial showing the changes in the moon's phases, or lunar cycles.

MOVEMENT: The machinery of any time piece.

NITROGEN NARCOSIS: This alcohol-like effect is often called 'rapture of the deep', whereas the body absorbs a toxic level of nitrogen, which in some cases can cause death.

OCTAGON CASE: A watch case having eight sides, shaped similar to that of a stop-sign.

OERSTED: The centimeter-gram-second electromagnetic unit of magnetic intensity, equal to the magnetic intensity one centimeter from a unit magnetic pole. [After Hans Christian Oersted (1777-1851).] - *The American Heritage Dictionary*, Second College Edition. Copyright © 1985 by Houghton Mifflin Company. All rights reserved.

OFFICIALLY CERTIFIED CHRONOMETER: Around 1949, Rolex introduced this wording on the dials of their chronometer-rated models.

OVETTONE (or Ovetto, or Ovitone): Italian for 'little egg', this nickname was associated with the *Bubbleback* models due to their rounded shape.

PEDOMETER: The first self-winding pocket watch design, invented by Abraham-Louis Perrelet in 1770, thus named after the source of its power (i.e. a weighted lever that jerks as a man walks).

PRECISION: Term used by Rolex to describe their watch movements which had not received a timing certificate, thus were not rated as chronometers.

PERPETUAL MOVEMENT: Another term for an automatic or self-winding movement with a winding rotor that travels a full 360 degrees.

PIVOT: The turned down part of an arbor. This part commonly projects through the hole in watch jewels.

PLATE: The portion of the movement which supports the bridges and other plates.

PRESIDENT (also Presidential): This nickname is often used to describe the Rolex *Day-Date* models, since one was given to *then* President Dwight D. Eisenhower in 1956, to celebrate his re-election and nearly every President since Franklin D. Roosevelt has worn one. However, the name 'President' is officially only used to describe the bracelet style featured on the *Day-Date* model.

QUARTZ MOVEMENT: Quartz watches use a tiny energy cell (or battery) to replace the mainspring as the power source. The oscillating mass is replaced by a tiny piece of shaped quartz crystal, which is tuned to a frequency of 32,768 Hz (cycles per second)—this is often called the piezoelectric effect and is similar to that of a tuning fork. A system of integrated circuits then divides the frequency into one-second pulses to drive a tiny motor, which in turn drives the hands.

QUICK SET: Introduced in late 1970, this feature allows the date to be rapidly set via the winding crown, without having the hour hand pass over the 'midnight' position—See also **double quick set**.

RADIUM: Radioactive luminous material first used on the hands of watches around 1913. This material was subsequently replaced by *Tritium* around 1950.

REFERENCE NUMBER: The case or model number of a watch, usually engraved between the lugs, and/or inside/outside the case back.

REGISTERS: Term used to describe the subsidiary 'extra-function' dials positioned on the face of a chronograph watch.

ROLESIUM: A Rolex term used to describe the case metal mixture of stainless steel and platinum, trademarked on May 21, 1932. This configuration is currently seen on the Rolex Yacht-Master.

ROLLESOR: A Rolex term used to describe the case metal mixture of stainless steel and gold, trademarked on April 1, 1933.

ROMAN-ARABIC DIAL: See also **California Dial**.

ROTATING BEZEL: Often used on sports watches like divers' or aviator models, it is used to perform an additional function, such as checking decompression times, or telling the time in different time-zones—See also **bi-directional rotating bezel** and **uni-directional rotating bezel**.

ROTOR: The oscillating weight used in an automatic movement.

RUBY: See also **Jewel**.

SAPPHIRE CRYSTAL: First introduced in 1970, on the *Rolex Quartz*, these synthetic crystals are now used in most watches, due to the fact that they are highly scratch resistant.

SELF WINDING: See also **Automatic Winding**.

SERIAL NUMBER: An identification number of a watch, usually engraved between the lugs, and/or inside/outside the case back. This number can often be used to date the production of the watch.

SHOCK ABSORBER: A system where the jewels on the balance staff are spring mounted, thereby protecting the balance staff from damage, in the event that the watch is dropped.

SKELETON HANDS (or Skellete): Term used by Rolex to describe the hands on a watch that are 'cut-out' so they only feature an outline of the hands. Some of these hands are nicknamed *Mercedes-style*.

SKELETON CASE: Also known as a 'clear back' model. It features a transparent front or back, thus permitting a view of the internal workings of the watch.

SPELEOLOGY: The study and exploration of caves. It was for these 'cave dwellers' (or speleologists) that the Rolex *Explorer II* was designed, whereby one could distinguish day from night with the use of a special 24-hour hand and bezel.

SPRING BAR: A small spring-loaded pushpin, which passes through the end piece into either side of the lugs, thus holding the bracelet onto the case.

SUBSIDIARY SECONDS (or Sunk Seconds): The small seconds dial, usually positioned at the 6 o'clock and is sunken so as not to impede the hour and minute hand.

SUPER BALANCE: Balance wheel design for the Auto Rotor Perpetual movement, patented by Rolex in 1935.

SUPERLATIVE CHRONOMETER OFFICIALLY CERTIFIED: Starting in 1957, Rolex introduced this wording to replace 'Officially Certified Chronometer' on the dials of their chronometer-rated models and it is still used to this day.

SWEEPING MOVEMENT: Also known as the 'step' or 'action'. Sweep refers to the movement of the second hand quickly 'ticking' at approximately 5-8 times per second, thus giving the illusion of sweeping.

TACHYMETER (or Tachometer): A special scale printed on the outside of a chronograph, used to calculate the average speed traveled over a measured distance. Frequently used in auto racing to determine 'lap times'.

TELEMETER: A special scale printed on the outside of a chronograph, used to determine the distance of an object from the wearer by measuring how long it takes sound to travel that distance.

THUNDERBIRD BEZEL: Also called the Turn-O-Graph bezel in the U.K., thus named after the Turn-O-Graph watch where it was first introduced. The bezel is now fitted to select Rolex Datejust models.

TOOL WATCH: This concept refers to watches created for use in specific sports or professional activities.

TONNUEAU CASE: Barrel-shaped case, whereas the ends are squared and the sides bow out in a rounded convex shape.

TRAVEL CLOCK: Also called portfolio or purse watches. This refers to early covered, folding or protected clocks, some of which were carried in women's purses around the early 1900s.

TRIPLOCK: Rolex screw-down crown, which features a triple seal against water and dust. First patented on July 22, 1952, it features the Rolex *crown* underscored with three 'dots'.

TRITIUM: Luminous material used on the hands and hour markers of a watch since the 1950s. This radioactive material was discontinued by Rolex around 1998, in favor of a safer material *LumiNova*. Modern watches containing Tritium will be marked "T", "T 25", or "T<25" on the bottom of the dial. (*Please Note: The radiation content is extremely small and is not a direct hazard to the wearer.*)

TWINLOCK: Rolex screw-down crown, which features a twin seal against water and dust. First patented on April 20, 1953, it features the Rolex *crown* underscored with a single horizontal 'line'.

TWO-TONE (also 2-tone or tu-tone): Refers to a watch case featuring two different metals (e.g. stainless steel and yellow gold).

UNI-DIRECTIONAL ROTATING BEZEL: Introduced in the 1980s, this elapse time bezel is often found on divers' models, and only moves in the counterclockwise direction. Thus, protecting the diver from an erroneous (and potentially dangerous) reading when measuring decompression times, since any accidental movement could only err on the side of safety.

WINDING STEM: Shaft on which the crown is fixed on an end.

SUBJECT INDEX

BIBLIOGRAPHY

Books

Borer, Emil. *Modern Watch Repairing & Adjusting*. London: N.A.G. Press, 1942.

Bruton, Eric. *Clocks & Watches*. Italy: The Hamlyn Publishing Group Ltd, 1968.

Bruton, Eric. *The History of Clocks and Watches*. New York: Crescent Books, 1982.

Dowling, James and Jeffrey P. Hess. *The Best of Time: Rolex Wristwatches*. Atglen, Pennsylvania: Schiffer Publishing Ltd, 2001.

Ehrhardt, Sherry and Roy Ehrhardt. *Wrist Watch Price Guide*. Kansas City, Missouri: Heart of America Press, 2002.

Gordon, George. *Timeless Elegance: Rolex*. Hong Kong: Zie Yongder Co, 1989.

Milham, Willis I. *Time and Timekeepers*. New York: The Macmillan Company, 1944.

Patrizzi, Osvaldo. *Collecting Rolex Wristwatches*. Genova, Italy: Guido Mondani Editore, 1998.

Rolex Watch Company. *Four Hundred Years of Watchmaking: An Historic Exhibition*. New York: 1974.

Rolex Watch Company. *Rolex Jubilee Vade Mecum*. Zurich: Fetz Brothers, 1946.

Rolex Watch Company. *Talking Points*. New York: 1992.

Rolex Watch Company. *The Anatomy of Time*. Manchester England: Jesse Broad & Co. Ltd, 1955.

Shugart, Cooksey, Tom Engle and Richard E. Gilbert. *Complete Price Guide to Watches*. Cleveland, Tennessee: Cooksey Shugart Publications, 2002.

Skeet, Martin and Nick Urul. *Vintage Rolex Sports Models*. Atglen, Pennsylvania: Schiffer Publishing Ltd, 2002.

Viola, Gerald and Gisbert L. Brunner. *Time in Gold: Wristwatches*. Atglen, Pennsylvania: Schiffer Publishing Ltd, 1988.

Periodicals

Christie's auction catalogues, Geneva, London and New York, 1990 to date.

Cigar Aficionado, New York, New York: M. Shanken Communications Inc, 1997 to date.

Fortune Magazine, London, 1941-1950.

Geographical, London: Royal Geographical Society, 1941-1957.

Horological Journal, London: The British Horological Institute, 1920-1968.

L'Illustration Magazine, France, 1930-1936.

National Geographic, Washington D.C.: National Geographic Society, 1953 to date.

Rolex watch catalogs, Geneva and New York, 1972 to date.

Sotheby's auction catalogues, Geneva, London and New York, 1990 to date.

Other sources include dozens of *Rolex Spare Parts Catalogues*, *Pamphlets*, *Price Lists*, *Service Manuals* and *Advertisements*, as well as numerous personal interviews with retired Rolex employees and authorized dealers.

PHOTO CREDITS

While many of the images in this book were taken by the author, some images were provided by the following sources:

Generalwar.com: Numerous late model Rolexes, including: Day-Date, Yacht-Master and Daytona, including the Daytona image used on the cover.

Master Piece Jewelry: Rolex watch bracelets.

Passions.com.sg: Vintage Rolex models, including: Chronograph, *Comex* Submariner, Military Sub mariner and Prince.

Watchcommander.com: Vintage Rolex models, including: Milgauss, Daytona, Datejust (Ovettone), Quartz and Prince.

Michael J. Rosenman: Late model Rolex Datejusts.

Bjsonline.com: Vintage Rolex models, including: Milgauss, Explorer and *Comex* Sea-Dweller.

Rarerolex.com: Counterfeit Rolex lug markings.

Northerntime.com: Vintage Rolex Prince models.

Michael Benson: WWI vintage Rolex wristlet.

Christie's Images, New York: Catalog images, including: 'Deep Sea Special', Piccard, Mercedes Gleitz Oyster watch, Milgauss and 'James Bond' Submariner.

Syd Cain: James Bond Submariner production drawing.

National Geographic Magazine: Historical picture from the Mt. Everest expedition.

Some magazine advertisements from the following sources:

National Geographic Magazine.
Geographical Magazine.
L'Illustration Magazine.
Fortune Magazine.
Cigar Aficionado Magazine.

It is important to note that the aforementioned sources did NOT provide images of the 'counterfeit' watches shown in this book (except where noted). Therefore, these sources should not be considered associated with counterfeit watches in any way whatsoever.

RECOMMENDED WEBSITES

antiquorum.com	Antiquorum Auctioneers
awi-net.org	American Watchmakers-Clockmakers Institute
bhi.co.uk	British Horological Institute
bjsonline.com	Commercial website with good Rolex information
collectingwatches.com	Supplemental website for the book: *Collecting Rolex Wristwatches*
europastar.com	Europa Star Online
fhs.ch	Federation of the Swiss Watch Industry
hessfineart.com	Jeffrey P. Hess' website
horology.com	Horology "The Index" — Enough said!
hrwatches.com	HR: Watches Magazine
iq-enterprises.com	InfoQuest Publishing— supplemental website for *The Rolex Report*
iwjg.com	International Watch & Jewelry Guild
nawcc.org	National Association of Watch & Clock Collectors
rolex.com	Official Rolex website
rolexawards.com	The Rolex Awards for Enterprise
timezone.com	Watch Resource website
tudorwatch.com	Official Rolex Tudor website
newturfers.com	The Ultimate Rolex Forum
ukwatches.com	James M. Dowling's website
watchnet.com	Watch Resource website
watchzone.com	Watch Resource website

POST SCRIPT

I would like to thank you again for purchasing this book, and I hope you enjoyed it as much as I enjoyed writing it. Being an *informational reference book* of sorts, it is updated and improved with constructive criticism and input from readers like yourself. Therefore, we respectfully request that you send us your comments, corrections, compliments and complaints (via e-mail to **jb247@hotmail.com**) so we can make improvements to the next edition.

Furthermore, if you have any information or resources which could benefit this book, we would love to hear from you. This would include: information, images, out-of-print Rolex catalogs and manuals, price guides, vintage advertisements, etc...

Please visit our website at **http://www.iq-enterprises.com** for a supplemental resource to this book, including corrections as they are identified.

Again, thanks for your purchase and we hope to see you again when we release The Rolex Report 5th Edition.

Sincerely,

John E. Brozek

John E. Brozek
InfoQuest Publishing, Inc.

288

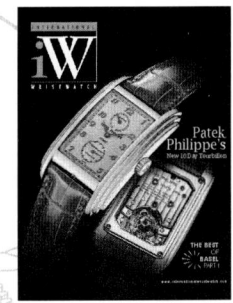

The
American Watch Guild
announces
the creation of the

International Watch Collectors Society

The **Society** will provide its members with the following

- Calendar of major watch sales & auctions.
  - Antiquorum, Christie's, Phillips & Sotheby's
  - The previews of upcoming auctions.
  - Reports: photographs, prices and auction results.
- Announcements from significant watch firms of new releases and limited editions.
- Information about emerging new master watchmakers and their creations
- Establishment of regional chapters where the collectors can meet and have guest speakers from noteworthy watchmaking factories.
- Question and Answer service by Stewart Unger, noted watch authority & author.
- Annual meeting at the Concours d'Elegance at the summer Jewelers of America Show held at the Javits Center in New York.
- A book club.
- Plus Free Booklets: *How to Buy a Watch (and its Functions)*
  The Care and Service of Timepieces
  Where to Find the World's Finest Watches
  How to Detect a Counterfeit Watch

Membership	1 year - $65	2 years - $120	6 Issues of Collectors Corner per year Invitation to the Concours d'Elegance
Master Collector	1 year - $120	2 years - $220	the above plus: 10% discount from the Book Club Rebate coupons from Manufacturers

Membership Application   Name_____Phone_____

Address_____City_____State_____Zip:_____

Make check payable to: ## International Watch Collectors Society, LLC
244 Madison Ave., #258 New York, NY 10016 • *Fax: 516-374-5060*

Hess Fine Art

Buying & Selling Rolex, Hamilton, Patek Philippe and other fine watches.

Founded in 1984, Hess Fine Art specializes in fine watches, diamonds, Fine jewelry, art and collectibles. We are a Sothebys.com founding member, Ebay power seller gold, NBC affiliate regulars, and Museum appraisers and decommission agents.

Hess Fine Art is dedicated to providing each of our customers with a safe, friendly and convenient internet purchasing experience. With 130 years of in house watch making experience, you can count on the quality of our merchandise and the honesty of our descriptions.

Jeffrey Hess has over 30 years in the horology (watch) trade, and is a world renowned watch researcher, watch historian and co-author of the best selling book: "The Best of Time: Rolex Wristwatches An Unauthorized History".

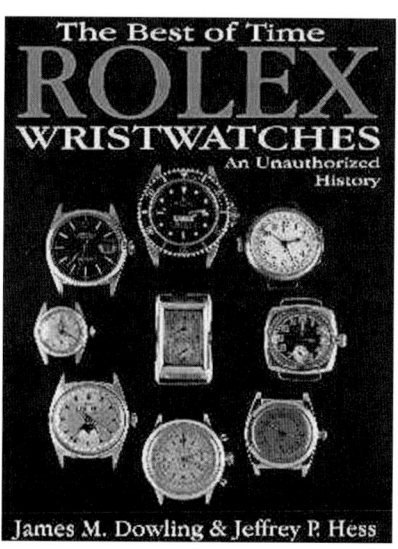

We are also proud to offer full-servicing for your Rolex and other fine mechanical watches.

HESS FINE ART

1131 4th Street North
St. Petersburg, Florida 33701
Hours: M-F 9:00-5:00 EST
(727) 896-0622 • (800) 922-4377 • FAX: (727) 822-8899
E-Mail: hessfine@hessfineart.com

Please visit our website at: www.hessfineart.com

Central Cigars is located in downtown Saint Petersburg, Florida at 273 Central Avenue and features the largest selection and best prices on the most sought after cigars, humidors and accessories including… Arturo Fuente, Opus "X", Davidoff White Label, Padron, Ashton, Diamond Crown, Macanudo, Partagas and introducing the "C" which is hand-rolled on location by Head Master Roller, Roberto Ramirez. Mr. Ramirez was also named "Cuba's top Roller" by Fidel Castro and is recognized as one of the top 10 rollers in the world!

Next time you're in town, make sure to visit our cigar bar complete with overstuffed leather chairs and couches, private lockers, TV's, and cigar reading material… a great place to enjoy a drink, smoke a cigar and relax! We offer an extensive selection of ports, fine wine, and imported beer for your enjoyment.

We have a full-service website to process your order, or just call our toll-free number. When ordering, make sure to mention this book along with the promotional offer: *We will never rush the hands of time* to receive a free Arturo Fuente cigar with your order.

Central Cigars & Cigar Bar

273 Central Avenue
Saint Petersburg, Florida

(toll free) 888.898.8994

www.centralcigars.com

ADVERTISE IN THIS BOOK

ATTENTION DEALERS AND ORGANIZATIONS: This book is circulated <u>world-wide</u>. It is marketed directly to individuals, as well as through numerous bookstores and upscale jewelers. *The Rolex Report* has received critical acclaim and is used regularly by serious collectors, pawn shops and organizations alike.

We are currently accepting advertisements for the next printing. Ads are printed for a <u>minimum</u> 1-year run of the publication, and ad space is limited.

AD SIZES

FULL PAGE: 9" HIGH x 6 $\frac{1}{2}$" WIDE
HALF PAGE: 4 $\frac{1}{4}$" HIGH x 6 $\frac{1}{2}$" WIDE

For ad rates or information on placing your ad please contact:

InfoQuest Publishing, Inc.
10460 North Roosevelt Blvd #377
Saint Petersburg, FL 33716
www.iq-enterprises.com
Phone: 727.204.1184 — E-Mail: jb247@hotmail.com

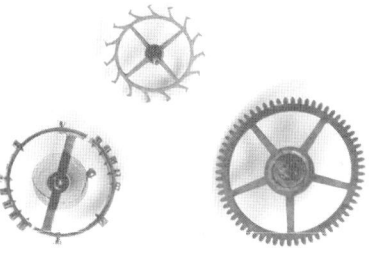

All ads must be professionally produced with 'camera-ready' artwork and submitted on white paper in the actual ad size.

Have you visited our website lately?

http://www.iq-enterprises.com

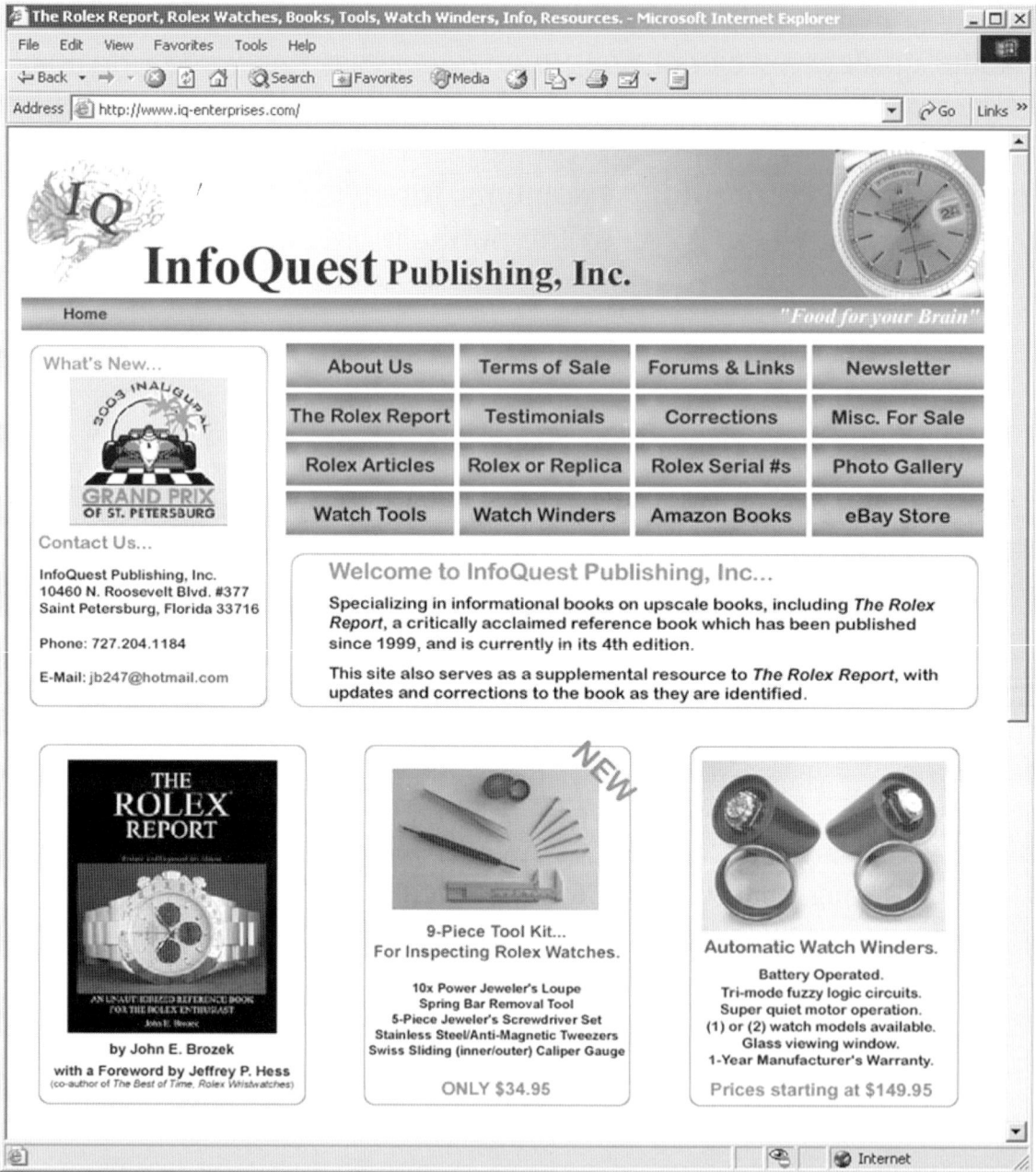

Your one stop source for Rolex news and information, as well as a supplemental resource to *The Rolex Report*, with updates and corrections as they are identified... Rolex articles, watch winders, tools, auctions, books, web links, a photo gallery, and much more...

AUTOMATIC WATCH WINDERS

- Our Automatic Watch Winders properly maintain all automatic watches, and meet the winding requirements of all watch manufacturers, including: Rolex, Tudor, Omega, Breitling, Patek Philippe, and many others.
- Very quick on/off spring loaded watch mounts, holds any wrist size watches securely in place, with no chance of disengagement from rotating cups.
- Tri-mode fuzzy logic operation: user programmable, for clockwise, counter-clockwise, or bi-directional winding.
- The programmed cycle repeats daily without user intervention.
- Super quiet operation.
- Operates up to 1 year on batteries — perfect for storing the winder in a safe.
- Glass viewing window (Dust Cover).
- Pilot light cycle indicator.
- Packaging includes protective cloth bag, box and user's manual.
- 1 year USA manufacturer's warranty.

* Batteries not included.

InfoQuest Publishing, Inc.
10460 North Roosevelt Blvd #377
Saint Petersburg, FL 33716

E-Mail: jb247@hotmail.com
Phone: 727.204.1184

Visit our online catalog at:
www.iq-enterprises.com

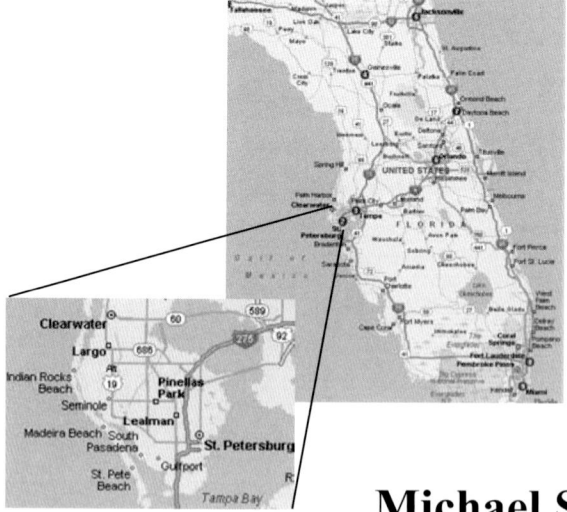

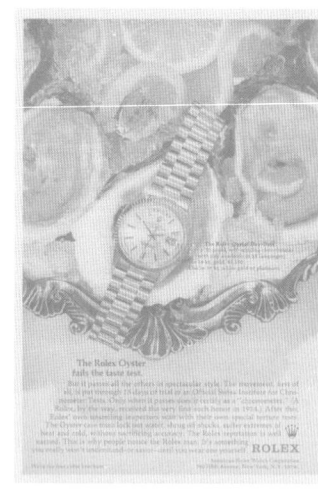

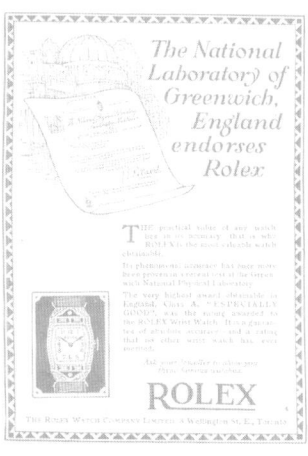

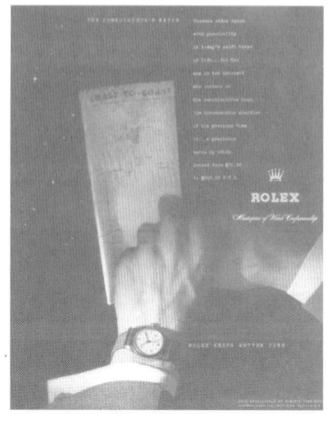